Orwell Your Orwell

Other Books by David Ramsay Steele

From Marx to Mises: Post-Capitalist Society and the Challenge of Economic Calculation, 1992.

Three Minute Therapy: Change Your Thinking, Change Your Life (with Michael R. Edelstein), 1997.

Atheism Explained: From Folly to Philosophy, 2008.

Therapy Breakthrough: Why Some Psychotherapies Work Better than Others (with Michael R. Edelstein and Richard K. Kujoth), 2013.

Orwell Your Orwell
A Worldview on the Slab

David Ramsay Steele

St. Augustine's Press
South Bend, Indiana

Manufactured in the United States of America

1 2 3 4 5 6 24 23 22 21 20 19 18 17

Library of Congress Cataloging in Publication Data
Steele, David Ramsay, author.
Orwell your Orwell: a worldview on the slab / David Ramsay Steele.
South Bend, Indiana: St. Augustine's Press, 2017.
Includes bibliographical references and index.
LCCN 2016033727 | ISBN 9781587316104 (hardback)
LCSH: Orwell, George, 1903–1950 – Criticism and interpretation.
BISAC: LITERARY CRITICISM / General.
LCC PR6029.R8 Z793 2017
DDC 828/.91209–dc23 LC
record available at https://lccn.loc.gov/2016033727

∞ The paper used in this publication meets the minimum requirements of the American National Standard for Information Sciences - Permanence of Paper for Printed Materials, ANSI Z39.48-1984.

St. Augustine's Press
www.staugustine.net

For Dan McCloskey

But I say unto you, That every idle word that men shall speak, they shall give account thereof in the day of judgement. For by thy words thou shalt be justified, and by thy words thou shalt be condemned.

Matthew 12:36–37 (A.V.)

Contents

Preface

On January 23rd, 1984, millions of Super Bowl viewers were diverted or fazed by a TV ad with the concluding line, "On January 24th, Apple Computer will introduce Macintosh. And you'll see why 1984 won't be like *Nineteen Eighty-Four*." This advertisement, aired just that one time as a genuine commercial, but many times since as a work of art, has been hailed as "the greatest TV commercial of all time." And those who delivered some such judgment would often add: "And it didn't even show the product!" What's even more remarkable, however, is that it didn't need to explain the setting: rows of wretched uniformed persons with drawn faces, a giant screen with a giant face spouting ideological gobbledygook.

If we consider that portion of the population which reads books, or remembers a time when they used to read books, we find that there are a few books, at most a dozen, which the overwhelming majority, probably as many as ninety percent, of these book readers have all read. Two of these dozen books were written by George Orwell. To have written one such book might be put down largely to chance. To have written two of them seems to betoken some kind of talent.

Prior to 17th August 1945, Orwell was familiar to those who followed English writing, but he was not one of the more outstanding figures. On that date *Animal Farm* appeared. It was an immediate success, and brought Orwell fame and income beyond anything he had known. In June 1949 *Nineteen Eighty-Four* came out, and quickly became a popular success dwarfing even *Animal Farm*. A very sick man, unable to write much more, though bursting with new ideas, Orwell died six months after its release.

These two colossal best sellers stimulated interest in Orwell's earlier writing. His *Homage to Catalonia*, a flop when it appeared in 1938, now sells hundreds of copies every week, and is by far the most widely-read non-fiction book on the Spanish Civil War. His two outstanding novels, *Burmese Days* (1934) and *Coming Up for Air* (1939) are popular and even his inferior novels, *A Clergyman's Daughter* (1935) and *Keep the Aspidistra Flying* (1936) continue to find new readers. His works of observation and commentary on the poor, *Down and Out in Paris and London* (1933) and *The Road to Wigan Pier* (1937) are now more widely read than ever. But for those who have really fallen under Orwell's spell, his essays and reviews, assembled in various collections, usually become the most-loved of his writings.

Although Orwell's works other than *Animal Farm* and *Nineteen Eighty-Four* might have disappeared from popular awareness but for the enormous and enduring fame of those two works, readers who pursue the other Orwell are not disappointed, for Orwell is a capable and entertaining writer who comes across as a warm and sympathetic personality. And since all of Orwell's works of fiction are consciously designed to make political points, the ideological connection between his fiction and his essays is unusually tight.

This book is not a biography, nor is it a contribution to literary criticism, nor a study of Orwell's psychology. It's a book about Orwell's ideas—his beliefs—in the context of the changes in prevailing ideas which have taken place over the past two hundred years or so. If Orwell says something, I try to make sense of it in terms of his framework of ideas or "web of belief" rather than primarily in terms of his psychology or circumstances, and I try to relate it to similar or dissimilar ideas prevalent among Orwell's contemporaries and predecessors. My initial motivation for writing on this topic was my conviction that Orwell's actual stated beliefs are often mischaracterized.

Much of this book is concerned to pin down just what Orwell believed and advocated, and how this relates to what his predecessors and contemporaries believed and advocated. I often disagree with Orwell, and where this is so, I often criticize his views. But my factual claims about Orwell's positions stand or fall independently of my evaluations of those positions. The test is: "Would Orwell himself agree that, where his views are reported, they are characterized accurately?"

Orwell is an uncommonly charming writer and his readers usually find themselves nodding in agreement, though this is partly because people who read Orwell sometimes make him say what they are already predisposed to agree with. Hence there has arisen the strange spectacle of various ideological groups striving to "steal" or "appropriate" Orwell. This seems pointless to me, for opinions are not made one smidgen more worthy by the fact that some outstanding writer agrees with them, and anyone who looks closely at Orwell's writings will accept that he was often badly mistaken.

A key to some of the widespread misunderstandings of Orwell is that on more than one occasion he quite radically changed his views. Orwell's commentators have been slow to perceive this, and therefore they tend to mix together disparate ideas from different periods in his life. There were also periods when Orwell maintained a rigid position with an air of confidence, despite actually being subject to doubts, occasionally expressed, about that position, and there were other contexts in which his views were gradually modified over several years.

As an example of what may come from ignoring Orwell's ideological *volte-faces*, consider the following. In early 1938, Orwell wrote the words: "if someone drops a bomb on your mother, go and drop two bombs on his mother" (XI, 113). In January 1983 Norman Podhoretz quoted this as showing Orwell's repudiation of pacifism. Christopher Hitchens responded to Podhoretz with caustic ridicule: how could Podhoretz so grievously distort Orwell by attributing to him a sentiment which Orwell was ironically putting into the mouth of someone else? (Hitchens 2002, 99).

Now, Orwell is not, with the quoted words, straightforwardly asserting his own view. On this narrow point Hitchens is right. But neither is Orwell ironically characterizing the outlook of an opponent. The drift of Orwell's argument here is that modern war faces us with a choice between doing terrible things and, if we won't do those terrible things, being overrun by people who will do those terrible things. This is a dreadful predicament, and Orwell admits he has no satisfactory answer.

But what both Podhoretz and Hitchens have clearly overlooked is that this quotation comes from Orwell's "pacifist," revolutionary leftist, or anti-war period, which lasted two years and two months, from June 1937 to August 1939, and this remark is very closely tied to his militant opposition, at that time, to any "imperialist" war between capitalist nations, and *especially* to the anticipated "anti-fascist" war against Germany. Orwell at this point definitely does not believe that Britain faces the choice between dropping bombs on German mothers and having bombs dropped on British mothers. The application of the remark is to Republican Spain which does (he believes) face such a choice because of the Nationalist rebellion.

In August 1939 Orwell's view of the coming war with Germany was suddenly and comprehensively transformed, and in the years that followed, Orwell scathingly denounced precisely the opinions he had voiced during his earlier anti-war period, though almost always without mentioning that the views he was attacking are the views he formerly held. Podhoretz understands that Orwell had an anti-war, a so-called pacifist, period, and that he then repudiated it, but Podhoretz mistakenly dates this repudiation before Orwell wrote the quoted words. From what we know of Podhoretz and Hitchens, we can be sure that they both agreed with Orwell's pro-war stance after August 1939, and disagreed with the anti-war (but pro-revolution) stance illustrated by this Orwell quotation.

During the war, Orwell unequivocally defended, against criticisms from Vera Brittain, the Allied policy of so called "strategic bombing," actually extermination bombing, of German civilians. Orwell argued that it was a good thing that wartime slaughter was no longer confined to combatants, and in any case, it was impracticable to outlaw any specific kind of killing (XVI, 193). So in practice Orwell had arrived at a position of agreeing, non-ironically, with "If someone drops a bomb on your mother, go and drop two bombs on his mother"—except that Orwell was now going further, for it was the Allies who initiated and remorselessly pursued the policy of deliberately targeting civilian housing, with the object of killing as many non-combatants as possible.

And so, Podhoretz, not Hitchens, turns out to be more right than wrong, in the sense that the Orwell they both admired most, the later pro-war Orwell, would have endorsed, without irony, the quoted words, and even gone further. But Podhoretz gets there only by a sort of accidental canceling out of errors.

Although this book presents an Orwell quite different from the most common and conventional image of Orwell, it should not be seen as a debunking exercise. The first two chapters, which refute some of the prevalent misconceptions, do this only to clear away the debris and stake out something of the ground plan for a positive, bold, and highly specific account of Orwell's motivating ideas.

This work is concerned with tracing ideas held by people in the past and therefore it is unavoidably concerned, much of the time, with a small minority of the population known as "intellectuals." Orwell himself emphasizes that intellectuals live in a world different from that of the great mass of non-intellectuals. Opinions which would be disgraceful in either one of these worlds may be quite normal and even *de rigueur* in the other, though sometimes the two worlds interact.

Most of this book has turned out to be about politics (defined broadly enough to include abstract political concepts like capitalism, socialism, democracy, and totalitarianism). The bulk of what Orwell wrote is about politics. Up to 1936, though interested in political issues, Orwell saw himself as primarily a creative writer in the tradition of English literature, and especially a novelist in the mold of George Gissing. From mid-1936 on (the period in which something like ninety-five percent of his extant writings are produced) political issues had become his life: he could hardly write a line which didn't belong to a political polemic. This is apparently what Orwell was getting at when he wrote in 1948, "I am not a real novelist anyway" (XIX, 336), a sentiment he would never have voiced in 1935.

In arriving at an accurate picture of Orwell's beliefs, we must always begin with what Orwell himself states, but this has to be qualified in a number of ways. There are some issues on which Orwell says little or nothing, but which are quite important in his overall worldview, to take a few examples at random: his rejection of anarchism and syndicalism, his rejection of Keynesianism or of any "middle way" between capitalism and socialism, his conviction that Gissing is a much more important—as well as a better—writer than, say, George Eliot. And then, as a persuasive writer, Orwell trimmed what he said according to its acceptability to his target audience: chiefly leftwing intellectuals.

We should also bear in mind the hazard which afflicts writers of persuasive prose: you come up with a draft, probably a fifth or sixth draft, ask a few people to look it over, make amendments, carefully read the final draft through several times, then send it off. And months later you look at a sentence you've written and yelp, "What? I said that? What a blockhead!" Much of Orwell's output was written at great speed, with little or no rewriting, and in that context there are remarkably few inconsistencies or wayward remarks. But still, we ought not to build too much on anything he says only once.

A word about this book's main title and subtitle. In 1892, William Ernest Henley (the model for Stevenson's character, Long John Silver) published his poem, "Pro Rege Nostro," with its celebrated opening lines, "What have I done for you, / England, my England?" The poem became popular during World War I, and was viewed by the narrow left as offensively jingoistic. During that war, D. H. Lawrence published a short story, "England, My England," which became part of a 1924 collection with the same title. In 1941 George Orwell wrote an essay about the English people, and entitled it "England Your England" (no comma). Among the overtones of this resonant title are: make what you will of this England of yours.

Too many people have made what they would of this Orwell of theirs, and in that sense my title is a mild reproof. Yet it also carries the affectionate sense: even when Orwell's opinions are correctly understood and you find yourself in clear disagreement with him, you will still want to make him your own, just as you do Jonathan Swift, Mark Twain, Samuel Butler, H. G. Wells, Bernard Shaw, or H. L. Mencken. As for the subtitle, the thing to bear in mind is that it is, not Orwell himself, but Orwell's ideas about politics, society, and culture which are on the mortuary slab undergoing my autopsy. Orwell changed his mind on important issues several times and died at the age of forty-six; if he had lived longer, his worldview would not have been frozen in January 1950.

My intention has been, where Orwell is quoted, to give the original spelling and grammar, which are mostly British but occasionally American (when he wrote for American publications). My own writing, while consistent in every specific usage, is predominantly American with some Britishisms. I do however hold that proper names should not be amended. Thus, it is "Labour Party," not "Labor Party" (just as, to a writer of British English, it should be "Pearl Harbor," not "Pearl Harbour").

The title of Orwell's last book is *Nineteen Eighty-Four*, never *1984*. First, the written-out form was Orwell's expressed preference, though he acceded to the numerical title for the American edition (XX, 26–27). (Orwell did not capitalize "four," but I put this down to the editorial convention for written-out numbers that he was used to, and this convention now no longer predominates.) Second, the written-out form has a somber resonance in the reader's mind's ear, like the long strokes of a great plague-warning bell, while a succession of four numerals conveys a quite different atmosphere.

In 1968 there appeared the *Collected Essays, Journalism, and Letters of George Orwell*. The editors did a very good job of selection, and these four volumes contain the majority of Orwell's most interesting writings other than his nine book-length works. The editors did not hesitate to call it "Collected." They could hardly have dreamt that interest in Orwell would explode to such an extent that within forty years there would be a truly 'collected' or 'complete' compilation in twenty volumes, eleven of them quite fat, carrying Orwell's every surviving jot and scribble. In this book, I have reluctantly decided not to give any references to the much-loved *Collected Essays, Journalism, and Letters*, but only to the *Complete Works*.

The first nine volumes of the *Complete Works*, edited by Peter Davison, are Orwell's nine book-length works. These appeared in the *Complete Works* hardback in 1986 and 1987. The remaining eleven volumes are a chronologically arranged collection of Orwell's other extant writings. These appeared, as part of the set of twenty hardback volumes, in 1998. In 2000–2002, Volumes X–XX appeared in paperback, with additions and updatings. The publishers evidently decided to sell the rights to the first nine volumes to Penguin, and then to package the paperback Volumes X–XX so as to downplay the existence of the *Complete Works*. No reference to the *Complete Works* appears on the covers or title pages of these books, and thus in many cases no reference to the *Complete Works* appears in various online listings of them. To add to the confusion, there are several writers named Peter Davison (none of whom, as far as I know, is the Fifth Doctor). You may be able to pick up the full 1998 boxed set for a few thousand dollars, and that does not, of course, include the updatings to the paperback volumes X–XX. It may help the reader to know that, for the first nine volumes, the pagination of the main Orwell work is nearly always identical with recent Penguin editions, though some accompanying commentary is omitted from those, and different material added. If you want to get hold of all twenty volumes of the *Complete Works* in their best editions, the best approach is to look for each volume individually in used book channels. In this book, all my references to Orwell's works are to the *Complete Works*, Volumes I–IX in hardback and Volumes X–XX in the superior paperback edition, and are signified simply by the volume number in capital Roman numerals. There is also *The Lost Orwell*, a supplementary volume of more recently discovered writings not included in the twenty volumes of the *Complete Works*, listed in my bibliography as Orwell 2006 (and not to be confused with *Orwell: the Lost Writings*, an earlier compilation whose parts are all now contained in the *Complete Works*).

A draft of the manuscript was read by Stephen Berry and David Gordon, both of whom offered numerous helpful criticisms which led to editorial changes, though in some cases I stubbornly failed to see reason.

An Orwell Timeline

370 B.C.E. *Republic* by Plato.

426 *The City of God* by Augustine of Hippo.

1308–1321 *The Divine Comedy* by Dante Alighieri.

1516 *Utopia* by Thomas More.

1644 *Areopagitica* by John Milton.

1689 Bill of Rights: the core of the British constitution is settled. The British state is monarchical, parliamentary, and anti-Papist.

1726 28th October. *Gulliver's Travels* by Jonathan Swift.

1772 *The Year 2440* by Louis-Sébastien Mercier.

1757–1858 British interests gain control of most of India.

1778 Beginning of Catholic Emancipation: The Papists Act, first of a series of Acts removing legal disabilities of Roman Catholics in Britain.

1780 The Gordon Riots: popular demonstrations in London against the Papists Act.

1801 1st January. Following abolition of the Irish parliament, the

United Kingdom of Great Britain and Ireland comes into existence.

1813 *A New View of Society* by Robert Owen.

1826 *The Last Man* by Mary Shelley.

1830 *The Doctrine of Saint-Simon: An Exposition, First Year, 1828–1829* by Saint-Amand Bazard, Prosper Enfantin, Olinde Rodrigues, Hippolyte Carnot, and others.

1831 27th December. Charles Darwin begins his five-year voyage on *The Beagle*.

1848 *Manifesto of the Communist Party* by Karl Marx and Friedrich Engels.
Revolutionary uprisings across continental Europe.

1857–1858 Indian Mutiny. Soldiers of the British East India Company revolt against the company. Though defeated, the mutiny leads to the winding up of the company and the introduction of British imperial rule to most of India.

1859 *The Origin of Species* by Charles Darwin.
On Liberty by John Stuart Mill.

1867 *Capital*, Volume I, by Karl Marx.

1872 *Erewhon* by Samuel Butler.

1876 1st May. Queen Victoria adopts the title "Empress of India."

1882 The British government gains control of the Suez Canal.

1883 Karl Marx dies.

1886 *Demos: A Story of English Socialism* by George Gissing.

1888 *Looking Backward: 2000–1887* by Edward Bellamy.

1891 *News from Nowhere* by William Morris.
New Grub Street by George Gissing.
Papal encyclical *Rerum Novarum*.

1893 13th January. Independent Labour Party (ILP) founded.
Mohandas Gandhi begins non-violent campaign by Indians in South Africa.

1893 *Merrie England* by Robert Blatchford.

1895 *The Time Machine* by H. G. Wells.
Degeneration by Max Nordau.
The Psychology of Crowds by Gustave Le Bon.

1896 Eduard Bernstein, leading German Social Democrat and friend of the late Marx and Engels, begins to publish controversial articles advocating Revisionism.

1898 Marie and Pierre Curie discover radium.
The Sleeper Awakes (later revised and retitled *When the Sleeper Wakes*) by H. G. Wells.

1899 *The Presuppositions of Socialism and the Tasks of Social Democracy* (*Evolutionary Socialism*) by Eduard Bernstein.
11th October. Beginning of the Boer War (Engelse Oorlog).

1900 27th February. Labour Representation Committee formed.
25th September–24th October. “Khaki” election, held during the Boer War; intense patriotic sentiment; Conservatives returned with a big majority.
The Interpretation of Dreams by Sigmund Freud.

1901 *Anticipations of the Reaction of Mechanical and Scientific Progress upon Human Life and Thought* by H. G. Wells.

1902 31st May. Close of Boer War with victory to Britain.
What Is to Be Done? by "Nikolai Lenin."

1903 25th June. Eric Arthur Blair born in Motihari, Bengal.
17th December. The Brothers Wright accomplish the first extended manned flight of a powered, fixed-wing, heavier-than-air flying craft.
28th December. George Gissing dies of lung disease, aged forty-six.

1904 Blair, his mother, and his sister move to England.
The Napoleon of Notting Hill by G. K. Chesterton (novel set in London, 1984).

1905 *A Modern Utopia* by H. G. Wells.
"On the Electrodynamics of Moving Bodies" by Albert Einstein.

1905–1907 Failed revolution in Russia.

1906 The Labour Representation Committee is renamed the Labour Party.

1907 *The Story of a Social War* (later retitled *The Secret of the League*) by Ernest Bramah.
The Iron Heel by Jack London.

1908 *Reflections on Violence* by Georges Sorel.
The War in the Air by H. G. Wells.
The Man Who Was Thursday: A Nightmare by G. K. Chesterton.

1909 "The Machine Stops" by E. M. Forster.

1914 *The Ragged-Trousered Philanthropists* by Robert Tressell.

1911 Blair starts at St. Cyprian's, a private "prep" boarding school.
Political Parties by Robert Michels.

1912 *The Servile State* by Hilaire Belloc.
15th April. *Titanic* sinks.

1914 28th July. The Great War begins.
2nd October. Eleven-year-old Blair publishes a patriotic poem in a local newspaper.
October. Benito Mussolini, Italy's leading socialist, switches from an anti-war to a pro-war position.

1915 Gandhi returns to India and agitates for Indian independence.

1916 24th–30th April. Easter Rising in Dublin proclaims the Irish Republic.
November 22nd. Jack London dies, aged forty-one.
December. Blair finishes at St. Cyprian's.

1917 March. Overthrow of the Tsar and establishment of a democratic provisional government of Russia.
May. Blair enters Eton College as a King's Scholar.
November. The Bolshevik Party, led by Lenin and Trotsky, seizes power and stamps out all civil and democratic liberties in Russia. Opposition to the minority Bolshevik *coup* leads to a civil war.

1918 The Great War ends.
Russian Bolshevik government begins the rapid introduction of socialism, conceived as the abolition of money and institution of "production for use."
Eminent Victorians by Lytton Strachey.
New Labour Party constitution: formation of constituency branches with individual membership, and commitment to "common ownership of the means of production, distribution, and exchange."

Meccania, the Super-State by Owen Gregory.
14th December. General election. The Labour Party gets three million votes (giving them fifty-seven MPs).

1919 2nd–6th March. Formation of the Communist or Third International (Comintern), with affiliated Communist Parties in all countries, subordinate to Moscow directions.
23rd March. Together with other revolutionary syndicalists and former Marxists, Mussolini launches the Fascist movement.
The Outline of History by H. G. Wells.
Government of India Act. India is given some internal self-government within the British empire.

1920 End of Russian Civil War with complete victory to the Bolsheviks, now renamed the Russian Communist Party. Intensification in Russia of the drive to abolish money and introduce socialism. Widespread Russian starvation and appeals for international aid.
"Economic Calculation in the Socialist Commonwealth" by Ludwig von Mises.
June. *Leftwing Communism: An Infantile Disorder*, by V. I. Lenin.
The Practice and Theory of Bolshevism by Bertrand Russell and Dora Black.
31st July. Communist Party of Great Britain founded.

1921 The Russian Communist government of Lenin and Trotsky massacres the striking Kronstadt workers.
"New Economic Policy" in Russia: the Soviet government retreats, calls off the failed attempt to abolish the market, and permits some commercial activities to re-emerge.
Blair leaves Eton College and joins the Indian Imperial Police, to be stationed in Burma.
R.U.R. (Rossum's Universal Robots) by Karel Čapek.
6th December. Anglo-Irish Treaty gives dominion status to Southern Ireland.

1922 *The Waste Land* by T. S. Eliot.
Die Gemeinwirtschaft (*Socialism*) by Ludwig von Mises.
Ulysses by James Joyce.
31st October. The King of Italy appoints Mussolini Prime Minister.
15th November. General election. Labour Party gets 142 MPs and becomes the official Opposition.
29th November. New recruit to the Imperial Police, Eric Blair arrives in Mandalay, Burma.

1923 April. Lenin appoints Joseph Stalin General Secretary of the Communist Party of the Soviet Union.
May. Lenin suffers the first of several strokes and is no longer active in government.
8th–9th November. Beer Hall Putsch: Adolf Hitler fails to seize power in Bavaria, is imprisoned, concludes that the electoral road to power looks more promising, and begins to write *My Struggle.*
6th December. General election, leading to the First Labour government (January 1924), with the Labour Party a minority and therefore dependent on Liberal support.

1924 *We* by Yevgeny Zamyiatin.
21st January. Lenin dies.
10th June. Murder of Italian Socialist Deputy Giacomo Matteotti by Fascists.
29th October. General election: Conservative victory ends first Labour government.

1925 Mussolini dismantles constitutional checks, to become dictator of Italy.

1925–1926 *My Struggle* by Adolf Hitler.

1926 4th–12th May. General Strike in Britain.
28th May. Military coup in Portugal.

1927 September. On leave in England, Blair decides not to return to Burma, but to live in England and devote his life to writing.
Metropolis, silent movie by Fritz Lang.
Blair lives briefly among down-and-outs in the East End of London.
November. Trotsky expelled from the Communist Party of the Soviet Union.

1928 First Soviet Five-Year Plan begins.
Blair passes himself off as a tramp and lives temporarily as a tramp.
Spring. Blair goes to live in modest circumstances in Paris.
Memoirs of a Fox-Hunting Man by Siegfried Sassoon.

1929 Blair works as a dishwasher in a Paris restaurant.
Blair returns to England.
Death of a Hero by Richard Aldington.
Trotsky is expelled from the Soviet Union.
30th May. General election. Second minority Labour government under Ramsay MacDonald.
Im Westen Nichts Neues (*All Quiet on the Western Front*) by Erich Maria Remarque.

1930 2nd March. D. H. Lawrence dies of lung disease, aged forty-two.
The Castle, first publication of an English translation of Franz Kafka.

1931 12th April. A coalition of Republicans and Socialists wins the Spanish elections; two days later Spain is proclaimed a republic.
Papal encyclical *Quadragesimo Anno*.
24th August. "The Great Betrayal." In response to the economic crisis, Labour Prime Minister MacDonald forms a "National" coalition government with mainly Conservative members, and is henceforth regarded by the Labour Party faithful as a traitor.

1932 *Brave New World* by Aldous Huxley.
Antonio de Oliveira Salazar becomes prime minister of Portugal.

1933 9th January. Blair publishes his first book, *Down and Out in Paris and London*, under the carelessly assumed name "George Orwell."
30th January. Adolf Hitler appointed Chancellor of Germany.
5th March. National Socialist German Workers' Party wins 43.9 percent of the national vote in Germany.
New constitution for Portugal confirms the dictatorship of Salazar.
The Shape of Things to Come by H. G. Wells.

1934 *Winter in Moscow* by Malcolm Muggeridge.
25th October. *Burmese Days* published.

1935 11th March. *A Clergyman's Daughter* published.

1936 January–March. Aiming to write a book about living conditions among the poor, Orwell stays with poor families in the North of England.
20th January. King George V dies; his son becomes King Edward VIII.
18th January. Rudyard Kipling dies.
16th February. Spanish elections: Popular Front government elected by a narrow majority.
February. *The General Theory of Employment, Interest, and Money* by John Maynard Keynes.
20th April. *Keep the Aspidistra Flying* published.
Things to Come, movie with an H. G. Wells screenplay predicts the bombing of London in 1940, followed by the collapse of civilization.
9th June. Orwell marries Eileen O'Shaughnessy.
Which Way to Peace? by Bertrand Russell.
"Burnt Norton" by T. S. Eliot.
Modern Times, mostly-silent movie by Charlie Chaplin.
14th June. G. K. Chesterton dies.

The War with the Newts by Karel Čapek.
13th July. Murder of José Calvo Sotelo
17th July. Spain's African army rebels, beginning the Spanish Civil War.
10th–11th December. King Edward VIII abdicates; his brother becomes King George VI.
30th December. Arriving at the Lenin Barracks in Barcelona, Orwell enlists in the POUM militia and serves on the Aragón front.

1937 8th March. *The Road to Wigan Pier* published.
3rd May. On leave in Barcelona, Orwell is caught up in the outbreak of fighting between Communists and the Left (the CNT and the POUM) in Barcelona.
20th May. Back at the front, Orwell is wounded in the throat by a Nationalist sniper bullet and is hospitalized.
15th–16th June. Arrest, torture, and murder of POUM supporters in Catalonia, on instructions from Moscow.
23rd June. Orwell and his wife, on the run from the Communist police, escape into France.
Swastika Night by "Murray Constantine" (Katharine Burdekin).
"Spain" by W. H. Auden.

1938 January. "Year Nine" by Cyril Connolly.
25th April. *Homage to Catalonia* published.
13th June. Orwell joins the Independent Labour Party (ILP).
Hitler proclaims right of Germans in Czechoslovakia to self-determination. Growing war scare.
29th–30th September. Munich conference: By agreement with Britain, France, and Italy, Germany acquires the ethnically German part of Czechoslovakia.
Power: A New Social Analysis by Bertrand Russell.
30th October. Thousands of Americans, hearing an Orson Welles radio adaptation of H. G. Wells's *The War of the Worlds*, are convinced for several hours that the United States has been invaded (by Martians or by Germans).

1939 26th January. Barcelona falls to the Nationalists.

March. In breach of the Munich agreement, Germany occupies Bohemia and Moravia.

29th March. Franco's Nationalists enter Madrid.

1st April. End of the Spanish Civil War; Francisco Franco becomes dictator.

12th June. *Coming Up for Air* published.

The End of Economic Man by Peter Drucker.

The School for Dictators by Ignazio Silone.

22nd August. Orwell switches from opposition to support for the coming war against Germany.

24th August. Pact of Friendship between Germany and Russia, secretly dividing Poland between them; in every Western country, Communist Party members now become militantly antiwar and warmly tolerant of Nazism.

1st September. Germany invades Poland.

3rd September. Britain and France declare war on Germany.

September. Orwell leaves the anti-war ILP, making public his newly adopted pro-war views.

1940 11th March. *Inside the Whale and Other Essays* published.

29th March. Orwell starts writing for *Tribune*.

"East Coker" by T. S. Eliot.

Soviet government massacres twenty thousand Polish officers and intellectuals in the Katyn Forest.

10th May. Germany invades France.

26th May–3rd June. Evacuation of British troops from France via Dunkirk.

14th June. Germans occupy Paris.

The Totalitarian Enemy by Franz Borkenau.

The Last Man by Alfred Noyes.

Darkness at Noon by Arthur Koestler.

The Great Dictator, movie by Charlie Chaplin.

21st August. Trotsky assassinated in Mexico City by a Soviet agent.

1941 19th February. *The Lion and the Unicorn* published.
3rd March. *The Betrayal of the Left* by Victor Gollancz and others, with two chapters by Orwell.
22nd June. Germany invades Russia. In every Western country, all Communist Party members promptly become militantly pro-war and "anti-fascist."
18th August. Orwell starts at the BBC, working on broadcasts to India.
Arrests of Jews in German-occupied Europe and their transportation to camps in Poland.

1942 15th February. Japanese troops occupy Singapore; the British garrison surrenders without a fight.
23rd August. Battle of Stalingrad begins.
The 1946 Ms by Robin Maugham.
3rd October. First successful test-flight of a long-range rocket by Wernher von Braun's team at Peenemunde.
Implementation of the Final Solution: systematic extermination of Jews and others in German-occupied Poland.

1943 2nd February. Battle of Stalingrad ends with German surrender.
The Machiavellians: Defenders of Freedom by James Burnham.
23rd November. Orwell leaves the BBC to become Literary Editor of *Tribune*, and starts writing *Animal Farm*.

1944 February. *Animal Farm* is completed but is rejected by some publishers because of its anti-Soviet message.
6th June. Allied invasion of Normandy.
13th June. Beginning of bombing of London by rocket-propelled missiles launched from German bases in France and Holland.
June. Orwell and his wife Eileen adopt a child, Richard Blair.
The Road to Serfdom by F. A. Hayek.
The Managerial Revolution by James Burnham.

July–August. *Animal Farm* accepted for publication by Warburg.

1945 February. Orwell resigns as Literary Editor of *Tribune* and goes to France as a war correspondent.
29th March. Eileen Blair dies unexpectedly during an operation.
28th April. Mussolini killed by Communist partisans.
30th April. Hitler kills himself.
8th May. The Allies announce Victory in Europe.
5th July. General election. Sweeping Labour victory. The first majority Labour government is formed under Clement Attlee.
16th July. Explosion of the first atomic bomb at White Sands, New Mexico.
July–August. Orwell starts to write *Nineteen Eighty-Four*.
6th August. Atomic bombing of Hiroshima.
9th August. Atomic bombing of Nagasaki.
14th August. Japan surrenders.
17th August. *Animal Farm* published.
December. *That Hideous Strength: A Modern Fairy-Tale for Grown-Ups* by C. S. Lewis.

1946 23rd May. Orwell moves to a cottage on the Isle of Jura, Scotland.
Nationalization of British coal industry.
13th August. H. G. Wells dies.

1947 15th August. India becomes independent.

1948 4th January. Burma becomes independent and elects not to join the Commonwealth.
30th January. Gandhi is assassinated by a militant Hindu.
Nationalization of British railways.
February. Communist coup in Czechoslovakia.
24th June–12th May 1949. Soviet Union blockades Berlin.
November. Orwell completes *Nineteen Eighty-Four*.

1949 6th January. Seriously ill, Orwell enters the Cotswold Sanatorium.
January. Mao Zedong captures power in China.
4th April. Britain signs the NATO treaty.
8th June. *Nineteen Eighty-Four* published.
September. Having acquired the know-how from some of its hundreds of spies in the United States and Britain, the Soviet Union detonates an atomic bomb.
13th October. Orwell marries Sonia Brownell.

1950 21st January. George Orwell (Eric Arthur Blair) dies of lung disease, aged forty-six.
23rd February. General Election. The Labour Party retains power with a slender majority.
2nd November. Bernard Shaw dies.

1951 25th October. General Election. Conservatives gain power.

1953 5th March. Joseph Stalin dies.

1956 The Hungarian uprising is crushed by Soviet tanks.
Soviet head of state Nikita Khrushchev's "Secret Speech" acknowledges some of the atrocities committed under Stalin. Many members of Western Communist parties leave these parties, forming the "New Left."

1960 1st January. Fidel Castro takes power in Cuba.

1961 The Berlin Wall is built, to stop workers migrating from East Germany to West Germany.

1962 The People's Republic of China discloses that Yugoslavia is fascist; the Soviet Union discloses that Albania is fascist.

1963 The People's Republic of China discloses that the Soviet

Union is fascist; the Soviet Union discloses that the People's Republic of China is fascist.
22nd November. Aldous Huxley dies.

1968 *Collected Essays, Journalism, and Letters of George Orwell* (four volumes) published.
Prague Spring: the democratic movement in Czechoslovakia is crushed by Soviet tanks.
Popular British journalist Bernard Levin predicts that the Soviet Union will fall in 1988; shortly after this, Levin amends the predicted date of downfall to 14th July, 1989.
In Portugal, dictator Salazar is replaced by Marcelo Caetano.

1970 2nd February. Bertrand Russell dies.
Will the Soviet Union Survive until 1984? by Andrei Amalrik.

1973 *The Gulag Archipelago* by Alexander Solzhenitsyn.

1974 25th April. In Portugal, a military coup overthrows Caetano, precipitating a period of revolutionary unrest.

1975 The ILP renames itself Independent Labour Publications, and becomes a campaigning organization within the Labour Party, committed to "market socialism."
20th November. Franco dies. The restored monarch, Juan Carlos de Borbón, moves to democratize Spain as a constitutional monarchy.

1976 2nd April. New constitution for Portugal terminates the "revolutionary" period and confirms liberal democracy.

1977 Karol Wojtyla, Archbishop of Krakow (later to become Pope John Paul II) orders that *Nineteen Eighty-Four* be read in churches.

1979 3rd May. A Conservative government is elected under Margaret Thatcher.

1980 Newly-elected US President Ronald Reagan, evidently unhinged, predicts the imminent downfall of "Marxism"; reputable Western scholars hasten to reassure the public that the Soviet Union is in no danger of collapsing and will endure indefinitely.

1984 The year awaited by hundreds of millions of Orwell readers across the world: thousands of books and articles referring to Orwell appear.

23rd January. During the Super Bowl, Apple Computer runs a startling ad: "On January 24th, Apple Computer will introduce Macintosh. And you'll see why 1984 won't be like *Nineteen Eighty-Four*."

1986–1998 *The Complete Works of George Orwell* (twenty volumes).

1989 9th November. The Berlin Wall is torn down.

1991 The Union of Soviet Socialist Republics is dissolved.

November. The Communist Party of Great Britain dissolves itself, its leading members forming the Democratic Left.

1995 April. The Labour Party changes its constitution, replacing its seventy-seven-year-old commitment to "common ownership of the means of production, distribution, and exchange" with "a community in which power, wealth and opportunity are in the hands of the many, not the few."

1997 1st May. Election of "New Labour" government, with Tony Blair as Prime Minister. Growing awareness that the British population's subjection to state-promoted video surveillance is the most intensive and intrusive in the world.

2010 6th May. Election leads to a coalition Conservative and Liberal Democrat government headed by David Cameron, pledged to make big reductions in government interference.

1
The Purveyor of Orthodoxies

Saints should always be judged guilty until they are proved innocent.
—George Orwell, January 1949 (XX, 5)

The usual view of George Orwell is that he spoke out fearlessly against the fashionable fallacies of his day. Because he was not blinded by any doctrinaire creed, he could see what others would not see. He was right where the fashionable herd was wrong, and he, almost alone, dared to go against the herd. He was the conscience of his generation of intellectuals, because he faced facts which more conformist writers found too uncomfortable to face. And he suffered because of his outspokenness, an outsider to all cliques and parties.

Here is Richard Rovere, in his Introduction to *The Orwell Reader*: "Orwell arrived on the scene in the middle 'thirties and proceeded to fire the camps of the orthodox wherever he found them."[1] Rovere tells us that the "brains" of 1930s intellectuals were "addled," and that Orwell was a critic of this brain-addling, though Rovere leaves obscure exactly what this means, except that Orwell was critical of Communism. According to Philip Bounds, Orwell "was the ultimate outsider in politics—insecure, scornful of orthodoxies, cussedly independent."[2]

David Lebedoff writes of Orwell's "aversion to fashionable orthodoxy." According to Lebedoff, Orwell was "uncontaminated by political

1 Orwell 1956, xvii.
2 Bounds 2009, 2. Bounds could here perhaps be read as describing a general reaction to Orwell, not giving his own judgment, and that would substantiate my point in a different way.

correctness" and "[u]nfettered by any orthodoxy."[3] Lebedoff further maintains:

> Orwell paid a terrible price for his failure to conform to the political correctness of the Left. His fervent anticommunism made him a pariah to many of his fellow socialists, and crippled his career. (185–86)

If we look closely at these assertions (and others like them[4]) we find that there are four distinct claims about Orwell: 1. Orwell was frequently right where others (perhaps the majority) were wrong; 2. Orwell was unusually candid or outspoken, fearlessly telling the truth where others were more circumspect; 3. Orwell rejected all orthodoxies—all creedal systems or packages of belief; 4. Orwell suffered discrimination or even ostracism because of his views.

All four claims are mistaken. The picture of Orwell as an outspoken outsider is radically misleading. All of Orwell's general political opinions were commonplaces among leftwing intellectuals of the 1930s and 1940s. Orwell was a preacher of well-worn, widely-promoted social and political positions; he was committed to very definite orthodoxies, and he meticulously crafted what he chose to say and to refrain from saying. Orwell was never isolated, never ostracized, never suppressed. He never climbed out on a limb or adopted a dangerously unpopular standpoint. As an Old Etonian, Orwell was *ex officio* a member of the British ruling class. Many doors were always open to him, and most of those few that were shut, he himself chose to shut.

The picture of Orwell as a maverick, a loose cannon, or a holy pariah would not have become so prevalent if it did not seem to fit very well with a quick skim of some of his more popular writings. Anyone reading Orwell soon finds that, though a man of the Left, he frequently attacks people on the Left; as some leftists have sourly noted, he attacks people on the Left far more than he attacks the Right. His persuasive prose often conveys the assumption that the objects of his attack are powerful and

3 Lebedoff 2008, 118.

4 For example Slater 1985, 132–33.

he is the dissident; this is one of his standard rhetorical postures. He frequently refers contemptuously to "orthodoxies," most memorably in his phrase, "smelly little orthodoxies," so it might be natural for a careless reader, especially at a later date when the odor-free and gargantuan orthodoxies Orwell was promoting are no longer so familiar, to suppose that he was averse to all orthodoxies. Above all, it is usually mentioned that Orwell sharply criticized the Soviet dictatorship at a time when Communism was most fashionable among Western intellectuals, and it is now vaguely supposed by many readers that British intellectuals in the 1930s were predominantly pro-Communist.

Orwell and the Left

From mid-1936 until his death Orwell called himself a socialist and identified with the Left. But as well as advocating leftwing ideas, Orwell also commented on the Left in general terms. He was intrigued by the fact that the Left dominated intellectual life, so that the class of intellectuals held characteristic ideas alien to those of the majority of the population. In early 1941 Orwell writes that "there is now no intelligentsia that is not in some sense 'Left'" (XII, 405), and later in the same year, that "in the last ten years there has been no intelligentsia in England that is not more or less 'Left'" (XIII, 70).[5] In 1948, he estimates that leftist domination of the intelligentsia has been in place for about fifteen years (XIX, 289).

As so often, Orwell knows he is exaggerating to point up an accurate observation. There were always a few literary intellectuals who were outside the Left. Orwell was aware of C. S. Lewis and Colm Brogan, whom he might not have rated fully-fledged "intellectuals." He was probably not aware, or only very dimly aware, of Tolkien or Peake. Yet he certainly

5 This is from a transcribed speech by Orwell, whose publication without his editorial input he vigorously protested. I make sure I quote from it only where what it says is stated by him elsewhere. In fact, though, the prose of this piece is very lively and Orwellian, and his protests were probably more due to its incautious frankness than to anything in it he did not mean to say at the time.

knew about Anthony Powell, Hugh Kingsmill, and Evelyn Waugh, not to mention T. S. Eliot and Wyndham Lewis. He also knew of impressive literary figures who were, from a typical leftist point of view, apolitical, like James Joyce, Virginia Woolf, P. G. Wodehouse, Henry Miller, or Henry Green. But shorn of Orwell's habitual exaggeration, the essential point is correct: the overwhelming majority of those intellectuals whose politics can be easily identified as left or right are left.

Today we know that the dominance of the Left over intellectual life has continued for more than eighty years and shows no sign of terminating. However, what defines the boundaries of "the Left" is always changing, at least in subtle details. Broadly speaking, the Left since Orwell's day has retained its dominance over the opinions of intellectuals but has shifted steadily rightward. And the small minority of intellectuals who don't fall within the Left is now somewhat more numerous in comparison to the Left, and somewhat better organized, than eighty years ago. To Orwell the intellectual dominance of the Left appeared as something of a historical novelty. He could recall a time when it was not so, or did not appear to be obviously so.

As a consequence of leftist dominance of the intellectuals, Orwell observes that writers can say things that most British people would find shocking, knowing that saying these things is very safe, while an intellectual can say something that wouldn't raise an eyebrow among non-intellectuals, but would be outrageous among the literary intelligentsia.

> A modern literary intellectual lives and writes in constant dread—not, indeed, of public opinion in the wider sense, but of public opinion within his own group. As a rule, luckily, there is more than one group, but also at any moment there is a dominant orthodoxy, to offend against which needs a thick skin and sometimes means cutting one's income in half for years on end. (XIX, 289)

In this passage, written after the war, Orwell recognizes the Left as a whole as the dominant "group." He is identifying with the fundamental beliefs of that group, whilst pleading for the recognition of certain "facts" which the inherited beliefs of the Left cause leftists to be reluctant to admit.

At the same time, Orwell routinely displays his awareness that the Left is segmented into various ideological factions, and that the dominant orthodoxy he identifies is, not so much the Left as a whole, as one segment within the Left. After mid-1936, Orwell's political views are always in line with some prominent segment of the Left and his key political views are never very remote from those of the currently dominant segment of the Left.

The impression that Orwell "attacked the Left" and is therefore a kind of misfit or deviant on the Left is a superficial misunderstanding. After all, leftists are always complaining about the Left, just as rightists are always complaining about the Right, and just as, for instance, the most nondescript Christian ministers are always complaining about the behavior of Christians. But Orwell does not very often "attack the Left." Most often, he attacks one segment of the Left from the standpoint of another segment of the Left. And the latter, the segment with which Orwell identifies (and which sometimes changes, as his opinions change) is always a substantial and consequential segment. Since something like nine-tenths of intellectuals with perceptible political allegiances were leftist, Orwell always had plenty of targets within the Left.

It's true that Orwell also occasionally complains about leftwing intellectuals in very general terms. But when these complaints are examined closely, they are usually either covers for his attacks on a particular segment of the Left or they are criticisms of leftist intellectuals of a kind which many leftists could be expected to applaud.

Asked by the Duchess of Atholl in November 1945 to speak at a meeting protesting Soviet actions in Europe, Orwell refused, explaining that the people associated with the meeting (the League for European Freedom) were supporters of the British Empire. He therefore did not feel he could be associated with them. "I belong to the Left and must work inside it," he wrote in response, "much as I hate Russian totalitarianism and its poisonous influence in this country" (XVII, 385). Probably Her Grace understood what Orwell was getting at: that if he addressed this meeting, leftists might begin to think of him as rightwing, and then he would not be able to attack Communism from within the Left, where his attacks on it would be more effective. If we take what Orwell writes here at face value, and suppose that there was symmetry in his opposition to the British Empire and to the Soviet Union, then we would expect Orwell to refuse to endorse actions on behalf of people who were friendly to Soviet Communism. But Orwell did not adopt that stance, as shown by his signing of the petition of protest against the sentence of the Communist spy Alan Nunn May (XVIII, 367).

Orwell's Orthodoxies

If Orwell had been a man averse to all orthodoxies, then this would tend to imply one of two things: either that he arrived at original positions unique to himself, or very uncommonly held, or that he was an eclectic who adopted bits and pieces of different orthodoxies, without paying any attention to whether his overall position would meet with approval from any of the major schools of intellectual opinion. Yet either of these characterizations is quite provably inaccurate. In broad outline, Orwell's views on political and social matters are off-the-peg, and Orwell always attaches himself to an ideological faction with a numerous following. There is nothing discreditable in this. It just happens to be the truth about Orwell, and it's advisable (if we're to understand his thinking) not to assume the contrary.

In all major matters of political positioning, Orwell chooses among already well-defined points of view, and he opts for a point of view that has a substantial following. Let's look briefly at one example. By 1936 Orwell had adopted the term "totalitarian," and from mid-1937 employed it frequently to denote both Communist and fascist regimes. The term had become current among intellectuals some years before this. The view that Communism and fascism in practice possess an essential similarity which can be indicated by the term "totalitarianism" had a growing following, and Orwell attached himself to this current of opinion. As it happens, I agree with this view: the point I'm making is not that Orwell is at fault, but that he is, as always, running with a pack. Now, is there a distinctive Orwellian take on totalitarianism? Well, we can certainly summarize what Orwell thought about totalitarianism, though it will not be sharply distinguished from the views of Silone, or Koestler, or Borkenau—writers all widely read by leftists at the time. But then, far more people now read Orwell on totalitarianism than have read Koestler, or have even heard of Silone or Borkenau.

There aren't many important arguments or notions which may, even possibly and debatably, have ever been distinctive to Orwell. One is the link Orwell claimed to identify between corruption of language and totalitarianism. Another is his conviction that popular culture, such as comic postcards, children's comics, and Edgar Wallace thrillers, is worth serious analysis. But notice that, in these two cases where Orwell's approach was indeed somewhat distinctive, the positions he took were perfectly compatible with the prevailing ideology of democratic socialism and did not make him any enemies. His writings expounding these approaches did not arouse any great interest at the time, but neither did they arouse any hostility. They were widely acceptable and sometimes applauded.

It may be asked, if Orwell was orthodox, what were his orthodoxies? The answer is fairly straightforward, provided we bear in mind that Orwell several times undergoes a change of political outlook on specific clusters of issues, and provided we remember that Orwell's general social outlook and political views before mid-1936 are somewhat obscure because only patchily documented. In or around mid-1936, Orwell experienced a fairly sudden conversion to socialism and to identifying himself as a member of the Left (though many views, such as his general attitude to the British Empire or his hostility to birth control, remained the same as before). His views immediately prior to this conversion were explicitly anti-socialist and anti-Left. Over ninety-five percent of Orwell's extant writing dates from after this conversion to socialism. Leaving aside his earlier, pre-socialist views, we can characterize his positions after mid-1936 in these ways:

> *Specific political program*. From mid-1936 until June 1937, Orwell's positions were fairly typical of non-Communist leftists who favored a Popular Front policy of co-operation with the Communists. In May–June 1937 Orwell abruptly shifted his position and became what the Communists would have characterized as "ultra-left," and very much opposed to a Popular Front. From June 1937 until August 1939, Orwell

adhered to the revolutionary anti-Stalinist Left of the "London Bureau," which entailed opposition to the coming war against Germany (and Orwell in the latter half of this period was actually a member of the ILP, affiliated with the London Bureau). In August 1939 Orwell had a sudden conversion from an anti-war to a pro-war position, and thereafter supported the war against Germany, whilst maintaining that a socialist revolution would enable the war to be fought more effectively. From August 1939 until the end of his life, Orwell's policy views gradually evolved, but he remained to the left of the Labour Party. He strongly supported the Labour government which was elected in July 1945, yet regretted that its policies were not left enough. Thus he ended his life a Labour leftwinger, a Bevanite.

In all these ways, Orwell's views are fairly typical of left-wing intellectuals of the time, and, precise details of timing and nuances of emphasis aside, the direction of his evolution (for example, from so-called pacifism to support for the war) is the most common one.

Now, even the above brief summary tends to understate the utter ordinariness of Orwell's political views, because it focuses on differences among various segments of the Left. All sizeable segments of the 1930s Left shared far more of their views than they disagreed on, and Orwell dogmatically endorsed this shared leftist credo (as we will see many times over in Chapter 3 and elsewhere below).

When Orwell is actually quoted as denouncing orthodoxy, a major source is the essay "Inside the Whale," from April 1940. Here Orwell employs the term "orthodoxy" in a rather narrow sense, to mean adherence to the position of a specific organization (XII, 105). He is arguing that a writer ought not to be tied to any official platform or program. The examples he mentions are Communism and Catholicism—he doesn't cite his own strict adherence to the doctrine of the London Bureau, which he had abandoned quite recently. In this narrow, organizational sense, Orwell had thrown off adherence

> to any "orthodoxy," yet in doing so he had become more "orthodox" in the sense normally understood: he had arrived at a position more in conformity with the precise beliefs of the typical leftwing intellectual at that moment. Specifically, he was now on board with the concept of a "war against fascism," which he had previously rejected.
>
> *General political philosophy.* From mid-1936 until his death, Orwell was a democratic socialist in the tradition of Robert Blatchford, Keir Hardie, Bernard Shaw, Bertrand Russell, and R. H. Tawney. He was never a Marxist (though like most non-Marxist leftists of the period, he had eclectically absorbed some elements of Marxist thinking and terminology into his socialist outlook). Being a democratic socialist did not rule out hoping for an armed workers' uprising, which was Orwell's stance from June 1937 to the end of 1942.
>
> *Key values for social philosophy.* Orwell's broader social thinking is a confluence of two streams, each of them highly influential at the time. One is the view predominant on the Left: rationalism, materialism, secularism, heavily indebted to the writings of people like T. H. Huxley, H. G. Wells, Winwood Reade, and Grant Allen. The other is a cluster of ideas deriving from the fin de siècle and earlier, which I label Post-Socialism and Anti-Degeneratism, and which I look at in Chapters 4 and 5.

Orwell after mid-1936 consciously writes for the Left. He understands that the Left is his audience and the market for his writings. He is well aware that the kind of literary career he has staked out for himself would be at risk if he became known as possessing right-wing affinities. The intellectual Left are the people he wants to persuade, and he avoids antagonizing them. He often says things that leftists would take to be somewhat shocking, in a bold and adventurous spirit that they can identify with. He avoids saying the kind of thing that would cause leftist intellectuals to classify the writer as someone who was not one of themselves.

It's one thing to criticize the Left from within its ranks; it's quite another to be hailed by the Right as an effective critic of the Left's beliefs. At the end of Orwell's life, he had two extraordinary best-sellers within four years, and a lot of rightwing people, with the breathtaking effrontery we have come to expect of them, professed a liking for these two books. What happened to Orwell is like the situation of a person who is in the habit of whispering sympathetically and persuasively to a close confidant, and who abruptly realizes that his carefully nuanced words have been picked up by a public address system, and are being listened to by hundreds of assorted neighbors, many with outlooks at variance with the person he had thought he was addressing. Orwell suddenly found he had a huge audience beyond the narrow confines of the leftist intelligentsia, and for all that this was gratifying, it must have been embarrassing too.

Confirmation by Contrary Instance

In a phrase that has been widely quoted, Orwell said of himself that he had "a power of facing unpleasant facts."[6] As we will see in later chapters, most of the facts Orwell credited himself with facing were actually falsehoods. But that is unremarkable: Orwell, like anyone else, made mistakes.

Why would a fact be unpleasant? Two notions may be mixed up in the concept of an unpleasant fact, first that the fact implies that certain hopes you might have had are doomed to disappointment, that the situation is grimmer than you might have supposed, and second, that the fact casts doubt upon your cherished belief system. To keep mentioning "unpleasant facts" therefore tends to reinforce an impression of fearless candor. However, Orwell's habit of mentioning unpleasant facts is a technique of persuasion; it serves a propagandistic purpose.

As an example, Orwell, the committed socialist, often asserts that socialism in Britain will involve Britain giving up its empire, and since British workers' living standards are as high as they are (he supposes)

6 XVIII, 316. Orwell often employed this clumsy expression "power of," for instance XII, 393; XVI, 493; XVII, 386. It may show the influence of French, where "pouvoir" can mean ability to do something.

because of the empire, this means that the introduction of socialism must cause an immediate and substantial drop in workers' living standards. Now Orwell was just mistaken about this, as we will see in Chapter 6: the empire did not increase British workers' living standards; it decreased them. Britain's giving up its empire could not (and, as it turned out, did not) reduce the real incomes of British workers.

However, if we step back from any question of factual accuracy, what the "power of facing unpleasant facts" amounts to is that when arguing for a position, Orwell often makes a point which looks to be at odds with that position. Though it might seem that this would blunt the force of his main argument for the position, it actually makes his main argument more convincing. It's an effective persuasive ploy.

It is persuasive in a number of ways. First, it makes his position seem less extreme, more moderate, and for many readers that is a recommendation. Second, it conveys that the writer is judicious, not over-hasty or dogmatic, and thus is reasonable. Third, it informs us that the writer is candid, an honest fellow who is not afraid to acknowledge facts which seem to go against his position, and is therefore someone we can trust. Fourth, it shows that the argument is not simple-minded, and therefore flatters the reader in advance: if he accepts the writer's conclusions, he can feel he is more discerning both than those who don't accept these conclusions and than most of those who do. Fifth, since it is the writer who chooses which "unpleasant facts" to emphasize and which to ignore, it distracts attention from other "unpleasant facts," which go unmentioned and might be more serious objections to the main argument.

We can call this effective persuasive stratagem "confirmation by contrary instance." I do not maintain that Orwell initially adopted this device simply because it was an effective persuasive technique. Rather, I surmise that it was a deep-rooted mental habit with him, to embrace a theoretical position and to go on worrying about some "fact" that seemed to threaten the tenability of that position. But as he developed his skill as a persuasive writer, he found that this mental habit could be the basis for a useful rhetorical technique.

This device is particularly effective when employed by someone who makes a practice of sweeping, exaggerated contentions, as Orwell does. An unbroken series of such assertions is liable to arouse the reader's skeptical instincts. But if occasionally one of these sweeping claims is balanced by mention of a contrary consideration, an admitted problem or serious anomaly, the reader may drop his critical guard.

Orwell's habit of always giving attention to some contrary consideration led him into an argumentative stratagem that was to stand him in good stead: he had a reason to attack anyone who took either side on an issue. If a writer showed any concern to increase the living standards of the masses, Orwell would attack that writer as being a hedonist who was powerless against fanatical creeds like Communism and fascism (XII, 178; XV, 291–92).[7] If any writer suggested that increasing the living standards of the masses was not of supreme importance, Orwell would attack them as privileged scoundrels who didn't have the elementary decency to allow the workers the basic amenities the bourgeoisie took for granted (XIII, 509–510; XV, 215). If someone failed to demand independence for the colonies, Orwell would attack them as self-interested beneficiaries of evil imperialism (V, 148; XI, 358–361). If someone proposed independence for the colonies, Orwell would berate them for advocating something manifestly impracticable (XV, 48–49). Against people who considered that Communism and National Socialism were mutually opposed, Orwell would point out that they were essentially the same (XI, 158–160; XII, 159, 461–62); if someone considered Communism and National Socialism essentially the same, Orwell would rebuke them for such a crude oversimplification (XVIII, 58; XX, 46). When we add to this even-handed oppositionism Orwell's habit of attacking people for what he surmised they were really thinking rather than for what they actually stated, we understand why someone today who reads Orwell without much awareness of actual intellectual trends of the 1930s and 1940s may get the impression that Orwell was against nearly everyone, and therefore must have been an isolated figure.

The Style of Propaganda

Originally, "orthodox" meant holding true or correct beliefs, but by the nineteenth century it had come to be used (outside theology) mainly to

7 I look at Orwell's anti-hedonism in Chapter 5 below.

mean something like "adhering closely to some standard belief system," whatever the merits or demerits of that belief-system. By extension, the term could also be employed in a derogatory sense, to imply that the orthodox believer is parroting some pre-packaged set of beliefs without having thought seriously about them.

One reason why many people find it easy to accept that Orwell is an independent-minded fellow, his own man, boldly bursting through all crimping ideological constraints, is that we're familiar with the kind of convert to a belief system who thinks and speaks in the special terminology of that belief system. If we run into an Evangelical Christian, a Scientologist, a Randian Objectivist, or an adherent of Lyndon LaRouche, we often get the feeling that the special jargon of the belief system seems to have infected the speech-centers in the believer's brain. A Communist in the 1930s or a Maoist in the 1970s would also fill the bill.

Orwell, by contrast, writes in plain English. His prose is direct and unpretentious. There's a no-nonsense, down-to-earth quality in the way he constructs his sentences and sometimes an intimate, chatty tone. However, Orwell's approach here is actually that of some successful propagandists for well-defined belief systems. Alongside the orthodox propagandist who talks in a peculiar jargon, there is also the orthodox propagandist who smoothly passes himself off as a real person.

In Orwell's youth, he had witnessed the concerted onslaught of Catholic propaganda in England, by such writers as G. K. Chesterton, E. C. Bentley, Hilaire Belloc, and Father (later Monsignor) Ronald Knox. We don't know any details of Orwell's immediate reactions to this episode, but we do know that it left a deep impression on Orwell, that thereafter he was strongly anti-Catholic (in retrospect he refers to these Catholic literary activists as "the Catholic gang"), and that (consciously or unconsciously) he emulated much of Chesterton's style of argument. Both Chesterton and Orwell present themselves to the reader as plain, commonsensical Englishmen. In person, neither Chesterton nor Orwell were plain or normal Englishmen; anyone who met either of them for five minutes would forever remember them as decidedly queer birds. But normal Englishmen is just what the timbre of their prose ceaselessly proclaims them to be.

That Orwell's self-projection in his prose is different from Orwell the real person has been pointed out by many commentators, most notably by Raymond Williams, who makes it sound almost like a consciously deceptive pose.[8] My view is that presenting one's own character in a selective light is a natural result of striving to be persuasive. The specific point I am making, however, is that taking this misleading self-projection at face value leads readers to think of Orwell as holding opinions at variance with those of the modish Left, when actually his views, broadly characterized, are quite commonplace on the Left. It is striking, for instance, how many commentators will use the word "orthodox" to explain what Orwell is against, taking their cue from Orwell's own frequent use of this term, and how many will mention the term "decency," which Orwell frequently employs as a positive value-judgment. Orwell frequently appeals to "decency" but this doesn't demonstrate that he's any more committed to decency as a value than other writers who don't employ this particular verbal device.

In detailed applications of his ideological positions, and especially in ways of formulating pre-existing ideas so that they become subtly new and challenging, Orwell is often strikingly original. However this is sometimes the way with the most accomplished propagandists for an orthodoxy. They breathe new life into the orthodoxy by the way they present it. They make the orthodoxy appear fresh and exciting. They draw daring conclusions as to matters of minor detail which may evoke consternation among the already confirmed orthodox, who don't themselves feel the need for this updated packaging.

Orwell's Artful Honesty

Readers of Orwell's essays and reviews are often impressed by his "honesty," a word one hears from their lips again and again. Orwell is a virtuoso rhetorician, who, along with other persuasive techniques, adroitly displays his own honesty, as if to say: "See how brutally honest I am: I dare you to be courageously honest too—by accepting my conclusions." Readers of Orwell who judge him to be unusually honest have been taken

8 Williams 1971, 51, 89.

in by his sales pitch. As Daphne Patai wrote, "a passion for appearing honest and actually being honest are very different things."[9]

Orwell's non-fiction prose has been described as like someone "thinking aloud." This is perfectly true of the effect, the tone of delivery, but not of the method of composition. It's like observing that Bach's fugues sound so fluent that you would think they were being improvised by the performer. An impression of spontaneity is achieved by meticulous application of well-honed technique.

Orwell doesn't reveal his raw thoughts or his anguished doubts, or rather, he reveals them selectively, as it suits his propagandistic purposes. His prose often engages the reader by enacting the process of coming to a particular conclusion, but the enactment is probably not the way in which Orwell came to that conclusion, and may not disclose the decisive reason why he currently accepts that conclusion. You can be sure that Orwell believes in the conclusions he is trying to get you to accept, but beyond that, if you want to know what Orwell is "really thinking," you have to speculate.

One of his favorite ploys is to make a sweeping assertion, more extreme than the reader would ever entertain if it were stated coldly, with such verve and with such a disarming air of uncompromising candor that the reader is bowled over and accepts it, moving on to the next stage in the argument. As Raymond Williams pointed out, Orwell probably picked up this persuasive technique from Chesterton.

Orwell often tells you candidly what he has thought and felt, but he does this selectively, to suit the case he is arguing at the moment. In fact, even when he is living his life, generating the experiences he will draw upon in his writing, he is already processing it for use in making a case. We can be sure, for example, that when he was shot in the throat in Spain in May 1937, his very *first* thought was something like this: "Pay close attention, Eric. This could be really handy material, if you survive to write it up." (Probably his second thought was to recall the passage in *Memoirs of a Fox-Hunting Man*, where Dick is shot in the throat and dies a few hours later.[10])

9 Patai 1984, ix.
10 Sassoon 1929, 364.

I could defend my claim that Orwell reveals his thoughts selectively by analyzing a particular passage and giving my own account of what Orwell was really thinking, but of course this might easily be disputed in any particular case. However, we can sometimes compare what Orwell wrote for publication with what he wrote in private letters. An example is a review Orwell wrote in March 1944 of a book by Harold J. Laski (XVI, 122–23). In this review, Orwell praises Laski but gently raises a critical point: Laski is too little inclined to criticize the USSR. Orwell's approach in this review is influenced by the pro-Soviet climate of the time, he is trying to concede as much to the prevailing wartime Russophilia as he can, in order to get his review published. It didn't work and the review was rejected, but Orwell sent a copy to Dwight Macdonald; he and Macdonald discussed the review in their next couple of letters. Here Orwell refers to Laski's book as "pernicious tripe" (XVI, 298).

No doubt Orwell meant every single specific thing he said in the review, but he didn't hold the view of Laski his readers would tend to attribute to him. Orwell despised Laski as a disgusting apologist for totalitarianism, but was prepared to leave the impression that he greatly respected him. I don't see anything culpably disingenuous here; my point is simply that Orwell was no blurter. He was a cool and deft shaper of persuasive prose.

As for the general question of Orwell's honesty, most writers are predominantly honest, and I don't believe that Orwell was significantly more or less honest than the majority of writers. Orwell took a job as propagandist for the British government during wartime, and partly based the Ministry of Truth in *Nineteen Eighty-Four* on his work at the BBC. As he himself reported, he disseminated untruths on behalf of the war effort, and was quite pleased with himself for having done so. Many people would say that lying in the anti-Nazi cause was justified, but that's not the point here. Readers of Orwell, because of the way he parades his own outspokenness as a persuasive ploy, often attribute to him the standpoint that we should always speak the truth, even if it hurts our own political cause. While in some places Orwell argues for that position, in others he rejects it, and in practice he sometimes goes against it.

"All propaganda is lies, even when one is telling the truth" is one of Orwell's well-known pronouncements. No doubt many people take this remark to illustrate Orwell's lofty standards: he must be so principled that he considers the selectivity and partiality involved in propaganda to be just as bad as outright lies. In fact, the remark is uttered by Orwell in justification of his own admitted lies in behalf of the British war effort (XIII, 229). The burden is that since all propaganda is equivalent to lies, it's okay for him to literally tell lies. The particular lie here is the claim that Japan is about to attack Soviet Russia. Orwell reports that he does not believe this at all, but has repeated it several times in his radio newsletters. He's pleased with himself for deliberately spreading this falsehood, which might be useful to the British war against Germany.

Do the Lower Classes Smell?

In much of his writing which innocent readers may take as strictly factual narrative, Orwell invents, distorts, and suppresses: this is true of his short pieces, "Such, Such Were the Joys," "How the Poor Die," "A Hanging," and "Shooting an Elephant," the volume *Down and Out in Paris and London*, and to a lesser extent of his descriptions of Northern working-class squalor in *The Road to Wigan Pier*.[11] The effect he is aiming for is more important than any correspondence with literal truth. Much of Orwell's purported non-fiction should actually be classified as fiction. Again, many people would say that this creative re-ordering of the facts is an unexceptionable form of artistic license, and again, that's not my point. Willingness to allow fiction to be read as documentary does not fit well with Orwell's image as unusually scrupulous.

We can put the matter of Orwell's candor, and occasional lack of it, in perspective by looking closely at one particular incident.

When Orwell's *Road to Wigan Pier* came out in March 1937, it was panned by Communists and some fellow travelers. Harry Pollitt's review in the *Daily Worker* claimed that in *The Road to Wigan Pier*, Orwell disclosed that he had a problem with the working class because working-class people

11 These works are probably no closer to literal reportage than Isherwood's Berlin stories or Miller's *Tropic of Cancer*, which are uncontroversially viewed as fiction. For discussion of departures from literal accuracy in various Orwell works, see Crick 1992, 35–37, 64–80, 186–88, 583–590.

smelled. Orwell branded this a "lie" and persuaded his publisher Victor Gollancz to make a fuss about it.

Since then, numerous admirers of Orwell have defended him against the calumny that he said that the workers smelled. They have repeated his own later protestations that he had said no such thing. He had instead said no more than that middle-class people of his own background had been brought up to believe that the workers smelled. However, Orwell was not telling the whole truth; he had indeed intimated that working-class people did smell.

It's true that he does say that people of his own social position have been brought up to believe that the workers smell, and it's no doubt true that this is the most important point he's trying to make, and yet he also clearly acknowledges that working-class people do smell. Whether his later denials arise from cold-blooded deceit or from being muddled about what he had actually written, they do not reflect the scrupulous respect for truth and unusual candor often ascribed to him. To become more aware of the emotive charge of this issue, it may help to contemplate the hypothetical example of a white supporter of the American Civil Rights movement in the 1960s, who wrote something similar about black people smelling.

A succession of writers have defended Orwell on this matter. Many of them simply point out that, after all, the 1930s workers did smell, so why the fuss? Exactly—but this implies that Orwell's denials are not entirely candid. Writing in 2002, Christopher Hitchens takes the other tack in defending Orwell. Hitchens indignantly denies that Orwell wrote the sentence, "The working classes smell," vouchsafing that this would be a "damning" sentence, a "statement of combined snobbery and heresy." According to Hitchens, Orwell "only says that middle-class people, such as his own immediate forebears, were convinced that the working classes smelled" (Hitchens 2002, p. 46). Orwell certainly says that, but does he "only" say that? According to Hitchens, to accuse Orwell of saying that the workers smelled is a "simple—or at any rate a simple-minded—confusion of categories," and he refers readers to *The Road to Wigan Pier*, where what Orwell says about the odiferous working classes can be "checked and consulted" (46).

A pity, then, that Hitchens did not take a minute or two to check or consult it. Orwell broaches the topic of proletarian smelliness by stating that in his childhood "four frightful words" were "bandied about quite freely. The words were: *The lower classes smell.*"[12] So far this is consistent with Hitchens's reading, and must have been where Hitchens stopped. Orwell now pursues this theme for three pages.

At first he does not strongly commit himself on the factual issue of plebeian redolence, though he does casually imply that the comparative uncleanliness of navvies, tramps, and domestic servants is a matter of observation. He quotes from a Somerset Maugham travel book: "I do not blame the working man because he stinks, but stink he does. It makes social intercourse difficult to persons of sensitive nostril." (Though difficult, Maugham evidently did not find intercourse with working-class youths altogether beyond his powers.) Then Orwell confronts the inevitable factual question:

> Meanwhile, *do* the "lower classes" smell? Of course, as a whole, they are dirtier than the upper classes. They are bound to be, considering the circumstances in which they live, for even at this late date less than half the houses in England have bathrooms. Besides, the habit of washing yourself all over every day is a very recent one in Europe, and the working classes are generally more conservative than the bourgeoisie. . . . It is a pity that those who idealise the working class so often think it necessary to praise every working-class characteristic and therefore to pretend that it is meritorious in itself.[13]

There's no way to escape Orwell's acknowledgment, in this passage, that the lower classes do smell. (Of course, all humans smell, if you get close enough to them, some of them quite nicely, and "smell" in this context is short for "smell more strongly or more offensively than those of

12 V, 119. Orwell's italics.

13 V, 121. Orwell is using "bathroom" in the traditional British sense, to mean a room with a bathtub installed in it. At this time the British did not use the word "bathroom" in the American way as a euphemism for "toilet," and, it so happens, it was fairly common in British houses to have separate rooms for the toilet and the bath.

cleaner habits.") The word "Meanwhile" indicates that though Orwell feels he can't evade answering the question, he wants to put it in its unimportant place, as an aside to his main argument. He avoids answering it directly or literally, while making his meaning quite clear: the smelliness of the lower classes is not *merely* a belief held by the upper and middle classes, but also an objective fact.

A little later Orwell mentions the notion "that working-class people are dirty from choice and not from necessity," again accepting that they are dirty while trying to leave that point in peripheral vision. "Actually, people who have access to a bath will generally use it" (122). He has already told us that most British households don't have bathrooms, which means that the great majority of working-class people don't have bathtubs installed in their homes (though many working-class families in homes without bathrooms possessed a galvanized zinc tub which they might use once a week). Earlier, Orwell has closely identified being dirty with smelling (119–120), so there's no room to interpret him as accepting the griminess of the lower orders without also acknowledging the olfactory corollary.

We see then, that despite some references by Orwell to the middle-class belief that the lower classes smell, worded almost as though this belief were in itself nothing more than snobbish prejudice, Orwell ultimately does not flinch from the objective fact that the English working classes of 1936 are dirtier than their social superiors like himself, and that they therefore smell—though he adds that it's not their fault. This is not an invention of Orwell's detractors, as Hitchens heatedly asseverates, but something clearly indicated by what Orwell says.

And Orwell's opinion on this point is factually correct. We did smell. As an English working-class child in the 1940s and 1950s, when things were a lot better than twenty years before, I can recall that, though most homes by then had bathtubs, it was out of the question to pay for hot water to be available all the time. The water was heated for the occasion, and when it was bath night, once a week at most, barely enough was heated for one bath per person; this meant that if the depth of water in the tub exceeded about two inches, it would get uncomfortably cold. (Until the 1960s almost no British working-class homes had central heating and very few had showers.)

Working-class people in the 1930s had limited access to hot water. It would be a fairly genteel working-class family where everyone could have a hot bath once a week (without going to the municipal public baths, which some did). You didn't wash your hair as often as you had a bath (so the shoulders of jackets and coats were always greasy, as therefore were places like chairbacks that they frequently touched), and you "could not afford" (the opportunity cost was too high, because of your low income) to change your socks, underwear, or shirt every day. Clothes had to be washed by the housewife, by hand, in a sink, with soap flakes (the dramatically more effective detergents were still to be marketed), and then hung on a line, every Monday unless it rained, to dry in the wind.

Wearing the same clothes for many days or weeks at a stretch is probably more conducive to a noticeable smell than not bathing. Even someone who washes very thoroughly will be comparatively smelly if he can't change his socks, underpants, undershirt, and shirt very often. To change all these daily, which is now taken for granted across Europe and North America, would have been an unthinkable extravagance for many working-class people in 1930s Britain. The same would apply to many middle-class people too.

Pollitt's way of alluding to this issue in his review is misleading—just as misleading as Orwell's, and Gollancz's, and Hitchens's, disavowals. If Orwell had been utterly candid, lacking all guile, he might have responded along these lines:

> Mr. Pollitt has given a misleading account of my discussion in *The Road to Wigan Pier*. My main concern was the way members of the middle class perceive the working class, and the obstacle this raises to inter-class collaboration in pursuit of the goal of socialism. As for the factual question of whether the workers smell, this was not the focus of my discussion, but I did intimate in passing that the workers, or a big proportion of them, do smell. My defense of this assertion is that it's true. However, I also pointed out that this was not the workers' fault, for reasons both of limited access to baths and historical tradition.

Instead, Orwell blusters, not quite candidly, parsing his written words, trying to make something of the fact that he had never literally said "the lower classes smell," except in attributing these words to middle-class snobs. Yet Orwell had unmistakably intimated that the working classes smelled.

Eight years later, this issue was revived as a contentious topic in the correspondence columns of the socialist weekly *Tribune*, and Orwell responded. His carefully worded letter does not explicitly retract his earlier untruthful denials that he had asserted that the workers do smell, but leaves open the possible interpretation of implicit retraction. Some of the correspondents had defended Orwell by accepting that Orwell had said that the workers do smell and asserting that it was a fact that they do. Orwell did not correct them (XVII, 201–04). The implication is that he knew he had been fibbing in 1937.

Why Orwell Matters, Really

Many people who write about Orwell suppose that he is an important writer because, on certain crucial political issues, he was right when others were wrong. Some even think that he was distinguished by exceptional moral goodness—I can just hear Orwell's sarcastic guffaw if he had heard anyone coming out with that. I, however, do not believe that Orwell's importance is linked to his good character or to the correctness of his opinions on the political events of his day.

No one thinks of evaluating, say, Jonathan Swift by itemizing the ways in which he was right in disputes with his contemporaries. Most of Swift's admirers don't care about such matters at all. Perhaps they should, but if they did, though they might learn some interesting things, they wouldn't discover anything which would change their evaluation of Swift's stature as a writer. It's the same with Orwell: he is a great writer, but his greatness does not reside in his being right while others were wrong. As the reader of this book will find out, Orwell was frequently wrong, sometimes wrong to the point of silliness, where some of his contemporaries were right. And Orwell never—not once—adopted a dangerously isolated position.

My view that Orwell's key positions were held by many on the Left, and usually by the majority, does not make me think less of him as a writer, because those qualities for which I value his work do not depend upon his being right or upon his being both right and in the minority. Orwell's importance as a writer resides not only in his nine book-length works, at least four of which are superb achievements, but even more in his numerous short pieces, the essays and reviews he turned out rapid-fire, week by week, to put bread on the table. Although Orwell was not an original thinker, and his ideas, broadly characterized, were all fairly standard for his time and social position, he had a superb gift for formulating these ideas sharply, so that their implications appeared fresh and startling. These writings sparkle with polemical virtuosity; they throb with life. They will make entertaining and enlightening reading for centuries to come.

2
The Follower of Intellectual Fashion

> It is perhaps the most characteristic feature of the intellectual that he judges new ideas not by their specific merits but by the readiness with which they fit into his general conceptions, into the picture of the world he regards as modern or advanced.
>
> —F. A. Hayek, "The Intellectuals and Socialism" (1949)

If, as so many people suppose, Orwell is at odds with the conventional thinking of his day, just where does he dissent? What, specifically, are the points on which Orwell strays from the intellectual flock?

Christopher Hitchens has a shot at answering this question. According to Hitchens, in his book on Orwell,

> The three great subjects of the twentieth century were imperialism, fascism, and Stalinism. . . . Most of the intellectual class were fatally compromised by accommodation with one or the other, and some by more than one. (Hitchens 2002, 5)

"Most" means more than fifty percent, so this claim by Hitchens doesn't literally imply that Orwell's views on the three great subjects were unusual. But Hitchens does seem to be implying that they were unusual. For instance, he maintains that Orwell was "uncommonly prescient" on these three topics and on other issues too (10). This suggests that not just slightly more than fifty percent of the intellectual class, but much, much more than fifty percent might have been fatally compromised.

But is it even true that, in the 1930s, more than fifty percent of members of the British intellectual class were fatally compromised with at least one of these ideological movements? I would say: definitely not. But to defend that denial might lead me into a wearisome statistical and methodological labyrinth. Part of the problem is what degree of toleration of Communism counts as fatal compromise with Stalinism.

Does support for the Popular Front policy in the relevant period (1934–1939) constitute a fatally compromising accommodation with Stalinism? If so, then people like Sir Stafford Cripps and Aneurin Bevan were fatally compromised. Yet still, the vast majority of Labour Party members were clearly opposed to the Popular Front (which is why Cripps and Bevan were expelled from the Party), so it's not immediately evident that the majority of the Left, let alone of all intellectuals, could be so classified. But then, the narrow Left had more intellectuals per head than the broad Left, so maybe the majority of Labour Party members should not be counted. Yet even if we decided that most intellectuals were Popular Frontists and therefore fatally compromised, we're still left with the "unpleasant fact" that Orwell, when he wrote *The Road to Wigan Pier* in April–December of 1936, and right up until 3rd May 1937, was himself a Popular Frontist! To defend what Hitchens claims, we might perhaps have to say that Orwell's avoidance of fatal compromise consists in the fact that he abandoned Popular Frontism while it was still quite fashionable (though already demonstrably losing its luster).

Alternatively, we could deny that advocacy of a Popular Front was a fatal compromise with Communism—my guess is that this would have been Hitchens's position. But if support for a Popular Front doesn't qualify, then what does? The Popular Front dominated the Communist Party's activities, and its relations with the non-Communist Left, until the Nazi-Soviet pact, and with that pact, the overwhelming majority of non-Communist leftists who had been fellow-travelers quickly ceased to be so (at least until 22nd June 1941).

Hitchens says that "most" intellectuals were fatally compromised by accommodation with at least one of the evils, so we would have to add in those intellectuals who accommodated with the empire or fascism. But since (as I am about to explain) almost no one on the 1930s Left was pro-empire or pro-fascist, and since leftwing intellectuals greatly outnumbered rightwing intellectuals, it seems difficult to arrive at a plausible percentage total consistent with Hitchens's claim.

As this brief discussion shows, there's no simple formula or easy answer (although Hitchens's claim about "most" does look dubious). And so, instead of seeking to directly refute the claim that "most" 1930s intellectuals were fatally compromised by accommodation with one of the three great evils, I will advance a more modest and easily provable counter-claim. *Throughout the 1930s a very large segment of the Left was simultaneously opposed to the British Empire, to fascism, and to Communism.*

In sooth, if we look at Hitchens's "three great subjects"—what Orwell thinks about them and what the intellectual Left thinks about them—we clearly see how very typical Orwell is. On these three great subjects, Orwell's positions were not very unusual, and nor was he even slightly prescient. And on the issues of the empire and Communism, Orwell himself sometimes wobbled, in a way that many other leftists did not wobble. Accepting Hitchens's three great subjects as a test exactly as Hitchens defines them, not only were there many left intellectuals in the 1930s who scored as well as Orwell, there were many who scored a bit better.

The Left and the Empire

When Orwell wrote about the British Empire, he was primarily thinking of India, or India and Burma together.[1] As he remarked in May 1944, "Imperialism means India" (XVI, 186). There were good reasons for this. The British Empire in the 1930s consisted of various countries with very different degrees of economic development and of self-government. The highest level of self-government was the "dominion": the status reached at that time by Canada, Australia, New Zealand, South Africa, and Southern Ireland. Though often casually considered components of "the empire," these countries were in fact independent sovereign states, voluntarily associated in "the Commonwealth." The Statute of Westminster of 1931 formally recognized what was already the fact: that Britain

1 When Orwell was in Burma in 1922–27 it was administratively part of India. In 1937, when India was given more internal self-government, Burma was separated from India.

could not legislate for the dominions without their consent. A declaration of war by Britain would not commit the dominions. So in September 1939 all the dominions except Ireland (formerly the Irish Free State) voluntarily declared war on Germany. Ireland chose to be neutral. India and Burma, having some degree of internal self-government but not yet dominion status, found themselves at war with Germany, without having been consulted.

As an example of their genuine independence, the dominions operated protective tariffs against imports from Britain, and there was simply nothing Britain could do about this. Continual British immigration to Australia was a well-known traditional fact of life, but when the depression struck in 1930, raising unemployment in Australia, the Australian government suspended emigration from Britain, and again, there was nothing Britain could do about it. A dominion could at any moment, if its government so chose, break all connection by leaving the Commonwealth, as the association of dominions and Britain was called.

The dominions along with Britain itself were a voluntary association of equal and independent states. It goes without saying that there was considerable emotional and political importance in the fact that the dominions were all predominately white (or in the case of South Africa, completely controlled by a substantial white minority), and that all the dominions except South Africa and Ireland were populated mainly by British-descended people who still thought of themselves as British.

British India (including what are now Pakistan, Bangladesh, and Myanmar) was not only by far the most highly-populated part of the 1930s British Empire; it also had a significant degree of internal self-government, by a Congress elected by Indians of property. Taxes and other internal policies were determined by this "Government of India," with only occasional interference by the British government at Westminster. India already operated protective tariffs against British manufacturing. When British people in the 1930s talk about Indian self-rule they are usually talking about advancing India rapidly to dominion status, which while nominally keeping India within the Commonwealth would effectively amount to independence (precisely what happened in 1947). Most British political opinion adopted a perspective of continued future expansion of Indian self-government leading ultimately to dominion status, though some Conservatives expected that this might take many generations.

Orwell had spent five years in Burma in the imperial police and after he returned to England he made a point of reviewing books on Burma and commenting on Burmese issues. Burma, like India, had a significant nationalist movement for independence. Most of the other non-white imperial possessions harbored no such movements before the Second World War, and were at lower levels of economic and cultural development, which according to the thinking of the time implied that they were less ready for self-rule.

By the 1930s, the further extension of Indian self-rule, with eventual dominion status, was hardly controversial among Labourites, Liberals, and most Conservatives. The only real issue was how quickly India should be advanced to dominion status. Many people in all three major parties believed that the mission of the British Empire was to gradually bring about its own extinction. This was the clearly expressed view, for example, of the Conservative Stanley Baldwin, three times Prime Minister. There were die-hard imperialists in the Conservative Party who wanted to limit or slow down further extensions of self-rule, but they were in a minority even in their own party. (What I have stated here was the reality, and the view of well-informed people. Much of the general British public were proud of the empire and thought of everything colored pink on the map as "ours." Explicit anti-imperialism was therefore not popular with the broad public, or even familiar to them, but it was the almost unanimous view on the Left.)

Orwell acknowledged that, in advocating Indian self-rule, he was agreeing with the vast majority of intellectuals. For example, in the course of defending his friend the Indian novelist Mulk Raj Anand against the charge of being prejudicially anti-British, Orwell wrote in 1942: "if Mr. Anand makes it plain that he is anti-imperialist and thinks India ought to be independent, is he not saying something which almost any English intellectual would echo as a matter of course?"[2]

2 XIII, 338. And, for instance: "If there is one point . . . that . . . is not disputed, outside the ranks of the British Conservative Party—it is that Britain ought to stop ruling India as early as possible" (XV, 332).

An indication that the Left and much of the Right was overwhelmingly in favor of self-rule for India is that the Labour government which came to power in July 1945 quickly moved to give dominion status to India, Pakistan, Burma, and Ceylon, all of which had been effectively granted independence by 1947, fully implemented for all of them by early 1948. These enactments were disliked by Churchill and some other Conservatives, but were virtually uncontroversial among Labour Party supporters. The Conservative opposition in Parliament did not feel emboldened to bring the issue to a vote: even regretful Conservative politicians accepted quickly and quietly that the matter was settled and irreversible.

As evidence of the intellectuals' fatal compromise on the empire issue, Hitchens cites—Sidney and Beatrice Webb! On this issue, by the 1930s, the Webbs' following was minute. Not one percent of the broad or the narrow Left had any sympathy with the Webbs' pro-empire position. On the issue of empire, the Webbs had been left behind, while Orwell sailed in the great mainstream.

Yet, for all his anti-imperial rhetoric, and unlike most of the Left, Orwell was not an unqualified proponent of independence for India and Burma. Orwell several times criticized leftist assertions that India and Burma should be given immediate independence, asserting that these countries could never become truly independent and that the Nationalist movements were sham movements, led by people who did not really want independence. I'll come back to this point shortly (and in more detail in Chapter 6).

Leftwing Anti-Fascism in the 1930s

Although the roots of Fascism lay in the Left, and Mussolini had been the pre-eminent leader of Italian socialism, the Left in the late 1920s and 1930s was united in being hostile to Fascism. Only a very few writers, like Georges Sorel and Bernard Shaw, had welcomed Fascism from within a leftist perspective, and to those leftists who knew of it, this generally appeared grotesque. There were many leftists who became Fascists or National Socialists, but this was viewed by everyone, including these persons themselves, as their quitting the Left and becoming adherents of the Right. As Mussolini, the former Marxist revolutionary, famously announced in 1922, "The world is turning to the right."

In leftist writing at the time, including Orwell's, references to "fascism" are most commonly references to National Socialist Germany, which in point of fact was not Fascist at all. Later the term "fascist" was also applied by the Left to the Nationalist forces in Spain, though most of these were closely akin to neither Fascism nor National Socialism. Thus, "fascism," as we most commonly encounter the term, is a theoretical construct of the Left, and a way of referring collectively to Hitler's Germany, Mussolini's Italy, the Spanish Nationalists, and several other regimes and movements. I will use "Fascism" with a capital F to denote real Fascism (Mussolini's movement or its close imitators) and "fascism" with a small f to denote those who are labeled "fascists" in this influential leftist theory.

Although the Left in the 1930s were virtually all strongly anti-fascist, there was a serious and consequential division within the Left on how to combat fascism. I have to say something about this here, because Orwell, after August 1939, often attacks leftists who, he claims, are not truly anti-fascist or are covertly pro-fascist, and Hitchens or some of his readers may have these attacks in mind when Hitchens raises the possibility that Orwell was remarkable in not being fatally compromised by accommodation with fascism.

Most of the broad Left (consisting mainly of the great bulk of the Labour Party) had supported the First World War, while most of the narrow Left had opposed it. In the period 1928–1933, however, the opinion gained ground among the broad Left that the narrow Left had been correct: the war should never have been supported, and neither should any future war. The Left became dominated by anti-war enthusiasm which was usually loosely called "pacifism."

And so, in the early 1930s, we have the large phenomenon of leftists who were both strongly opposed to fascism and strongly opposed to rearmament which would make Britain ready to wage war against the fascist powers. In the years 1937–39 George Orwell was an adherent of this anti-war view, even as this view was rapidly losing ground in the Left. Then, in a dramatic conversion, literally overnight, on August 22nd 1939, Orwell switched to a pro-war position. For the next six years he criticized, denounced, and ridiculed the "pacifists," whom he sometimes accused of being pro-fascist. The people he was now attacking were maintaining the position he had himself taken, until 22nd August 1939.

I look more closely at these developments, both on the Left and in Orwell's life, in later chapters. Here it's enough to be clear that there was a momentous change in Orwell's attitude to the war on a specific date, that the direction of change of Orwell's ideas was one that many leftists had taken, from anti-war to pro-war—though Orwell's switch of position was unusually abrupt and unusually late—and that when Orwell, after August 1939, attacked the "pacifists" for being objectively pro-fascist, he was attacking a minority left view from the standpoint of the majority left view.

Again, we see that Orwell was identified with mainstream leftwing positions, and in no way isolated.

Orwell and Communism

So obvious is it that the overwhelming majority of politically-minded 1930s intellectuals were both anti-empire and anti-fascist that it is tempting to unpack Hitchens's contention in the following simple way: Orwell is unusual in being both leftwing and anti-Communist. Certainly, writers other than Hitchens have thought so, and many of Hitchens's readers may get this impression.

In the 1930s, there was nothing unusual in being leftwing and anti-Communist. In 1936, when some notable leftists were already decidedly anti-Communist, Orwell had some criticisms of Communists but despite that was a supporter of the Popular Front policy promoted by the Communists. After May 1937, following his experiences in Spain, Orwell adopted a more hostile attitude to the Communists and to the Popular Front, roughly the same hostile attitude already held by many people on the Left, such as Bertrand Russell, Fenner Brockway, Clifford Allen, John Middleton Murry, and the bulk of the Labour Party.

A legend has developed around Communist influence in the 1930s. As a result, many writers now routinely make two mistakes: they greatly exaggerate the influence of the Communists, and they tend to equate "left" with "pro-Communist," when in fact most of the British

Left were never pro-Communist. It was by no means anomalous to be extremely leftwing and strongly anti-Communist. This, however, is a complex issue requiring some clarification, which I provide in Chapter 9 below.

Unlike some countries, Britain never had a big Communist Party: CPGB membership had a roller-coaster of ups and downs but never at any point came close to a hundred thousand, and the CP never had more than two Members of Parliament (a figure which exaggerates rather than understates their popular support, as these two were in highly anomalous constituencies; in the vast majority of constituencies the Communist vote could never hope to rise to triple digits).[3] The Labour Party, publicly committed to socialism, was the main opposition party in Britain, the only serious electoral alternative to the National government. Since the 1920s the Labour Party had proscribed the Communist Party and all its front organizations, expelled individuals and branches who were found to be entangled with Communists, and harshly criticized the Communists in pamphlets and other literature.

Orwell was not isolated in his anti-Communism. His critical view of Soviet Russia and its Communist Party supporters was widely shared on the Left.

Russell and Orwell

I could compare Orwell with a sample of leftwing writers of the 1930s, but for a simple, revealing comparison, we can look at the positions taken by Bertrand Russell, possibly the most influential British leftwing writer of the time. He wrote numerous books with major sales, as well as many articles and speeches. He was an indefatigable advocate and agitator for various leftwing causes.

Russell, like Orwell, was a firm opponent of "fascism." He consistently denounced both Nazi Germany and the Spanish Nationalists.[4]

3 In Britain, "constituency" is the term for an electoral district at the national level. The number of seats in the British House of Commons is not fixed by constitutional law. In 1935 it was 615 and in 1945, 640.

4 Russell 2002, 107–08, 111–12.

Like Orwell and numerous other leftwing intellectuals, Russell moved from a "pacifist" or anti-war position to one of support for the war against Hitler (and Russell did so five months before Orwell did). Russell had been imprisoned during World War I for his anti-war activities (technically, for insulting the United States, a wartime ally). In 1936 he published *Which Way to Peace?*, a detailed argument against a second British war with Germany. As with many others who decided, after opposing the coming war, that the war has to be fought after all, the event which changed his mind was Hitler's action in March 1939 in occupying Bohemia and Moravia, in breach of the Munich agreement. Russell made no public statement about his change of mind until after the war had started—the same was true of Orwell.

Russell was an active campaigner for independence for the colonies. He was Chairman of the India League. Russell, along with other British leftists, notably Fenner Brockway, threw a great deal of his energies into campaigning for Indian self-rule, something Orwell never did.

Bertrand Russell had become a strong critic of Soviet Russia and opponent of Communism by 1920. His *Practice and Theory of Bolshevism* was influential throughout the 1920s and 1930s. Later writers have sometimes under-rated Russell's strong anti-Communism because they have carelessly read back into the 1930s what they know of Russell in the 1960s and 1970s. Beginning around 1958 (eight years after Orwell's death), Russell became so impressed by the danger of nuclear war that he favored a neutralist position for Britain in the Cold War, and called for unilateral nuclear disarmament by Britain and France (though not by the United States or the Soviet Union). Russell even tilted to the Soviet side, because Russia seemed more willing than the West to back down to avoid nuclear war, as in the Cuban missile crisis. But earlier, from 1920 to the late 1950s, Russell was a consistent opponent of Communism. In 1944 he wrote that Communism was even more evil than Nazism, and after the war, he suggested pre-emptively bombing Soviet Russia before the Russians could get nuclear weapons.

Russell, who spent some years in the United States, was alarmed by the dangers to civil liberty evident in the phenomenon usually termed "McCarthyism," and in this context made some statements that sound somewhat favorable to Soviet Russia. At the same time he sharply attacked various aspects of Soviet policy, such as the persecution of scientists who would not endorse Lysenkoism. Taking Russell overall and Orwell overall, Russell was more staunchly and unwaveringly anti-Communist in the period up to Orwell's death.

Russell prior to 1950 was at least as much opposed to the empire, to fascism, and to Communism as Orwell. However, while Russell maintained a fairly steadfast and consistent position on these three issues, Orwell wobbled seriously on the empire and his opposition to Communism was qualified by his conviction that it represented the probable future. (Again, let's be clear, I am not berating Orwell for his vacillations or hesitations; I am merely controverting the factual claim implied by Hitchens, that Orwell was unusual in being anti-fascist, anti-imperialist, and anti-Communist.)

Although Orwell was committed in principle to self-rule for the colonies, he repeatedly stated that independence for India and Burma was impracticable, and that the Indians and Burmese wouldn't really want independence if it were offered to them.[5] On this point, Orwell was untypical of the Left, who usually demanded full self-rule for India and Burma as soon as possible, and were quite sure the Indians and Burmese would want it. So Hitchens had it exactly the wrong way around: the vast bulk of the Left and a sizeable chunk of the Right (meaning here people who would vote Conservative) favored prompt self-rule for India and Burma after the war, while Orwell went out of his way to question and denigrate this policy goal. Independence arrived for both India and Burma just a few years after Orwell had pronounced this to be manifestly impracticable.

Orwell's hostility to Communism, though generally powerful, was clouded by a deep-rooted ambivalence. Aside from his brief period of Popular Front support in 1936–37, even after Orwell had become an open enemy of the Communists he continued to think of Communism as being somehow progressive and laudable. Orwell made occasional statements suggesting that the Soviet Union and the Communist movement might have the potential to evolve into something better. While not

5 See my discussion in Chapter 6 below.

wanting the Soviet system to spread west, he did not look forward to the downfall of the Soviet state in Russia.[6]

By the standard of Hitchens's "three great subjects," Bertrand Russell scores somewhat better than George Orwell. Yet no one has ever considered Russell (in the period 1920–1958) an isolated or politically unorthodox figure. No one has singled him out as the conscience of the Left or considered his broad views on policy as being anything other than commonplace within the Left. The fact that Russell in this period is never viewed as a maverick while Orwell most commonly is so viewed has little to do with the content of their respective positions. It arises mainly from the fact that Orwell, in the techniques and mannerisms of his persuasive prose, frequently adopts a rhetorical posture of presenting himself as a brave dissident from conventional leftist orthodoxy, whereas Russell doesn't do this.

The Reception of *Wigan Pier*

When people mention Orwell's isolated, maverick, or unorthodox status, they usually appeal to at least one of three episodes in his life. Each of these three episodes (and no other) is often appealed to in support of the popular view that Orwell was a fearless deviant, an unusually non-conforming individual who spoke his mind without fear or favor. They are:

1. March 1936–March 1937. The circumstances surrounding the publication of *The Road to Wigan Pier*.

2. June–July 1937. The rejection by the *New Statesman* of Orwell's writings on Spain.

3. March–August 1944. The delay in acceptance for publication of *Animal Farm*, because of its anti-Soviet message.

Let's consider these three episodes in turn. It's not essential to my case that Orwell was never at any time out of step with most of the Left,

6 See my discussion in Chapter 9 below.

or with the dominant faction of the Left; what I do maintain is that he is always, when articulating a political position, expressing a view in conformity with at least one major segment of the Left.

The once-standard account of the origin of *The Road to Wigan Pier*, repeated in early books and articles about Orwell, is that Orwell was commissioned by Victor Gollancz for the Left Book Club to go to the North of England, observe the poor, and write an account of what he discovered.[7] But when he turned in his manuscript, it was found to be so strongly critical of socialism and of the Communists that there was a lot of nervousness about publishing it, and when it did appear, the book included a foreword by Gollancz, apologizing for some of the unfortunate statements, highly critical of socialism and Communism, made in the book. Despite this, we're told, the book upset many socialists because of its forthright criticisms of socialism.

After this story had been repeated several times in commentaries on Orwell, it was eventually pointed out that Orwell's work could not have been commissioned by the Left Book Club, which had not been founded, nor definitely decided to be founded, when Orwell left for the North. The topic of the Distressed Areas was a fashionable preoccupation, because of the highly publicized marches of the unemployed and Walter Greenwood's meteoric best-seller, *Love on the Dole*. For the author of *Down and Out in Paris and London* to make first-hand observations in the Distressed Areas and write a book about his observations was a very natural publishing move.

Orwell embarked upon writing what was to become *The Road to Wigan Pier* without any thought of the Left Book Club. The publisher Victor Gollancz may have assumed that the book, by someone who had recently been an openly-declared non-socialist with an apparently apolitical stance, would, like *Down and Out in Paris and London*, draw no political conclusions.

Gollancz later suggested to Orwell—apparently after having the entire manuscript—that the book be included in the Left Book Club. Orwell's immediate reaction to Gollancz's suggestion was that he doubted the book would be considered leftwing enough. But Gollancz wanted

7 Rovere 1965, xv.

the book in the Left Book Club, and Orwell agreed, despite his misgivings. A different picture now emerges.

The period from 1934 to August 1939 was the period of the Popular Front campaign, the time when the Communist Party attained the peak of its intellectual influence on the non-Communist Left. The Left Book Club was the highest achievement of the CPGB in its bid, during the Popular Front phase, to achieve sway over the British Left. The Left Book Club was not just a book club, but a continual stream of pamphlets, magazines, public meetings, discussion meetings, weekend schools, dances, socials, and other events. The Left Book Club was a vibrant church.

The selection committee of the Left Book Club consisted of three individuals, each of whom was at this time a reliable Communist fellow-traveler: Victor Gollancz, John Strachey, and Harold Laski. Since Gollancz owned the publishing company, he was a bit more equal than the other two. (The Gollancz firm was well fixed, because of its popular Lord Peter Wimsey novels.) Though none of these three was ever a member of the CPGB, they were at this time all in favor of intimate collaboration with it, and Strachey was being regularly coached on what to write by Palme Dutt[8]—though Strachey could say it so much more elegantly and persuasively than Dutt ever did. None of the three, of course, vetoed the choice of *The Road to Wigan Pier* as a Left Book Club selection, as each of them was empowered to do.

The Road to Wigan Pier falls into two parts of approximately equal length. The first part consists of reportage of the lives of some of the Lancashire and Yorkshire poor, mainly focused on the squalid and the harsh. It is vivid, impassioned, replete with horrifying observations of squalor, just the thing that morally indignant socialists would find agreeable. The second part consists of remarks, partly autobiographical and partly commentary on the socialist movement and on general social issues. Here Orwell says harsh things about some socialists and makes a few snippy remarks about the Communists.

8 Thomas 1973, 120–96. Dutt was not only the leading ideological authority in the Communist Party of Great Britain but also a leading ideological authority in the Communist International.

We don't know precisely what conversations Orwell had with Gollancz before going to the North to collect material for the as yet unnamed book. But if the understanding was that Orwell would produce a study of living conditions in the North, then it would be natural for the publisher to insist that most or all of the second part of the book be eliminated or greatly condensed. To the present-day student of Orwell's thinking, this second part is a goldmine, the most extended piece of systematic exposition of his views on general social issues that Orwell had ever penned. To readers at the time, it might have seemed a self-indulgent exercise by a very minor writer, with a streak of sanctimonious, self-obsessed whining, volubly declaiming his distinctly unoriginal thoughts on the world.

The Road to Wigan Pier was published in its entirety as both a trade edition and as a selection in the Left Book Club, and was a considerable success. (There was also an abridged edition with only the documentary first part, omitting Orwell's opinionated second part, but this was a very minor spin-off: the complete edition was by far the bigger seller, both to Left Book Club members and in the book trade.) The book was one of the biggest-selling volumes of the Left Book Club, and up to 1944 (when Penguin brought out a cheap paperback edition of *Down and Out in Paris and London*) was Orwell's largest-selling book and his only commercial success.

It is repeatedly stated in commentary on Orwell that the second half of *The Road to Wigan Pier* contains serious and damaging criticisms of socialism. What an outspoken and awkward chap this Orwell must be, offering devastating criticisms of socialism at the very point where he is passionately advocating socialism!

The truth is that *The Road to Wigan Pier* advances *absolutely no* serious criticisms of *socialism*. It mentions such serious criticisms in passing only to ridicule and dismiss them with a superficial wave of the hand.[9] It accepts the necessity and workability of socialism in an extraordinarily naive and uncritical fashion. Compare it, for example, with G. D. H. Cole's *The Simple Case for Socialism* (1935), which takes up considerable space addressing criticisms of socialism. *Wigan Pier* does

9 See my discussion in Chapter 3 below.

contain harsh criticisms of *the lifestyles and personal foibles of some socialists*, and these criticisms would have seemed a tad excessive to some leftists at the time, while highly gratifying to others.

And what of Orwell's attitude to the Communists? The most negative comment is his mention of "Bolshevik commissars (half gangster, half gramophone)" (201). However, this comes near the end of a section dealing with ugly stereotypes of socialists held by non-socialists who ought to be recruitable for the socialist movement. The phrase is one of a series of unfortunate "pictures" of socialists in the minds of non-socialists. Orwell displays considerable sympathy with these non-socialists, but still, the phrase is implicitly attributed to them, not to himself. He also mentions "the stupid cult of Russia" (201). He had earlier made clear that what he primarily objected to about this cult was its emphasis on industrial achievements. A major theme of the second part of the book is that the socialist movement has suffered because of its identification with rapid industrial development.

In two places (V, 160, 199) Orwell mentions the fact that just a few years earlier, the Communists had been attacking "democratic forces" whom they were now trying to ally themselves with. This might seem surprising, especially in light of Orwell's later statements that he had no understanding of the differences among leftwing groups and viewed them with impatience (VI, 188). However, in 1934–35 Orwell had been getting his view of socialism mainly from ILP members,[10] and then on his visit to the North, from leftists of different affiliations. Thus, he would undoubtedly have repeatedly heard of the fact that, up to 1934, the Communist Party was denouncing the ILP and the Labour Party as "social fascist," and that the CP had then dropped this hostility in favor of co-operation. *Wigan Pier* was written near the end of the period when the CP was cozying up to the ILP, and when many people even expected these two parties to unite to form a single revolutionary party. Communist vilification of the ILP as "Trotskyist" lay just a few months in the future. In 1936 Orwell evidently shared the view of many on the Left that the Communist Party had once been obtusely "sectarian" but had

10 The ILP (Independent Labour Party), the only party Orwell ever joined, is discussed in Chapters 3, 7, 8, and 9 below.

now turned over a new leaf and could be trusted as a firm ally in the pre-eminent task of the moment: fighting fascism.

Orwell makes clear (202–06) that he endorses the movement for a Popular Front. This means the co-operation of all antifascist parties, both socialist and non-socialist, against fascism, which in practical effect in 1936 Britain would mean that the Labour Party should lift its ban on the Communist Party, giving the CP free rein to infiltrate and capture positions in the Labour Party. Orwell remarks that the Socialist movement does not want to attract "the type of humbug who passes resolutions 'against Fascism and Communism,' i.e. against rats and rat poison" (206). Here Orwell recognizes the existence of people who condemn fascism and Communism alike, and emphatically repudiates this position,[11] endorsing Communism as an effective agency against the great evil of fascism.

The Road to Wigan Pier is the work of a Communist fellow-traveler. This is hardly surprising, since to have one's work appear in the Left Book Club in 1936 was *ipso facto* the act of a fellow traveler (or of a Communist).[12] (After Spain, Orwell denounced the Left Book Club along with the Popular Front movement in general, and his 1939 novel *Coming Up for Air* has an uncomplimentary vignette of a Left Book Club meeting.) Orwell's superficial criticisms of Communism in 1936 were not unusual among fellow travelers of the period; indeed, they were milder than many. Orwell did not actually say anything against the Soviet

11 He makes a similar remark at X, 534. After May 1937 he would draw attention to the essential similarity of fascist and Communist systems (XI, 159–60) while sometimes pointing out that it is over-simple to regard them as identical.

12 Leading Labour Party figures criticized the Left Book Club because it did not include any books by mainstream Labourites. To neutralize such criticism, the Club adopted as a token the distinctly uninspiring book by Clement Attlee, *The Labour Party in Perspective*. Aside from that, about a third of all Left Book Club selections were by Communists, the rest by carefully monitored fellow travelers. It was out of the question for Trotskyist works to appear in the Left Book Club before August 1939, after which the Club continued, greatly reduced in membership and permitting some anti-Communist works.

social or political order itself (except implicitly, as an example of the evils of machine production). There is no suggestion that Russia is not socialist. There is no mention of the fact that Russia is a brutal dictatorship without any democracy or free speech—though such observations can easily be found in the contemporaneous writings of acknowledged fellow-travelers such as Harold J. Laski.

It is striking that, as early as *The Road to Wigan Pier*, Orwell mentions the possibility of a future "totalitarian world," a collectivist "slave-world," no longer capitalist, with all power in the hands of "a small caste of rulers and their bravos" (200). But Orwell presents this simply as something that could come from fascism; there is no hint that it could come from Communism or that it could be the unintended consequence of attempts by the Left to institute socialism in Britain.

At this stage the Comintern quite deliberately courted leftists who voiced criticisms of the Soviet Union, provided they were prepared to accept the Communists as legitimate members of the Left and allies in the struggle against fascism. Orwell accepted them as much more than that. *The Road to Wigan Pier* was published on 8th March 1937, while Orwell was fighting in Spain. Right up until the point where he unexpectedly found himself involved in the Barcelona street battles of May 1937, Orwell never wavered in his desire to be transferred from the POUM militia to the Communist-controlled International Brigade.

To be acceptable to the Communists, fellow-travelers had to be non-Trotskyists, and they had to be supporters of the Popular Front policy, but since no Trotskyist would support the Popular Front, and in any case the number of real Trotskyists in Britain was tiny (three or four hundred at most, none of them prominent figures), this was not a serious problem. A source of possible friction was the issue of the show trials of former leading Bolsheviks. Any leftist who suggested these trials might be frame-ups risked being attacked by the Communists as a "Trotskyist"` and therefore an agent of fascism. The first Moscow Trial, the Trial of Sixteen, occurred to great publicity in August 1936, while Orwell was working on *Wigan Pier*. But, while many on the Left, including the major leftist weekly *The New Statesman*, were already criticizing these sham trials, Orwell (as far as we can determine) voiced no skepticism about them until nearly two years later, a year after he returned from Spain (XI, 158).

The Communist Party leader Harry Pollitt wrote a hostile review of *The Road to Wigan Pier*, published in the *Daily Worker* on 17th March 1937. Most writers on Orwell misunderstand the significance of this. By the time the book was printed, Pollitt knew that Orwell was fighting in the POUM militia, and was therefore a "Trotsky-fascist." Pollitt would have remembered that Orwell had refused to commit himself to joining the International Brigade and would not have known that Orwell was at heart a fellow traveler who was now trying to get out of the POUM militia and into the International Brigade. When he saw Pollitt's review, Orwell immediately concluded that his POUM connection was the reason for its hostility (XI, 16).

If a few accidental circumstances had turned out differently, and Orwell had been fighting (as he would have preferred) for the International Brigade instead of the POUM militia, the *Daily Worker* would never have panned the book, and very likely Pollitt would have praised it to the skies. The same goes for all subsequent references to the book by Communists and their close allies. These do not show that there is something in *The Road to Wigan Pier* that upset the Left. They merely show that, around the time of the book's release, but not earlier, the Communist Party classified Orwell as a Trotskyist and therefore a target for demonization and destruction, whatever he had written or not written. To take another counterfactual, if the timing had been a bit different, and Orwell had already been fighting for the POUM militia when the volume came up for consideration, and the Communists had already entered upon their final conspiracy to liquidate the POUM, there is no way that the Left Book Club would have selected the book, or Gollancz would have published it, even outside the Left Book Club. Gollancz and the Left Book Club were effectively under the thumb of the CPGB; they were not open to anything the CPGB viewed as Trotskyism.[13]

13 Because of his perceived eminence at the time, Stephen Spender was shown unusual latitude. His *Forward from Liberalism* contained remarks critical of the Moscow trials, but the harshest of these was added by Spender during proof corrections and therefore escaped the notice of the LBC triumvirate until the book was out (Sutherland 2005, 207). *Forward from Liberalism* was the instrument for converting many to Communism, and no doubt some of them were impressed by the broad-mindedness that allowed such friendly but severe criticisms of the Soviet government into print.

During the Popular Front period, some notable individuals were expelled from the Labour Party for agitating for a Popular Front. And yet, if we look closely at those leftists who supported the Popular Front, we see that the great majority of them retained some suspicion of the Communists and some critical distance. They were not tempted to vote for, much less to join, the CP. They considered the CP (as representative of the reliably anti-fascist Soviet Union) a valuable ally in the fight against fascism, but an ally which deserved criticism and needed to be watched. Orwell's public attitude to Communism in late 1936 and early 1937 was not out of line with the fashionable attitude of these Popular Front leftists.

Gollancz added a foreword to *The Road to Wigan Pier* which now seems fussy and pathetically over-anxious. But this ill-advised foreword should also be seen as a more tolerant alternative than requiring Orwell to drop the second part of the book. And although Gollancz's foreword is indeed a bit silly, the Left Book Club was fairly new at this time, and Gollancz explains that what concerns him is that members have reacted to earlier volumes by supposing that everything stated in them is an official Left Book Club line. Gollancz could have published *The Road to Wigan Pier* outside the Left Book Club, since it was solely at his initiative and insistence that it had been considered for the Left Book Club. But he must have judged that its appeal to Club members would outweigh any qualms some members might have had, and he was right.

It's easy to read Gollancz's foreword, assume without corroboration that it reflects widespread disquiet among socialists about *The Road to Wigan Pier*, and then see the Communist-instigated hostility to the book after its release as a continuation of the same disquiet. Looking at it in this superficial way, we infer that Orwell's book scandalized a major portion of the Left. But once we understand that the Communist-instigated hostility was independent of what was in the book, we can put the book's reception in proper perspective. *The Road to Wigan Pier* was a hit with leftist readers, and there is no evidence that more than a tiny handful of them were at all discomfited by it, and even those who were (like Gollancz and Laski) mostly considered it a positive contribution on balance.

The Road to Wigan Pier does not reveal an Orwell who was isolated or out of place on the fashionable Left, but a Popular Front leftist with very typical views on current policy. Of course, it is merely his *broadly characterized political views* which are typical, not his talent as a writer nor all of his specific detailed comments.

Dirty Spanish Linen

When he came back to England from Spain in June 1937, Orwell was sharply critical of the account widely accepted by British leftists of the Spanish Civil War. Here is certainly a genuine instance where Orwell has a serious difference with the dominant faction within the Left. Yet Orwell's was not an isolated voice, and a close look at this episode reveals it in a different light than that normally shed upon it by Orwell's more uncritical admirers.

In the early part of the Spanish Civil War, the Republican military forces arrayed against the Nationalists were divided according to political affiliation. Orwell fought in the militia of the POUM, an anti-Stalinist Marxist party which had an appreciable following only in the province of Catalonia, and even there was not a major force. In May 1937, the Communists, who had come to be the effective government of Catalonia, liquidated the POUM. Its members were arrested and many of them were tortured and killed. Orwell and his wife Eileen (who had got a job in Barcelona) had to escape from Spain, just one jump ahead of their murderous Communist-led pursuers. It was a close call: Orwell and Eileen could easily have been caught and killed, and when Orwell arrived back in England, many POUM people were still in Communist-controlled government jails.

The Communists disseminated the story that the POUM had been secretly working for the Nationalists (or "the fascists," as the Left always misleadingly referred to the Franco forces). This was untrue; it was something the Communists had simply made up. (Individual Communists in the know might reconcile themselves to such mendacity by reasoning that the POUM, though not directed by fascists, was acting in a way which, in the judgment of the Communists, objectively helped the fascists. Since these issues needed to be simplified for the backward masses, it was therefore smart tactics to say that the POUM were conscious fascist agents.) All these accusations of fascism acquire a certain irony from the fact that, within a couple of years, the Soviet Union and its CPGB instrument were to align themselves with Hitler (though they omitted to congratulate Trotsky for having been right all along). At the time, the Communists presented the events in Barcelona in May 1937 as a fascist-backed POUM uprising against the Republican government. In fact it was (though Orwell apparently didn't see this) part of a Communist plan to physically eliminate all the Communists' leftist critics. The POUM was taken by surprise by the street fighting and, although bound to support the CNT workers against the police, played a minor role in the action.

Back in England, Orwell found that the Communist account was repeated uncritically in mainstream news sources such as the *News Chronicle*. He submitted an article and a book review to the leading leftwing intellectual weekly, the *New Statesman and Nation* (usually referred to just as the *New Statesman*). These submissions were rejected, and the *New Statesman* people made it clear to Orwell that they would not publish anything exposing the role of the Communist Party in Spain, not even in their correspondence columns.[14] Orwell then announced that he would refuse to write anything further for the *New Statesman*. This certainly shows Orwell disagreeing with an influential leftist institution.

Although the *New Statesman* refused to publish anything examining the "civil war within the Left" in Spain, and although the CP line was being disseminated by major newspapers such as the *News Chronicle*, as well as by the *New Statesman*, and of course by the *Daily Worker*, *Labour Monthly*, and other organs directly controlled by the Communists, books and articles taking essentially the same view as Orwell continued to appear. Orwell's articles on Spain could not appear in the *New Statesman*. His rejected article appeared in *Controversy*,[15] while the rejected review of Borkenau appeared in *Time and Tide*, a very well-known liberal publication. Another article, "Spilling the Spanish Beans,"

14 Just a few weeks earlier, in June 1937, Orwell had written (in a private letter) praising the *New Statesman* for giving space to non-Communist views on Spain (XI, 27).

15 *Controversy* (which later became *Left Forum*) had grown out of the ILP's internal discussion journal to become a well-respected forum for diverse leftwing views.

appeared in *New English Weekly* (XI, 41–46). *The New English Weekly* had informed Orwell they would publish anything by him (though because they didn't pay, and Orwell depended on his writing for his livelihood, he didn't send them much).

Lebedoff considers that Orwell "wrote so few articles before the war because no one would publish them" and no one would publish them because he was a leftist who was "known to be fiercely anticommunist."[16] This is a misreading of the actual circumstances. Between coming back from Spain and the start of the war (two years and two months), Orwell wrote two complete books, *Homage to Catalonia* and *Coming Up for Air*, and he gave them priority. He also wrote much of the book of essays *Inside the Whale*, completed in December 1939. Yet despite distraction by serious illness requiring several months' hospitalization,[17] and despite other activities such as writing his (subsequently lost) anti-war pamphlet and visiting Morocco for his health, he additionally wrote and published during this period thirty book reviews (substantial, not brief notices) and six articles, which averages about one published piece every three weeks. He could easily have written and published a lot more, had he elected to spend less time on writing the books, or had he been in better health. In October 1937, Orwell wrote that he was getting "letters from all quarters" asking him to write something (a new experience for him) but he was turning them down because by contract he had to complete *Homage to Catalonia* (XI, 93). Being outspokenly anti-Communist was not a serious career liability for a leftist writer in Britain in the 1930s.

Orwell's *Homage to Catalonia* was published in April 1938, not by the fellow-traveler Gollancz but by the more independent-minded leftist publisher, Secker and Warburg. Although the book turned out to be a flop in terms of immediate sales, it was reviewed quite widely, including a few extremely favorable reviews in prominent places. The review in *The Observer* (a respected national Sunday paper) was little short of rapturous. British leftists who wanted the truth to come out about Spain included not only anarchists, syndicalists, and Trotskyists, all pretty negligible in numerical following, but also the ILP (Independent Labour

16 Lebedoff 2008, 115.
17 Taylor 2003, 251.

Party), which at this time, though in steep decline, still had several Members of Parliament and a bigger membership than the Communist Party.

The ILP in 1937 had a "Socialist Bookshop," a mail-order book service which they hoped to boost into a sort of anti-Stalinist rival of the Left Book Club, and approached Secker and Warburg, as a publisher open to leftwing works of a non-Comintern orientation, to make a deal through this "Bookshop" to publish a number of specific named works, including what would become *Homage to Catalonia*. Nothing came of this idea. A segment of the English left was well informed of the interpretation which dissented from the CP line, and agreed with it. Orwell himself wrote a letter to the editor of the *Manchester Guardian* (a private letter, not for publication), congratulating that paper on its reporting of events in Spain (XI, 82). (*The Manchester Guardian* had already attained the status of a prestigious national newspaper, and later would become simply *The Guardian*.) *The Daily Herald* (a major national daily perceived as the voice of the Labour Party) also gave space to the non-CP version of events in Barcelona.[18]

The *New Statesman* continued to welcome Orwell's writings. They were happy to publish Orwell's articles on any topic other than Spain, while Orwell published his articles on Spain in other outlets. The refusal to write any more for the *New Statesman* was purely a decision of Orwell's. Orwell maintained his boycott for only a few months: he began writing for the *New Statesman* again after the outbreak of war, though he always thereafter privately viewed the journal and its editor with contempt.

18 Many Irish workers were resident in England and voted for the Labour Party. These Irish Catholics were continually being bombarded by the Catholic clergy with pro-Franco propaganda. (This was a time when nearly all Irish Catholics would attend mass every week.) While this did not, of course, make Labour Party leaders or officials qualify their support for the Spanish Republic, it did make Labour Party writers more careful about what they said, and no doubt contributed to the fact that the *Daily Herald* was somewhat fairer to all sides in Spain, and therefore incidentally would give more mention to the Spanish leftist critics of the Communist Party. The fact that the ILP was still greatly respected within the Labour Party also helped.

What was at issue between Orwell and Kingsley Martin, editor of the *New Statesman*? I don't at all dispute that Martin and others harbored some serious illusions about the Communists from which Orwell, by this time, had freed himself. But both Orwell and Martin wanted a Republican victory in Spain. Both styled the Nationalists as "fascists," and identified fascism with the defense of capitalism. Both Orwell and Martin were broadly "pacifist" with respect to the impending war with Germany. And lest we exaggerate the *New Statesman*'s pro-Soviet tilt, we should recall that this periodical was already vigorously denouncing the Moscow Trials and the purges as outrageous frame-ups and atrocities, a matter on which Orwell had not yet pronounced.

Martin's argument against publishing Orwell's pieces on Spain was that this would objectively weaken the Republican side and make a Nationalist victory more likely. Orwell's reply was that exposure of the facts would *not* weaken the Republican side. Although there are some places where Orwell maintains that it's best to tell the truth even where it is to the disadvantage of "our side," there are other places where he takes the opposite view. In one letter, Orwell states: "I would keep silent about the whole affair if I thought it would help the Spanish government" (XI, 118).

One urgent motive for Orwell to spill the beans was the hope of getting some of the leftist political prisoners released. However, Orwell mentions that some of these very prisoners had urged him not to publicize the facts, because they believed it would hurt the Republican cause (XI, 118). Still, it remains true that dozens of imprisoned leftists were butchered by the Communists and their Socialist Party enablers, and many of them might have been released if the British Left had been more vocally critical.

Orwell's claim that exposure of the facts would not hurt the Republican side in Spain is dubious. If the behavior of the Communists had become better known outside Spain, this surely would have diminished the considerable flow of men and materials into Spain in support of the Republic. At this time Orwell believed that the Republic still might win, or that a stalemate between the two sides was the probable outcome. The Republic was already doomed, but Orwell didn't think so. Martin was probably right on the narrow counterfactual question: the Spanish Republic's demise would have been made more certain and more swift by a wider international knowledge of the Communists' treacherous and brutal actions against the Spanish Left. Although Orwell's writings on this topic, referring to the threatened death of objective truth, are penetrating and disturbing and foreshadow *Nineteen Eighty-Four*, what was at stake at the time was a tactical dispute between leftists who were agreed on nearly all their objectives and presuppositions, and both of whom were ready to be less than fully candid in print if this helped the Left against the Right. And on the purely factual issue of the probable results of various tactics, Orwell was very likely mistaken.

Aside from the prevalence of the Communist account of the events in Barcelona, we should bear in mind the inherent difficulty of explaining what had really happened. To begin with, you had to grasp the fact that in its Spanish policies the Communist Party was on the right wing of the Republican camp. This would appear incredible to most British people who might take an interest. Then you had to get some idea of the differences between the Communists (and their Socialist Party allies) and leftwing anti-Communists like the POUM. It would be difficult to outline these differences without provoking the thought that on these matters the POUM line was reckless and unlikely to succeed, while the Communist line was more sensible. That would not excuse the imprisonments, the tortures, the murders, and the lies of the Communists, but it might reduce the incentive to expose them.

Orwell was right to help to expose the facts. But today we can say that cheaply, because we can see that almost the entire Left, Orwell included, was seriously deluded about Spain. They believed that the outcome in Spain would be decisive for the future of world civilization. The main leftist theory was that capitalism was in terminal crisis because of the ineluctable declining rate of profit and that the capitalists had paid the fascists to take power and reduce workers' wages, thus prolonging the lifespan of senescent capitalism. All that now seems quite incredible to everyone, but it was firmly believed at the time. And if you believed that, you would be tempted to let the embarrassing facts lie uncovered for a while, in the interests of winning the immediate struggle against the great evil—fascism.

Looked at in a broader context, Orwell's turning against Popular Frontism because of Communist behavior in Spain was part of a general process of leftist disenchantment with the Popular Front. The Communists were promoting the Popular Front at the same time that they were conducting a ferocious struggle against what they defined as "Trotskyism," mostly a product of their imagination. They defended the Moscow Trials and the purges and attacked everyone to the left of them in Spain as Trotskyists and agents of fascism. Between 1936 and 1939, the Popular Front campaign was losing much of its luster, and many leftists who had at first welcomed cooperation with the Communists had second thoughts.[19] The period of the Popular Front, from 1934 to 1939, was a time when a major segment of the Left made fellow-traveling into a principle. Yet it was also a period of growing disillusionment, indicated by some of the books that appeared: Malcolm Muggeridge's *Winter in Moscow* (1934), Boris Souvarine's *Nightmare in the USSR* (1937), Eugene Lyons's *Assignment in Utopia* (1937), and—probably most effective of all because its author was such an outstanding writer and formerly so well-known as a vocal fellow-traveler, André Gide's *Return from the USSR* (1936). Published later, but still symptomatic of disillusionment during this period, was Ante Ciliga's *The Russian Enigma* (1940).

Again we see that Orwell's ideological development is in line with a broad trend within the Left.

The Delayed Acceptance of *Animal Farm*

My final example is the fact that after completing *Animal Farm*, Orwell did not immediately find a publisher for it. Publishers rejected it because it is an obvious allegory of the Russian revolution, putting the Soviet Union in an unfavorable light and likening Joseph Stalin to a pig. When the book was finally placed with a publisher, production was then delayed a year because of the government's wartime limitations on the use of paper by private publishers.

19 See Symons 1960, 129–138. Corthorn's study (2006) includes a detailed account of how the narrow Left became gradually less pro-Soviet during this period, in response to Soviet behavior. Like many writers, Corthorn calls the narrow Left (the Left of the Left) "the Left," a problematic usage which implies that people like Bertrand Russell, J. B. Priestley, or Kingsley Martin were not of the Left.

This episode is normally presented as one more illustration of Orwell the lone voice speaking out against totalitarianism, fighting against the entrenched pro-Communist intellectual establishment. Zwerdling writes that "The book was effectively suppressed for so long that Orwell wrote to his agent that he was ready to publish it at his own expense."[20] But this is surely stretching the meaning of the term "suppressed." Orwell was free to submit the typescript to any publisher, and any publisher was free to accept or reject it. Failing that, Orwell could self-publish it. Expressing a common misunderstanding, Gardner says that the "eighteen-month gap" between completion of the work and publication was caused by "the book's political purpose."[21]

Six or seven British publishers in succession rejected the book,[22] though the first of these doesn't really count, because Orwell was obliged by prior contract to submit the book first to Gollancz, and did so fully expecting that Gollancz would reject it. *Animal Farm* was accepted for publication by the seventh or eighth British publisher approached, less than five months after Orwell began submitting it, an outcome that most authors would regard with envy. The formal convention (often discreetly flouted) is that an author must wait for a rejection from one publisher before showing the work in question to another publisher.

Later, Orwell would write that the book "had to be peddled around from publisher to publisher over a year or so" (XVIII, 442). Although some have taken Orwell's recollection at face value,[23] it is inaccurate. Orwell completed *Animal Farm*, and still had to prepare a typescript that

20 Zwerdling 1974, 52. In a related vein, Ian Williams writes of "determined efforts to thwart" publication of *Animal Farm* (Williams 2007, 108).

21 Gardner 1995, 97.

22 The five definites are Gollancz, Nicolson and Watson, Hutchinson, Jonathan Cape, and Faber and Faber (XVI, 131, 142, 155, 182, 282–83). Apparently Orwell's agent showed it to Hutchinson while Nicolson and Watson were considering it. According to Michael Meyer, the work was also rejected by William Collins on the grounds that it was too short. Without formal submission, it was also shown to the anarchist Freedom Press, who understandably rejected it because of Orwell's statist political position.

23 Steinhoff 1975, 117.

could be sent to publishers, on 19th March 1944 (XVI, 126–27). At some point before 29th August, Warburg was committed to publishing it (XVI, 335, 358). So that is an outside limit of five months and ten days. But if we allow time for Orwell to get the work typed up and delivered to Gollancz, and take into consideration the fact that Warburg expressed definite willingness to publish it earlier than August 29th (XVI, 335), a closer estimate would be decidedly less than five months. Furthermore, Orwell wrote to his agent as early as 18th July that Warburg had "again" expressed his willingness to publish the book "if he can see his way to getting the paper" (XVI, 292), and Orwell certainly knew that getting the paper was a matter of when rather than if. If we count this as acceptance, then the delay falls below four months.

Orwell pointed out that he had a track record as an author and that "normally I have no difficulty in publishing my stuff" (XVI, 174). As against that, two things should be borne in mind. First, there was a general reduction in the quantity of new works accepted for publication during the war years, caused by the government's stringent rationing of paper supplies available to private publishers. Second, all of Orwell's previous books had been works of a familiar and easily classifiable type: realistic novels, muck-raking social commentary, or eye-witness reportage. Publishers are notoriously hesitant in making decisions about books which they cannot relate mechanically to earlier titles with a clear track record. *Animal Farm* is a fairy story, a parable, almost too short to make a real book. Nothing closely similar had been seen before—perhaps the nearest precursor is Anatole France's *Penguin Island* (1908). It still evokes mirth that the American publisher, Dial Press, in rejecting *Animal Farm*, stated that the American reading public didn't go for "animal stories," but it's entirely possible that the publisher's reader who wrote those words completely understood the purpose of the book. He was doing what publishers routinely do, trying to evaluate the sales prospects of a new manuscript by relating it to some familiar category of previously published works.

The fact remains that six or seven publishers in succession rejected *Animal Farm*, four of these clearly because of its anti-Soviet message. But three of those four demonstrably had no fondness for Communism. The fundamental reason for these rejections is that Soviet soldiers were dying by the thousands every day, making a huge contribution to the war against Germany. Orwell began submitting the work before the Normandy landing. It was widely held in Britain that nothing should be said to upset the Russians. This was not mere gratitude—there was the reasonable concern that Russia might conclude a separate peace with Germany. The view that nothing should be publicly said against the Russians prevailed on the Right as well as the Left: for instance, Lord Beaverbrook (Max Aitken, rightwing Conservative newspaper magnate, wartime Minister of Supply, and confidant of Churchill) tried to curb the collectivist implications of wartime controls while praising Stalin lavishly and squelching even the slightest criticism of the Soviet Union. Orwell himself observed that the Conservatives were more pro-Soviet than the Left (XVI, 300). So, although it's true that the rather modest delay in settling on a publisher for *Animal Farm* was partly due to a kind of bias, this bias was *not* that of a pro-Communist tilt among leftist intellectuals.

Orwell had quit his job at the BBC and begun writing *Animal Farm* because he was convinced the war was safely won, but this opinion had not yet become predominant in Britain. From what we know of Orwell's general views, we can reasonably surmise that if *Animal Farm* had been the work of another writer, and if it had appeared in, say, October 1941, he would have opposed its immediate publication.

Despite a climate protective of the Soviet image, an understandable outcome of the military situation, Jonathan Cape accepted the book, whereupon the editor there had a conversation with a senior man at the wartime Ministry of Information, who persuaded him to change his mind. Cape thereupon reversed itself and withdrew its acceptance of the book. We now know that that Ministry man, Harry Peter Smollett, was a Soviet agent. Smollett's effective argument to Cape was that our Russian allies would be upset.[24] The reputable liberal journal *Time and Tide* expressed interest in serializing the work, but (according to Crick)

24 Without knowing that Smollett (formerly Hans Peter Smolka) was the one responsible for persuading Cape to reject *Animal Farm* and without of course knowing that Smollett was a spy, Orwell named him in the list of politically suspect individuals he later gave to Celia Kirwan. See Chapter 9 below.

Orwell rejected this approach because he considered *Time and Tide* too rightwing.[25]

During the whole period when six or seven publishers were rejecting the work, Warburg knew about the existence of the work and repeatedly asked to see it. Within days of having the manuscript, the Warburg firm agreed to publish *Animal Farm*. It seems clear enough that the same result would have occurred if the work had been offered to Warburg immediately on completion. So the entire four-or-five-month delay was avoidable and Orwell had to have known this.[26] Secker and Warburg was the obvious choice, as this firm (run by Warburg alone) had published *Homage to Catalonia* after Gollancz had rejected it. However, upon completing *Animal Farm*, Orwell told his agent not to bother with Secker and Warburg, as Warburg would reject the book for political reasons ("probably wouldn't touch anything of this tendency") and in any case Orwell had heard that Warburg did not have supplies of paper (XVI, 126). But any publisher accepting the book would very likely have had too little paper to be able to proceed for some time, and *Animal Farm* does not represent any political "tendency" that Warburg would have been likely to object to.

Five years earlier, when Orwell had suspected Gollancz might reject *Coming Up for Air* because of its anti-war, anti-Popular Front viewpoint, and the possibility arose of giving it to Warburg, Orwell had written to his agent: "I suppose it would be better to go to one of the big ones [publishers] if they will have me, but meanwhile there will I suppose be considerable delays" (XI, 352), and so he was ready to opt for the small and unprestigious Secker and Warburg (who had published *Homage to Catalonia*), though that turned out to be unnecessary, as Gollancz did accept *Coming Up for Air*. In 1944, Orwell was eager to get *Animal Farm* published as soon as possible, and the main barrier was the government's

25 Crick 1992, 456. If true this is remarkable, because Orwell had written for *Time and Tide*, and unlike publication in book form, publication in *Time and Tide* would have been prompt. Orwell also instructed his agent not to show the manuscript to two named "Catholic" publishers, because it would do him "permanent harm" to be published by them (XVI, 130–31).

26 This is more or less acknowledged by Crick (1992, 459).

restriction on use of paper. Orwell could easily have avoided *any* delay (even the modest less-than-five-month delay) in acceptance of *Animal Farm*; his motive for incurring the delay was his ambition to break into the big-time publishing league by acquiring a more impressive publisher than Warburg.[27] There's no solid evidence that it was any harder to find a publisher for *Animal Farm* than it had been for *Homage to Catalonia*—the difference lay in Orwell's changed attitude to the rinky-dink Warburg firm, now that he considered himself a more established writer.

By the time the book appeared, the war in alliance with Russia was won and the Cold War was beginning. Within a year, the perception of *Animal Farm* had been transformed from an outrageous attack on a gallant ally to an amusing and rather sympathetic account of how the best of intentions had been tragically perverted in Russia. The six or seven rejectors paid dearly. *Animal Farm* came with an option on Orwell's next book, which would be *Nineteen Eighty-Four*. Instead of finding a major publisher, Orwell made one.

What the brief delay in acceptance of *Animal Farm* illustrates is that there was widespread reluctance to pillory a valuable wartime ally while the outcome of the war was perceived to hang in the balance, and that therefore Orwell had to give up his immediate ambition to move up to a major-league publishing house. The big publishers' reluctance did not amount to censorship or suppression, and did not arise because of Communist sympathies among the leftist intelligentsia.

A Typical Leftwing Intellectual?

Can it really be the case that Orwell voiced completely orthodox leftist views while consistently maintaining the pretense that his views were unorthodox? No, of course not. Although Orwell often employed rhetorical expressions suggesting that he was a beleaguered dissident or

27 Some years later (and therefore maybe not perfectly accurately), Warburg recollected that he was concerned about the anti-Soviet aspect of the book in the wartime situation and that his wife threatened to leave him if he published it (Warburg 1973, 47–49). But he met with other members of his firm who were enthusiastic to go ahead, and they quickly agreed. (His wife didn't leave him.)

persecuted heretic, there are also many occasions where Orwell matter-of-factly acknowledged, often casually and in passing, that his views were entirely typical of a leftwing intellectual.

A telling example is Orwell's unfinished article on Evelyn Waugh (XX, 74–79). Here he points out that "the literary intelligentsia has grown large enough to constitute a world in itself." It has different beliefs from those predominant in the population as a whole. "What is heterodox for the wider culture may be orthodox for the intelligentsia." Consequently, there is nothing "daring or original" in being an anarchist, an atheist, or a pacifist. (Orwell is an atheist but not an anarchist or a pacifist, but as he recognizes, several mutually exclusive views co-exist within the literary intelligentsia, whereas certain views held by numerous people outside the literary intelligentsia are unacceptable within it.) "The daring thing," he continues, "is to believe in God or to approve of the capitalist system. . . . The English novelist who has most conspicuously defied his contemporaries is Evelyn Waugh." He later remarks in what might perhaps have become the punch-line of the completed article, "Waugh is about as good a novelist as one can be . . . while holding untenable opinions" (79). Orwell exaggerates the handicap to a writer of fiction in embracing unfashionable opinions. Several notable fiction writers of the day, such as Anthony Powell or Hugh Kingsmill, were non-leftists without obvious disability.

It's clear from the context that there was no irony in Orwell's employment of the term "untenable." The opinions Orwell judges untenable include belief in God and in the capitalist system. They are not just mistaken but untenable, and adhering to them reduces one's potential as a novelist. Orwell makes the acute observation that only he, among leftists, would be liable to make, that these are the daring or original views within the literary world, yet he also makes it clear that he shares the literary world's judgment of these views. Orwell acknowledges that he largely shares the ideological worldview of the literary intelligentsia, even while he is accurately noting that views quite conventional among non-intellectuals are "daring" among intellectuals.

The fashionable quality of Orwell's views was not confined to his politics. He was an atheist imbued with the secular worldview of T. H. Huxley, Wells, Shaw, and Winwood Reade. Yet he saw Roman Catholicism as peculiarly threatening, Protestantism far less so, the usual stereotype among progressive Anglo-Saxon intellectuals of the time. And he thought that modern man has "lost his soul," paying an emotional price for the absence of religious faith. None of this is at all unusual for British intellectuals of the period. Orwell was a "Protestant atheist," steeped in the traditional British view of the Catholic Church as the great enemy of liberty. His conviction that modern man suffers from a deficit of religious sustenance, a "loss of soul," was commonplace at the time and Orwell did not add any novel elaborations to it.

Orwell saw himself as a writer, a contributor to the stream of English literature. When leading literary pundits of the day took notice of Orwell, their remarks were broadly favorable.[28] Orwell's strictures on the correct use of English reflect the prevalent, ill-informed belief among schoolteachers and other pedants of the 1930s that most of current linguistic change is degeneration (Bolton 1984).

Orwell's outspoken opposition to homosexuality, vegetarianism, and birth control (which I consider in Chapter 5 below) would not go down so well with today's leftist intellectuals. From an Orwellian viewpoint, the deviants he saw as a crackpot minority discrediting the Left have since largely taken over the Left, just as he feared. These views of Orwell's were not shocking to most of his contemporary leftist readers, however. In fact they were very much in harmony with a distaste for effete and effeminate middle-class manners, a distaste which tended to go along with glorification of the mores and lifestyle of manual workers. R-r-r-revolutionary romanticism most often has a flavor of *machismo*, and Orwell's *macho* attitudes were in themselves not considered remarkable. A glorification of tough manliness was a common bond among many hard leftists, militant Communists and militant anti-Communists alike. And in the 1930s, the conception of homosexuality as a pathological form of degenerate abnormality was still the dominant orthodoxy, on the Left as well as the Right.

28 See some of the reviews collected in Meyers 1975.

3
The Socialist

> Socialism is usually defined as "common ownership of the means of production." Crudely: the State, representing the whole nation, owns everything, and everyone is a State employee. . . . It is not certain that Socialism is in all ways superior to capitalism, but it is certain that, unlike capitalism, it can solve the problems of production and consumption.
> —George Orwell, February 1941 (XII, 410)

Writers who visit the poor in order to write about them go to places fabled for their poverty. In 1902 the American Jack London went to live in the slums of London to write *The People of the Abyss*. There were equally squalid slums in New York, but the slums of the English capital were world-famous. In February 1936 Orwell went to the North of England to observe the poor. There were poor in the Home Counties and there was extreme industrial-type poverty closer to hand in South Wales, but the poor in the North were *fabulously* poor.

In the 1920s, when most of the world experienced a boom, Britain was in slump.[1] In the 1930s, Britain was further hit by the world slump, made in the USA, yet in some parts of the country there was buoyant growth. Most British people in the 1930s enjoyed increasing incomes. New industries were developing and a "new middle class" was growing rapidly along with increasing home ownership, spearheaded by the "building societies" (equivalent of American savings and loans). Britain was becoming suburbanized and predominantly middle class. But

1 The most commonly-offered explanation is sharp deflation because of Britain's return to the gold standard at the pre-war price of gold.

because of the continuing effects of the 1920s slump and the impact of the new world slump, total unemployment rose, heavily concentrated in certain regions.

Most British people in the 1930s were better off than they had been earlier, while there was a visible concentration of ugly poverty in old industrial locations, labeled "the Distressed Areas." Lancashire, Yorkshire, South Wales, Northern Ireland, Clydeside, and Tyneside contained examples of visible squalor more extreme than could now be found in the Home Counties—the area around London, the only part of Britain that Orwell knew well. The highly-publicized marches of the unemployed, climaxing with the Jarrow Crusade of October 1936 (when Orwell was in the closing stretch of writing *The Road to Wigan Pier*), dramatized the situation in which the majority of the population were concerned spectators of shockingly bad conditions in the Distressed Areas. The novel *Love on the Dole* (1933), written by an unemployed man from Salford—the classic slum—won a huge readership. The wretched spectacle of slum life had become eminently marketable to the comfortable reading public. Just as, thirty years earlier, *The People of the Abyss* had followed *A Child of the Jago*, so *The Road to Wigan Pier* now followed *Love on the Dole*.

When Orwell returned to the South on April 2nd 1936, he sat down to write *The Road to Wigan Pier*. It took him nearly ten months to complete. The title has several layers of meaning. Everyone in Britain knew "The Road to Mandalay," the wildly popular poem by Kipling set to music and turned into a music-hall hit song[2] and parlor standard. Orwell had come *from* Mandalay in Burma to Wigan in Lancashire and thus the title emphasizes how very personal is his view of the North, and points up his parallel between exploited colonial populations abroad and oppressed working populations within Britain itself. "Pier" has the nostalgic, glamorous resonance of American "boardwalk." Blackpool Pier, for instance, instantly conjures up glitter, glamour, and a rare old good time for working-class folk. Few had gone to Wigan for a good time, and the facetiously nicknamed Wigan Pier, once a broken-down jetty on the Leeds-Liverpool Canal, used for loading coal onto barges, had become

2 British "music hall" corresponds to American "vaudeville."

the occasional butt of music-hall jokes for its extreme absence of glitter or glamour. It had been torn down before Orwell got there. The title of Orwell's book also has an inadvertent resonance. Kipling knew a thing or two about India, but his knowledge of Burma was that of an ill-informed tourist, and "The Road to Mandalay," while superficially appearing knowledgably authentic, is an outsider's, one might say a tourist's, impression.[3]

The Road to Wigan Pier is in two parts of equal length. Part I is an account of scandalous poverty in the poorest parts of Lancashire and Yorkshire. Part II is a statement of Orwell's views on the working class, socialism, socialists, and modern civilization in general, including a sketchy intellectual autobiography. Before *Wigan Pier*, Orwell's general views are often a matter of uncheckable conjecture. With this work, we suddenly have a much more complete and precise account of his worldview.

The Orwell of *Wigan Pier*, completed in December 1936, is a new convert to socialism. One of the purposes of his visit to the North was to help make up his mind about whether to become a socialist (V, 113). Orwell must have decided to commit himself to socialism either while in the North or (more likely) after his return from the North, even as he was immersed in writing *The Road to Wigan Pier*. This narrows the date of his conversion to the period from February to December 1936, though the first few months and the last few months of this period are much less likely. I have adopted the convention of referring to the date of his conversion to socialism as "mid-1936."

Before his trip to the North, Orwell rejected socialism. We can see this from his novel *Keep the Aspidistra Flying*, which he completed immediately before leaving for the North. He checked the proofs (with a final opportunity to make changes) while in Wigan. *Keep the Aspidistra Flying* is not a straightforwardly antisocialist work, but, together with a few other clues, it provides evidence that Orwell in early 1936 finds socialism wanting. It is an anticapitalist work, in the sense that the main character, Gordon Comstock, hates capitalism and no one in the novel, certainly not the narrator, has a word to say in capitalism's favor. It is,

3 Gilmour 2002, 75.

however, a narrative in which there are some explicit arguments about socialism, and these arguments are presented in such a way as to convey that socialism is both unsavory and unconvincing.[4]

We're told in the novel that Comstock had briefly been a socialist at sixteen. "Every intelligent boy of sixteen is a Socialist. At that age one does not see the hook sticking out of the rather stodgy bait" (IV, 46). We also know that Orwell had briefly called himself a "Socialist" at the age of "seventeen or eighteen" (V, 130–31).

We therefore have clear evidence that Orwell definitely and somewhat scornfully rejected socialism as late as early 1936, but since so little is known about his political opinions in earlier years, we can't say for sure whether his anti-socialism of early 1936 had been maintained at about the same level for some years, or whether his views had undergone fluctuations, so that he might have been somewhat more favorable to socialism at some points before 1936.[5] Some early writings, like "Unemployment" (1928) could easily have been written by a socialist (X, 122–27), though also possibly by an antisocialist and anticapitalist like the author of *Keep the Aspidistra Flying*.

In 1933 he had written (in a private letter):

> A few years ago I thought it rather fun to reflect that our civilisation is doomed, but now it fills me above all else with boredom to think of the horrors that will be happening within ten years—either some appalling calamity, with revolution or famine, or else all-round trustification and Fordification, with the entire population reduced to docile wage-slaves, our lives utterly in the hands of the bankers, and a fearful tribe of Lady Astors and Lady Rhonddas et hoc genus riding us like succubi in the name of Progress. (X, 317)

4 The specific points are identified in the next chapter.

5 This might explain his statement in March 1947: "Up to 1930 I did not on the whole look upon myself as a Socialist" (XIX, 87), which readers would naturally suppose implied that this had changed in 1930. Alternatively, this way of putting it might have been designed to conceal from leftist readers of *Animal Farm* how recently he had joined the Left.

This doesn't have the stamp of socialist thinking. Concern about trustification and Fordification was widespread, and accentuated by *Brave New World*. The idea that the bankers ruled was prominent in the Single Tax and Social Credit movements. Mention of Lady Astor and Lady Rhondda would conjure up not so much capitalist exploitation as enthusiastic advocacy of women's rights and healthy living.

What "Socialism" Meant in 1936

In saying that Orwell became a socialist in 1936, we have to bear in mind what this meant at the time. Later on, the meaning of such a literal assertion would become diluted. To be a socialist in 1936 meant favoring the swift abolition of private ownership of factories, mines, big farms, railroads, and banks. This was not questioned for a moment, even by people we now think of as being on the right wing of the Labour Party (Ernest Bevin or Herbert Morrison). After about 1950, to quickly convey to someone what happened to Orwell's political orientation in 1936, you would have to say: "he became an extreme, hardcore, leftwing socialist."

To become a socialist in 1936 was not to espouse some vague attitudes about the direction of desirable change, but to accept the replacement of the present capitalist system by something very clearly defined. After 1945, the entire Left moved right. By the 1960s, anyone who had proposed to implement the proposals in Harold Macmillan's *The Middle Way*, the 1938 program of moderate, socially-conscious Conservatism, would have been perceived as a radical leftist.

Socialism in 1936 is an imaginary type of social order which socialists believe will come into being in the near future. Quite varied conceptions of socialism had been prevalent in the mid-nineteenth century, but after about 1880 most of these had died away, and there was little disagreement among socialists about the defining characteristics of a socialist society. In 1908 Mikhail Tugan-Baranowsky identified eight types of socialism (socialism and communism, each further divided into centralized, corporate, federal, and anarchical varieties) and characterized one of these, centralized socialism, as "the reigning tendency of the socialist movement at the present time," exemplified in the Saint-

Simonians, Pecqueur, Rodbertus, the Marxists, and Bellamy (Tugan-Baranowski 1966, 18). In the following decades, centralized socialism became even more dominant, despite the upsurge of syndicalism in the early twentieth century. If asked in 1936 to define socialism, the Labour Party, the ILP, the Communist Party, H. G. Wells, Bernard Shaw, and George Orwell would have given substantially the same answer. These people had sharp differences on many issues, but not on the defining features of a socialist society.[6]

In the 1880s and 1890s, the conception of socialist society held by continental Marxism (Social Democracy), was brought into conformity with that of mainstream non-Marxist socialism. The traditional Marxist view that money and the state would disappear in the revolution was abandoned or relegated to the distant future, long after the socialist capture of political power. Bellamy's *Looking Backward* (1887) does not strikingly conflict with Bebel's *Woman and Socialism* (1879), the major popular Marxist text discussing what a socialist system would look like. Bellamy was no Marxist and knew little of Marxism, but it was possible for *Looking Backward* and its sequel *Equality* to be translated into German and widely read by Social Democrats, with an undisturbed assumption that Bellamy and Social Democracy were on the same side.

According to this common view of socialism, large-scale productive enterprises would no longer be owned by individuals, either singly or in association, but by "the community as a whole." The direction of production would not be left to the anarchic processes of market competition, but would be consciously planned for the benefit of the entire population.

Although socialism in Britain was always preponderantly non-Marxist, British socialism did not disagree with German Social Democracy on the basic conception of what a socialist society would look like. A

6 The closest thing to any serious difference might be the question of income equality, but this was not a hotly debated issue. Shaw specified absolute equality whereas Cole held that differences in wages would continue. There was a lot of vagueness. Orwell often referred to "approximate equality," but at one point said that no one should receive more than ten times the after-tax income of anyone else (XII, 422), a surprisingly wide range. All socialists agreed that property income would be abolished.

representative and influential statement of socialism as it was generally understood was Robert Blatchford's *Merrie England* (1894). The popularity of *Merrie England* was phenomenal. Most prominent British socialists of the early twentieth century would later attribute their conversion to socialism to Blatchford.[7] *Merrie England* captures the conception of socialism advocated in many hundreds of socialist publications between 1894 and 1939.

Merrie England sets out very clearly what socialism is. Instead of being owned by private individuals, industrial undertakings will be owned and run by the state, just as the postal service is already. "The postal service is the standing proof of the capacity of the state to manage the public business with economy and success" (Blatchford 1897, 80). Pointing to the post office as the model for the whole of socialist industry is not unusual for the time—it even appears in Lenin's *The State and Revolution*.

Merrie England distinguishes between "Practical Socialism," in which everyone works for wages, and a more distant "Ideal Socialism," where goods and services are provided free, so that wages no longer exist. After socialism is up and running, the government will begin providing some goods and services free, and this system of free distribution—Ideal Socialism—will expand and eventually supplant the wages system. So even here, English socialism parallels German Social Democracy, with its occasional references to free distribution of goods, rather than wages from government-owned industries, in the more remote future. However, *Merrie England* rests its case for the immediate desirability of socialism on Practical Socialism.

Orwell mainly acquired his conception of socialism from conversations with ILP members who in the early 1930s were still imbued with the socialism of *Merrie England*, though as the 1930s wore on, eager to be "revolutionary" so that they could be ready for the collapse of capitalism, many ILPers adopted more Marxist and Leninist language. Orwell never referred to Blatchford, and not being knowledgeable about

7 Blatchford himself had been converted to socialism upon reading *A Summary of the Principles of Socialism* (1884) by the two Marxists H. M. Hyndman and William Morris.

the history of socialism, was probably only hazily aware of him. Despite Blatchford's enormous past influence, which left its mark on the thinking of all active socialists, he was no longer respected by the Left or read by new adherents to socialism. Blatchford prefigured Orwell in being an ILP socialist who then became patriotically pro-war during the Boer War. As a pro-war apostate, Blatchford was rarely mentioned in the early twentieth century (he also supported Britain in the First and Second World Wars, and by this time the narrow Left paid him no heed).

The Doctrinaire Socialist

Under socialism, the form of future society embraced by Orwell in mid-1936 and quite demonstrably retained until the end of his life, all, or nearly all, of industry will become state-owned. Property incomes, such as dividends and rent, will be abolished. Wages (including salaries) will be made equal, or at least much less unequal than they are under capitalism. Central economic planning will replace competition as the method for allocating resources to all the various branches of industry. There will be no capital markets or money markets because these can have no conceivable function. National institutions favoring class privilege, such as the House of Lords and the public schools,[8] will be abolished.

Some minor alternative varieties of socialism are ignored and thereby tacitly ruled out: Orwell does not want to immediately abolish money, or the police or military, nor does he exhibit any interest in producers' co-operatives (later termed "workers' self-management") or federations of communes. Not in *Wigan Pier*, but later, he would briefly allude to a more remote future society of "pure communism" (XII, 459), again in line with *Merrie England*.

Orwell assumes that in his desired form of socialism, freedom of speech, freedom of assembly, and all the other liberties associated with liberal capitalism will be retained, and most likely enhanced. Democracy

8 In Britain "public school" refers to a private secondary school, usually an elite private boarding school (which in the 1930s would always be single-sex), while "state school" is the term corresponding to U.S. "public school."

too is part of Orwell's picture of socialism, though when he employs the term "democracy," he is usually referring to civil liberties rather than to decisions by majority vote—not that he rejects majoritarian rule, but that when he talks about "democracy," this is not uppermost in his mind. Orwell also mentions a possible "Slave-state" which would be planned and collectivist, but would not merit the name "socialism" (V, 175).

Public ownership of industry (collectivism) plus democracy and "approximate" economic equality define Orwell's conception of socialism (XII, 410). If he subsequently had doubts that this was the kind of future society he wanted to see, no explicit record of any such doubts has survived. The most striking thing about Orwell's view of socialist society, then, is its unrelieved ordinariness. This can be confirmed by comparing Part II of *Wigan Pier* with Cole's *The Simple Case for Socialism* (1935). Although the rhetorical styles are very different, and although Orwell utters many views on other matters, not shared by Cole, and of course Cole expounds at much greater length, when it comes to the basic conception of how we define socialism and what we need to do to bring it about, Orwell is in agreement with Cole. We reach the same conclusion if we compare Part II of *Wigan Pier* with Strachey's *The Theory and Practice of Socialism* (1936).

Stansky and Abrahams are seriously mistaken when they contend that: "Unorthodoxy is written all over Part II of *The Road to Wigan Pier*" (Stansky and Abrahams 1980, 194). There are a few somewhat unusual aspects of Orwell's account, but when it comes to Orwell's conception of a socialist society, there is not a chink of light between Orwell's view and that of the routine ILP or Fabian Society view. Orwell, just like most other socialists at the time, treats the general outlines of a socialist society as completely uncontentious. Even years later, despite Orwell's greater familiarity with anarchist, syndicalist, and other kinds of nonstandard socialist thinking, there is no glimmer of heterodoxy in his conception of the future socialist society.

The most notable absence is syndicalism. The years 1890–1914 had witnessed a dramatic upsurge of revolutionary syndicalism. It even erupted in the United States, in the form of the Wobblies. Syndicalism is the single major exception to the rule that "socialism" in the early twentieth century meant "centralized socialism" or neo-Saint-Simonianism.

Syndicalists criticized the mainstream socialists—the Social Democrats and Labourites—for placing their trust in parliamentary elections. Syndicalism was distinctive both for the definition of socialist society and for the means of achieving it. "Direct action" and strikes were the revolutionary means. Workers would seize control of separate industries, and then federate to form a nationwide, eventually worldwide, "industrial union."

The syndicalist movement withered away after 1917, as some syndicalists became supporters of Bolshevism, while others founded the Fascist movement. A few avoided both of these paths, but they were a tiny remnant. In a more general way, syndicalist ideas still had some life left in them in France and Spain, and continue to be propagated in the English-speaking world in the form of "Guild Socialism." Orwell repeatedly encountered syndicalist ideas while in Spain but he must also have been independently aware of them from other sources. Furthermore, before he became a socialist, Orwell was a "Tory anarchist," and later he was friendly with several anarchists. Despite all this, there is no evidence in his writing that anarchism had any appeal, or even any great interest, for him after 1935, or that he was at any time interested in syndicalism as a political program.[9]

Socialists in the 1930s often used terms like "common ownership" rather than state ownership. They generally accepted that in socialism there would be some enterprises owned by co-operatives, by municipalities, or in other ways not directly administered by the central government. But they assumed that the government would decide which enterprises would be owned by non-state entities, and the non-state entities would have to fit within the central plan, determined by the government. They also assumed there would be some privately-owned businesses, such as small farms, which might remain in private hands for a long time. All large-scale industrial undertakings would be taken over by the government.

9 In an otherwise fine article on Orwell, Eckstein (1992, 202–03) states that Orwell "always" gave his socialism "a strongly anarchist slant." Orwell never once gave his conception of the future socialist society even a slightly anarchist slant.

Socialists sometimes debated the question whether the former owners should be awarded compensation in the form of government bonds and whether (at least in the early stages of socialism) there should be any exceptions to the rule of state ownership of all assets. All such qualifications, however, go unmentioned by Orwell in *The Road to Wigan Pier*, and are only rarely and briefly mentioned in the whole of his written output. He does say in 1944 that under socialism people should own their own homes, and that it is "probably desirable" that a farmer should own as much land as he can actually farm. He mentions these points only as exceptions to his general view that private land ownership should be abolished (XVI, 336). In April 1947 he raises the question of how freedom of the press could be preserved in a collectivist system and proposes that only the "big Press" be nationalized, leaving small publications in private hands (XIX, 117). How these small presses might fare in a world where nearly all production, including that of paper and ink, is a coercively-imposed government monopoly, is an issue he doesn't pursue.

A widely read account of Orwell's political views is that of Raymond Williams, who was heavily influenced by Orwell and referred to him at different stages of his career, the references becoming steadily more hostile over time. Williams asserts that Orwell's socialism in 1936 was "undoctrinal," and that for him socialism was merely a matter of opposition to imperialism, fascism, and inequality.[10] He characterizes Orwell at the end of his life as "an ex-socialist."[11] It's not entirely clear just what Williams meant by these assertions, but in the sense that they would most naturally be taken by readers, they are misleading. As I document throughout this book, Orwell's socialism is rooted in his conviction that capitalism is doomed and can only be replaced by collectivism, whose advent is irresistible, mainly because a planned economy must be far more efficient than a competitive one (XII, 410). From mid-1936 until the end of his life, Orwell favors the replacement of private ownership of almost all industrial assets by the state, along with approximate equality of incomes, abolition of hereditary wealth, and the retention of

10 Williams 1971, 54–55.
11 Williams 1981, 390.

democracy. This is precisely the most orthodox Anglophone socialist doctrine of the 1930s.

Orwell recalls that while in Burma he had "worked out an anarchistic theory that all government is evil, that the punishment always does more harm than the crime and that people can be trusted to behave decently if only you will let them alone," but he now sees this to be impracticable (V, 137). This passage shows that Orwell's "Tory anarchism" had not been merely an unreflective posture but embodied a definite political theory. From 1936 on, however, Orwell always dismissed anarchism as utterly impracticable. He briefly mentioned anarchism in 1945, in his review of a book by his friend the anarchist Herbert Read (XVII, 403). Here, as against Read, Orwell asserts that anarchy is incompatible with high living standards because modern industry requires "a planned, centralised society." In another brief mention of anarchy he maintains that it substitutes pressure of public opinion for law, and is thus inherently totalitarian (XVIII, 424).

Socialism Means Central Planning

The complete orthodoxy of Orwell's conception of socialism, its conformity with that of the great majority of 1930s socialists, is sometimes disputed. Stansky and Abrahams say of Orwell: "What he wanted was a Socialism without planning—surely a contradiction in terms?—founded upon ideals of honor and decency" (Stansky and Abrahams 1980, 194). But Orwell, along with other 1930s socialists, assumes that socialism without central planning makes no sense and he never entertains such a notion. In his discussion of why he thinks capitalist Britain must lose militarily to collectivist Germany, he identifies Germany's economic planning as the reason (XII, 410–12; 460–62). For Orwell, socialism is a planned society by definition, as contrasted with capitalism, which is by definition unplanned. So closely was socialism identified with planning that socialists would sometimes use a phrase like "a planned society" as a synonym for socialism, and Orwell himself does this too (XIX, 87).

In addition to his general view that collectivism just has to be more efficient than capitalism because planning must be more efficient than competition, Orwell is also convinced of a prevailing popular theory known (though usually not by its adherents) as underconsumptionism. Capitalism is thought to suffer from a fatal flaw: the workers, being necessarily underpaid, can never afford to buy what they have produced, therefore capitalism is always in the desperate situation of being unable to sell all of its products. Capitalism, says Orwell, "makes it impossible to consume all the goods that are produced" (XVII. 27). This notion is superficially confirmed by the observation that at the outset of a typical slump, the immediate problem seems to be inventories of goods that can be sold only at a loss. A version of underconsumptionism had been widely disseminated by Henry George's *Progress and Poverty*—still read with excitement by millions as late as the 1930s. Other versions were promoted by J. A. Hobson and by the Social Credit movement. A simple form of underconsumptionist theory was widely accepted by socialists—we find it, for instance, presented as "Karl Marx's doctrine of surplus value," its exposition taking up an entire chapter, in *The Iron Heel*.[12] It is not, of course, Marx's doctrine. If any such theory were correct, it would be a puzzle how capitalism could last six weeks. A more complicated version of the same idea was propounded by 1930s Marxist economists, such as John Strachey, though underconsumptionism had been rejected by Marx.[13]

Arguments against Socialism

Describing Orwell's treatment of socialism in Part II of *The Road to Wigan Pier*, Richard Rovere says: "It was perhaps the most rigorous examination that any doctrine has ever received at the hands of an adherent" (Rovere 1956, xv). In fact, *Wigan Pier* does not critically examine *socialism* at all. It has sundry animadversions on the manners and morals of some *socialists*, including the famous denunciation of vegetarians, nudists, fruit-juice drinkers, and sandal-wearers (V, 161–62), but these are independent of the merits or demerits of a socialist society.

12 London 1948, 141–162.

13 For a refutation of one simple kind of underconsumptionism, see Marx 1974, Volume II, 334–343.

Opponents of socialism before World War II had two chief arguments: first, that the attempt to establish socialism would lead to something the socialists didn't want, an oppressive and regimented type of society in which liberty would be lost, and second, that socialism would be considerably less efficient than capitalism, so that the replacement of capitalism by socialism would lead to a drop in output, and therefore to general impoverishment. Both of these arguments had a history and were easily available to anyone interested.[14] Orwell dismisses the first argument without examination and never mentions the second (unless we count a single brief, dismissive reference to the contention that socialism "won't work").

The first argument is characterized by Orwell as "the beehive state" (V, 194). Orwell's acknowledges that this is a common argument against socialism yet dismisses it without serious attention. It's the very same argument—that a centralized economy leads to totalitarianism—which would soon come to preoccupy him for the rest of his life, culminating in *Nineteen Eighty-Four*, but in *Wigan Pier* he scoffs at fears of a beehive state. He does distinguish socialism from collectivism, and does (following Cole's *The Simple Case for Socialism*) mention the possibility of a future collectivist "Slave-State" (V, 175), but he doesn't connect this with the totalitarian beehive state that critics of socialism were claiming would be the actual outcome of any attempt to introduce socialism.

The second argument, about the economic inefficiency of socialism, was given a classic restatement in 1935 in Hayek's *Collectivist Economic Planning*, which was widely read and widely discussed. Orwell must at the very least have heard that some economists were claiming that socialism could never match the economic efficiency of capitalism, and that therefore the mass of people would end up permanently poorer under socialism. Yet Orwell never—not in *The Road to Wigan Pier* and not subsequently—mentioned this argument. Instead, Orwell often voiced the conviction that any planned economy must always be more economically efficient than capitalism, an opinion he never abandoned.

In the same year as *Wigan Pier*, there appeared a book titled *The Socialist Case*, by Douglas Jay. Although few suspected it, this volume presaged the ideological future of the Labour Party. There is no record that

14 Richter 1907; Mallock 1907; Hearnshaw 1929.

Orwell ever paid any attention to Jay's book or that it influenced him in the slightest. A few thoughtful Labour Party supporters had read Hayek's *Collectivist Economic Planning*, and been shaken by it. Although they did not stop regarding themselves as socialists, they became somewhat more skeptical about "planning," and insistent that market prices must be allowed to function under socialism. Their economic ideas were developed by the influential economist Evan Durbin, who died in 1948. The Keynesian Revolution was just what these Labour revisionists needed. And so, unusually for socialist advocacy at the time, *The Socialist Case* is Keynesian. Gradually, the kind of revisionist socialism propounded by Jay and Durbin gained ground within the Labour Party. Later it formed the basis of "Gaitskellism" (Hugh Gaitskell, an admirer of Austrian economics, was leader of the Labour Party during most of the fabled "thirteen years" of Conservative rule, from 1951 to 1964.) The new Labour Party thinking was summed up in 1956, in Anthony Crosland's book, *The Future of Socialism*.

At first the goal of bringing all of industry into "common ownership" was not questioned, but later Gaitskell tried to get "Clause Four," committing the Party to "common ownership" of industry, removed from the Party's constitution. Gaitskell failed, but more than thirty years later, in 1995, Tony Blair succeeded. Most leftist intellectuals of the 1930s barely noticed the beginning of this whole development, which lacked the chiliastic allure of more traditional socialism but was better suited to the policies of a party which could credibly assume office. Furthermore, if leftists had been asked about it, many of them would have been suspicious, for it was a tenet of 1930s leftwing thinking that any attempt to modify capitalism to make it more like socialism was incipiently fascist, and the Jay-Durbin approach would have appeared to them as modified capitalism. In retrospect, it would have been fascinating if Orwell had set down his reactions to Jay's *The Socialist Case*, but nothing was further from his mind.

The Non-Marxist

"I am not a Marxist," wrote Orwell, "and I don't hold with all this stuff that boils down to saying 'Anything is right which advances the cause of the Party'" (XI, 256). Although never a Marxist, Orwell's political positions were those of a typical socialist of the time, and thus overlapped with Marxism to a large extent. Many of Orwell's views were of a kind that, had we encountered them after about 1960, we would be inclined to suspect their proponent of being a Marxist. Marxists clung to such views after many others had discarded them.

Marxism is one current within a broader socialist tradition of thought we can call neo-Saint-Simonianism.[15] Neo-Saint-Simonianism is not an alternative to Marxism: it includes Marxism, at least the Marxism of the Second and Third Internationals, as one of its denominations. Neo-Saint-Simonianism excludes anarchism, syndicalism, or moneyless communism, though the tradition of neo-Saint-Simonianism may draw something from these doctrines. For instance, Robert Owen's thinking no doubt had some impact, at several removes, on the worldview of socialists like Robert Blatchford, Bernard Shaw, and R. H. Tawney, but Owen had advocated a communist form of association that was not favored by those later writers. Nationalizing industries and turning everyone into a government employee would have had no appeal for Owen, or for William Morris, but this is precisely the essence of socialism for Blatchford, the Webbs, Shaw, Tawney, and Orwell.

The socialism Orwell came to in 1936 was this mainstream type of neo-Saint-Simonian socialism. Like other British socialists, he knew of Marxism as a sub-variety within socialism, sharing all the most important assumptions, but distinguished by a number of key features: support for the USSR, a "scientific" terminology (some of which, like "proletariat," had been freely absorbed by non-Marxists), commitment to a disciplined and conspiratorial vanguard party, and a theoretical insistence upon the supreme role of economic self-interest in explaining people's actions. The Marxism known to Orwell in 1936 was Leninism-Stalinism, the Marxism of the Third International, the Marxism of Strachey's *The*

15 Saint-Simonianism is the frankly anti-democratic and oligarchical movement deriving from *The Doctrine of Saint-Simon* (1828–29; Iggers 1972). I am calling Neo-Saint-Simonianism the form this movement took in the 1840s, after it had been modified, under the influence of Pierre Leroux, to become democratic and equalitarian (see Bakunin 1976).

Coming Struggle for Power. There are numerous points of agreement between Orwell's outlook and this type of Marxism, but these are just those points where non-Marxist socialism agrees with Marxism. They are the common elements of neo-Saint-Simonianism.

Although Orwell wants what both he and the Marxists see as socialism, he believes, as Marxists do not, that society is in serious danger of settling into a malign form of collectivism, a stable slave state. Orwell holds that people in general are irrational, and tend to choose subordination to some cruel, self-sacrificing creed in preference to tolerance and self-interest. Orwell classifies Marxism along with Fabianism as belonging to that type of socialism which in his view lays too much emphasis on material improvement and industrial development. He does not accept that people are always dominated by their material interests (though he allows that the theory that they are so dominated is often a useful guide, as a first approximation). Although he is very interested in class, and sees socialism as primarily in the interest of the working class, he has no commitment to the Marxist or any other strict definition of class, and is therefore quite prepared to acknowledge new developments in class structure which many Marxists were inclined to deny or to explain away. He shows little interest in the Marxian labor theory of value and theory of surplus value, and when he refers to these, there are indications that he has misunderstood them (giving them an underconsumptionist slant, for example).

Orwell recognized much Comintern orthodoxy as "Marxism," and so he equated Marx's historical materialism with the theory that people are always primarily motivated by economic gain, and that the "superstructure" of morality and law is merely a hypocritical cover-up for this pursuit of financial gain (XII, 244). Orwell rejected this theory and saw himself as giving much more importance to people's conscious motivations than would be allowed by Marxism.

Richard Rees originated the story, since repeated by others, that Orwell showed by his intervention in a summer school discussion that he was an expert on Marxist theory (Rees 1962, 138–39). This account must be based on Rees's misunderstanding, because Orwell's acquaintance with Marxist theory was demonstrably thin. He knew only what he had picked up in passing references in ephemeral polemical writings. The sole exception to this is that, as Philip Bounds has documented, he closely followed the many works by British Communists on literature and culture, and even developed his own ideas on those topics in a sort of interior debate with these works,[16] but this would not have given him any understanding of fundamental Marxist ideas and would have confirmed his limited and simplistic conception of Marxist cultural theory.

Orwell took the Marxists of his day at their word, as having a scientific theory which would tell them what was going to happen next in world politics. Marx, says Orwell, is "a tipster who not only tells you which horse to back, but also provides the reason why the horse didn't win" (XI, 162), which is indeed an apt description for many 1930s Marxists, but even more for Orwell himself, with his numerous confident and mistaken predictions.

The Anti-Trotskyist

H. G. Wells referred to Orwell as "that Trotskyist with big feet," which is partly right: Orwell did have big feet.[17] Obviously, Orwell was not a Trotskyist, for the following elementary reasons:

1. A Trotskyist has to be a Marxist, and Orwell was not a Marxist.

2. Orwell asserts that he is no Trotskyist, and habitually describes Trotskyists in the third, not the first, person.

3. Orwell maintains that if Trotsky had beaten Stalin and gained the leadership, or if Lenin had lived longer, the subsequent history of Soviet Russia would probably have been no better.

16 Bounds 2009.

17 Orwell had big feet, big hands, unusual height, an increasingly bony face, and premature aging, all symptoms of the growth-hormone disorder, acromegaly.

> 4. Orwell rejects the Trotskyist classifications of both the Soviet Union and Nazi Germany.
>
> 5. Orwell supported the Allied side in World War II (even prior to 22nd June 1941), whereas the Trotskyist position is that this was an imperialist war which should be opposed by 'revolutionary defeatism' within the western countries, modified by defense of the Soviet Union after 22nd June 1941.
>
> 6. Orwell favored the western side in the Cold War, whereas the Trotskyist position was that Soviet Russia must always be supported against the capitalist West.

The Communist Party tended to label anyone as "Trotskyist" who criticized the Stalin regime from the left. In this sense, Orwell (like Fenner Brockway or James Maxton) was a "Trotskyist," at least by mid-1937, but it is not helpful to be so slapdash in our ideological categories. The Communists called the ILP Trotskyist, and Orwell was a supporter of the ILP, then an actual member, then someone who basically agreed with the ILP except on the issue of the current war. But few ILP members saw themselves as Trotskyist, and Trotskyists (including Trotsky himself) severely criticized the ILP.

There were few Trotskyists in Britain in the 1930s and 1940s—Orwell estimated the number in England as "about five hundred" (XVI, 158), probably a serious exaggeration, and Orwell says that he had "no contacts with them" (XVI, 497). None of them was a notable writer. Talented and well-known former Communist writers in New York often became Trotskyists, even if only briefly, but nothing like this occurred in London, probably because of the huge and politically relevant Labour Party.

In a 1946 letter to Dwight Macdonald, Orwell wrote:

> . . . Trotskyists . . . feel responsible for events in the USSR up to about 1926 and have to assume that a sudden degeneration took place about that date. Whereas I think the whole process was foreseeable—and was foreseen by a few people,

> e.g. Bertrand Russell—from the very nature of the Bolshevik party. (XVIII, 507)

This is somewhat charitable to Bolshevism, whose brutal, anti-working-class character did not have to be "foreseen" when Russell wrote about it in 1920. Nonetheless it is incompatible with Trotskyism. Discussing James Burnham's 1945 article, "Lenin's Heir," Orwell agrees with Burnham that the Russian regime would have turned out very similar without Stalin: "Well before 1923 the seeds of a totalitarian society were quite plainly there. Lenin, indeed, is one of those politicians who win an undeserved reputation by dying prematurely" (XVIII, 274). In his review of *Darkness at Noon*, Orwell states: "The Moscow trials were a horrible spectacle, but if one remembers what the history of the Old Bolsheviks had been it was difficult to feel sorry for them as individuals" (XII, 359). Orwell writes this anti-Trotskyist analysis into *Animal Farm*, where he makes clear that Snowball (corresponding partly to Trotsky and partly to all the Old Bolsheviks) took part in the early perversion of the Animalist revolution. Popular adaptations of *Animal Farm*, such as animated cartoons, often give the work a Trotskyist twist by changing this element of the story to make Snowball a genuinely hopeful alternative to Napoleon.

At no time was Orwell a Trotskyist in any literal sense. However, as a socialist who was, at least from June 1937 to August 1939, to the left of the Communist Party, Orwell often agreed with Trotskyists on practical political activities. Despite his un-Trotskyan view that if Trotsky had defeated Stalin the Soviet Union would still have become a horrible totalitarian dictatorship (XVII, 343), Orwell often spoke as though Bolshevism had started out hopefully and only later departed from an initially promising course. His experiences in Spain led to a considerable overlap with Trotskyist analyses: he looked forward to a revolutionary uprising in Britain. There was considerable common ground between Orwell and Trotskyism, but this was not because of any influence on Orwell from Trotsky or Trotskyism. Occasionally Orwell half-seriously refers to himself as a Trotskyist, (XI, 237–38) always implicitly indicating the loose usage in which any anti-Communist leftist is supposedly a Trotskyist. Similarly, Orwell sometimes explains that the POUM is not, correctly speaking, Trotskyist, but occasionally, depending on his context and his audience, refers to it without qualification as Trotskyist.

Seeking to claim Orwell for Trotskyism, John Newsinger asserts that Orwell's "last great book, *Nineteen Eighty-Four*, was decisively influenced by the Trotskyist critique of the Soviet Union."[18] Newsinger's judgment that *Nineteen Eighty-Four* owes something to Trotskyism is derived, not from any specifically Trotskyist element in *Nineteen Eighty-Four*, for there is none, but solely from Newsinger's surmise that Orwell's concept of "oligarchical collectivism" is derived from Dwight Macdonald's use of the term "bureaucratic collectivism."

It's a stretch to connect Orwell with Trotskyism because Orwell was supposedly influenced by a former Trotskyist to accept an idea that was flatly opposed to Trotskyism. In any case, Newsinger's surmise seems to be mistaken. Orwell's oligarchical collectivism is indeed the same concept as MacDonald's bureaucratic collectivism, but Orwell held this concept before he could have been influenced by Macdonald. The similarity is what we would expect from any socialist who concluded that the Soviet Union was not what socialists wanted but was nevertheless a stable non-capitalist form of society.

In 1941, Orwell started writing for the American journal *Partisan Review*, which at this time was edited by former Trotskyists. One of these, Dwight Macdonald (sometimes called "the American Orwell," for his witty political essays and interest in popular culture), corresponded with Orwell, and admired him as a writer, though disagreeing with him on various political issues, notably his support for the war. Macdonald took the "bureaucratic collectivism" label from Bruno Rizzi, who had coined it in 1938. Since Trotskyists habitually referred to the ruling group in Russia as "the bureaucracy," it was natural for those former Trotskyists who came to reject Trotsky's characterization of the Soviet Union as a deformed workers' state to call it "bureaucratic collectivism."

Orwell consistently referred to the USSR as "oligarchical collectivism" (never bureaucratic collectivism), from early 1940, which is too early for him to have been influenced by Macdonald. Macdonald's first major article about bureaucratic collectivism came in 1941 and he did

18 Newsinger 1999, 157.

not correspond with Orwell until later. The first recorded place where Orwell calls the Soviet system "oligarchical collectivism" is in his review, published in May 1940, of Borkenau's *The Totalitarian Enemy*. Orwell states that Nazi Germany and the Soviet Union "are rapidly evolving towards the same system—a form of oligarchical collectivism" (XII, 159). Orwell agreed with the main outlines of Borkenau's analysis, but Borkenau himself did not use the term "oligarchical collectivism." It seems likely that "oligarchical collectivism" is Orwell's own coinage: it captures what he sees as the essentials: that the Soviet and Nazi systems are not capitalist and not democratic. It may have been suggested by the Oligarch class in London's *The Iron Heel*, or perhaps by Robert Michels's "law of oligarchy," which Orwell would certainly have heard about and very likely read. Probably Borkenau's analysis, which Orwell would doubtless have heard from Borkenau in person before 1940, merely confirmed and amplified what Orwell already believed.

The Trotskyist position, as set out in *The Revolution Betrayed* and promoted even today by residual Trotskyist groupuscules, is that the Soviet Union from the 1920s until around 1990 was a "workers' state with bureaucratic deformations." Both orthodox Trotskyists and their critics agreed that this was incompatible with the bureaucratic collectivist label, which implies a new form of class society, neither capitalist nor socialist. With evident distaste, Newsinger describes Isaac Deutscher's views on Soviet Russia (123), without mentioning that these were precisely Trotsky's views too.[19]

Orwell, Borkenau, Rizzi, Macdonald, and Burnham all agreed, contrary to Trotskyism, that Soviet Russia was a new type of class society, neither capitalist nor what socialists wanted. They also all agreed on something else: that Nazi Germany was not capitalist, and was (or was rapidly becoming) a society of the same general type as the Soviet Union.

Someone who held that the Soviet Union was bureaucratic collectivist could, in theory, stay in Trotsky's Fourth International, and thus

19 One of these views, defense of the Soviet suppression of the 1956 Hungarian uprising, Trotsky did not live to express, but it would have been the only position consistent with his fundamental political analysis.

remain a Trotskyist in an organizational sense—though as a practical matter any Trotskyist who came to espouse the bureaucratic collectivist theory was probably on his way out of organized Trotskyism. But someone who held the Orwell-Macdonald view of Nazi Germany could not last for five seconds in any Trotskyist milieu. Trotskyism was wedded to the theory that National Socialism was an instrument of big business. The theory that Soviet Russia and Nazi Germany were essentially the same type of society was clearly incompatible with Trotskyism.

The ILP Member

Orwell joined the Independent Labour Party (ILP) in June 1938,[20] and left it in September 1939, purely on the issue of his newly-embraced support for Britain's war with Germany. Orwell had many discussions with ILP members in 1934–35, while working in a bookshop owned by ILP members. His general conception of socialism, both before and after he became a socialist, was always that of the ILP and therefore (whether he realized it or not) that of Blatchford's *Merrie England*. From November 1943 Orwell was literary editor of *Tribune*, the magazine of the left wing of the Labour Party, and he generally agreed with the *Tribune* outlook, except that after 1945, he considered *Tribune* too hesitant to openly take the side of NATO against the Soviet bloc.

The Independent Labour Party or ILP (so named because it pursued working-class representation in Parliament outside the Liberal and Conservative parties) had been founded in 1893. The ILP later played the leading role in setting up the Labour Party, and until the 1920s was the most powerful political component of the Labour Party.[21] All of the most prominent early leaders of the Labour Party were members of the ILP. Fyvel calls the ILP "an offshoot of the Labour Party."[22] It would be less inaccurate to say that the Labour Party was an offshoot of the ILP.

20 Another well-known writer who joined the ILP in the period of its sharp decline was Graham Greene.

21 The Independent Labour Party is nearly always referred to as the ILP. The Labour Party is almost never referred to as the LP, partly because this would not distinguish it from the Liberal Party.

22 Fyvel 1982, 52.

Until 1918, the Labour Party was so structured that no one could join it directly. The only way to join it was to join one of its affiliated organizations, a trade union or a political society. The vast majority of trade union members were also dues-paying members of the Labour Party simply because of their membership in a union, since virtually all unions chose to affiliate with the Labour Party and to hand over part of their membership dues to the Labour Party. In the reorganization of 1918 it became possible to join the Labour Party directly as a "constituency member." This seemed to imply that it was now pointless to join one of the affiliated societies, such as the ILP or the Fabian Society. Why join two or three organizations instead of just one?

The Fabian Society continued to play a significant role by becoming a research body—the kind of organization which would later be called a think tank. ILP membership declined but did not immediately collapse. The ILP had an impressive tradition, it had organizational and ideological ties with many Labour MPs, it had a nationwide organization of thousands of members (with the usual dances, cycling clubs, and so forth), and it was a home for Labour Party activists who felt (as most activists for any major party always feel) that the Party in Parliament was too soft and compromising. It also had a bit of money, from wealthy Quakers and other pacifists who had admired the ILP's anti-war stance in World War I. In 1932 the ILP voted to disaffiliate from the Labour Party, a disastrous move which accelerated the ILP's decline.[23]

As a home for leftwing activists, the ILP faced competition from the Moscow-subsidized Communist Party of Great Britain. In membership both the ILP and the CP always remained very small by comparison with the Labour Party. But neither were tiny groupuscules: both had thousands of members, and anyone who hung around a Lyons' Corner House (a chain of London tea houses), and kept an ear out for political conversation, would soon be made aware of the lively activity of both organizations. While the ILP was affiliated with the Labour Party until

23 In 1975 the ILP retained its initials but changed its name to Independent Labour Publications. Having re-assessed its socialism and its relation to practical politics, it went back into the Labour Party as an effective voice for market socialism.

1932, the CPGB made repeated attempts to affiliate with the Labour Party; these attempts were always decisively rebuffed.

Socialism and Workers' Living Conditions

Many references to workers' living standards are scattered throughout Orwell's writings. Considered together, these remarks often appear puzzling or contradictory. There are persistent themes, but Orwell's general assessment of the prospects for improvement (and even of the *desirability* of improvement) is liable to fluctuate.

The Road to Wigan Pier begins with an account of scandalous poverty and hardship, and then shifts to a discussion of socialism. It's natural to interpret the work as following the familiar socialist formula—presenting a case that socialism is required to improve the workers' living conditions. This is indeed one recurring element in Orwell's thinking. For example, in 1942 he responds to people who bemoan "materialism" (in the sense of desire for higher incomes) by saying that the workers are right to be materialist: all they want is to acquire some of the basic comforts already enjoyed by the people who preach against materialism (XIII, 509–510).

Yet Orwell was aware that the condition of Spanish and British workers, as of most European workers, had gradually improved over many decades under capitalism, and—this is the surprise—he often intimates that we cannot expect much improvement in the early decades or centuries of socialism. His most extreme, and quite startling, statement of this view occurs in the April 1941 essay "Will Freedom Die with Capitalism?" Here Orwell asserts that for a long period after the establishment of socialism, people's living conditions will not improve, and may worsen. The transition to socialism "may make life very nearly unbearable for a long period, perhaps for hundreds of years" (XII, 459). This is an odd thing to say in an article arguing *in favor* of socialism—and it is definitely not a statement about oligarchical collectivism (bad collectivism or totalitarianism), which will presumably be even closer to unbearable, but quite unambiguously about democratic socialism, the system Orwell fervently advocates.

Orwell did not subsequently repeat such a grim prognosis, and it may be that he only briefly assented to it in 1941. Yet it is the most extreme formulation of a point he reiterated more moderately from time to time: that we cannot expect any dramatic improvement in living standards under socialism, at least not for some generations. In "Will Freedom Die with Capitalism?," he proceeds to defend socialism despite its possibly making life nearly unbearable for centuries, on three grounds: that it is historically necessary, that it will eventually lead to "pure communism," and that, historically, capitalism did not improve living conditions when it first came in. As to historical necessity, Britain must become more socialist in order to win the war against Hitler's socialist Germany, but this is merely one instance of the fact that the entire modern world is irresistibly moving towards collectivism. "The forces making for centralised control and planned production and consumption are overwhelming" (460). Orwell's intimation that his beloved socialism could make life "almost unbearable" for centuries to come, and that this is no reason to oppose it, illuminates most starkly the consequence of Orwell's adamant conviction that capitalism is objectively doomed and collectivism objectively inevitable.

With his intimate knowledge of English and French realistic fiction, Orwell was in no doubt that working-class living conditions had markedly improved over the past hundred years and that inter-class hostility had diminished (XVIII, 77, 80–81). In one emphatic statement to this effect, he points out that nineteenth-century writers assumed that conditions would not improve, yet they have improved beyond anything that could have been imagined, because of "the enormous increase in the productivity of labour" (XVI, 14)—a highly exceptional remark, as elsewhere Orwell nearly always attributes high wages to imperial exploitation of the colonies and to the low birth rate.

Orwell was also keenly interested in factual reports of occupation, income, and similar trends (XVI, 214; XVIII, 39–40), and was readily able to accept the facts about Britain's increasingly middle-class character, unlike many Marxists who found these facts difficult to accommodate with their received doctrines.

In his famous essay on "dirty postcards," Orwell noted that these cartoons depict people brimming over with sex appeal until marriage, whereupon they mutate to unappetizing middle age, abruptly, with no transition. This reflected the reality of traditional working-class life, in contrast to the middle class, who retain their youthful good looks until much later. Orwell points out that this traditional pattern has recently given way to a working class which has become more like the middle class in postponing the visible symptoms of aging. But this recent development, Orwell says, "will probably disappear again when our standard of living drops and our birth rate rises" (XIII, 28).

Orwell often writes as though he believed that the improvement in working-class incomes was almost entirely due to two temporary influences—the decline in the birth rate, so that workers spent money on themselves they would earlier have spent on raising their children, and the financial gains from the empire. Since socialism would reverse both of these (giving independence to the colonies and raising the birth rate once again above replacement), recent gains would be largely canceled out.

In his last years, Orwell's comparative pessimism about prospects for improvement took the form of pointing out the need for increasing output rather than redistributing it (XIX, 290, 334), and was influenced by the assumption he shared with many other people, that, with the war over, capitalism's inherent propensity to chronic depression was likely to manifest itself once again.

The Labour Party Supporter

Orwell consistently supported the Labour Party while deploring its insufficiently leftwing attitudes and actions. His view of the Labour Party was entirely typical of ILP members and of 1930s leftwing intellectuals generally.

Before World War II, the Labour Party had been in office twice, in 1924 and 1929–31, on both occasions as a minority government dependent on Liberal support. The Labour landslide in 1945 came as a surprise to Orwell and to nearly everyone. However, Orwell and many others were not too far out in gauging public opinion. What they failed to take into account was that various technical details of the electoral situation at that time would convert a Labour edge over the Conservatives into a landslide in terms of Parliamentary seats. (The Labour Party got 49.7 percent of the votes, winning 61.4 percent of the seats.)

The Labour Party's 1945 election manifesto states that while the Party's ultimate aim is socialism, a Labour government will not immediately nationalize all of industry, but will begin by nationalizing transportation, power, and steel (with compensation to the former owners), and increase government control over the remaining privately-owned industries.

Shortly after the election Orwell wrote that

> A Labour government may be said to mean business if it (a) nationalises land, coalmines, railways, public utilities and banks, (b) offers India immediate Dominion status . . . (c) purges the bureaucracy, the army, the Diplomatic Service etc. so thoroughly as to forestall sabotage from the right. (XVII, 246)

In the event, the Labour government did some of these but not others, while doing other leftwing things not anticipated by Orwell. It did nationalize the mines, railways, and public utilities, but not the land or the banks (except the UK central bank, the Bank of England). It also nationalized steel and "road haulage" (trucking). Within a few years, a fifth of the economy was taken into state ownership. The government did quickly grant India, Pakistan, Burma, and Ceylon dominion status and thus independence. It did not purge the government services, but it did not need to: there was never any "sabotage from the right." It also introduced a free national health service and a vastly expanded system of welfare payments, and re-introduced rationing and other controls which had expired at the end of the war, in some cases intensifying them (bread, which had not been rationed during the war, was rationed for the first time in 1946). All this amounted to a social revolution, carried out peacefully and constitutionally by a government which had received less than fifty percent of the votes—though many Conservative voters favored or did not strongly oppose most of these measures.

The Labour government took part in the establishment of NATO, essentially a defensive pact to deter the Russians from rolling up Western Europe. The government also initiated the "independent nuclear deterrent," British-controlled nuclear weapons additional to the nuclear weapons available through NATO. Britain under Labour took part in the occupation of Germany and waged war on Communist insurgents in Malaya. Orwell supported Britain's cold-war alliance with the United States, though as a second-best to his more preferred option which he recognized as "a pipe dream" (XVII, 248): a democratic socialist Europe which would be independent of both Russia and America.

From mid-1936 until the end of his life, Orwell was a socialist who conceived of socialism as state ownership of industry combined with political democracy and equality. But there were changes in his chosen denomination within socialism. From mid-1936 until June 1937 he was a "generic" socialist, a fellow-traveler, and a supporter of the Popular Front. From June 1937 until August 1939 he was an adherent of the revolutionary anti-Stalinist Left (on which more in Chapters 7 and 8 below). When he abruptly switched to support for the anti-fascist war in August 1939, he continued to accept most of the principles of the revolutionary Left, then he abandoned some of these piecemeal during the course of the war. As late as February 1941, he states that it is probably impossible to introduce socialism by peaceful means, using existing democratic institutions (XII, 377), but by the end of the war in 1945 he had in effect given up on revolution by armed uprising and may fairly be characterized as a Bevanite—a supporter of the left wing of the Labour Party—even though the defining moment of "Bevanism," the Bevanite revolt over National Health Service prescription charges, did not occur until fifteen months after Orwell's death.

4
The Post-Socialist

Socialism? I believe it to be dead.
—Benedetto Croce, February 1911

George Orwell was a post-socialist before he became a socialist, and all the time he was a socialist, from 1936 until his death in 1950, he remained a post-socialist. What I mean by these strange statements is simply that early in his life Orwell came to accept a cluster of beliefs fashionable in the early twentieth century, these beliefs derived from the intellectual reaction against socialism in the 1880s and 1890s, and Orwell never completely abandoned these beliefs.

As we read works from the period 1880–1939, we often encounter a general outlook, a definite system of interlocking ideas, which sees socialism not as new and dangerous, but as naive and outmoded. We can call this system of ideas "post-socialism." Post-socialism accepts all or most of the socialist complaints against capitalism and liberalism, but lacks any confidence in a socialist future. Post-socialism agrees with socialism that modern humankind has lost its soul or its sense of meaning in life, because it has lost the pre-industrial sense of community. Post-socialism accepts socialism's claim to be the most advanced embodiment of progress, but sees progress itself as a clay-footed idol. Post-socialism holds that material improvements make people spiritually worse off and that humans are fundamentally irrational. Post-socialism is an adaptation and a reformulation of pre-socialist views which reject urbanization, mechanization, and progress.

An identifying mark of post-socialist thinking is the claim that socialism maintains all the illusions of liberalism, one version being that Marx is essentially like Bentham. Post-socialism sees liberalism as a creed of rationalism, progress, and happiness, and socialism as a more up-to-date creed of rationalism, progress, and happiness. Post-socialism agrees with the socialist rejection of liberalism but holds that any faith in rationalism, progress, and happiness is hopelessly naive.

This belief system was imbibed by many intellectuals in the late nineteenth and early twentieth centuries. Among intellectuals greatly interested in the arts and not very interested in politics, it was virtually the reigning orthodoxy. This helps to explain what might otherwise seem puzzling: that in the 1920s and 1930s socialism is highly fashionable among politically inclined intellectuals while the leading creative artists nearly all hold a "reactionary" political worldview deplored by socialists. The "reactionaries" shared the socialists' negative view of capitalism and liberalism, while rejecting the socialists' positive proposals. Most of the fundamental assumptions of the reactionaries and the progressives were the same. Orwell embraced the post-socialist doctrine in the years prior to 1936, and modified it only slightly when he became an avowed socialist in mid-1936. At the end of this chapter, I give a few indications of the origins of these beliefs and where Orwell probably picked them up from.

When we think of the post-socialist belief system, two points should be borne in mind. First, this constellation of beliefs would be encountered in many books and journals after about 1880, and would be adopted by many individuals regardless of whether those individuals had personally ever been socialists. Intellectuals growing up in the Edwardian period would absorb the assumptions of post-socialism. Second, this cluster of beliefs does not strictly determine any political allegiance. People holding these beliefs would most often be without political affiliation, though some of them might support leftist policies (with reservations about the unrealistic hopes of others who supported the same policies), or might view themselves as opponents of the left. We see, then, how it could be true that Orwell was a post-socialist before he became a socialist and remained a post-socialist after he had become a socialist.

From Post-Socialist Anti-Socialist to Post-Socialist Socialist

Prior to 1936, Orwell refused to identify himself as a socialist because of certain objections he had to socialism as a movement. When he took the plunge and started to call himself a socialist in *The Road to Wigan Pier*, these objections remained, little altered, but instead of being reasons why we should not be socialists, they became reasons why socialism should change its sales pitch and thereby change the type of people it recruits. Orwell's 1935 reasons for rejecting socialism become his 1936 reasons for rejecting what he sees as the usual way in which socialist advocacy is packaged. He continues to attack socialists—but no longer the idea of socialism itself—in the same terms as before, but now from the inside.

The novel *Keep the Aspidistra Flying* was Orwell's last work before he became a socialist. It shows signs of his growing preoccupation with socialism and of his refusal to embrace it. The protagonist of *Keep the Aspidistra Flying*, Gordon Comstock, is a lower-middle-class man of twenty-nine, who hates "the money system" so fiercely that he dreads being trapped by it, and chooses to live an impoverished life working in a shabby bookstore. He writes poems and half-heartedly aspires to make his name with a great work of poetry. He has turned down a more lucrative career writing advertising copy—advertising being "the dirtiest ramp that capitalism has yet produced" (55). He has a middle-upper-middle-class friend, Ravelston, who is a convinced socialist and funds a socialist magazine named *Antichrist*. Ravelston holds "the naive belief that in a little while Socialism is going to put things right" (92). When Ravelston says that Comstock ought to read Marx, Comstock replies that he would sooner read Mrs. Humphry Ward (94). When Ravelston asks Comstock for his view of socialism, Comstock replies:

> "Oh! Some kind of Aldous Huxley Brave New World; only not so amusing. Four hours a day in a model factory, tightening up bolt number 6003. Rations served out in greaseproof paper at the communal kitchen. Community-hikes from Marx Hostel to Lenin Hostel and back. Free abortion-clinics on all the corners. All very well in its way, of course. Only we don't want it." (IV, 97)

Brave New World had appeared three years before. Huxley's novel plays out the usual post-socialist critique of socialism with the addition of a few up-to-the-minute elements from science and popular culture. It depicts a socialist society dedicated to "hedonism" (what would later be termed materialism or consumerism), high output, and individual conformity. "Four hours a day" is mentioned by Comstock because it's a cliché of the time that socialism will be so much more efficient than capitalism that the normal working day can easily be halved without any reduction in output.

The contemptuous dismissal of socialism voiced both by Gordon Comstock and by the novel's narrative voice is also that of Orwell himself. In early- to mid-1936 this unfriendly characterization of socialism is first maintained by Orwell in complete earnest, and then becomes his picture of the unfortunate way in which socialism is envisioned by those misguided socialists who identify socialism with technology and growth, and by those decent people who reject socialism. As he moves from rejection to acceptance of socialism, Orwell remains convinced that this picture of socialism appeals to morally deficient people.

Orwell had been aware of socialism, as the most conspicuous political current among intellectuals, for several years, and had taken part in numerous political discussions with socialists, notably with Mr. and Mrs. Westrope, members of the ILP and owners of the bookshop where he worked part-time from October 1934. Victor Gollancz, the publisher of Orwell's first two books, was well-known as a socialist. While in the North, Orwell was mainly in the company of socialists. In the midst of writing *Wigan Pier*, he married Eileen O'Shaughnessy; she and her family were socialists. Orwell's intellectual situation prior to his conversion is that of someone opposed to socialism, but not on very rigorously worked-out grounds, who is being ceaselessly reminded that socialism is the burning intellectual issue of the moment. And so he was liable either to give more theoretical elaboration to his anti-socialism or to embrace socialism.

Both as antisocialist and then as socialist, Orwell professes himself disgusted by the effects of industrial progress. His antisocialism, like Gissing's, is bound up with a revulsion against modern technology and the *timbre* of modern urban life. In Part II of *Wigan Pier*, Orwell expresses this revulsion stridently, whilst fully accepting that an enormous increase in "mechanisation" is practically necessary.

The pre-1936 Orwell rejects socialism because he thinks of it as the embodiment of industrial progress, and he is appalled by some of the conspicuous symptoms of that progress. What precipitates his acceptance of socialism is that while still repelled by industrial progress, he has become convinced that it is inescapable.

What was Orwell's political outlook prior to 1936? The evidence is thin, because when Orwell converted to socialism, he was simultaneously converted to politics. Before 1936, politics was not an all-dominating feature of his mental landscape. After 1936, everything is political. "Every line of serious work that I have written since 1936 has been written, directly or indirectly, *against* totalitarianism and *for* democratic Socialism, as I understand it" (XVIII, 319).[1] Most people who quote this do so to specify Orwell's political position; what is often overlooked is that this statement implies that no line of serious work Orwell wrote after 1936 is non-political. While we know that *Animal Farm* and *Nineteen Eighty-Four* were coming, still, to me, this declaration has a certain sadness.

The pre-1936 Orwell is reported to have called himself a "Tory anarchist."[2] In no extant writing does Orwell apply this label to himself, but he does use it to characterize Jonathan Swift (XVIII, 425). Swift, of all writers, had the greatest influence on Orwell, and Swift—famously, in Part III of *Gulliver's Travels*—was an enemy of the machine. Swift was one of the greatest of pre-socialist enemies of progress.

The view propounded by some writers[3] that "Blair" and "Orwell" represent different personas or signify a character transition is baseless. "Orwell" was simply the name assumed by Blair, though he decidedly preferred his assumed name to his baptismal one. For example, Orwell's fateful conversion from largely apolitical antisocialist to committed

1 But then, wherever Orwell utters a generalization, we can expect it to be false. Something like 20 percent of his output after 1936 is concerned with purely literary matters, and something like 70 percent of that has no more connection with democratic socialism than any such work picked at random from a library catalog. So when Orwell says "every line," he ought to have said "somewhere between 80 and 86 percent of the lines."

2 Crick 1992, 174, 205.

3 Stansky and Abrahams 1980; Williams 1981, 3.

socialist ideologue occurs three and a half years after his adoption of the new name. No profound change of outlook is associated with the name change.

Most intellectuals are non-political. This doesn't mean that they have no political views—their political prejudices may be extremely strong. It means that they are not primarily interested in politics; they would never dream, for instance, of joining a political party. Politics doesn't fascinate them as much as other matters—chiefly the arts. When a non-political intellectual becomes a political intellectual, he normally adopts all the distinguishing doctrinal features of the political intellectual. But when Orwell became a political intellectual in mid-1936, he clung to the aesthetic and other standards dominant among non-political intellectuals, and judged the socialist movement by those standards.

Orwell on Technology

If we look at the thought of the Left in all its diversity, we find both positive and negative responses to technology, industrialization, and economic growth. In the twenty-first century, the hostile responses predominate. Anti-technology and anti-growth sentiments come mainly from the Left. In the 1930s, the balance of leftist opinion was different. The 1930s Left was predominantly pro-technology and pro-growth. In the Marxian terminology, we might put it this way: in the 1930s, most socialists complained that capitalism was failing to develop the forces of production as fast as they could be developed. This was the chief indictment of capitalism, dwarfing all others. Today, leftists (who can mostly no longer be called socialists) complain that capitalism is developing the forces of production far too fast. This is now the chief indictment of capitalism, dwarfing all others.

Since Orwell's death, the left has fallen out of love with technology. The progressives have turned against progress. In the 1930s, while there was some discernable leftist hostility to technological progress, generally the Left was strongly pro-technology. There are occasionally expressions of alarm by socialists that socialism is over-emphasizing material progress, as in Benedict's *The Larger Socialism* (1921). Orwell anticipates the later turn against technology, but the grounds for his anti-machine stance are not those of the twenty-first-century leftist. He is very little concerned, for example, with damage to the natural environment—though he does make a couple of brief reference to soil erosion, deforestation, and over-use of resources (XVII, 27–29; XIX, 397).

Orwell is slow to adopt the word "technology," and usually writes instead of "machine civilisation," "mechanical progress," "the machine," and (less frequently) "industry" and "industrialism." Orwell's vocabulary resists the newfangled. There are a few exceptions: he early takes up 'totalitarianism' and uses it frequently from 1936 on, and he is fond of "intelligentsia" (a term that pedants would restrict to pre-1917 Russia) to refer to the class of Western intellectuals. The word "technology" had already acquired its present meaning, as illustrated by its use in such works as Huxley's *Ends and Means* (1937). It's the kind of un-Saxon jargon word Orwell is generally slow to adopt even after it has become everyday usage among intellectuals and journalists.[4] I will sometimes refer to Orwell's statements about machinery in his own terminology, and sometimes in the more recent terminology of "technology" and "high-tech."

The Road to Wigan Pier was written four years after the appearance of *Brave New World* and cites that work approvingly. But Orwell's anti-technologism predates *Brave New World* and does not have exactly the same roots as Huxley's, though both Huxley and Orwell, in their individual ways, absorb and retransmit the anti-progress ideology of post-socialism which dominates early twentieth-century thinking.

Both Huxley and Orwell were responding to pro-technology socialism as conveyed in most socialist advocacy of the time. For both writers, the target is socialism as it appears in the utterances of socialists, and as far as technology goes, this is perceived as an extrapolation into the future of the most technologically-advanced capitalist culture, the United States. Neither Huxley nor Orwell display any doubt that collectivism *can* develop advanced technology even more effectively than capitalism,

4 In a broadcast talk given in June 1943, Orwell employs the words "technology" or "technological" several times (XV, 134). In later writings he returns to his normal practice and does not use those words again (for instance XVII, 171–72).

and they both accept that industrial development automatically tends to move society toward collectivism.

Both Huxley and Orwell accepted the necessity for continued technological advances, but the ways they reconciled this with their hostility to some of technology's consequences were different. Huxley wanted a culture in which technology would be guided by values other than hedonism. The Orwell of *Wigan Pier* agreed, but this is not the focus of his thinking. Instead, he emphasized his belief that the malign effects of technology are inseparable from technological progress itself. He not only maintains that technology has bad effects, he even appears to rule out the possibility that its good effects could outweigh these bad effects. He dismisses attempts to defend technology as making any net contribution to human wellbeing.

How can such a stance be harmonized with acceptance that continued technological progress is inevitable, and even to be guardedly welcomed? In *Wigan Pier* Orwell alternates between expressing his horror at technological progress itself and expressing his horror at technological progress as the key rhetorical feature of socialist advocacy. As for technological progress itself, in between denouncing it, Orwell asserts that it is practically unavoidable. And as for technological progress as the centerpiece of socialist propaganda, Orwell maintains that this approach repels decent people and attracts the worst (V, 176–182).

In *Wigan Pier* Orwell offers three main objections to modern technology: that it makes us soft, that it corrupts taste, and that it is not consciously controlled.

"The tendency of mechanical progress is to make your environment safe and soft; and yet you are striving to keep yourself brave and hard . . . softness is repulsive. . . . what is usually called progress also entails what is usually called degeneracy" (181–82). So, technology is bad because humans need hardship. Such worthy attributes as physical strength and courage cannot survive technological progress.

Orwell accepts that technology shortens working hours, but flatly rejects the view that this is in any way desirable (180–88). Orwell argues that, given more leisure, people will use it for worthless pursuits, and furthermore, that the goal of expanding leisure is self-defeating because people need work.

Next, Orwell gives examples of "the frightful debauchery of taste that has already been effected by a century of mechanization" (189). In the case of food, he instances canned food, artificial flavoring, and colorful but tasteless imported apples. This points to the incident in *Coming Up for Air*, where Bowling bites into a sausage and is outraged to find that it tastes of . . . fish. Orwell also attributes ugliness to the products of mechanization. "There is probably no one capable of thinking and feeling who has not occasionally looked at a gas-pipe chair and reflected that the machine is the enemy of human life" (178).

Finally, he claims that "there is a tendency for the mechanisation of the world to proceed as it were automatically, whether we want it or not. . . . the process of mechanisation is out of control" (191–92).

Why Orwell Was Wrong about Technology

Interspersed with Orwell's attacks on mechanization are numerous statements that mechanization is an unalterable fact that has to be accepted. In one passage, he even asserts (in standard 1930s socialist mode) that capitalism culpably holds back technical progress, along with an approving reference to the theory that capitalists buy up patents to prevent their being implemented. "Some years ago someone invented a gramophone needle that would last for decades. One of the big gramophone companies brought up the patent rights and that was the last that was ever heard of it" (192n). This legend was rife in socialist circles of the time—*The Man in the White Suit* (1951) later reflects and disseminates this kind of tale, and I recall the legend of the everlasting light bulb being generally accepted by British socialists as late as the 1960s (I believed it myself). I could take up several pages explaining why this sort of thing is unlikely to occur, but probably it's enough to mention that "some years ago" must have been less than twenty, after which time this hypothetical patent would expire and the super-durable gramophone needle would promptly flood the market.[5]

In this *Wigan Pier* passage we encounter, as we often do in writings hostile to technology, the claim that technological innovations are just

5 On the myth of the everlasting light bulb, see Steele 1992, 300–01.

made for the sake of it, whenever they can be made, along with the contradictory claim (or admission) that they are sometimes not made at all. The basic fallacy here is to think that technology alone is a limit on innovation, when there is also the limit imposed by scarcity of capital. Numerous hypothetical technical innovations are never implemented or are implemented after a long delay because they are not profitable,[6] and this must always be the case under any social system, including any type of socialism.

We are all borne along by the current of progress. Comparatively few people actively plan for this to happen. Now, it's quite true that, asked to contemplate the spectacle of industrial development—the machines, the smokestacks, the tedious factory routine—many people will give an unfavorable verdict. But they all want the fruits of industrialization. Whatever their tribal, religious, or national background or upbringing, people always want more and better goods and more leisure time, and the only possible way they can get these things is through industrial development, technological innovation, and economic growth.

Orwell repeatedly claims that the way in which socialists recommend socialism, by emphasizing mechanical progress, alienates sensitive people who may turn to fascism. However, Mussolini's Fascism was a modernizing doctrine, preoccupied with high-tech. There is not quite the same emphasis in National Socialism, which was somewhat less rhapsodic about high-tech than 1930s Fascism or 1930s Communism, but still, 1930s Nazism was decidedly pro-technology, and would never attract anyone appalled by the high-tech zeal of 1930s leftists. As a typical 1930s leftist, Orwell never examined Fascist or National Socialist theory or the actual nature of these doctrines' popular appeal, and so he supposed that they wanted to put the clock back.

Orwell denies that there is any improvement in people having higher incomes and shorter working hours. He denies that leisure is valuable in

6 In other words, implementing an innovation ("making a machine") has to withdraw resources from other uses, and in many cases the reduction in output from that withdrawal has a higher value than the additional output from the innovation itself; therefore the innovation, though technically feasible, should not be made, and will not be made except by error, until prices change.

itself, because it leaves open the question of what people might do with it. However, he has spent the entire first half of this very book depicting people who work long hours under terrible conditions and have inadequate incomes. If hardship and long hours are so easily tolerable, why all the fuss? Without exception, all the problems paraded so indignantly in Part I can be cured (and have largely been cured in today's Lancashire and Yorkshire) by economic growth, which is helped along by technological innovation. Oddly, Orwell discusses increased leisure without mentioning the fact that it goes along with increased output and higher incomes: he doesn't notice that people choose to take part of their gains from economic growth in more leisure and part in more goods (other than leisure).

Orwell says that human beings need work and that if they are not compelled by economic necessity to work such long hours, they will spend part of the time freed up by this to do some other kind of work, though the worker "may not call it work" (183). But the work that he does for his own enjoyment without payment yields him more satisfaction than the work he does only because he needs the money to live—that's why he chooses to do it. This is therefore a real gain in human wellbeing.

"The labourer set free from ditch-digging may want to spend his leisure, or part of it, in playing the piano, while the professional pianist may be only too glad to get out and dig a potato patch." This is literally true, but it does not imply that increased leisure is valueless. The laborer who plays the piano in his leisure time is doing something he prefers to do and he is happier, in his own estimation, for doing it. It doesn't count against this that someone else might be glad of a change from piano playing. Furthermore, the fact that instances may be cited where some people will use their leisure doing things that other people are paid to do doesn't imply that these leisure preferences are randomly distributed among activities. Few people find it an intrinsically enjoyable pastime to kneel in a cramped position and hack away at a coal face for hours on end, while many people want to sit on a river bank in summertime, snoozing fitfully and waiting for a fish to bite.

Orwell maintains that once a machine can produce something, no one will want to make that thing as a hobby, so that making things as a leisure time activity dies out (185–86). Exactly the opposite has occurred, with a vast expansion of do-it-yourself activity since Orwell wrote. Orwell himself made furniture by hand as a hobby, evidently not accepting his own argument that this would be wholly futile.

Orwell contends that ultimately all work can be done by machines, so that every opportunity to choose "creative work" will be ruled out. Here he claims that anything made by hand can be made better by machine (contradicting his claim that artifacts of machine production like the gas-pipe chair are necessarily ugly), and that you cannot derive any enjoyment from making something by hand if you know that it can more easily be made by a machine. It's strange to deny the value of mechanical improvement because of what will supposedly happen if it is projected many thousands of years into the future, and even then, it seems unlikely that those distant humans will be at a loss for something to do. They can still make music, tell stories, learn and extend scientific knowledge, play competitive games, or go hunting.

Orwell raises the prospect of replacing every human function with machines, for example eventually getting rid of human hands because everything they do can be done by machines. Here we have to distinguish between what might happen while humans are physically more or less the same as they are now, and what might happen over millions of years in which they gradually evolve into something unrecognizable as human. As long as humans are constituted roughly as they are now, they will want to exercise their hands and will look for ways to do so. Millions of years in the future, we can suppose that hands might have atrophied, and our descendants may have developed interests somewhat different to ours, but this isn't sufficient reason to consign today's third-world farmers to endless malnutrition and fourteen-hour workdays, especially as all of humankind will very likely be wiped out by some cosmic catastrophe before millions of years have passed.

Do industrialization and urbanization debauch taste? Rising real incomes mean a greater variety of consumer goods, and a greater range of choice, with choices made by some individuals considered bad in the opinion of other individuals. The examples given by Orwell are cases of widened choice. Some people buy brightly colored apples without much complexity of flavor, but the less visually prepossessing, more flavorful

English apples like Cox's Orange Pippin have continued to be available in England to this day. Stam's gas-pipe chair was one experimental event in 1926. It begat a wide range of cantilevered and tubular metal chairs, none of which has caused many people to despair for civilization, and all of which taken together remain a small segment of the range of available chairs.

In some instances, foodstuffs or other goods are prepared by cheaper methods, losing some of the subtlety of traditional fare, but becoming affordable by a wider section of the population. This will be particularly irksome to social groups which are descending, as other social groups are rising and expanding. Members of declining groups, like families of imperial civil servants in the 1930s, will compare what they had available in their childhoods with what has newly become available, and will probably discount the fact that the new is available to millions more people, and conclude that standards are declining generally. If we look at the economy as a whole, we observe that with economic growth, quality improves and the range of choices widens.

Orwell on Technology after *Wigan Pier*

In later years Orwell continued to make comments about technology and continued to combine general denunciations of machine production with statements about its necessity. Sometimes he contradicts his anti-technological arguments in *Wigan Pier*, and sometimes he reasserts them, even years after having contradicted them. But the balance of his emphasis changes, with gradually less mention of technology's bad effects and more assertions of its benefits.

As a consequence, *Nineteen Eighty-Four*, thirteen years after *The Road to Wigan Pier*, is very far from being an anti-technology dystopia in the tradition of *We*, "The Machine Stops," or *Brave New World*. Despite its intercontinental missiles and video surveillance, *Nineteen Eighty-Four* conveys the sense that technology, as it affects individual lives, is inadequately developed.

In November 1941 Orwell writes that there is a lot of ugliness because of "the impact of the machine" (XIII, 75). And yet here he concludes:

> I don't think there is any reason to be pessimistic about the long-term effects of the arrival of the machine. Ultimately we shall get used to the machine. We do, however, have to defend ourselves against the threat of totalitarianism, which might really bring a swift and final death to civilization. (XIII, 76)

But again in 1942 he is writing of "the squalor, even the meaninglessness of modern life after the triumph of the machine" (XIII, 215).

What changed was that in 1936 Orwell saw the machine as ineluctably corrupting, while toward the end of his life he had graduated to a slightly different view: hedonism, favored by the machine, is corrupting, but also unsustainable. The vacuity of hedonism leads to fanatics—who have an alternative to hedonism—taking power and instituting totalitarianism.

As late as March 1942, Orwell is still clearly anti-progress and anti-machine. Yet five months later he is indignantly affirming that the workers are obviously right to want higher incomes and shorter working hours (XIII, 509–510), and a few months after that he states: "Before you can despise the machine, the machine must set you free from brute labour" (XIV, 283), which is close to the standard contemporary leftwing view. In June 1943, he mentions the differences in living standards between 1900 and "today," and attributes them to the power of the machine to raise living standards (XV, 134), a contradiction with the position he most often states, that the rise in living standards is due almost entirely to exploitation of colored labor in the colonies and the fall in the birth rate. He opines that "We have invented machines that would have seemed magical only a hundred years ago, and we have used them almost solely to make war." This is a mistaken judgment which could only have been made by someone largely ignorant of industrial matters. Machinery has mainly been used to increase output of peaceful production, thus raising both population and real incomes, and only to a much smaller extent to wage war.

In *Wigan Pier* Orwell asserts that primitive people are finer specimens than modern workers, and ridicules John Beevers for questioning this (V, 179). Several times over the next few years he made the same point in passing—that tribal folks are both happier and more aesthetically pleasing than modern Western people (XII, 460; XIV, 185). In October 1944 he calls this view into question. "It is quite possible that a modern factory-worker is more individual, more intelligent, happier and more amiable than, say, a mediaeval serf or a Roman slave" (XVI, 434). A few months later he announces that "We live in an age in which the average human being in the highly-civilised countries is aesthetically inferior to the lowest savage. This state of affairs . . . is expected to right itself of its own accord as soon as society takes a comelier shape" (XVII, 77–78). So (unless this is an issue where Orwell vacillated back and forth), he accepts the possibility that modern workers are happier than ancient ones, while thinking them aesthetically inferior to savages. This gradual, hesitant movement on the issue of the noble savage is typical of Orwell's gradual shift from dislike of progress to acceptance of it. Some decades after Orwell's death, research would confirm what ought to be obvious: that happiness rises with income, that people in advanced industrial "market democracies" are predominantly happy, and that they are considerably happier than people in pre-industrial societies.[7]

Like all left-oriented intellectuals with a strong interest in literature, Orwell notices the unsettling fact that the consolidation of leftist identification among politically affiliated intellectuals coincides with the rise of modernist writers whose political outlooks is most often what the Left considers reactionary and rightwing. In Orwell's eyes, writers who have rejected the ideals of progress and liberalism have thereby acknowledged reality. They have become "grown up," but unfortunately their "revulsion from a shallow conception of progress drove them politically in the wrong direction" (XIII, 216). The leading modern writers (Lawrence, Joyce, Yeats, Eliot) share Orwell's fundamental post-socialist outlook without sharing his commitment to the Left. In trying to account for this, Orwell asserts that earlier writers (Shaw, Wells, Bennett, Galsworthy) were unaware of anything outside Britain. This is an embarrassing blunder, as others are quick to point out (217–220), but it is Orwell's confused

7 Eighty-five percent of people in the U.S. are above the neutral mid-point between unhappiness and happiness (Diener and Diener 1996); and the corresponding number for several Western European countries is slightly higher.

way of recognizing that when post-socialist ideas triumphed in England, they were seen as coming from France. There was home-grown post-socialism, and post-socialists looked back fondly to writers like Swift, Carlyle, Ruskin, and Samuel Butler, but English intellectuals of the time felt able to do this because they had, so to speak, gotten permission from Paris. Obeisance to Paris as the headquarters of intellectual advance took hold in Britain in the 1890s, along with fin-de-siècle disenchantment with progress.

The World Wells Made

The rise to dominance of the doctrine of post-socialism in the early twentieth century is dramatically captured in the reception and reputation of Herbert George Wells. Wells is mentioned more than any other writer in *The Road to Wigan Pier*—six or seven mentions (depending on how you count them) as compared with four mentions for each of runners-up Bernard Shaw and D. H. Lawrence. All but one of these Wells mentions identifies Wells with the evil worship of machines and progress.

Wells became famous in 1895 with *The Time Machine*, a work of science fiction, more than thirty years before the term "science fiction" would be coined. His early works, now his most widely read, are not really derived from science, in the manner of Jules Verne, but are romances with a horrific aspect and some scientific trappings. When Wells wrote *The Time Machine*, he was twenty-nine years old, and had been a keen socialist for more than a decade. The work reflects arguments over the different conceptions of socialism then prevalent. In 1887 Edward Bellamy had written *Looking Backward*, and in 1890, in reaction against Bellamy's depiction of socialism, William Morris wrote *News from Nowhere*, the glowing depiction of a low-tech socialist future where even literacy dies out. Wells's view of a possible future is a dry and sardonic comment on socialist predictions.

In 1901, for the new millennium, the now famous writer of fiction Wells published a non-fiction work, *Anticipations of the Reaction of Mechanical and Scientific Progress upon Human Life and Thought*. This was a commercial success and established him as an authority on the real-life repercussions of technology. At the same time, Wells was turning out works like *Kipps* and *The History of Mr. Polly*, outstanding novels with no science-fiction component. Some of his later novels are vehicles for clunky discussions of "ideas," to their detriment as works of narrative art. He later wrote *The Outline of History*, which has huge sales for many decades, and followed this up with similar "outline" works on biology and economics.

In the first few years of the twentieth century, Wells had a strong following among the popular reading public and among intellectuals. But then intellectual opinion began to swing against Wells, along with the general intellectual reaction against progress, science, and technology, so that after about 1920, while popular readers still thought of Wells as a great literary mind and social thinker, intellectuals tended to dismiss him as a facile popular entertainer and a naive promoter of high-tech utopia.

Wells accepted all the elements of standard socialism, what I have called neo-Saint-Simonianism. His main focus was on the prevention of war by a World State. As a member of the Fabian Society he tried, and naturally failed, to transform it into a cadre dedicated to his own specific opinions. Subsequently he hoped to call into being a "samurai" or dedicated elite of socialist intellectuals who would take over the world.

Wells never changed his fundamental political outlook, but having become a celebrity pundit, he tried out changes in the way he presented his message. He wavered somewhat over Communism but ultimately came down in qualified opposition, and he opposed Fascism sharply, as reflected in his novel *Meanwhile* (1927).

Wells once jokingly called himself a "liberal fascist," but the joke betrays a half-truth. When the movie *Things to Come* appeared in 1936, some members of the British Union of Fascists were puzzled. They knew that Wells was supposed to be an enemy, but here (in "Wings over the World") was a positive depiction of Fascism pretty much as British Fascists conceived it, even down to the black shirts.

Orwell's Attacks on Wells

To post-socialists, Wells was the embodiment of what they perceived as discredited liberal illusions. Throughout his life as a writer, Orwell frequently attacked Wells's worldview. Apart from Wells's alleged naive faith in science, Orwell's major criticism is that Wells failed to understand the power of totalitarianism, because he was "too sane to understand the modern world." Wells is one of those intellectuals who had never felt patriotic emotion, and therefore he cannot understand the emotional appeal of fascism. Wells is too sensible, and sensible men are not the most powerful. "The energy that actually shapes the world springs from emotions—racial pride, leader-worship, religious belief, love of war—which liberal intellectuals mechanically write off as anachronisms, and which they have usually destroyed so completely in themselves as to have lost all power of action" (XII, 538). Orwell is here faithfully intoning *fin-de-siècle* post-socialism. He is not applying himself to what Wells actually wrote.

Wells, writes Orwell, was not prone to patriotic emotions and therefore cannot understand fascism. "The thunder of guns, the jingle of spurs, the catch in the throat when the old flag goes by, leave him manifestly cold." Orwell contrasts Wells with Jack London. London had a fascist streak and was therefore able to understand fascism (before it came along). The implication is that Orwell too must have had a fascist streak. Orwell points out that the Nazis use technology. "Modern Germany is far more scientific than England and far more barbarous."

In his attacks on Wells, Orwell is applying a formula without making any serious attempt to grasp the ideas he is criticizing. Orwell had read Wells with intense excitement in his youth and had re-read him several times subsequently. And yet when he sits at his typewriter to write about Wells, he forgets what he has read. His picture of Wells is egregiously inaccurate—though these inaccuracies were standard among post-socialists.

Orwell commits the error which is a commonplace of post-socialist and *fin-de-siècle* criticisms of progress and rationality: assuming that people who enthusiastically embrace these values are unaware of any alternative. Having mistakenly imputed to advocates of progress the belief that progress is inevitable, opponents of progress deduce that they can refute progress by citing cases where progress has not occurred, which is like arguing against medicine by pointing to outbreaks of disease.

People who favor progress do not consider progress to be inevitable, but to be sometimes possible, and when possible, worth encouraging.

Wells was in favor of progress and rationality and from his youth he was acutely aware of the dangers of retrogression and the vitality of anti-progress ideologies. Wells was always mindful of the fragility, instability, and impermanence of civilized and tolerable human life, or of any human life at all. Most of Wells's early stories have often been considered morbidly pessimistic—think of *The Island of Doctor Moreau* or *The Sleeper Awakes*. *The Time Machine* depicts a future in which humankind has evolved into two races, mindless pretty things and horrible brutes, and a remoter future in which intelligent life will have died out. The deeper horror in *The War of the Worlds* comes from the realization that the Martian invaders are beings of the sort which (Wells anticipates) humans will evolve into. Every line of the book is written with this irony in mind. Back in the 1890s, Wells had foreseen that humans accustomed to high tech for millions of years would evolve into organisms without limbs. When Orwell in 1936 raised the issue of human-descended beings losing their hands, supposing he was making a point against Wells, he was half-recalling what he had read as a boy in Wells.[8] Orwell attributes to Wells the claim that all our problems will be solved by "science," which is the opposite of Wells's view that social and political changes are necessary to enable us to cope with the repercussions of scientific discovery.

Orwell throws out claims about Wells which he does not attempt to argue for and which are presumptively untrue. For example, he claims that Wells has never experienced patriotic emotions. As far as we can evaluate such a contention, the evidence is all the other way. Wells broke with his socialist comrades to enthusiastically whip up support for the Allies in the Great War (Wells coined the slogan, "The War to End War"). The standard ILP view of Wells after 1914 was that he was a sell-out to patriotic warmongering. Aside from this, it is a fallacy to assume that you need to share in the emotions associated with an ideology to understand it. For instance,

8 It's possible that Wells might have gotten this from Samuel Butler, and also possible that Orwell might have remembered reading this in Butler and forgot that he had also read it in Wells.

it's a reasonable surmise that Frederick the Great never experienced the slightest flicker of religious piety, but he was perfectly well able to understand the role of religious passions in the actions of other people, and manipulate them accordingly. Orwell did not propose any specific insight essential to understanding patriotism or fascism which Wells failed to appreciate. Whatever the shortcomings of his understanding of the emotional sources of mass support for fascism, the author of *The Sleeper Awakes*, *The New Machiavelli*, and *The Holy Terror* had a lot to say about psychological factors in politics, whereas Jack London and George Orwell contribute almost nothing on this topic.

Trying to explain Wells's appeal, Orwell refers to "journeys to the moon and to the bottom of the sea" (XIII, 213) and "the inhabitants of the planets and the bottom of the sea" (XII, 540). Wells wrote only one book about a journey to the moon, and that is more concerned with the peculiar social organization of beings who live inside the moon. He wrote nothing about the inhabitants of the planets except for the Martians who invade Earth in *War of the Worlds*—and they are schematic future-human-descendants. He wrote nothing about a journey to the bottom of the sea. Orwell is here so sloppy that he confuses Wells with the utterly different Verne. Orwell feels he has to account for the fact that in his youth he found Wells's early stories, with their bleak, merciless ethos, totally enthralling. But instead of really trying to remember, he relies on the clichés of post-socialist ideology to tell him what he must have been thinking at the time: the appeal of these stories must lie in their wonderfully imagined locales. This is pure tommyrot.

Orwell's contrast of Wells with Jack London is not apt. It's unconvincing to say that *The Iron Heel* shows a better grasp of the future totalitarianism than *The Sleeper Awakes*. Perhaps neither of them come particularly close, but if these works must be put to that test, then *The Sleeper Awakes* surely wins hands down. If this is so clear, why doesn't Orwell see it? Everything Orwell writes about Wells is written just as though Orwell had never read a single line of Wells. And Orwell links Wells's supposed illusions with those of the Marxists, despite the fact that London was a Marxist and Wells was not.

The notion that we can refute Wells by pointing out that barbarians are eager to adopt modern technology (XII, 191) is simply risible. This was a prominent theme in Wells's writing, for example the character of Ostrog in *The Sleeper Awakes*. Before Orwell was born, Wells was predicting the use of the most advanced modern technology by "reactionaries" and barbarians.

Orwell confuses advocacy with prediction. In his early writings Wells often depicts the horrors that might ensue, dwells on the "irrational" way in which people might behave, and emphasizes the fragility of human civilization (to cosmic events, to alien invasion, to totalitarianism). Later he was more inclined to develop scenarios depicting the best that might happen if people act, in his view, appropriately. Not for one moment did Wells suppose that he was predicting what was bound to happen, or was even particularly likely. He saw himself as laying out the kind of thing that might happen in the unlikely event that people (from his point of view) came to their senses.

The really serious flaw in Wells's thinking is one for which Orwell was unequipped to criticize him: his complete ignorance of economic principles. Wells wrote an entire textbook of economics, bereft of any glimmer of economic insight. Wells had never troubled to look inside Alfred Marshall's *Principles of Economics* (1890) nor had he learned anything from Walras, Jevons, Wicksteed, John Bates Clark, or Irving Fisher. The downward-sloping demand curve was as much beneath Wells's notice as the correct incantation to raise the Devil. Associated with this absolute and utterly comprehensive ignorance of the economy, Wells never doubted that it was feasible for a civilization to exist in which science and technological innovation could flourish in the absence of commerce and financial markets.

Some Writers Orwell Read

While Orwell was early captivated by Wells and then repudiated him as the epitome of machine worship, other early influences were absorbed and then qualified more hesitantly if at all.

Orwell read *Gulliver's Travels* the night before his eighth birthday (XVIII, 428) and remained enthralled for the rest of his life. And so, at the age of seven, the future author of *Nineteen Eighty-Four* fell in love with a story in which (in Part III) prose works are composed by machine, deviant individuals are corrected by operating on their brains, and evolved natural speech is replaced with a simplified artificial language.[9]

Swift's attacks on science and machinery impressed him, and we may surmise that at first they convinced him. In 1942 Orwell composed an imaginary interview with Swift brought back to life (XIV, 156–61). This is in effect a conversation between Orwell in 1942 and the pre-1936 Orwell represented by the resurrected Swift. The interviewer (the Orwell of 1942) accepts the necessity of the machine and the superiority in some respects of modern life. In questioning Swift (the pre-1936 Orwell), the interviewer also questions some of the arguments in *Wigan Pier*. Though Orwell has come around to the view that mechanical progress is unavoidable and even (gulp) positively desirable, his criticisms of Swift are less strident and much more sympathetic than his numerous thoughtless attacks on Wells.

Orwell greatly admired Samuel Butler, whose fame began posthumously, in Orwell's childhood. Butler surmised that machines were conscious and would eventually conspire to displace humans, unless they were stopped. In *Erewhon*, the citizens make it a serious crime to use any machine invented after a certain date, and even as late as 1945, Orwell was seriously suggesting that we might have to adopt a similar law, to prevent machines destroying civilization (XVII, 172).

In the 1920s, Orwell became thoroughly familiar with the Roman Catholic writers, including Chesterton, Belloc, and E. C. Bentley, who rejected industrialism and capitalism in favor of "distributism," a doctrine popularized in Chesterton's slogan that every man should have "three acres and a cow." We don't know the details of Orwell's immediate reactions to these writers. Looking back from the 1940s, he viewed this group—"the Catholic gang"—with hostility, while accepting some key elements of their worldview, such as their aversion to industrial development, capitalism, and eugenics.

In 1927 Orwell committed himself to the life of a full-time writer, with the assumption that his most significant works would be realistic, socially-conscious novels. George Gissing was Orwell's model. So neglected was Gissing at this time that most of his works were difficult to

9 Swift 1970, 132–164.

come by, but some that Orwell did manage to read, notably *The Odd Women*, crystallized for him the kind of novelist he aspired to become. Gissing wrote his first novel, *Workers in the Dawn*, in 1880, committed to socialism of the then fashionable type, Comtean Positivism. Gissing then rejected socialism, and wrote the anti-socialist—and less centrally but still quite decidedly, anti-progress and anti-machine—novel *Demos* in 1886.

In the 1920s, Anatole France was one of the most lavishly admired of contemporary writers, and Orwell shared in the prevailing estimation, though by the 1940s he came to share the general view that France had been over-rated (XVI, 261–62). France started writing in the 1860s as a skeptical, some would say cynical, anti-clerical conservative, his worldview shaped by Renan and Taine. A Dreyfusard, he gradually became committed to socialism, and near the end of his life, threw his support to the new Communist movement.[10] Yet some of his most widely read works, though written while he was a socialist, conveyed a sense of ultimate futility and therefore disappointed many socialists. At the same time, they gratified left-leaning intellectuals not so committed to socialism but imbued with the post-socialist worldview, who perceived recognition of futility as a mark of mature percipience.

Penguin Island (1908) depicts a population of penguins as an allegory for the history of France. Medieval horrors are succeeded by capitalist horrors, and then the story is continued into the future. The exploited workers lack the capacity to carry through a revolution, and so capitalism continues, increasingly horrific, until it collapses into primitive barbarism. Then progress begins again and the penguins go through a second medieval stage until they again arrive at capitalism, which again develops to a grotesque climax, with never any socialist salvation in sight. The implication is that atrocious capitalist progress and collapse into primitive wretchedness will alternate without end. As with *Animal Farm*, the reader's most immediate conclusion must be that this tragic outcome is due to the extreme stupidity of almost everyone.

Anatole France's novel of the French Revolution, *The Gods Are Thirsty* (thirsty for human blood, that is) has superficially little to do

10 Jefferson 1965.

with socialism, but discomfited many socialists because of its powerful depiction of hapless humans possessed by fanatical ideology. Extraordinary brutality is unproductive, unjustifiable, and disgusting, yet it is the natural outcome of the way people are.

Orwell was impressed by Karel Čapek's play *R.U.R. (Rossum's Universal Robots)*, which he cites in *Wigan Pier* (176) and mentions at other times. *R.U.R.*, which coined the word "robot," was written in 1920. It depicts a world in which soulless robots (actually human-looking replicants), dedicated to increasing production at all costs, rebel against their human makers and supplant them.

Orwell followed Aldous Huxley's writings as they appeared, as he followed all the fashionable British and French writing of the time. Huxley's novels and stories breathe the air of post-socialism: capitalism is beneath contempt, yet confidence in any benign transformation is not warranted. Orwell was at first deeply and favorably impressed by *Brave New World*, but he soon decided that *Brave New World* had misdiagnosed the modern world and misprognosed the probable future, and that he would one day write a better dystopian novel setting out the more accurate and even more horrific alternative.

Leavis's Post-Socialism

F. R. Leavis was the most powerful intellectual influence in literary criticism in the 1930s and 1940s. He was not a politically committed writer—he was never identified with leftwing causes—yet he advanced a very definite view of society with strong political implications. Leavis's general ideas on society closely correspond with Orwell's post-socialist worldview in 1935–36.

Orwell may have gotten some of these notions directly from Leavis (whom Orwell must certainly have read no later than about 1933) or they may both have picked them up from other sources. The most likely possibility is that Orwell read Leavis in the early 1930s, and strongly agreed with him because these ideas were a slightly more explicit formulation of ideas Orwell has learned from Swift, Butler, and Gissing, and from the general intellectual legacy of the *fin de siècle*. Leavis gives us a hint of what might probably have become of Orwell's beliefs if Orwell had not committed himself to the Left, and more generally to political ideology, in 1936. In sharing Leavis's views on culture, Orwell was not agreeing with Leavis on the specific merits of particular English writers—the one area in which Orwell was extremely knowledgeable, and where he had developed his own decisive likes and dislikes. Because Orwell certainly objected to many of Leavis's specific judgments about works of fiction, it's possible that Orwell underestimated the impact on himself of Leavis's social philosophy.

The Leavises (F. R. Leavis and his wife Q. D. Leavis, author of *Fiction and the Reading Public*) advanced a theory of literary criticism which entailed a particular conception of society and culture. They propounded this theory in belligerent tones, though some of its key tenets are elusive.

According to the Leavis view, English society underwent a disastrous transformation between the seventeenth and nineteenth centuries. The organic community of the traditional village was devastated by the machine, which debased taste by "leveling down" and destroyed old patterns of co-operation.[11] Up to the seventeenth century, people saw work as part of their lives, whereas after the disruption, they come to view work solely as the means to the end of the pleasure they will enjoy in their free time. Although Leavis blamed the machine, he considered it mistaken to strive to abolish or restrict machines or to attempt to restore older social conditions. He calls the modern worldview Benthamism, neo-Benthamism, or technologico-Benthamism. The embodiment of this malignant heresy is H. G. Wells. Referring to Hollywood, Leavis fears that the future "has been forecast in California."[12] Leavis would like to see a reversal of secularization, yet "while agreeing that the recovery of religious sanctions in some form seems necessary to the health of the world, we reply that they cannot be had for the wanting" (44). This view is the same as Orwell's: the disappearance of religious faith is a heavy loss but there doesn't seem to be anything we can do to bring it back, especially as we can't bring ourselves to give it any credence.

Leavis is an embattled foe of progress and modernity. He sees modern popular culture—popular novels, movies, newspapers, and

11 For a good general outline of Leavis's views, see Bilan 2010.
12 Leavis 1986, 42.

advertising—as the assembled battalions of the enemy. He thus tacitly holds that all observable dissemination of ideas outside a select group of intellectuals is toxic. He seems to believe that the influence of this ideology is what is most truly harmful, and that the alternative, healthy worldview, though it sprang in the past from village practice, can now be kept alive as an antidote to technologico-Benthamism, by high-minded intellectuals in the universities. Leavis was writing at a time when only a tiny fraction of the British population had any involvement with universities (though he lived to see, and thoroughly dislike, the great expansion of British tertiary education after World War II).

Leavis is well known for editing the journal *Scrutiny* (1932–1953), sometimes called the rostrum of the New Criticism, though this term is now usually reserved for the later American movement. For a British literary intellectual in the 1930s, the main alternative to *Scrutiny* was Marxism, or the simplistic Comintern Marxism that passed for Marxism at this time. *Scrutiny* contains many criticisms of Marxism, with occasional condescending nods of approval. In his 1932 essay "Under Which King, Bezonian?," Leavis gives his general appraisal of Marxism as an alternative to his own approach to culture. He is against "a formula . . . or any simple creed," and he rejects the "dogma of the priority of economic conditions." Anent Trotsky's *Literature and Revolution*, Leavis observes that Trotsky, "like all the Marxists, becomes indistinguishable from Mr. Wells" (40). Leavis's deeper point is the incongruity of the Marxists' obsession with the dependence of literature on the class struggle and the conditions of production, while they aim at a classless society in which there will be no class struggle and literature will be cut loose from production.

Later Marxists have generally argued that Leavis was closer to Marxism than he recognized. But they tend to miss Leavis's, and literary post-socialism's, boundless self-assurance and sense of superior understanding, an attitude which acquires piquancy from the fact that the *Scrutiny* crowd were generally of lower social rank (Leavis's father owned a musical instruments shop) than the public-school Marxists who were so garrulous in the 1930s. The title "Under Which King, Bezonian?" is a quotation from *Henry IV, Part 2*. A bezonian is an ill-equipped scoundrel and the aptness of this word to the subject-matter must have crossed Leavis's mind.

The Intellectual Crisis of Socialism

European socialism went through a harrowing crisis in the 1880s and 1890s, during which it was mortally wounded. On the continent this was known as "the Crisis of Marxism," a terminal crisis from which Marxism would and could never recover. We all know that early twentieth-century intellectuals perceived Christianity as an old and discredited faith to which they might, under the stress of circumstances, be tempted to return. But this was also most intellectuals' attitude to socialism. For them, socialism too was an old and discredited faith to which they might, under the stress of circumstances, be tempted to return. Less than thirty years separate Nietzsche's declaration that "God is dead" from Croce's announcement that socialism is dead. In both cases, "dead" means "unable to appear remotely plausible to most intellectuals."

A number of developments now made it more difficult for intellectuals to accept Marxism. The publication of Volume III of *Capital* in 1894, along with the criticisms of Eugen von Böhm-Bawerk (1884 and 1896) made it clear that Marx could not resolve the incompatibility of the theory of Volumes I–II with the observable reality of capitalism recognized in Volume III. Simultaneously in England, Wicksteed's criticism of Marx's labor theory of value and the ensuing debate in print showed British socialists that Marxist economic theory was untenable. Meanwhile, neoclassical price theory was coming into bloom as one of the most beautiful and empirically powerful theoretical systems in the history of science.

Near the end of the nineteenth century, social classes were developing in a way quite different to that anticipated by Marx: capital was not being centralized in ever fewer hands, but was being dispersed among wider sections of the population. Classes were not polarizing, but new sectional divisions and disparities were appearing among the working class, and ownership of substantial property was expanding, not shrinking. Furthermore, the working class was not becoming a "class for itself"—quite the contrary, national identification meant a lot to workers all over Europe, while international working-class solidarity meant nothing.

The intellectual crisis of socialist doctrine did not lead immediately to the rise of some affirmative alternative. Classical liberalism was at its nadir, and would not show clear signs of rebirth till 1944, with *The Road to Serfdom*. The immediate consequence of the intellectual decapitation of socialism was the growth of post-socialism among apolitical intellectuals.

The Fin-de-Siècle Background of Post-Socialism

The mortal crisis of socialism in the 1890s coincided with the vigorous growth of ideas we now call *fin-de-siècle*.[13] Even painting with broad strokes, it would be too much to say that these ideas represent a revulsion against rationality and progress. They do represent a qualification and limitation of those values, a revulsion against what had come to be seen as overconfidence in rationality and progress.

The theories of Tarde and Le Bon call human rationality into question—especially the rationality of non-intellectuals. The philosophy of Bergson maintains that the universe is not mechanistic, and is therefore only partly amenable to scientific method. There is a reaction against Comte's Positivism, which is both a socialist belief-system—a proto-Marxism—and an approach which applies science to everything and anticipates the extirpation of metaphysics.

Because the crisis of socialism coincided with the curtailment of the values of rationality and progress, loss of confidence in socialism did not predominantly take the liberal form of challenging socialism's claim to be the embodiment of rationality and progress. Instead, rationality and progress were called into question, and socialism was rejected precisely because it was seen as one more example of overconfidence in rationality and progress.

13 The direction of fin-de-siècle thinking has been charted by scholars, and in broad outline is not controversial. See, for example, Part IV, Chapter 5, of Baumer 1977.

The Myth of Mind Control

In the course of the nineteenth century, the novel theory gained ground that it was possible by natural methods to control people's minds against their will.

Before the French revolution, the main preoccupation of French intellectuals was Mesmerism,[14] something we would now find familiar as a "therapeutic cult." Mesmerism was at first conceived as a matter of purely physical "magnetic" effects, not as having anything specifically to do with the "mental." But it gradually came to be thought that some of the human feelings and behavior involved in Mesmerism were due to the strange persuasive influence of the practitioner on the patient, and Mesmerism was renamed "hypnosis." The early nineteenth century saw the growth of intense interest in hypnosis, and in the late nineteenth century, the new ideas about hypnosis were applied to broad social and political questions.

In the momentous popular novel *Trilby* (1894), George du Maurier takes the familiar idea of hypnotic suggestion and uses it to construct an allegory about art. The literally artless singer, Trilby, achieves fame as a concert performer, but can only sing when her mind is controlled by Svengali. The storyline of *Trilby* would only have been comprehensible earlier in history if Svengali had been a sorcerer and his influence just magical. Svengali, however, is not a magician. The underlying assumption of the story is that science has shown us that human minds can be manipulated. In popular readership at the close of the nineteenth century, *Trilby* was second only to *Dracula*, another novel in which several characters' minds are brought under the control of another person.

In 1895 Gustave Le Bon published *The Psychology of Crowds*. This adroitly written book was translated into all major languages and sold millions of copies over the next few decades. Le Bon's political stance was anti-democratic: the policies emerging in a democracy can have no rational basis, since they merely reflect the blind emotions of the populace. Le Bon unscrupulously concealed how much he owed to earlier writers.[15] His work was the culmination of two decades of scholarly

14 Darnton 1970.

15 Ginneken 1992, 130.

discussion of crowd behavior. It had become accepted by influential writers that when people gather in crowds, they are no longer rational beings with free will but are hypnotized by the crowd and behave unconsciously. So influential was this theory that in Italy rioters were successfully defended in court because they were not responsible for their actions, having been hypnotized by the crowd.[16]

The influence of the ideas preached by Le Bon was enormous. To mention only a few obvious examples, Freud, Pareto, and Durkheim were heavily indebted to Le Bon, or to the ideas of thinkers like Gabriel Tarde which Le Bon repackaged, and the section in *Mein Kampf* dealing with propaganda (the only lively portion of that dreary tome) might have been lifted from Le Bon.

In 1915 Wilfred Trotter published *Instincts of the Herd in Peace and War*. From the fact that people have firm beliefs about matters they are not qualified to investigate, Trotter concludes that people's beliefs must be largely irrational. Popular beliefs are manifestations of human gregariousness: humans have an instinct to accept the beliefs of the herd. They believe what the herd believes, and therefore their beliefs express the instinct of human gregariousness.[17] Trotter's ideas were further disseminated by Edward Bernays, author of *Propaganda* (1928) and founder of "public relations."

From Le Bon's predecessors, through Le Bon, to Trotter and Bernays, there is a deep theoretical shift. Starting from the view that people in a crowd behave differently than they do away from the crowd, the theory gradually moves to the position that most people's beliefs and behavior are unconsciously motivated and irrational all the time. Le Bon talks about "the crowd" but occasionally tells us that people do not have to physically assemble to be a crowd, and in practice he assumes that whenever members of the lower classes do anything political they are acting as a "crowd." Trotter has left behind the idea of a change in people's mental state in a crowd. He writes about "the herd," but this just means that people's gregarious instincts make them

16 Ginneken 1992, 69–73.

17 There's an echo of Trotter in Orwell's remark about "the tremendous urge to conformity in gregarious animals" (XVIII, 424).

conform to what they identify as the beliefs which embody the social group.

At least as early as the 1920s, it had become orthodoxy among intellectuals that the views of the majority of people are irrational. They may be manipulated by sinister groups, but their minds cannot be changed by reasoned argument. This theory supplies a ready explanation of the unpleasant fact that the masses do not hold the same opinions as the intellectuals.

In the 1930s and 1940s the theories of Pavlov became widely known. After World War II this interest quickly died down, while interest in Freud and Jung remained at a high level. However, in the 1930s, intellectuals who had embraced Freud with ease were quite shaken by Pavlov. In the 1930s and 1940s, Pavlov did more to assault intellectuals' confidence in human rationality.[18]

The view, popular among intellectuals, that non-intellectuals are victims of conditioning and propaganda, helped leftist intellectuals make sense of fascism: fascism gained mass support because the fascists had found the trick for controlling the minds of the non-intellectuals. Unlike the masses, the intellectuals are not irrational, and this explains why they have the correct opinions, to wit, why they are leftists. Serge Chakhotin took the obvious next step in *The Rape of the Masses* (1940). The leftist intellectuals will adapt and perfect new variants of the formerly fascist techniques of manipulation, and thus happily assume their natural role as rational officers at the head of the irrational proletarian infantry.

18 A passage in Huxley's novel *Eyeless in Gaza* (Huxley 1936, 63) indicates the impact of Pavlov at the time, even though Huxley paradoxically says here that Pavlov "restated free will." A later popular exposition of the Pavlovian view is Sargant 1959.

5
The Reactionary

> A generation ago every intelligent person was in some sense a revolutionary; nowadays it would be nearer the mark to say that every intelligent person is a reactionary.
> —George Orwell, 1937 (V, 187–88)

Orwell was strongly opposed to birth control, homosexuality, and vegetarianism. Most writers on Orwell either fail to notice these opinions or suggest that they are no more than embarrassing or amusing personal foibles. Yet these views cohere well with other elements in his worldview, and there is no reason to treat them any differently from, say, his reservations about technological progress or his high valuation of rural life and manual labor. They flow from a popular and powerful complex of ideas I will refer to as "anti-degeneratism."

Two Anti-Degeneratist Theories

If you had given 1930s intellectuals the kind of free-association exercise then at the height of its popularity as the basic investigative method of psychoanalysis, and if you had given them the word "progress," you would have found that the most popular response was "degeneracy." It had become a cliché that progress entails degeneracy (V, 182). In early twentieth-century writings, we find innumerable assertions that the race—human, white, or national—is deteriorating. Modern civilized life brings about enfeeblement and decline, leading to extinction or to a new Dark Ages.[1]

1 Much has been written about the prevalence of the notion of degeneracy in the nineteenth and early twentieth centuries. See Soloway 1990; Cham-

We might suppose at first glance that everyone who makes these kinds of statements shares the same underlying theory. But in fact there are at least two distinct theories of degeneracy, illustrated in the cases of Aldous Huxley and George Orwell. Both of these writers speak of progress being accompanied by degeneration, but their understanding of the reasons for this, and the precise nature of the degeneration, are different. Although Orwell is younger than Huxley, Orwell adheres to the older theory, Huxley to the newer. For the sake of simple labeling, I will refer to the two theories as the Huxley theory and the Orwell theory, though neither of these writers contributed anything fundamentally new or distinctive to these theories, but simply downloaded them from the Zeitgeist.

The Huxley theory explains degeneration as the outcome of differential reproduction and recommends government-imposed measures of racial hygiene. It reflects the advances in biology made by Darwin and Weismann. If inferior people produce more babies than superior people, then the quality of the population will decline. The remedy must be to reduce the fertility of the inferior people or to enhance the fertility of the superior people, or both. The former is preferred to the latter as it is considered easier to accomplish. And so we find that Aldous Huxley, in the 1920s and 1930s, is a "eugenist," a strong advocate of selective breeding of humans, particularly the sterilization of mental defectives or "half-wits," whom he sees as multiplying to an alarming extent.[2]

The Orwell theory is more compatible with the pre-Weismannian assumption that a person's life experience will not only affect their moral character but will also change the biological determinants of behavior they pass on to their offspring. The Orwell theory can be outlined as follows:

> Once upon a time, people dwelt naturally and happily in the organic community of the rural village. They lived close to the soil and married in their teens and therefore did not suffer

berlin and Gilman 1985. My take on this topic is highly selective in focusing on what is most relevant to Orwell, so I draw very little on such works as Pick 1989 or Hurley 1996.

2 Huxley 2001, Volume III, 400–05. Advocates of eugenics mostly preferred to be called "eugenists," though others usually called them 'eugenicists' and the latter term has stuck.

> from chronic loneliness or develop erotic perversions or other emotional pathologies. Because their social status was preordained, they did not suffer from agonizing conflicts about their life's purpose. Traditional religion was an adequate explanation of the individual's place in the universe and an adequate solace for the high level of suffering.
>
> And then along came the disaster of modernization: capitalism, urbanization, industrialization, and over-specialization. By contrast with the rural past, city life is rootless, alienating, and degrading. It separates individuals from each other and subjects them to artificial conditions, which precipitate strange, morbid mental states and unnatural yearnings. Social isolation and delayed marriage favor sundry vices. These conditions lead to widespread masturbation, which in turn causes all the perversions, notably homosexuality. The unnatural food consumed in cities also contributes to the breakdown of the harmonious human form, along with such artificial conditions as public lighting, regulation of life by the clock, the habit of reading, distilled spirits, opium, exotic luxuries such as granulated sugar, and increased preoccupation with money. Birth rates fall below the level required to maintain the population, so that the expansion of cities can only be maintained by continual immigration from the countryside—until the countryside is depopulated, which brings about a collapse of population, and therefore brings civilization to an end.

This theory can be traced back to the eighteenth century but it really caught fire in the 1880s. Orwell does not favor eugenic measures, which would contradict his opposition to birth control. Where Orwell derived his anti-eugenicist ideas is not documented, but on this point as on several others he may have been influenced by Chesterton and other writers in *G. K.'s Weekly*, which we know he read attentively in the 1920s. There was also a strong leftist tradition of anti-eugenicism, since eugenics was seen as blaming heredity for social problems caused by capitalism.

In the 1930s, the clash between the two anti-degeneratist theories is suddenly muted, as intellectuals become aware of a frightening new fact: civilized birth rates have declined to the point where they are below replacement. It can be foreseen by simple extrapolation that the British population will soon shrink dramatically and that a small proportion of the able-bodied will be supporting a growing population of old-age pensioners.[3] Population decline is the global warming of the 1930s. Eugenicists had mixed responses to this bad news.[4] In the 1920s many of them had put all the emphasis on reducing the fertility of half-wits, destitute drunks, and other obvious degenerates, but this message now seems to conflict with the desperately urgent need to raise the overall birth rate.

The Falling Birthrate

In 1942 Orwell gave a brief list of "qualities by which any society which is to last longer than a generation actually has to be sustained": "industry, courage, patriotism, frugality, philoprogenitiveness" (XIV, 65).

A recurring motif in Orwell's writing is the need to have babies and the threat to national survival posed by the falling birthrate (XVI, 151; XVII, 280–82; XIX, 81–82). Orwell agrees with the view prevalent among intellectuals in the 1930s that Western civilization is facing a looming crisis of underpopulation. This collapse of fertility is one more reason why Western capitalism has not long to live, and perhaps even civilization itself may not survive.

Although Orwell says at one point that "the first necessity is to find out *why* populations rise and fall" (XVI, 151), most of the time he writes as if he is sure he knows the answer: capitalism gives people higher living standards and encourages a "hedonist" mentality.

> Most of the breeding in the world is done in non-democratic countries. As soon as the standard of living rises beyond a

3 Enid Charles wrote the most effective popular presentation of population collapse as a serious problem in 1934 (re-issued with a scarier title in 1936). What some historians describe as a "panic" on the subject of population decline took hold in September 1936. See Soloway 1990, 241–45.

4 Overy 2009, 132–34.

> certain point and people have a certain power of doing what they want, the birth rate falls below replacement level. . . . due to . . . the principle of hedonism. . . . people are taught to have a consumer mentality . . . things like cars, refrigerators, movies, cigarettes, fur coats and silk stockings are more important than children. (XIII, 69)

Because "capitalist democracy" gives people a higher standard of living and teaches them to place a higher value on pleasure, the birth rate falls and eventually (except for mass immigration from less developed regions, which at this time no one seriously considered) population falls. Later Orwell opines that "the dearth of babies is partly due to the competing attraction of cars and radios, but its main cause is a typically English mixture of snobbishness and altruism" (XVI, 223). Since the dearth afflicted all or most industrialized countries, this last remark must be seen as a hasty extempore dictum. To prevent a "calamitous drop" in the British birthrate, the government will have to design taxation to penalize childlessness, "to encourage child-bearing and to save women with young children from being obliged to work outside the home" (XVI, 223). One reason to welcome the Beveridge proposals for a greatly expanded welfare system is that their implementation will raise the birth rate (XV, 10).

Orwell assumes that socialism will reverse the trend of falling birth rates. Raising the birth rate will reduce living standards, as parents have less money to spend on consumer goods, so this is another reason (along with the ending of exploitation of colored labor in the colonies) why socialism will initially reduce living standards. These two facts, the declining birth rate and British dependence on exploitation of colonial labor, are, says Orwell, the two big issues evaded by the Left (XVI, 301).

Orwell also observes that, with the opening up of educational opportunities for the majority, people have fewer children in order to give each child "the best possible education." As economists would later put it, child quality is a substitute for child quantity.[5] Fear of the future, he surmises, also depresses fertility (XVII, 280). These are all commonplaces of such discussions at the time.

5 See Schultz 1974, especially Becker and Lewis 1974.

The story of *Keep the Aspidistra Flying* hinges on fertility. Near the beginning of the novel, we're told that "*nothing ever happened* in the Comstock family," who had "lost all impulse to reproduce themselves." In "thirty long years, there was not a single birth in the family, only deaths" (IV, 41). The surprising resolution of the story is that, although Gordon Comstock sells out to the hated "money system" by giving up poetry writing and returning to his job as an advertising copy-writer, "once again things were happening in the Comstock family" (277). Having rejected birth control, Gordon and Elizabeth then reject abortion and embark upon a new life. Comstock's personal revolt against capitalism fails, yet the ending is unequivocally upbeat because of pregnancy and marriage. Gordon sells out to the horrible "money system" in order to assume his responsibilities as a husband and father. Orwell would probably have approved of the generalization of this scenario: if Western man can get his fertility back up, then there is hope for civilization, be it ever so sick and degenerate. Otherwise, not.[6]

The Manly Man

In Orwell's view, persons of the male sex should be tough, hard, and virile—as well as decent, just, and fair. As we saw in the previous chapter, a major part of his objection to technological progress is that it makes us soft. A true man, in Orwell's view, will engage in sex with young women (sex with older women is presented as revolting, as with the prostitute in *Nineteen Eighty-Four*), will drink alcoholic liquor, will smoke tobacco, will eat meat, and will not take aspirin. A life free from hardship is a threat to manliness.

Recalling how he came to despise his role as a servant of the empire in Burma, Orwell describes the reaction of an American Protestant missionary:

6 Orwell believed himself to be sterile. No doubt he drew this conclusion, which was almost certainly correct, from the fact that numerous sexual liaisons, including those with native women in Burma and with several English girlfriends and his long-term relationship with Eileen, had all failed to bear fruit. Orwell and Eileen adopted a son, whom Orwell devotedly cared for after Eileen's death.

> One of my native sub-inspectors was bullying a suspect. . . . The American watched it, and then turning to me said thoughtfully, "I wouldn't care to have your job." It made me horribly ashamed. . . . Even an ass of an American missionary, a teetotal cock-virgin from the Middle West, had the right to look down on me and pity me! (V, 136)

To abstain from alcohol is contemptible. To abstain from sex with young women is contemptible. To be pitied by someone who abstains from both is horribly shameful.

Orwell's doctrine of manliness is somewhat tailored to his own preferences. It is his personal selection from the prevailing manly mores. We can imagine some other imperial police officer taking the disapproval of an unworldly American missionary as an inadvertent compliment. Many exponents of manliness would have considered solicitude for the welfare of the colored peoples, or even simply being a writer, as marks of a sissy, as when the character John Yule in *New Grub Street* attacks literature in general, maintaining that physical exercise is preferable.[7] But to Orwell manliness is toughness, but more than just toughness; it also encompasses equitable treatment of other people. He equates manliness with decency (X, 265).

At a young age, Orwell conceived a dislike (or the pose of a dislike) for things Scottish, in reaction to the prevailing cult of Scottishness, the Scots being held up to English public-schoolboys as models of vigor and austerity. So Orwell's mature concept of manliness lacks the then customary philo-Scottishness. Other aesthetic postures, such as his distaste for Rackham's illustrations, are compatible with the standard view of manliness.

Orwell did not give a systematic exposition of his objections to vegetarianism, partly because he could assume that a considerable majority of his readers would already agree that it is ridiculous. His one definite argument is that the vegetarian is willing to cut himself off from normal human interaction because of overly precious concern with his health (V, 162; XVIII, 318–19). No other motive for being a vegetarian is

7 Gissing 1968, 53–55.

mentioned, though Orwell does elsewhere take the view that excessive concern for the welfare of animals is a symptom of the prevailing childlessness (XVI, 202), in its turn a symptom of hedonism and degeneracy.

The Anti-Homosexual

Orwell's anti-homosexual position (not "homophobia," which suggests unreflective fear) flows naturally from beliefs and values about which he was quite forthcoming, though he never provided a systematic exposition.

Hitchens attributes Orwell's anti-homosexual position to an "involuntary shudder," which Orwell was unable to suppress.[8] But in concrete and personal terms, Orwell was entirely blasé about homosexuality.[9] He was intellectually and morally opposed to it, as, for example, he was intellectually and morally opposed to wide differences in incomes. Orwell did not fight to suppress any feelings of revulsion for homosexuality, any more than he fought to suppress his feelings of revulsion for inequalities of income. And in his personal relations he was entirely friendly with individuals he knew or suspected to be homosexual.

Orwell saw homosexuality as a product of modern civilization, and more particularly of capitalism and industrialism. His intellectual outlook, the theories he embraced, informed him that homosexuality is pathological. This view was very popular and quite unremarkable at the time, but Orwell was well aware of alternative views, and rejected them. For example, he made a dismissive comment about the admiration of some socialists for the writings of the "pious sodomite" Edward Carpenter (X, 471).

Orwell frequently makes deprecating remarks about homosexuals, referring to them as "sodomites." Reviewing a novel by his friend Cyril Connolly, he considers it a sign of "spiritual inadequacy" to write about

8 Hitchens 2002, 9.

9 See his account of being homosexually approached either in his sleep or while trying to sleep (I, 148). Although he says this was "a nasty experience in a locked, pitch-dark cell," having been woken up or kept awake, he then had a long and amicable conversation with the thwarted seducer. Everything in *Down and Out* is liable to be fictional; my point is not so much what actually happened as how Orwell thought it natural and defensible to describe what had happened.

"so-called artists who spend on sodomy what they have gained by sponging" (X, 491). He refers to the Auden group as "the nancy poets" and to pacifists as "the pansy left." Once he had adopted a pro-war position in August 1939, he implied that pacifists were homosexuals, insinuating that their opposition to the war derived from cowardice and cowardice from homosexuality (XV, 143).

These numerous but scattered remarks do not amount to an elaborate theory, and Orwell never had occasion to discuss homosexuality at length, but we can glean something more from his essay on Salvador Dali. Dali was not a homosexual but did pursue, or affect to pursue, various non-standard sexual practices such as sadism and a love for rotting corpses. Orwell was mainly concerned to insist that we should never cease to regard many of Dali's pictures as "diseased and disgusting" (XVI, 240). He referred to Dali's preoccupations as "the perversion of instinct that has been made possible by the machine age" (XVI, 233) and asserted that "Dali's fantasies probably cast useful light on the decay of capitalist civilization" (238). He rejected what he took to be the standard Marxist characterization of the proliferation of perversions in decadent bourgeois culture, in part because, he says, such an explanation cannot tell us why Dali exhibits these perversions instead of homosexuality. Orwell holds that Dali's proclivities are comparable with homosexuality, all such perversions being diseases of industrialized capitalism. Psychology and social science ought to be able to tell us why industrialized capitalism sometimes produces homosexuality and other times produces different perversions, but the Marxists are unable to do this (240).

Orwell's views on homosexuality and a few other matters were widely held in the 1930s and 1940s, but they were often not those of the most up-to-date intellectuals. Their vogue had crested earlier. These views thus appear to fit with Orwell's self-advertising as a representative of the ordinary man, as against the effete intellectual, the opinions of the ordinary man being usually the distillation of the views of the most advanced intellectuals of fifty to a hundred years earlier.[10]

10 To keep a sense of perspective here, we should remind ourselves that the American Psychiatric Association classified homosexuality as an illness until 1974 and the World Health Organization until 1990.

A facile (but not therefore necessarily incorrect) way to account for Orwell's views on such matters is biographical. Orwell was that *rara avis*, an Etonian intellectual who never went to Oxford or Cambridge. Much has been made of the informal homoerotic climate in English boys' public schools, and the young Orwell was not untouched by this: an extant note shows his romantic interest in another boy (Taylor 2003, 49). Publicly and in formal disciplinary policy, Eton College was of course hostile to "vice," whether solitary or collaborative. Orwell's general ideas on manliness and sex did not depart from this "official" Etonian position. Orwell went from Eton into the imperial police, where the *pukka* attitude was much the same. For a formative five years of his life, Orwell was a colonial policeman, away from home and from intellectual discussion. And thus, some of Orwell's intellectual attitudes are those of an earlier period than those of many of his contemporaries. Orwell was never quite "finished" as a 1930s intellectual; he retained a whiff of an earlier era—sometimes the Edwardian, sometimes even the Victorian. In some of his views, including his disparaging of homosexuality and his praise of manliness, it occasionally seems as if we're listening to someone assailing the most advanced ideas of the 1920s from the standpoint of the most advanced ideas of the 1880s.

Why the Anti-Degeneratists Were Wrong about Homosexuality

In his influential work *Psychopathia Sexualis* (1886), Richard Krafft-Ebing identified homosexuality as a disease caused by a number of factors including hereditary degeneracy and early masturbation. In the final edition (1912), Krafft-Ebing revised his opinion, and stated that homosexuality is not a disease. But by this time, Freud's ideas had become fashionable, and Freud reverted to the earlier view of homosexuality (as well as masturbation and oral sex) as pathological symptoms. Krafft-Ebing lost influence just as he arrived at an acceptance of homosexuality as part of the normal range of behavior. Despite some dissenting voices, the theory that homosexuality is pathological would remain dominant until the 1970s.

Cities give minorities of all kinds—chess players, pigeon fanciers, and poets— more opportunities to meet. The individual of minority tastes, etiolated in the claustrophobic imbecility of the village, finds joyful liberation in that wondrous amphitheater of anonymity, the city. If a constant minority of humans have homosexual inclinations, we may therefore observe a higher incidence of active homosexual encounters in the city than in the village. This is not because city life makes people homosexual but because it affords more opportunities, as it does for all encounters of like-minded persons. Homosexuality has been observed in many different cultures and we have no evidence that the incidence of people with homosexual preferences is higher in industrialized than in pre-industrial societies. What we do observe is compatible with the theory that a homosexual disposition is, like left-handedness, a genetically fixed constant in human populations, not a matter of nurture or personal choice and not a special product of any particular social system.

The Degenerate Middle Class

Attaching himself to the socialist movement, Orwell found himself in the midst of an uneasy relationship between middle-class and working-class socialists. The best way for modern Americans to think about this is by analogy with the relations between white middle-class civil rights workers and Blacks in the 1950s and 1960s. The English working class and middle class in the 1930s had separate dialects, table manners, values, life expectations, and schooling. There was awkwardness and frustration in their interactions within the socialist movement, though this was rarely talked about.

Socialism was, as Orwell was well aware, at its heart a middle-class movement, but a movement in which the working-class was accorded a special role, and which saw itself as a movement "of," as well as "for" the working class. Part II of *Wigan Pier* is addressed to middle-class socialists. It recommends greater respect for members of both classes: middle-class socialists should consider emulating working-class habits (as Orwell does, or thinks he does, by drinking his tea out of his saucer), and socialists should stop excoriating the middle class, which has the effect of repelling them from socialism and turning them into fascists.

Orwell's denunciations of sandal-wearers, fruit-juice drinkers, nudists and vegetarians clearly identify these obnoxious deviants as middle class (V, 169), implying that the working class, at least in some important respects, has healthier attitudes, as well as the merit of higher fertility. And if we want to recruit working-class people to socialism, then these deviants, the middle-class cranks, become an embarrassing liability (X, 471; XII, 228). Orwell never loses sight of the practical political impact of his statements; his hostile remarks about homosexuals, vegetarians, and others are designed to help unite middle-class and working-class on a platform of manliness and decency.

In his personal life, unless practical considerations went strongly against it, Orwell chose to live in the country and to raise chickens and goats. This personal preference was at least thoroughly harmonious with his conviction that urban living is inherently corrupting and morally inferior to traditional agriculture.

The Anti-Hedonist

Throughout Orwell's life as a writer, he attacked what he called "hedonism." In this he followed F. R. Leavis, Aldous Huxley, and other post-socialist writers of the time. He thought of hedonism as a doctrine favored by believers in progress, and particularly by socialists. In *Wigan Pier* he associated hedonism with technological progress, which he judged to be horrible and at the same time ineluctable, and he mainly objected to hedonism because it makes us soft. Softness is abhorrent because it saps manly virtues like courage and fortitude.

As Orwell's thinking evolves, in the fourteen years between *Wigan Pier* and his death, these themes recur, but he gradually ceases to attack hedonism primarily because it leads to softness. His later argument is that hedonism is feeble and perhaps has no future because it cannot withstand the attacks of the non-hedonists, fanatics like Nazis and Communists (XII, 118, 211; XV, 292).

At the same time, Orwell amends his view of technology. Instead of technology's being merely disgusting yet inescapable, there is more emphasis on mechanical progress as the means to improve the lives of the mass of people, so that they can cease to be preoccupied with hardship and turn their minds to nobler matters. This is one of Orwell's "unpleasant facts": technology is ugly, noxious, and dangerous, yet essential for any improvement. Implicitly, we should hold our noses and go for economic growth—whilst letting it be known that we're sensitive souls who do have to hold our noses.

And so Orwell eventually arrives with difficulty and hesitation at the entirely commonplace. For champions of industrial progress—the people whom Orwell attacks and misrepresents in *Wigan Pier*—have generally held that technology is valuable because it enables individuals, released from severe hardship and acquiring more leisure time, to turn their minds to nobler matters. To read some of Orwell's remarks, especially in *Wigan Pier*, you might think that his pro-technology arch-villains, such as Wells, Shaw, and John Strachey, believe that daily life in the socialist future would consist in a perpetual romp of sybaritic titillation. But this is not at all what these writers had in mind.

Confusion about Hedonism

Hedonism is the doctrine that pleasure—including the avoidance of discomfort—ought to be the sole or supreme goal of life. Pleasure can be simple and physical, like eating and drinking, or refined and cultivated, like reading Proust or appreciating a mathematical proof. Epicureanism is a form of hedonism which emphasizes the prudent pursuit of policies to maximize pleasure in the long run, a strategy which can lead to something that looks very like asceticism, though ultimately governed by long-run maximization of pleasure and minimization of pain. But even most non-Epicurean forms of hedonism don't recommend endless carousing. So, getting drunk is not intrinsically any more hedonistic than listening to the Brahms *Requiem*, and strictly speaking neither of these activities is necessarily hedonistic at all, if they occur within an ethical framework that does not make pleasure the sole or supreme goal of life.

Hedonism can be a goal of social policy or an individual ethical rule. Neither implies the other. For example, the founders or rulers or social engineers of a particular society may want to maximize pleasure for members of that society, but may decide to set up the ground rules of that society so that the members are not motivated entirely by pursuit of pleasure, figuring that this will have the outcome of maximizing pleasure.

A general presumption in favor of reducing misery and increasing comforts and enjoyments is not intrinsically hedonistic. Most non-hedonists would consider these important (but not all-important) goals. Yet Orwell routinely takes any evidence that someone favors economic growth—higher real incomes—as evidence of their hedonism, despite the fact that he himself favors economic growth while claiming to reject hedonism. Huxley is usually not quite so careless, but he tends to assume that any pursuit of pleasurable activities traditionally frowned upon is hedonistic. Thus, in *Brave New World*, sex and the drug Soma are approved by the official doctrine, and Huxley thinks of this as "hedonistic," while Shakespeare and the reading of history are both forbidden, though these are no less "hedonistic."

It's often supposed that, as incomes increase, and people have access to a richer diversity of pleasures, such as greater quantity and quality of food and drink, they become "more hedonistic." But first, there may strictly be no hedonism involved at all, if these pursuits are not part of a ruling philosophy that sees pleasure as the sole or supreme value. And second, if we define "hedonism" loosely, to mean the extent of preoccupation with pleasure (including removal of discomfort), we would normally expect to see the prevalence of so-called "hedonism" decrease. At a very primitive level, suppose that people spend ninety-nine percent of their efforts on acquiring the necessities of life (something totally "hedonistic" since it avoids the discomfort of starvation) and one percent on goals not dictated by "pleasure." At a higher level of income, they spend fifty percent on necessities, forty percent on luxuries, and ten percent on non-pleasure-determined goals. The proportion of human effort directed to "non-hedonistic" goals has increased tenfold, though people lead much more pleasurable and therefore happier lives. The illusion that there is less "hedonism" in the poorer society may be encouraged by the fact that here there are few choices: people have little alternative but to do what they and their ancestors have always done. Higher incomes bring more choices, so that people's pursuit of pleasure or of non-pleasure-determined goals becomes more deliberate, more calculating.

Aldous Huxley, F. R. Leavis, and following them Orwell, frequently use the word "hedonism" to characterize something they disapprove of in modern capitalism and in utopian depictions of the socialist future, but they don't mean hedonism in the strict sense, or in any coherent sense that can be easily identified. A later coinage would be "consumerism," but this term too, beyond the unsurprising fact that if people have higher incomes they get more of what they want, is muddled and elusive.

Both Huxley and Orwell claim that the socialist utopias of Wells and others are hedonistic, that *Brave New World* is hedonistic, and that the newest developments in capitalism (represented by the entertainment industry in the United States) are hedonistic. None of these societies is actually hedonistic, and even in the loose sense of being largely dedicated to pleasure, we see that in *Brave New World*, some pleasures are prohibited because of the ideology of the rulers. We also see that in Orwell's ideal of manliness, which he presents as the antithesis of hedonism, dedicated pursuit of some pleasures (food, sex with young women, alcohol, tobacco, and physical endurance) is obligatory.

The development of modern capitalism brings higher real incomes and with these a wider range of choices. Anti-capitalist writers respond with disapproval to the choices most people actually make. The underlying meaning of the writers' concern with "hedonism" is that the mass of the people have appalling taste: they like the wrong literature, the wrong music, the wrong leisure pastimes. The masses perversely prefer *Show Boat* to *Symphony of Psalms*, *The Ringer* to *Ulysses*, football to ballet, and therefore their lives must be hollow and base.

Numerous works describe Huxley's *Brave New World* as an assault upon the Wellsian utopias, and Huxley sometimes characterizes the book in just such a manner. Allied with the fact that Huxley often describes what's wrong with *Brave New World* as "hedonism,", and attributes hedonism to Wells, we get the conclusion that Wells is an arch-hedonist and Huxley and Orwell are his anti-hedonist critics. The whole truth is not quite so simple.

Huxley in the 1930s endorsed Wells's socialist World State and Wells's recommendation that an elite "samurai" class of intellectuals be formed to promote the World State.[11] Huxley repudiated democracy as

11 Huxley 1994, 31–43.

a failed system and looked forward to the authoritarian rule of a scientific minority, a system he saw imperfectly prefigured in Bolshevism and fascism.[12] At the same time, Huxley explicitly rejected "dictatorship.". What he would have preferred, it appears, was neither democracy nor dictatorship, but rule by committees of intellectuals like himself, camouflaged in the formal trappings of democracy.

Although Huxley became a pacifist and a proponent of mysticism, which Wells never did, Huxley too believed that the only hope for enduring peace lay in the establishment of a World State. Huxley, like Wells was a socialist, though unlike Wells's, Huxley's socialism was conceived within post-socialist assumptions. All these writers—Wells, Huxley, Orwell, and most writers at the time—just assumed uncritically that socialism could develop technology at least as well as, if not considerably better than, capitalism—notwithstanding that no one had seen socialism do this and that serious arguments had been propounded as to why this could never be feasible.

The horrifying features of *Brave New World* were put there by Huxley, and are not present in the Wellsian utopias. In fact these features are often similar to ones which Wells himself famously warns against—for example, the division of the population into separate castes and the use of reiterated slogans as instruments of conditioning.

When Huxley wrote *Brave New World* he intended it as a combination of good and bad features of the future society, not as purely bad. But it was taken by readers as a pure dystopia, a nightmare, and Huxley, who made his fortune with *Brave New World*, soon obligingly fell in with this way of talking about it. A prolific author of controversial articles, Huxley often referred to *Brave New World* but didn't go out of his way to remind his later readers that at the time he wrote it he had strongly advocated some of its more shocking elements, such as selective breeding of humans.

The society depicted in *Brave New World* is certainly horrifying, and some readers are horrified by its emphasis on pleasure, but even those readers would not say that this is the most horrifying aspect. *Brave New World* is a collectivist society in which there is no market economy and

12 Huxley 2001, Volume III, 191–92.

individual autonomy is not highly valued. The political rulers have found that drugs, genetic planning, and conditioning are more effective techniques of control than physical coercion. The rulers have outlawed history and most of the arts. Independent thinking is viewed as illness. All these things are not self-evidently connected with the primacy of pleasure—some of them involve curtailing pleasure—and they are the main reasons *Brave New World* has appeared to readers as a nightmare.

Orwell was ready to attribute hedonism to any ideological opponent who favored improvement of the human condition, so he saw hedonism everywhere. He contended that hedonists were at a disadvantage because they could not understand the appeal of fanaticism and irrational emotion. He attributes the appeal of fascism (meaning mainly National Socialism) to the fascists' ability to tap into a part of the human psyche which the hedonists were incapable of addressing. In the 1930s, leftists believed that fascism was arranged by the capitalists as a desperate last-ditch attempt to save capitalism from economic collapse, but this theory left unexplained the fact that the fascists had popular mass followings without which they would be of no consequence. The general leftist response to this fact was to maintain that fascism employed techniques of persuasion which appealed to irrational emotion. Hence we arrive at the remarkable fact that in the 1930s there are virtually no attempts by leftists to criticize the ideas the fascists are actually asserting, or even to understand their thinking. Orwell is entirely typical: he displays little curiosity about the origins of fascist ideas or the actual arguments employed by fascists in winning popular support. Fascism is paid for by the capitalists because capitalism is about to collapse, and fascism wins over the masses by some tricky form of hypnotic manipulation (which is inexplicably not available to fascism's rivals)—and that's that.

Orwell accepts this general leftist theory, making it slightly more pointed: the fascists (and, Orwell would add, the Communists too) appealed to an aspect of the human personality which traditional liberals neglected and could not even understand. Fascists had connected with something that socialists ought to connect with too, though the only definite content Orwell gives to this something is patriotism and self-sacrifice.

It's true that the ideas of the originating theoreticians of both Italian Fascism and German National Socialism include elements of anti-rationalism and of the same kind of antipathy to "hedonism" expressed by leftists like Orwell. Post-socialism, with its diminished rhetorical emphasis on the liberal objective of improved living standards was the common ideological heritage of Fascism, National Socialism, Leavis, Huxley, and Orwell. However, the Fascist and National Socialist parties acquired mass support in the course of election campaigns, and in these campaigns they always argued that their policies would raise living standards. No one would ever guess, from reading Orwell and other leftists of the time, that Italian Fascism was a self-consciously modernizing ideology, obsessed with high-tech and preoccupied with accelerating Italy's economic growth, or that the Nazis had acquired a popular following primarily because they had pledged to restore full employment.

The Vacuity of Orwell's Anti-Hedonism

Orwell asserts that "hedonistic societies do not endure" (XII, 211). Because people are irrational and want to sacrifice themselves rather than pursue pleasure, "The future is with the fanatics . . ." (XII, 179). The new slavery of *Nineteen Eighty-Four* threatens to win because hedonism cannot withstand the appeal of irrational self-sacrifice.

Orwell frequently charges people with "hedonism" when it's unclear why they would be considered any more hedonistic than he is. He takes any concern, on the part of the people he is criticizing, with improving living conditions, as evidence that they are hedonists, whereas his own commitment to raising living standards has no such implication. He applies this most often to Wells. He also applies it to C. E. M. Joad (a philosopher and well-known media pundit at the time), claiming that Joad can't grasp what's happening politically because he assumes that people are motivated by "hedonism" (XII, 178). Reviewing another book by Joad, he accepts that it is "sensible" (he does not voice any objection to its policy recommendations) while berating Joad because fanaticism and "folly" are prevalent in the world (XV, 292). He does not offer a fanatical belief system of his own, nor does he mention any antidote to fanaticism. Orwell doesn't let us know in what way he is any less guilty of "intelligent hedonism" than Joad.

Orwell finds a hedonistic strain in Koestler (XVI, 392–400). Because of this, he says, Koestler can't find "a political position" after breaking with Communism. Now if we tabulate Orwell's and Koestler's specific political positions, we find that they agree on almost everything except Zionism. Orwell doesn't identify any specific positions which supposedly flow from Koestler's hedonist strain. Orwell states that Koestler's position is "not far removed from pessimistic Conservatism." This is not fair, but if it can be applied to Koestler, it can be applied to Orwell, as indeed it has been by some detractors. Other than ordinary patriotism, Orwell doesn't identify any non-hedonistic principles, apart from fanatical creeds like Communism and National Socialism, which he perceives as the enemy, and traditional religion which he dismisses as untenable and "not grown up."

Orwell counterposes the fanaticism of Communism and fascism to hedonism. But there may be fanatical adherents of a "hedonistic" doctrine. Chief among fanatical totalitarian creeds is Soviet Marxism, which Orwell therefore insists is not hedonistic. Yet Marxism looks towards the fullest development of the productive forces, the development of technology to satisfy human wants. Marxism is therefore just as "hedonistic" as the "sensible" creeds Orwell dismisses as impotent. In the loose sense of "hedonism," Marx and Lenin are no less hedonistic than Wells, Joad, or Koestler, arguably even more so. (In the strict philosophical sense, none of these is hedonistic at all.) A political ideology explicitly calling for general immiseration cannot have a promising future, and that is the only type of political ideology which Orwell would not be liable to stigmatize as hedonistic. Indeed, while asserting that Communism and fascism succeed because they appeal to non-hedonistic motives, he also assumes that they can guarantee people's "security," which capitalism is unable to do.

The Anti-Rationalist

In the post-socialist and anti-degeneratist worldviews, the rejection of hedonism is tightly linked with anti-rationalism. We can distinguish two forms of anti-rationalism, epistemological and practical. Epistemological anti-rationalism is the view that something other than reason should be employed in deciding factual questions. Practical anti-rationalism is the view that, purely as a matter of sober recognition of reality, humans are not chiefly motivated by rational calculation but more by irrational emotional factors. Therefore, if you want to understand and influence people's behavior, you had better acknowledge that they are not rational calculators (and, a distinct question, but usually accepted concomitantly, not dominated by self-interest). Instead, people are gripped and moved by what come to be called "myths." Epistemological anti-rationalism gained some following in the fin de siècle, but much more influential was practical anti-rationalism.

Orwell endlessly reiterates that in the twentieth century, "intelligent hedonism" or the appeal to rational self-interest has been found wanting. Orwell claims that "political behaviour is largely non-rational, that the world is suffering from some kind of mental disease which must be diagnosed before it can be cured" (XVIII, 503). This view, that human motivation is non-rational, and that therefore economic motives cannot account for people's behavior, is a standard component of the early twentieth-century ideology of post-socialism.

Orwell's and Huxley's Anti-Hedonism

Orwell's specific attitude to hedonism is crystallized in his rejection of Huxley's *Brave New World*. From 1932 on, Orwell had a strong interest in dystopian stories, believed that he would one day write one, and he soon became concerned to develop a dystopia decidedly different from *Brave New World*. Both Huxley and Orwell were convinced anti-hedonists. *Brave New World* and *Nineteen Eighty-Four* both include a theme of anti-hedonism. Yet they oppose hedonism in different ways and for different reasons.

Huxley sees unbridled hedonism as an enemy. He sees a society dedicated to the gratification of material wants as a serious danger. For Huxley, the harsh discipline of Communism and fascism are transitory phenomena; he expects them to give way to a more affluent, more comfortable, more contented, if empty, way of life. In Huxley's judgment, persuasion and conditioning are ultimately more efficient, as methods of controlling people, than brutal repression, so brutal repression will tend to give way to persuasion and conditioning. Manifestly, Huxley had a more accurate grasp than Orwell of the way that industrialized society would develop, at least for the following century or so.

To Orwell, hedonism does represent a threat, but it is the threat of softness and enfeeblement, which prepares the way for the real enemy. Quite unlike Huxley, Orwell believes there is a serious danger that grim, brutal, and stable totalitarianism is the immediate and long-term future for the entire world. Orwell thinks that any group which gives itself over to hedonism must ultimately become easy meat for fanatical ideological enemies, which are more self-sacrificing, more dedicated, and more remorseless. The real enemy is not the lover of pleasure but the fanatic who is against pleasure, and the former is conceived as defenseless in face of the latter. A ruling class which puts pleasure above power will be replaced by a more fanatical ruling class, while an ideology of social reform which holds nothing higher than material wellbeing will ultimately be no match for more "irrational" movements like Communism and fascism.

The disappearance of traditional religious belief has the unwelcome result of removing a once-potent alternative to hedonism. Orwell mentions the need to develop a non-religious philosophy of life which will not be hedonistic, but he doesn't offer any suggestions as to what such a philosophy might include. Huxley pursued this quest at greater length with works like *The Perennial Philosophy*. Both Orwell and Huxley were fundamentally opposed to extreme asceticism and accepted pursuit of pleasure as a valuable end in itself. Both considered that a life wholly devoted to pleasure-seeking would prove unstable and unsustainable. Whereas for Huxley, this unsustainability would emerge through a kind of widespread inchoate appetite for pain and suffering, Orwell sees the unsustainability emerging by a different route: the vulnerability of pure pleasure-seeking to fanatical political movements, which will capture power and then wage war on pleasure.

Both these lines of thought are responses to the idea, widely aired in the 1930s, that Communism, and even more so "fascism," are movements which appeal to the self-abnegating, non-self-interested side of human nature. This view is popularly summed up in the cliché that the

Nazis had offered the Germans "guns before butter," and the Germans had accepted this choice. Whereas Huxley believed that these totalitarian movements were a temporary phase which would give way to a more hedonistic culture, Orwell assumed that the appeal of the totalitarian ideologies had become a more or less permanent condition of modern life. This divergence has parallels with our own day, when "anti-secularizers" see "fundamentalist Islam" as something capable of exercising greater appeal than the fruits of modernization, while "secularizers" see all forms of intolerant fundamentalism as liable to wither before the advance of economic growth and high real incomes.

The Nostalgic Atheist

Orwell rejected belief in God, an afterlife, or any supernatural forces. Reporting his own sighting of a ghost, he comments "presumably an hallucination" (X, 211). In discussing the phenomenon of poltergeists, he rules out supernatural explanation (XII, 247–48). Orwell tells us that he believed in God up to the age of fourteen, and adds that, even when he believed in God's existence, he had no love for God (XIX, 379).

At the same time, he maintains that the disappearance of religious belief is a serious loss, and that something needs to be formed to replace it. Yet he has little idea of what that something might be, except that it cannot be either "hedonism" or anything supernatural. He implies that the decline of belief in an afterlife weakens the sense of right and wrong (XVI, 112–13), but there is surely something paradoxical about an atheist intellectual with a strong sense of right and wrong, addressing other atheist intellectuals whom he assumes have a strong sense of right and wrong, raising a concern about the weakening of the moral sense because of the growth of unbelief.

Orwell's feeling that religious belief was untenable but its disappearance disquieting was a commonplace of British intellectuals in the early twentieth century. Jonathan Rose has well described how this idea, and the consequent hankering for some secular substitute for religion, dominated the Edwardian mindset.[13]

13 Rose 1986.

Occasionally people have attributed some religious belief to Orwell. Jacintha Buddicom recollected that Orwell held a "faith in some sort of after-life" and that Orwell stated in a letter comforting her on the death of her mother, that "nothing ever dies" (XX, 119–120). Given Orwell's many comments on theistic religion and the supernatural, Buddicom must be mistaken. Orwell and Buddicom were closely acquainted in their teens and briefly corresponded near the end of his life. Orwell, no doubt, was disingenuous in the latter case in order to offer consolation,[14] and in the former case to present himself in an attractive light for the usual male motive.

In 1932 there occurred the "odd episode" where Orwell befriended the curate of a High Anglican church and took an active part in church affairs, as well as partaking in Holy Communion.[15] Crick hints that there may have been some genuine religious motivation here, despite Orwell's clear statements that it was a pretense. Surely, if Orwell actually had harbored some religious feeling about Holy Communion, this would have made him less, not more, likely to participate when he did not fully believe in it. And there is a ready explanation for his cold-blooded deception: we can surmise that Orwell had decided to do undercover fieldwork in a milieu that he could use in a novel (*A Clergyman's Daughter*). Posing as a believing High Anglican is no more inexplicable, and somewhat less blameworthy, than posing as a destitute hobo.

Orwell often asserts that something has been lost because of the decline of religious belief. In 1942 he states that "The major problem of our time is the decay of the belief in personal immortality" (XIII, 510). Orwell is fond of the metaphor of the wasp, which he once observed eating, oblivious of the fact that the lower half of its body was missing, as a metaphor for modern man, unaware that he has lost his soul (X, 404; XII, 124).

Discussing Baudelaire's attitude to religion, Orwell says that Baudelaire "perceived that such notions as sin, damnation, etc., were in a sense truer and more real than anything he could get from sloppy humanitarian

14 David Gordon pointed out to me that Orwell might have been thinking of Horace, "Non omnis moriar," which refers to the survival of verse (and, by possible extension, of a person's influence) rather than personal survival.

15 Crick 1992, 226–27; X, 249, 269, 271.

atheism" (X, 343). All such statements by Orwell have a hollow sound. Orwell certainly does not think that *he* is suffering from any loss of his soul and he betrays absolutely no inclination to discuss any issues in terms of sin and damnation. He never comes up with any positive alternative to sloppy humanitarian atheism except (we can only assume) somewhat more rigorous humanitarian atheism. Orwell thinks that the modern world suffers from the decline of religious belief and needs something to put in its place, but he has no definite suggestions as to what that something might be, and he cannot even pin down what's missing.

If we look at Orwell's many references to religion in the last fifteen years of his life, we see that over time assertions of pure atheism and humanism tend to win out over assertions of what we have lost with the decline of religious belief. So, in March 1947, Orwell gives us a strong positive case for being concerned with this world, rather than any hypothetical other world. He holds that the two attitudes are not reconcilable: "one must choose between this world and the next. And the enormous majority of human beings, if they understood the issue, would choose this world" (XIX, 64). Here Orwell suggests that it is the Christian attitude "which is self-interested and hedonistic" because of its appeal to rewards and punishments in the afterlife. This conclusion is self-refuting: he maintains that the disappearance of traditional religion has left a gap which mere "hedonism" cannot fill, and then decides that traditional religion was at heart purely hedonistic all along.

Orwell has a special dislike for the Catholic Church. In one letter, he refers to someone as "a stinking RC" and self-mockingly refers to "my hideous prejudice against women, my obsession about RCs" (X, 268). He maintains the traditional English view that Catholicism is a threat to liberty, and at one point even applauds (though humorously) the efforts of the "No Popery" type of fundamentalist Protestants to combat the Catholic Church (X, 212). He often asserts that Catholicism is inherently pro-fascist (XII, 548–49; XVII, 176).

Reservations about Jews

On attending Orwell's funeral, Malcolm Muggeridge noted in his diary that most of those attending were Jewish, which was "interesting" in view of the fact that Orwell "was at heart strongly anti-Semitic." Muggeridge, who had many personal conversations with Orwell, cites no instances of Orwell's antisemitism.[16]

Orwell often condemned antisemitism and discussed its causes (XVI, 83–84; XVII, 64–70; XIX, 464–65). He asserts that antisemitism is a neurosis, an aspect of nationalism, which is itself a disease (XVII, 68), that he does not have a "hard and fast theory" about antisemitism's cause, but that he does insist that it is not purely economic in origin, nor is it a hangover from the Middle Ages (XVI, 83–84, 91–92). Thus it would be possible to extract from Orwell's works a substantial body of writing which makes him seem a determined yet reflective foe of antisemitism. At the same time, Orwell also delivers occasional remarks which by today's standards would usually be classed as antisemitic (for instance X, 516), though such remarks become less frequent over time.

Anti-degeneratists may be liable to antisemitism, because Jews often symbolize the corrupting commercial and urban mode of life, but there is no indication that this is at the root of Orwell's attitude to Jews. Orwell strives, as a writer, to make sharp observations, and he does not exempt any group of human beings. Taylor refers to these remarks as "insulting Jews," but this is surely anachronistic. Orwell no more thinks of himself as insulting Jews than he considers it insulting the English to point out that they are hypocritical, unartistic, and over-sentimental about animals (XII, 392–400; XVI, 200–04). The modern convention that no group of people may be pejoratively characterized (except for heterosexual males of northern European descent, who are fair game) had not come into force in Orwell's lifetime.

When Orwell's friend Tosco Fyvel found antisemitism in T. S. Eliot, Orwell dismissed this as "nonsense" (XIX, 461), arguing that a distinction had to be made between what was said before and after 1934 (presumably a reference to Hitler's June purge). A dislike of large groups of people, such as the hostility to things English which Orwell finds in much American writing, is not in itself culpable, he claims, but this

16 Muggeridge 1981, 376. Muggeridge himself has been suspected of antisemitism because of uncomplimentary references to Jews in his powerful anti-Communist novel, *Winter in Moscow* (1934).

would be different if the same things were said while English people were being systematically killed.

Orwell wrote (in a personal letter to Julian Symons), "I have no doubt Fyvel thinks I am antisemitic" (XIX, 461). Tosco Fyvel, who knew Orwell well, later commented on this remark that he had never considered Orwell antisemitic, but somewhat insensitive in the way he chose to phrase his references to Jews, as well as far from knowledgeable about the European Jewish experience.[17]

17 Fyvel 1983, 178–182. See also Walton 1982.

6
The Anti-Imperialist

At the age of twenty-four, after five years as an imperial police inspector in Burma, Orwell had become a bitter foe of the British Empire. His first novel, *Burmese Days*, displays the reasons for his hostility. He was appalled by the racial arrogance, the hypocrisy, the unfairness, the philistinism, and the brutality inherent in the everyday workings of the empire. However most of his non-fiction writing on the empire is preoccupied with one narrow issue: his contention that people in Britain are better off, and people in the colonies much worse off, because of the existence of the empire.

> . . . we are standing on the backs of half-starved Asiatic coolies. The standard of living of the British working class has been and is artificially high because it is based on a parasitic economy . . . (XIII, 69)

This is one of the constants of Orwell's outlook, maintained throughout all of his active life as a writer.[1] He keeps insisting that the immediate effect of giving up the colonies must be a serious drop in the incomes of British workers. Orwell berates the Left for failing to acknowledge this "fact." He also accuses the Left of bad faith, suggesting that leftists really do know that British wages are high because of colonial exploitation, but keep quiet about it (XI, 358–361). It's a point in Rudyard Kipling's favor, writes Orwell, that unlike the Left

1 A few among the many places where Orwell advances this theory are: V, 148; X, 27; XI, 358–61; XIII, 69, 150, 187–89; XV, 32; XVI, 23–24, 210; XVII, 246–47; XIX, 165, 290.

he took responsibility for the empire. "All left-wing parties in the highly industrialized countries are at bottom a sham, because they make it their business to fight against something which they do not really wish to destroy" (XIII, 153). And yet Kipling "never had any grasp of the economic forces underlying imperial expansion." because he "does not seem to realize . . . that an empire is primarily a money-making scheme" (150).

Worse than National Socialism?

In his revolutionary anti-war period (June 1937–August 1939), Orwell claims that the British Empire is worse than Nazi Germany because of its exploitation and oppression of the colored peoples. He maintains that the injustice of the British Empire and other European empires is "far vaster" than that of "Fascism" (meaning National Socialism) (XI, 360). His argument for the greater injustice of the British Empire is the low incomes of its non-white subjects, illustrated by the report that annual British income per head is over £80 and the Indian figure is £7. Hitler is unable to reduce wages to a penny an hour, but that is "perfectly normal in India, and we are at great pains to keep it so" (XI, 360). Orwell says nothing to suggest what these "great pains" might be. (One of the features of nearly all leftist discussions of the empire at the time, not just Orwell's, is the frequent claim that the empire is doing such and such, without any concrete examples of just how it is supposed to be doing it.) Orwell writes as if he is assuming that, without the Raj (British rule in India), Indian incomes would somehow naturally have been as high as British incomes. But in reality (as we shall see) low incomes in India predated the coming of the British, and Indian per capita income rose steadily (if disappointingly slowly) under the Raj.

In his pro-war period (from August 1939 on) Orwell changed his mind and maintained that "Nazism . . . is definitely worse than British imperialism" (XVI, 330), though the evidence he offers for this is reports of National Socialist outrages from before the war, which would have been equally well known to him when he wrote the earlier comparison in Nazism's favor.

The Movement for Indian Independence

In the 1930s, educated opinion in Britain and government policy assumed that all the countries in the empire would gradually acquire more and more self-government as they advanced economically and culturally. The highest level of self-government was that of a "dominion," and had already been attained by Australia, New Zealand, and Canada (and by Southern Ireland and South Africa, which later voluntarily left the Commonwealth). Although people often spoke of the dominions as parts of the empire, in fact the dominions along with Britain itself formed the Commonwealth, a voluntary association of sovereign states.

The self-governing dominions were mostly white-populated and (except for Southern Ireland and South Africa) largely populated by people of British descent, who at this time considered themselves to be British. There was a general expectation that the colonies with predominantly non-white populations, beginning with India, would eventually attain dominion status. Though not yet a dominion, India was sometimes treated more like a dominion, being represented at the 1932 imperial conference in Ottawa. The prevalent view was that the task of the British Empire was to bring about its own extinction by gradually turning all its colonies into dominions, though some people expected this to take generations. The minority of die-hard imperialists in the Conservative Party were most prominently represented by Winston Churchill, which mainly accounts for Churchill's years "in the wilderness" up to 1939.

India and Burma were the first parts of the empire to have substantial organized movements for independence. The leading Indian organization, the Indian National Congress (INC), often referred to as "Congress" was founded in 1885, and soon came out for independence. Later, when Indian Muslims decided they would not be safe under Hindu rule, the Muslim League was founded, and eventually came to advocate the creation of a separate Muslim state, Pakistan. The INC came under the influence of Mohandas Gandhi in 1915. In 1919 troops fired on unarmed demonstrators in Amritsar, a gift to the Nationalist movement. In a succession of civil disobedience campaigns, some of which turned violent despite Gandhi's influence, the INC, with growing popular support, agitated against the Raj. Hoping to get the Nationalists and others to agree upon a plan for gradually increased Indian self-government leading to eventual dominion status, the British government hosted a number of Round Table discussions in 1930–1932, but these broke down. The British government then put through its own unilateral legislation giving India an increased measure of self-government, the Government of India Act of 1935.

Under this Act there was a two-chamber governing body, elected by property-qualified voters (fourteen percent of the Indian population). The provinces of India had some autonomy. The Government of India handled nearly all internal affairs. The British government retained complete control of foreign policy, so that India abruptly found itself at war with Germany in September 1939, without having been consulted, to the annoyance of Indian nationalists. Some undemocratic features of this Act had been put in to encourage the Indian princes (bound by treaty to Britain but not under direct British rule) to voluntarily federate with British India, but as it turned out, none of them chose to do so.

During the war, the INC did not hesitate to take advantage of Britain's weakened position in the war to press for their own goals, and sometimes voiced the view that the Japanese or Germans would be no worse as rulers than the British. Under Gandhi's inspiration the INC launched the Quit India movement in 1942. The Japanese army occupied Burma and seemed about to invade India. Many demonstrations against British rule were suppressed and thousands of INC leaders were detained by the British until 1945.

Orwell's Equivocations on Independence

When Orwell became a socialist in 1936, his view of the empire did not change, and the anti-imperialism he took from his Burmese years remained central to his political thinking. He conceived of the situation of the British working class in *The Road to Wigan Pier* on the model of the exploited colonies, and his conception of *Animal Farm* arises from the thought that, seen from the viewpoint of farm animals, the class struggles among humans are a sham, just as, to colored colonial subjects, the class struggles within the white race are a sham.

Orwell often verbally assailed the British Empire and appeared to be calling for the colonies to be given their independence. If this had been Orwell's consistent position, it would have been the same as that of almost all of the Left (and of much non-left opinion). But in fact Orwell's position was not so straightforward, for he also simultaneously asserted that independence for the colonies was out of the question. Orwell continually alternates between apparently affirming that the colonies must have their independence and asserting categorically that they can never get it. He fiercely assaults those who defend the empire, whilst equally ferociously attacking those who demand independence for the colonies.

In early 1941, when he is arguing for a socialist revolution in England as the only way to win the war, which capitalism has shown it cannot win, his six-point program contains the provision "Immediate Dominion status for India, with power to secede when the war is over" (XII, 422). This would be accepted with a yawn by virtually all of the Left. But two pages later when he gives his detailed exposition of this point, he asserts that the Indians would refuse an offer of independence: "When a British government offers them unconditional independence, they will refuse it" (XII, 424; XIII, 259). The reason he gives is that India relies on British military protection and technical assistance.

A year later Orwell favors the same policy: immediate dominion status for India, "with the right to secede after the war, if she so desires" (XIII, 189). This formula, strictly considered, betrays a misunderstanding, for dominion status, in law and in fact, encompassed the right to "secede" at any moment, and "secession" was in any case of little importance, since a dominion was an independent sovereign state (which could opt to be neutral in a British war, for example). What the wording really meant, then, was that the INC should be promised dominion status when the war was over, and was expected in return to make no trouble while the war was still going on. Essentially this offer was conveyed to the INC in different ways on several occasions, and the INC always turned it down. However, the position of Attlee and other Labour Party leaders was that India would be given dominion status even though the INC had made trouble, though this fact was not often stated quite so boldly, because of the Labour Party's role in the wartime coalition. Orwell agreed with the British government that India could not be offered independence while the war was on, because this would be inviting the

Japanese to take over. Orwell assumed that India would want British military protection against occupation by Japan. But if India had announced that, as a dominion, it was exercising its right to pull out of the war and become neutral, Japan would probably have been delighted, and might have been just as willing to respect India's neutrality as Germany was to respect Southern Ireland's neutrality. However, Indian troops made a major contribution to the Allied war effort; for example, more Japanese troops (over 200,000) were killed by British imperial forces (mainly Indian) in World War II than by any other Allied formation.[2] And India was a major producer of steel for British war supplies.

In 1943, commenting in *Tribune* on the proposal that Burma (then occupied by Japan) be offered its independence from Britain after the defeat of Japan, Orwell says that Burma, a small agricultural country, "will never be independent."[3] Entirely reasonably, a correspondent wrote: "I began to wonder whether I had stumbled on the [diehard imperialist] *Daily Telegraph* instead of *Tribune*." Orwell responded: "If Burma is to be independent, what about Lithuania or Luxembourg? . . . The plain fact is that small countries cannot be independent because they cannot defend themselves" (49). A little later Orwell wrote that if the Burmese want dominion status, "let them have it" (50) again showing that he failed to understand—or intermittently forgot—that dominion status was independence. The only differences between a dominion and a "foreign" country were ceremonial and sentimental, and any dominion could become purely "foreign" (leave the Commonwealth) at any moment that it chose, as Southern Ireland did in 1949, and South Africa in 1961.

Again in September 1943 he is writing that "India is very unlikely to be independent in the sense in which Britain or Germany is now independent. . . . What is now called independence means the power to manufacture aeroplanes in large numbers. Already there are only five genuinely independent States in the world, and if present trends continue there will in the end be only three" (211).

2 Jackson 2006, 2.

3 XV, 48. Earlier than this he had made the same claim about Burma (XII, 419) and twice made a similar assertion about Morocco (XIV, 186, 208).

In 1947 India, Pakistan, Burma, and Ceylon—the biggest chunk of the empire, by all important measures—were given their independence, and, of course, their nationalist movements eagerly embraced independence. Even without that hindsight, it's clear that Orwell's view of these matters needed more work. Orwell persistently confused being independent with being able to do what you like in international relations at no cost. He was convinced by James Burnham's theory that the world was lining up into three great camps, with apparently negligible wiggle room for component parts of these camps. This theory soon turned out to be false. Orwell was over-influenced by temporary wartime conditions: for example, uncomfortably situated Belgium lost its independence for a while in 1914 and again in 1940, but it was never in serious doubt that Belgium would get back its independence when each of these wars was over.

On the general question of national independence, Orwell oscillates confusingly between the assertion that only a few big countries can be independent and the claim that no country can be "fully independent." Orwell tacitly assumes that if one country can subjugate another, it is almost bound to do so, overlooking the possibility that subjugation might be entirely feasible but just not worth it. Even during World War II, when many countries were temporarily occupied for strategic reasons, Southern Ireland, Sweden, Spain, Portugal, and Switzerland remained neutral and their neutrality was respected by both sides.

It is odd that in this context Orwell paid no attention to the example of Ireland, which had been so central to British politics for his entire lifetime. Southern Ireland became a dominion within the Commonwealth in 1922, chose to be neutral (as every dominion could freely have chosen) in 1939, and left the Commonwealth in 1949.[4] Southern Ireland was a small agricultural country (much smaller than Burma) and could easily have been reconquered by industrialized Britain. But aside from the fact that most British people accepted the general notion that people should not have a government imposed on them by force from outside,[5]

4 The country's official name was the Irish Free State from 1922 to 1937, Ireland (or Eire) from 1937 to 1949, and the Republic of Ireland thereafter.

5 Churchill and other imperialist die-hards, for example, always argued that the Indian nationalists were Brahmin intellectuals, isolated from the lower-

the reconquest and indefinite occupation of Southern Ireland would have been too costly to be worth the trouble. Southern Ireland's independence from Britain is proved by the fact that it had its own laws which it could change at will and which increasingly diverged from those of the UK, as well as its own law enforcement and military, securely under its own control, and its own currency and economic and social policies (such as prohibition of divorce and contraception and the banning of many sexually explicit books and movies freely available in the UK).

Orwell's way of resolving the seeming contradiction in his views on independence for the colonies is to suggest some new international arrangement by which the colonies would voluntarily co-operate with Britain. His notion of this new arrangement is vague and changeable. At one point he refers to "world federation," at another to a federation of socialist republics. But if this new arrangement were to be truly voluntary, then the former colonies would have become independent states and it is confusing to deny this. And that being so, we can't just assume that they would automatically accept the new arrangement.

Not long after the momentous British election results of 5th July 1945, Orwell still asserts that no country can be "fully independent" (XVII, 230), yet in the next breath he states that "India . . . is likely to become independent in the fairly near future," and adds that "after a few years of re-adjustment the results will probably be beneficial to Britain" (232). Orwell has moved, at least verbally, from the position that Indian independence can never happen to the view, standard on the Left, that Indian independence is likely to happen fairly soon. The very next month, he restates his longstanding view that Britain "lives partly by exploiting the coloured peoples" and to stop exploiting them "would entail a difficult reconstruction period in which our own standard of living might fall catastrophically" (XVII, 247).

caste Hindu masses who favored British rule, though admittedly the diehards were in no hurry to put this proposition to the test by extending the franchise to those Hindu masses. Churchill's speeches depict the INC as a movement of elitist Brahmins who want to oppress the Untouchables, the Muslims, and other disadvantaged groups, protected from Brahmin ill-treatment by the Raj.

We have no record of Orwell's thoughts as he came to realize that what he had been saying for years about the impossibility of Indian independence was mistaken. There must have been some point at which he was astonished, and this must have been around the time of the election of the Labour government. One month before that election, he was writing that "it is very unlikely that Attlee, Morrison and the rest of them can make any offer that the Indian nationalists would accept" (XVII, 162). Looking back from 1949 he remarks that "the British did get out of India without fighting, an event which very few observers indeed would have predicted until about a year before it happened" (XX, 10). In actuality quite a large number of people had been expecting just this for some years, and with the election of the Labour government in July 1945, it had become, in some quarters, almost a foregone conclusion.

A Money Racket

Orwell's belief that British workers gained materially from the exploitation of the poor colored colonies was not in itself unusual. Militant defenders of the empire from Cecil Rhodes and Joseph Chamberlain to Winston Churchill had continually asserted that the British working man's wages were as high as they were because of the empire. It seemed like common sense to many people, and was a key component of Lenin's theory of imperialism, preached by the Communist Party with almost no critical opposition from the Left.

On the other hand, the traditional liberal view (also shared by Karl Marx) was that while a small class of British people benefited from the empire, for most classes in Britain it was a burden rather than a bonus. In his spectacular best-seller, *The Great Illusion* (1909), Norman Angell had argued persuasively that Britain did not gain from the empire, except in the sense that all countries in the world gained by trade. Bertrand Russell (himself a staunch anti-imperialist) presented arguments against the theory that Britain as a whole benefited from the colonies.[6] And those socialists who did accept the theory that British workers derived some gain from the empire might assume that the immediate benefits of

6 Russell 1936, 164–65.

introducing socialism into Britain would more than make up for any reduction in working-class income due to loss of empire. So while these socialists nearly always held that the introduction of socialism would be accompanied by withdrawal from the empire, they did not necessarily conclude that the British worker would suffer a net loss as a result. Where Orwell was unusual was in stridently proclaiming, almost every time the topic of empire came up, that the working class must seriously suffer if the empire were abandoned.

Given Orwell's numerous and emphatic assertions that the British Empire enriched everyone in Britain by holding down colonial wages, it's a surprise to find him raising a doubt about this proposition on two occasions. In 1943, reviewing a book on India by the well-known leftist writer Henry Noel Brailsford, Orwell comments that the author "gives no very definite answer to the difficult question of whether, in balance, the British have done India more good than harm" (XV, 333). This is an isolated remark—and not quite the same question, though it's hard to imagine someone holding both that the British had done India more good than harm and that the British made themselves better off by holding down incomes in India. The notion that a "difficult question" is involved contrasts with Orwell's usual assumption that the benefit of colonial exploitation to British workers at the expense of colonial workers is so manifest that anyone who denies it must be disingenuous.

Then in 1946, we find Orwell raising the question "Do Our Colonies Pay?," the title of an article he wrote for *Tribune*. In this brief piece Orwell quickly skims over a lot of theoretical ground. He draws attention to the fact that there are two points of view on this question, on both the Right and the Left. He touches on a number of the arguments on both sides. He points out that it might be the case that a small minority benefits from the exploitation of India without Britain's prosperity as a whole depending on this exploitation—the traditional liberal view. He states that the question could be settled by ascertaining "the statistical facts," and yet he makes no attempt to ascertain these, and never subsequently did. He then states his own opinion without presenting any argument for it:

> My own view has always been (a) that over a long period we have definitely exploited, i.e. robbed, our colonial possessions,

> (b) that to some extent the whole British nation has benefited from this, in an economic sense, and (c) that we cannot make restitution to the colonial peoples without lowering our own standard of living for several years at the least. (XVIII, 143)

Did British Workers Gain from the Empire?

The claim that the British people as a whole, and especially British wage-workers, profited at the expense of Britain's colonies raises a number of fairly obvious puzzles, which Orwell never mentions.

If British wages were high because of British colonies, why were wages also high in some European countries which had no colonies, such as Sweden and Switzerland? And why were wages so very low, by European standards, in Portugal, which had a substantial overseas empire?

Around the end of the nineteenth century, both Germany and the United States began to approach Britain in average wages, this despite the fact that Britain had very many colonies, America and Germany very few. In the 1920s, the Fascist regime in Italy went to great expense to acquire colonies, notably Abyssinia, yet Italy's economy, and Italian wages, grew rapidly both before the Fascist episode (when Italy had very few and minor colonies) and after (when Italy had none). Indeed if we look at both Italy and Germany, it's not easy to dismiss the obvious conjecture that, rather than possession of colonies being an aid to economic growth, economic growth makes it possible to think about being able to afford the costly luxury of colonies (which, being a costly luxury, retard economic growth). Furthermore, there were a few non-European countries not ruled by foreigners at the time Orwell writes, which were economically backward and poor, just like the colonies. These never-colonized countries (like Abyssinia) or long-independent countries (like Bolivia) were generally among the very poorest, which is one illustration of a broader pattern that strikes anyone who looks at the facts: the poorest countries are those with the least contact with the developed industrial countries.

Within the British empire of the 1930s and 1940s, we can also compare the poor, colored colonies with the comparatively wealthy, white-populated countries, the dominions. Orwell maintains that high wages in Britain are somehow made possible by low wages in places like India and Burma. Wages in Australia, New Zealand, and Canada were at this time somewhat lower than British wages, but still very high by world or by historical standards. Does this mean that British workers benefited from India but didn't benefit from Australia and Canada? Might it also mean that Australian and Canadian workers shared in the higher wages due to exploitation of cheap labor in other parts of the empire? To ask questions like these is to lay bare the fact that we don't know how to begin to answer them, within Orwell's theory, because the mechanism by which British people are supposed to benefit from low wages in the colonies has not been specified.

Suppose that you're a British resident in the early twentieth century. You have savings which you could invest in Britain, in the United States, in Mexico, in Australia, or in India. Orwell's view implies that if you invest in India, you thereby raise British wages and reduce Indian wages, whereas if you invest in any of the other four places, there is no such effect (with Australia as a doubtful case, since he never addressed this). How could that possibly work? Notice that it won't do to say that the same effect will ensue in (comparatively poor) Mexico (or, for that matter, comparatively poor Mississippi), because Orwell makes it very explicit that (he predicts) the moment Britain stops ruling India, Indian wages will rise and British wages will fall as a direct result of India's political independence.

An Assumption in Search of an Explanation

Orwell calls the British Empire "a money racket" and applies to it words like "robbery," "pillage," and "plunder" (X, 145–46; XVII, 340). This may evoke an image of British people roaming around the colonies on looting sprees. Orwell knows perfectly well that nothing like this happened, and in any case that couldn't explain why British workers' wages would be high. If there were any robbery of the colonies, it must somehow have occurred in the normal course of business.

Orwell's account of the British Empire as a money racket explicitly relates to the routine operation of the empire at the time he's writing. So here we're considering only the way the empire operated after, say, 1858 (the year that the British government took over the administration of the Indian territories formerly held by the East India Company). And we're confining ourselves to the question which Orwell judges to be all-important: is the British Empire primarily a financial arrangement for benefiting British people, including British wage-workers, at the expense of poor people in the colonies?

What makes Orwell so sure that the answer is yes? Usually, Orwell simply points out that some British people made money by investing in the colonies and paying their colonial employees wages which were very low by British standards, as though this were enough to make his case.

Some British people invested in the colonies and got rich. But then, some British people invested in Britain and got rich, and some British people invested in foreign countries such as the United States, Argentina, or Germany, and got rich. (And, of course, some British people invested in all these places and just squeaked by or lost their shirts.) Every type of business activity which British investors undertook in the low-wage colored colonies, they also undertook in foreign countries; in the high-wage dominions; and in Britain. So fortunes made in the colonies hardly demonstrate that these fortunes were due to the existence of the empire, or of that part of the empire with predominantly low-income populations.

Those British investors in the colonies who got rich did so by their productive activity in the colonies, which paid incomes to some of the natives, thereby raising the incomes of people in the colonies. Though the natives' wages were often low by comparison with British wages, they were higher than they would have been in the absence of this investment from Britain. We can call British investment in the colonies a money racket, but it was no more a money racket than British investment in Britain, or the United States, or Germany, and it was no more a money racket than the work of a bricklayer or than Orwell's writing of book reviews. And it was no more a money racket than investment in the colonies by native entrepreneurs, such as the growing class of Indian capitalists.

British people with savings were free to invest in the poor colored colonies, in the rich white dominions, in foreign countries, or in Britain itself. If the poor colored colonies were such an engine of enrichment for the whole population of Britain, why did so little investment go there? This may not have been clear to Orwell, but we now know that about 30 percent of British investment capital was invested in Britain itself, another 45 percent in foreign countries, and about 16–17 percent in the dominions. So about 8–9 percent went to the poor colored colonies,[7] and some of this would still have gone to those places if they had not been in the empire. Viewed from the point of view of financial impact on Britain, the poor colored colonies were of little importance.

Following Orwell's article in *Tribune*, a correspondent wrote that "Of course Colonies pay" (XVIII, 145), arguing that since British investors drew dividends from their colonial investments (fancifully, "from 50% to 90%"), these dividends must come at the expense of the underpaid colonial workers. The reasoning must presumably be that if wages are low, more of the income from sales will be left over for the investors, which assumes that product prices are determined independently of wage costs. This would still not explain how British workers' wages would thereby be increased. However, the reasoning is wrong. Under competitive conditions, which prevailed throughout the empire, lower wages would not affect the rate of return to investors. Lower wages would translate into lower product prices and the rate of return to investors would be unaffected. And in fact profits were no higher on investments in the colonies than investments anywhere else.[8]

We might next consider that British workers benefited because the goods they consumed were cheaper than they might have been, but this

7 Davis and Huttenback 1986, 71–72, 308. Considerably more British investment went to the comparatively poor, politically independent countries of Latin America than to Britain's poor colored colonies, despite the risk of political expropriation in Latin America. These figures relate to the period ending 1912, but there was no dramatic movement after 1912 which would have helped Orwell's argument.

8 They were slightly higher before 1880, slightly lower from 1880 to 1905, and about the same after 1905 (Davis and Huttenback 1986, 109–110). If capital is free to move between different areas (however defined), we expect the rate of return to be the same from investments in all those areas, except that higher risk will mean higher return.

doesn't explain why goods produced in India as part of the empire would be any cheaper than goods produced in a hypothetical India outside the empire. We would still need to explain how the empire reduced wages in the colonies.

Believers in British exploitation of the colonies often mention "markets and sources of raw materials" and Orwell occasionally echoes these phrases. In 1948, three years into the Labour government, with postwar hardship in Britain and with a large chunk of the empire newly independent, Orwell mentions interest from foreign investments, cheap sources of raw materials from the colonies, and assured markets in the colonies as sources of Britain's past prosperity (XIX, 290, 439). The implication might be that the recent withdrawal from the major part of the empire means the loss of these benefits, and therefore helps to account for the current hard times, though it's not clear that this is what Orwell is claiming. If this really were what he was driving at, however, it would raise the question: How was Britain's trade with India in 1948 any different to what it would have been if India had not just become independent? There could have been no significant difference. Trade continued as before.

Interest from "foreign" investments did not come from the empire. Neither markets nor sources of raw materials readily harmonize with the usual assumption of Orwell's statements on the subject that the yield from the empire is connected with investment into the colonies. A British exporting firm was no more assured of a market in India than in Australia, Canada, the United States, or Argentina. And if export markets were the source of benefit to Britain, then the more affluent those markets the better, so this contradicts the theory that Britain benefited from low colonial incomes. The poor colored colonies accounted for a small portion of Britain's exports, and British firms had to pay for raw materials from the empire, just as they had to pay for raw materials from outside the empire. They would not be any cheaper just because they came from within the empire.

After the war, the Labour government re-imposed and extended wartime controls in Britain, such as rationing of consumer goods. These controls were eventually lifted, and from the late 1950s the British economy bounded forward in a burst of economic growth, dramatically raising the real incomes of the working class. By this time, Orwell was dead.

Over the next twenty years, Britain continued to give independence, one by one, to its former colonies (by 1970 the remaining colonies were few and tiny; the most important by far was Hong Kong) and British real wages continued to increase year upon year.

Neither colonial markets nor colonial sources of raw materials do anything to explain how British workers could enjoy high wages by keeping wages in the colonies low. Wages were low in India and Africa compared with Europe, because Europe was more industrialized. Low wages in India resulted automatically from the fact that the productivity of the Indian worker was low. Political arrangements cannot affect this underlying reality, except that they can prepare conditions which affect future investment, and therefore cause wages to rise faster or slower in the long term.

Were British Workers Living off the Backs of Starving Coolies?

The question of whether the empire was a net benefit or a net burden to Britain has always been controversial. The 1986 study by Davis and Huttenback employed more rigorous methods than previous analyses, and concluded: "The British as a whole certainly did not benefit economically from the Empire."[9] The British taxpayer subsidized the empire and on balance lost by it. The "colonies with responsible government" (dominions) seem to have been substantial net gainers and the poor colonies less dramatic gainers, in purely financial terms. The existence of the empire was always contrary to the interests of the British population taken as a whole, including the working class, though of course a few people (including those who got imperial jobs and those whose investments in the empire were subsidized) did very well out of it. I conclude that the British Empire was not a money racket but a national glory racket, in which British people of all classes seriously reduced their incomes and sometimes gave their lives for the sublime satisfaction of belonging to a great empire.

9 Davis and Huttenback 1986, p. 306. Their study examines the period from 1860 to 1912, but I have found nothing to suggest that British benefit increased after 1912.

Orwell makes a remark revealing something of his thinking: "There is no solution until the living standards of the thousand million people who are not 'white' can be forced up to the same level as our own" (XVI, 24). Orwell has not grasped the fact that the general level of wages can never be forced up; this has never occurred in any country at any time, and never could happen. The general level of wages is mainly governed by the productivity of labor. The wages of a section of the workforce can sometimes be forced up slightly, by restricting employment in that section, thus lowering the wages of workers in other sections (and slightly reducing wages overall). With just a few minor qualifications, the only way to raise the general level of wages is to increase the productivity of labor, and this occurs by capital investment, gradually over a long period. This gradual rise in real wages is typical and normal for any developed capitalist economy; it happens automatically and indefinitely, without requiring any political action. There is no way to force wages up.

Imagine that in, say, 1938, the government of India had imposed a minimum wage for laborers on Indian tea plantations—to pick an example where a high proportion of the output was consumed by British workers. (The government of India would have been legally entitled to do this. The British government would have been in theory legally entitled to over-rule it, but in practice would almost certainly not have done so.) It's true that British workers would have then had to pay more for their cherished pot of tea. But the greater sufferers would be Indian workers no longer employable on tea plantations because of the reduction in output of those plantations. Wages on tea plantations would increase, the number of workers employed on tea plantations would fall, output of tea would fall, and total wages of Indians as a whole would fall. Both British and Indian workers as a whole would suffer (though the lowest paid of those Indian workers who kept their jobs on the tea plantations would benefit).

Did the Empire Hold Back Development in the Colonies?

If British business investment in the colonies did not benefit the British worker at the expense of the colonial worker, it still remains possible that British government policy somehow benefited the British population in a way which harmed the colonial population. However, these two things don't automatically go together: if British policy harmed the colonies, it might have harmed Britain too, and if it helped Britain, it might have helped the colonies too.

Alongside his claims that ordinary money-making investment by British people in the colonies benefited all classes of British society while depressing wages in the colonies, Orwell also argued that British tariff policy, and other policies retarding Indian industrialization, hurt the colonies. It's not disputed that some British policies did discourage Indian development, though it doesn't follow that they thereby conferred any benefit on British workers.

In the context of discussions of India, Orwell assumes that industrialization is a good thing because it raises people's living standards. But if that's so, why not consider the possibility that British wages were higher than Indian wages because Britain, the first country to undergo an industrial revolution, was more industrialized than India? Then it needn't have been true that higher wages in Britain were due to the exploitation of half-starved coolies. Instead, the coolies were half-starved because they lived in a country that was insufficiently industrialized. While it might conceivably then be true that British policy was responsible for the insufficient industrialization, British workers would not necessarily benefit from this fact, and we will see that British policy, taken as a whole, was not responsible for the insufficient industrialization.

Here, Orwell fell back on his assumption that if a few countries have industrialized, then industrialization in other countries would be a threat to those early-industrialized countries (XIX, 436), therefore holding back colonial industrialization would benefit Britain. This fallacy is common in writings of the period. It is as if writers assumed that international trade only occurs at all because some countries are industrialized and others not. Orwell even expected that Britain would become a predominantly agricultural country after the war, because of the industrialization of Asian countries (XIII, 519).

The truth is almost the exact opposite: as industrialized countries pull ahead of unindustrialized countries, with occasional new recruits to the industrialized, the industrialized countries do more and more trade with each other and less and less with the unindustrialized world. The range and variety of manufactured goods increases, so that each industrialized country exports some kinds of manufactures while importing others. Put crudely, the industrialized countries don't need the unindustrialized countries but the unindustrialized countries, if they are to improve their situation rapidly, do need the industrialized countries.

Orwell, as we saw in Chapter 4, often bemoans the impact of industrial progress on British society. In that context, he implies (in different terminology) that "retarding industrialization" would be a fine thing. But Orwell seems to suppose that industrialization would be pure gain to India; there is none of his lamentation about the dire spiritual effects of "mechanical progress" in the context of industrialized Britain, though Mohandas Gandhi would have appreciated those remarks.

Before the First World War, Britain practiced free trade. Then some tariffs were imposed, yet even as late as 1931, most imports from all sources entered Britain duty-free. At this time countries everywhere were rapidly becoming protectionist, and the British Empire began to become protectionist too. As soon as parts of the empire acquired some elements of self-government, they erected protective tariffs against imports from Britain, as India did. In the early 1930s there was a campaign for "Empire Free Trade," which really meant protectionism against non-empire imports. In 1932 an empire and commonwealth conference was held in Ottawa; the participants were Britain, India, and four of the five dominions. The Ottawa conference led to numerous bilateral agreements between these countries and the colonies, to give each other 'preference', in other words to impose a higher tariff on imports from outside the empire than on imports from each other, whilst not attacking the right of the self-governing parts of the empire to operate protective tariffs against British manufactures.

The De-industrialization that Probably Never Happened

Indian nationalists have blamed the Raj for all the woes of independent India. Nationalists tell the story of a once-prosperous India devastated by British rule, which "de-industrialized" the country by exposing it to free trade.[10] Nationalist claims were echoed by Marxists (in contrast to

10 Dutt 1902; Dutt 1904.

the views of Marx himself, who welcomed British rule in India as a progressive force) and by the Left generally. But over the years, work by more scrupulous scholars has gradually put together a very different picture. British policies in India were far from optimal,[11] but on balance they favored industrialization, and they look good by comparison with any of the conceivable alternatives: a restoration of the Mughal empire, a continuation of the violent disorder following the breakup of Mughal rule, colonization by the French or the Portuguese, or imposition of all the policies favored by Indian nationalists themselves. Some of the more harmful elements of later British policy (such as import tariffs and restrictive labor laws) were in line with nationalist thinking and were maintained and extended after independence with continued and magnified harmful consequences.

The Raj covered India with railroads, introduced irrigation to the dry western zones, eliminated the brigandage which had been rife following Mughal collapse, installed an objective rule of law, initiated major new industries such as jute and tea, and provided education for an increasing number of Indians who were recruited to administer the Raj (even though there was grotesquely unfair discrimination in the recruitment and promotion of Indians compared with British civil servants).

In nineteenth-century India, some traditional textile crafts shrank because of competition from production in modern mills, but that is what industrialization means. Modern factories replace domestic output because of the factories' superior efficiency, leading to more and better goods in the hands of more consumers. At first the factory output came from Britain, but modern mills were set up in India in the 1850s, replacing the British imports and by the 1870s yielding Indian exports (Lal 2005, 206–24), to the increasing annoyance of trade unionists in Lancashire. These mills were owned and managed by Indians.

It remains controversial whether there was ever a period of net de-industrialization in India. However, there is no dispute that any net de-industrialization must have been over by the late nineteenth century. Furthermore, if there were earlier de-industrialization, and if it were

11 The sub-optimality of these policies is beyond the scope of the present discussion.

partly caused by cheap imports of textiles from British factories, this does not imply that the existence of the empire was responsible, for these cheap imports could still have occurred in an India outside British political control, as they occurred in many other foreign countries, where local industry was hit by cheap British imports, in that brief historical interlude when British factory production was far in advance of factory production anywhere else.

Rapid industrial development was effected by both Indian and British entrepreneurs. The industrial sector in India grew at more than 4 percent from the 1860s to 1930. Real incomes of Indians grew too, though slowly because most Indians remained in agriculture and population increased. From ancient times until the eighteenth century, Indian income per capita remained roughly constant, and fell following the collapse of the Mughal empire. It rose steadily from the 1860s until 1930, at 0.6 percent annually, a slow rate of growth by recent standards, but cumulatively amounting to 40 percent over the entire period.[12] British rule ended more than two thousand years of stagnation and India experienced vastly more gains in human wellbeing than it had ever seen up to that point. After 1930 per capita income declined slightly because of rapid population growth resulting from public health and anti-famine measures instituted by the Raj.

On the debit side, India bore an imperial burden second only to that borne by Britain, because Indian taxes paid for the large Indian army, which could be deployed anywhere in the empire. However, in 1939 Britain agreed to pay India for any use of Indian troops other than to defend India itself, so that by the end of the war, Britain owed India 1.3 billion pounds (since paid off, of course). The fact that British government employees in India, of which Orwell's father was typical, sent much of their salaries to dependants in Britain, and then retired to Britain, also constituted a drain on the Indian economy. Even so, taxes in India were far lower than they had been under the Mughals, and far lower than taxation in Britain itself, and (aside from the upkeep of the army) largely went to pay for infrastructure and other benign purposes in India. Britain was the most heavily taxed nation in the world, in large part because of the empire.

12 Heston 1983.

The Parsi entrepreneur Jamsetji Tata successfully installed state-of-the-art textile mills in India, beginning in 1869. He then conceived the plan to begin production of steel in India, something that had already failed several times with British entrepreneurs. London investors had no confidence in an ambitious and purely Indian initiative, so in 1907 (three years after Jamsetji's death) his firm Tata Steel sold stock in India. This coincided with the enthusiastic *swadeshi* movement (producing more things within India, to avoid being dependent on Britain). The Tata stock issue was quickly taken up by thousands of Indians, rich and poor. After many dramatic ups and downs, the Tata Steel Mills became by the 1930s the biggest steel producer in the British empire.[13] As Orwell says, there was some British "discouragement" and "obstruction" of Tata Steel (XVII, 217), but these were primarily a matter of lack of investor confidence, and as soon as Tata showed it could deliver the goods, the Raj itself guaranteed large and continuous purchases of Tata steel. (Tata Steel is still one of the world's largest steel producers and has acquired considerable industrial holdings in several countries including the UK.)

Orwell made much of the fact that there was no auto industry in India (XV, 333; XVI, 186–87). A car manufacturing firm relies upon numerous smaller suppliers of parts. An auto industry requires close proximity to a large pool of small or medium-sized manufacturing firms and experienced engineers. For comparison, Russia in 1913, when it was the world's fifth industrial producer, and considerably more developed than India in the 1940s, had only one small specialist auto maker, and an issue in Russian national debate was whether it was better to buy cars from Europe or from America.

Hobson and Lenin

By the 1930s, socialism had become associated with anti-imperialism, but this was a comparatively recent development. Early socialists were not necessarily anti-imperialist. The Webbs had been very much in favor of empire. Marx and the early Marxists saw empire primarily as a progressive force, bringing capitalism, and therefore rapid economic

13 Keenan 1943.

growth, to backward countries. More recently, this traditional Marxist view has been revived.[14]

When Orwell wrote, anti-imperialism, and the theory that European workers benefited by the exploitation of the colonies, were dominant on the Left. The older socialist idea that imperialism was the advance guard of capitalist modernization of the less developed world and the vehicle for future socialist modernization was largely dead. This was chiefly due to the enormous influence of John A. Hobson's theory of imperialism, which did not convince economists but did convince the political Left. Orwell didn't make a special study of the economics of imperialism and he probably never read Hobson, but Hobson's influence was pervasive in leftist intellectual circles, and when Orwell attended events like ILP weekend schools, he could not have escaped it.

Hobson's views evolved and shifted and are sometimes obscure.[15] Here we're not concerned so much with what Hobson "really thought," as with what the 1930s intellectual Left took from Hobson. Hobson started from the traditional liberal view that the empire benefited a few special interests, but was generally injurious to the British population. What he added to this was a theory that the British capitalist system as a whole had an inherent need for imperialist expansion, because of a built-in tendency to underconsumption. He concluded that the people who masterminded the imperial policy were the lords of finance, whose motivation was the thirst for investment outlets outside Britain. Hobson's own solution to the problem was "social reform," by which he meant measures to change the distribution of income in Britain, so that poorer people got more money and richer people less. This would reduce total saving and increase total spending on consumption, thus eliminating underconsumption and therefore the dangerous impetus to imperialism.

Hobson's theory was crudely adapted and simplified by Lenin, and this version became part of what the 1930s came to see as "Marxism." Orwell does not repeat all the elements of Hobson's theory, but he does accept underconsumptionism—the notion that capitalism has a problem because workers can't buy all that they have produced (XVII, 27).

14 Warren 1980.
15 Cain 2002.

Although Orwell propounds both the idea that the colonies are exploited and the idea of underconsumption, he does not suggest that these two things are tightly linked, and this is the crux of Hobson's theory. Hobson's specific idea that there is too much saving in Britain, which therefore needs the empire as an outlet for "surplus capital," is never voiced by Orwell.

The historical facts run counter to the Hobson-Lenin theory, though some of these facts have only become easily available since Hobson's day. The poor colored empire accounted for less than ten percent of investment of British savings, and investment in this part of the empire was not especially profitable in the relevant time-period. Both Hobson and Lenin gave statistics showing that European countries invested a large portion of their savings overseas, leaving their readers with the impression that these went to the colonies.[16] But since most of this overseas investment was in fact in the richer industrial countries, these statistics actually contradict their theory rather than confirming it. In any case, Hobson's approach is fundamentally misconceived. The "need" of a country to export capital does not make export of capital profitable. And if export of capital were profitable, the "need" for it would be immaterial.

Two Remaining Theories

To round off this consideration of ways in which people in Britain might have benefited from the empire, we can touch on two remaining theories—though neither of these was articulated by Orwell. First, there is the theory that mere trade between rich and poor countries—with or without an empire—benefits the rich countries at the expense of poor countries. Second, there is the theory that an empire yields general benefits (what economists call positive externalities), so that although there

16 Hobson 1965, 51–63; Lenin 1964, 242. For the same fallacious argument in support of one presentation of Hobsonianism which strongly influenced leftwing thought, see Brailsford 1918, 77–78. Lenin holds that imperialist investors realize "superprofits," out of which they bribe the labor leaders. Hobson and Brailsford take the view that only a few privileged groups benefit from imperialism and that British workers don't benefit at all.

is no unfair extraction of resources from the colonies to the benefit of the imperial power, residents of that power benefit anyway, because of the general expansion of trade and output.

Orwell did not live to observe the Communist theory of "neocolonialism." As Britain and other European colonial powers handed over political power to their former possessions, the inhabitants of these former possessions did not enjoy any immediate or dramatic improvement from self-rule. Where they had been desperately poor before independence, they remained desperately poor after independence. They became the "third world." This is what we should expect if their desperate poverty were not inflicted on them by their imperial rulers.

Actual decolonization appeared to falsify Lenin's claim that imperialism was "the highest stage of capitalism." The Communist theory was therefore adapted to say that imperialism was somehow still going on, even when the colonies had become independent nations. The opinion of leftwing intellectuals moved from the theory that imperial rule made the colonies poor to the theory that whenever rich countries trade with poor countries, this makes the poor countries poor and is therefore, mysteriously, a form of imperial rule. The rich countries, including especially their wage-workers, were still supposed to be living high off the exploitation of the poor countries. To some extent, this theory was implicit in earlier analyses, for example Lenin's *Imperialism* seems to assume that the independent Latin American countries where British investments were prominent were effectively part of the British empire.

But if rich countries can so easily exploit poor countries just by trading with them, without political rule over them, then this exploitation is independent of imperial rule and implies that imperial rule is not needed. However we observe that, whether poor countries are colonies or independent, they experience more economic growth and therefore more improvement in the people's living standards, the more involvement they have with the advanced industrial countries. The worst thing that could happen to a poor country, later to be called a third-world country, was to have no intercourse with the advanced industrial countries. This stark fact is the precise opposite of what we would expect if there were anything in the theory of neocolonialism.

The remaining possibility is that Britain and other European colonial countries benefited from their empires indirectly, by bringing new populations into the trading area. For example, it seems probable that British trade with India was greater than it would have been if India had been a disunited conglomeration of warring principalities lacking any common legal framework. In this scenario, Britain did benefit from the empire, but so did the populations of the empire themselves, and the other countries of the world. There were no losers, except the former brigands and warlords of post-Mughal India.

According to this type of theory, it might well be true that the empire cost Britain more than it yielded directly (as Davis and Huttenback's analysis indicates), and yet Britain would be better off because of the empire's indirect effects. By imposing respect for property and contract across a very wide area, guaranteeing free trade, and perhaps also establishing a certain minimum of cultural uniformity (reducing transactions costs) there would be a general enhancement of trade and therefore a cumulative increase in output. Net benefits would accrue to the inhabitants of the imperial country, the colonies, and the rest of the world. In this way, an empire would confer a general benefit on all of humankind. Broadly this kind of theory seems to be accepted by Lal.[17]

Whether there is anything in such a theory depends upon whether the improvement in respect for property and contract in the area of the empire, minus the costs of the empire, is sufficiently great, and that in turn depends largely upon whether numerous uncentralized agreements between traders and local rulers would be able to achieve much of the safety and security that could be achieved by central imposition. Here again we come up against the stark fact that in terms of volume of output or trade, the poorest countries are simply rather unimportant in the world economic system, and all theories which imply that these countries are somehow crucial to the system must be mistaken. This theory is also weakened because precisely those territories which would benefit most from imperial rule would be those where output and trade would be paltry for a long time to come. The ninety years of the Raj benefited Indian development but the Raj was a direct burden on Britain. India accounted

17 Lal 2004.

for such a modest part of British trade that it seems unlikely that the indirect benefits to Britain of ruling India could have recouped the costs to the British taxpayers.

Orwell was mistaken in supposing that the British working class benefited from the empire, and he was mistaken in supposing that small or industrially less-developed countries cannot be politically independent. If he had gotten beyond these errors, he would have been able to do what many other British people did: press for rapid decolonization as a matter of both self-interest and conscience. For, after all,

> The truth is that no modern man, in his heart of hearts, believes that it is right to invade a foreign country and hold the population down by force. (V, 135)

7
The Spanish Soldier

> Pray look better, Sir, quoth *Sancho*; those things yonder are no Giants, but Wind-mills . . .
> —Miguel de Cervantes, *Don Quixote*, Part I, Book I, VIII

When Orwell left England for Spain at the end of 1936, though no admirer of Soviet Russia, he endorsed the idea of a Popular Front, was happy with the Left Book Club, and viewed the Communist Party, for all its faults, as a valuable ally in the struggle against fascism. After he returned from Spain in June 1937, he opposed any Popular Front, despised the Left Book Club, considered the Popular Front Left a likely vehicle for the introduction of fascism in Britain, and was militantly opposed to any British "anti-fascist" war against Germany. His novel *Coming Up for Air* reflects this anti-Popular Front and anti-war position, so that Orwell surmised (mistakenly) that the fellow-traveler Victor Gollancz might refuse to publish it.

In the six months of his sojourn in Spain, Orwell's political views had undergone a considerable transformation, and actually this transformation perceptibly took hold in a much shorter period, a few weeks or even days near the end of that six months. So Orwell experienced two conversions, about a year apart. From mid-1936 (as we saw in Chapter 3), Orwell was a new convert to socialism and at that point he was impatient with the factional divisions inside the socialist movement. A year later he was a new convert to one of these very factions. In May–June 1937 he attached himself to a narrowly-delineated ideological system—that of the revolutionary anti-Stalinist Left.

This newly acquired orthodoxy was to last twenty-six months, from June 1937 up to August 1939. In all his many writings during this period,

Orwell's political orientation was constant and unwavering. In its outlines this orientation was in no way distinctive to Orwell. It was an off-the-peg suit of ideological clothes. It was substantially the same as that of the POUM in Spain and of the ILP in Britain. This ILP view is expounded at length, for example, by leading ILP member Fenner Brockway in his 1938 book, *Workers' Front*.[1] In June 1938, Orwell joined the ILP, and wrote a brief piece explaining why he had done so (XI, 167–69); Orwell at this time saw eye-to-eye with prominent ILP members on all key political issues.

When we speak of "the revolutionary anti-Stalinist Left," some readers may immediately think of Trotskyism, and the label "Trotskyist" would sometimes be loosely applied to the revolutionary Left as a whole. But Trotskyism properly defined was a part—and not the major part—of the revolutionary anti-Stalinist Left in the 1930s. In both Britain and Spain, for example, the ILP and the POUM, though small parties on a national scale, vastly outnumbered the tiny handful of Trotskyists in each country. Trotskyists were affiliated with Trotsky's Fourth International, while the ILP and the POUM were affiliated with the London Bureau (sometimes facetiously called "the Three-and-a-Half International"). Trotsky repeatedly denounced the activities of the POUM and ILP in angry and abusive terms.[2]

Trotsky's sharp criticisms illustrate the fact that what I am calling "the revolutionary anti-Stalinist Left," though a narrow sliver of the Left, still had room for important internal differences. Orwell wrote a five-to-six-thousand-word anti-war pamphlet which was never printed (though reportedly mimeographed) and has been lost (XI, 169, 223, 241–42). We can infer most of what it must have said, not just about war but about socialism, capitalism, fascism, and revolution from numerous Orwell writings around this time. According to one source, the ILP declined to publish it because it was "too long and absolutist" (XI, 169). Six thousand words is not terribly long by the standards of 1930s pamphlets and it's difficult to come up with a sense of "absolutist" in which Orwell's approach would be more absolutist than that of the leading ILPers, Brockway, Maxton, and McGovern.

1 The title is doubtless a rebuke to G. D. H. Cole's *The People's Front* (1937).
2 For example, Trotsky 1973, 209–210, 248–250, 342–44.

Good writing about controversial matters tends to upset people, because it conveys sharply and therefore provocatively what many readers prefer to leave in soft focus. Since Orwell would certainly have submitted this pamphlet to the ILP, the likeliest specific reason for rejection is Orwell's precise characterization at that time of the USSR and the Communist Party. He had not yet expressed his later view that the Third Reich was rapidly becoming the same type of system as the USSR, but perhaps the pamphlet contained early intimations of this thesis, which many in the ILP were far from ready to accept. Since Orwell was to spend a good bit of energy in the period 1939–1945 denigrating and reviling the antiwar views he had propounded in the period 1937–1939, he was no doubt glad that the pamphlet had never made it into print (and perhaps he played a conscious role in ensuring that it would be lost to history).

During the twenty-six months from June 1937 till August 1939, Orwell was a consistent ideologue of a precise and elaborate orthodoxy. What caused him to embrace this revolutionary leftist orthodoxy, in place of the more ecumenical socialism of *Wigan Pier*, was his interpretation of his experiences in Spain.

Civil War in Spain

The great cause of the Left in the 1930s was Spain. There has been nothing to equal it in the imagination of the Left before or since. The cause of Spain loomed much larger than the cause of Vietnam thirty years later, for example. Thirty-five thousand foreign leftists went to fight as volunteers for the Spanish Republic, and nearly five thousand of them died—many at the hands of commissars and the NKVD rather than the Nationalist enemy (XI, 35).

The Spanish Civil War officially began on 17th July 1936, with an attempted military coup, though this was the culmination of months of escalating violence in which normal government had broken down. The war officially ended on 1st April 1939, when the last remaining Republican forces surrendered.

At the outset, everyone expected one of two outcomes: either the generals' bid for power would succeed in a matter of days, as a military coup had done in 1923, or it would be quashed in a matter of days, as in

August 1932. Instead, after a few days of fighting and intriguing, province by province and town by town, the insurgent generals found themselves in secure control of less than half the country and the Republic retained control of the rest. Roughly speaking, the rightwing military rebels—the Nationalists—controlled those areas where their popular support was strongest, but they also enjoyed substantial support among the population in the Republican-controlled territory. Alluding to the considerable popular support for the Nationalist cause behind Republican lines, General Franco coined the term "Fifth Column."

There were thus two rival governments in Spain, each preoccupied with subjugating the half of Spain under the control of the other. Neither side was disposed to compromise. This was a war of territorial conquest, with trench warfare along a front, rather like World War I. Decisive battles occurred at particular points, moving a part of the front, but against the backdrop of a largely unchanging front.

It was a war of extermination of political opponents, and of categories of people judged to be objective enemies. When the Nationalists gained control of a town, they rounded up all known supporters of the Republic, and also people in such categories as trade union official. Some of these were shot immediately. Some were imprisoned and shot later. A few were imprisoned and eventually released. When the Republicans took a town they rounded up all supporters of the Nationalists and also people in such categories as priest or substantial property-owner. Some were shot immediately. Some were imprisoned and shot later. A few were imprisoned and eventually released. In some cases more imaginative methods than shooting were employed. The main reason that the Nationalists ended up having committed far more atrocities than the Republicans was that the Nationalists were usually winning.[3]

Each side was an alliance of disparate groups, brought together by fear of a victory for the other side. The main groups on the Republican side were Liberal Republicans, Socialists, anarchists, Communists, and (only in Catalonia) the POUM. The main groups on the Nationalist side were rightist military officers of no clear political affiliation, monarchists, Carlists, Falangists, and Catholics.

3 On the number of killings on each side, see Thomas 2001, 900–01.

A War between Two Coalitions

The Communist Party was tiny at the beginning of the war, but by the end of 1937 had almost complete control of the Republican side. The Communist Party achieved this in part by being allied with the Socialist Party and adroitly manipulating it,[4] in part because the Soviet Union was selling substantial military supplies to the Republic, and in part by publicly advocating an apparently sensible strategy that was attractive to a lot of middle-class Spaniards.

Spain was unusual in having a large anarchist movement, with millions of committed adherents. Anarchocommunists in the mold of Bakunin—fiercely anti-Church and favoring the abolition of money—were powerful among the farm workers in some areas. Anarchosyndicalists controlled the major federation of trade unions, the CNT. The POUM were Leninists critical of the Stalin regime in Russia, and were therefore inaccurately viewed by many as "Trotskyists." They were a small group, but dedicated, and were just big enough in Catalonia to be significant there. Orwell happened to fight for their militia only because they were linked with the ILP, who provided him with his introductory credentials.

Carlists, with their red berets, have been defined since 1833 as supporters of a dissident line claiming the Spanish throne, but in substance Carlism is a consciously anti-modern ideology. The Falange Española (Spanish Phalanx) was a broadly fascist movement, formed by admirers of Mussolini's Italy, though it had some more traditionalist elements, and was headed by Jose Antonio Primo de Rivera, son of the dictator who had ruled Spain (in the name of the king) from 1923 to 1930. The Falangists did not have a sizeable following at first and were a small component of the Nationalist side, though Franco played up the superficial fascist affinities of his movement to encourage material support from Mussolini and Hitler. Though always small, Falange membership

4 In most of Spain "the Socialist Party" refers to the PSOE. In autonomous Catalonia, the corresponding organization was the PSUC. Both parties came under Communist control, the PSUC more directly than the PSOE. Full names of all organizations mentioned, in Spanish and English, are given in the Index.

grew at a rapid rate in 1936, as people alarmed by leftist violence began to despair of any democratic solution.

To think of the Nationalist side as "Fascist" is as ill-informed as to think of the Republican side as "Communist"—or more so, as the Communists did succeed, for a few months, in gaining effective control of the Republic, while the original Falangists were always a subordinate part of the Nationalist coalition, and eventually became marginalized despite their increased numbers. The Nationalist rebellion was planned and instigated by generals who were not themselves Falangists or Carlists but who recognized that these and other groups would be useful allies, and so they brought the leaders of these groups into the rebel movement.

As far as we can tell from prior election returns and other indications, total public opinion in Spain gave approximately equal support to "Left" and "Right," to those disposed to support the Republic and those disposed to support the Nationalists. The leftist Popular Front won a big election victory in February 1936, but with less than fifty percent of the popular vote.[5] Due to the mechanics of the electoral system, the Popular Front gained a substantial majority of seats in the parliament (Payne 2006, 170–84). Support for each side was regionally concentrated—Orwell himself later remarked that the main determinant of whether someone would be a Republican or a Nationalist was what part of Spain they came from. Popular opinion swung from Republicans to Nationalists as the war progressed, because superior Nationalist organization avoided the high inflation and food shortages that plagued the Republican zone.

This doesn't mean that Franco was ever a hugely popular figure. We now know that the majority of Spaniards didn't care deeply one way or the other about Left versus Right; they viewed the whole thing as a wretched nuisance. Orwell recollected:

5 Because of the complex peculiarities of the electoral system and the loss of some information, different numbers can be produced, but all experts agree that the Popular Front received a minority of the popular vote. See the discussion in Payne 2006, 175–180. The Popular Front vote exceeded the vote for the right, but not the right plus the center.

> Looking back on casual contacts with peasants, shopkeepers, street-hawkers, even militiamen, I now suspect that great numbers of these people had no feelings about the war whatever, except a wish that it were over. (XI, 416)

Orwell's impression has been more than borne out by Michael Seidman's remarkable study focusing on the politically unenthusiastic majority (Seidman 2002). Much of the front, as in the First World War, was "quiet"—there was a tacit agreement between the conscripted rank-and-file soldiers on the two sides to fire off rounds without effect and avoid any actual damage. Desertions were heavy from the armies of both sides, but heavier from the Republicans, with a significant number of Republican deserters successfully recycled as Nationalist troops. Corruption, cynicism, and self-interested actions to the detriment of the military struggle were also more conspicuous on the Republican side.

In the Civil War, those we might loosely call moderates predictably lost influence, as extremists came to the fore on both sides. Of those people who would have preferred a democracy without political assassinations, priest-killings, or "social revolution," the ones on the Republican side were reduced to impotence while many were impelled to support the Nationalists as the lesser of two evils.

While both sides were coalitions of disparate groups, the Nationalists quickly sank their differences and subordinated politics to the military campaign. Carlists and Falangists hated each other just as much as anarchists and Communists, but the Nationalists did better at keeping the lid on such antagonisms. Supreme leadership was awarded to Francisco Franco Bahamonde in October 1936. Franco's unchallenged authority was favored by accidental circumstances: his likely rivals were older and were all dead by 1939. The suppression of internal strife and the undisputed primacy of Franco helped the Nationalists win the war—and helped ensure that the outcome was something which would have been the first choice of no Nationalists in 1936: Franco's dictatorship for life.

Those within the Republican coalition maintained their separate identities and never ceased to fight each other. Along with the bloody civil war between Left and Right, there was a bloody civil war within the Left, which contributed to the defeat of the Republic. Strife within the Left was most pronounced in Catalonia, the independent-minded Spanish province, with its own language, whose capital is the great Mediterranean seaport and industrial center of Barcelona.

Both Germany and Italy sold military equipment and personnel to the Nationalists, while Soviet Russia sold military equipment and personnel to the Republic. Military equipment for the Republic also came across the border from France, both at the beginning of the war and for a period in 1938, though most of the time France enforced the policy of non-intervention promoted by Britain (a policy which ruled out shipments of arms to either side in Spain). To pay for Soviet military supplies, Spain's gold reserves were early shipped to Moscow. This accentuated the Republic's dependence on Russia and therefore on the Communists, since the Republic had no gold left, its currency was not trusted, and its credit was bad. Stalin was aggrieved that the hundreds of millions of dollars in gold he had received was still, by his reckoning, tens of millions short.

Orwell in Spain

After delivering the manuscript of *The Road to Wigan Pier* to the publisher, Orwell left for Spain in the last few days of 1936. He wanted to write about what was going on there, but was unclear at first about whether he would go primarily as an observer or as a combatant. Seeking a letter of introduction from a leftwing organization, he met with the CPGB leader Harry Pollitt (XI, 136). Because Orwell would not give an undertaking that he would join the International Brigade, Pollitt declined to give Orwell a letter (and thereby inadvertently saved the life of the individual who would do more than any other to bring about the total worldwide defeat of Communism). If Pollitt had provided the letter, Orwell would no doubt have enlisted in the International Brigade and would then have been killed.

Instead of going to Spain with an introduction from the CPGB, Orwell obtained one from the ILP, which meant that he would enroll in the militia of the POUM. Orwell was posted on the Aragón front, to the west of Catalonia. At this point, many of the Republican fighting forces were still divided along political lines. Each political tendency of note had its own militia, responsible for a different part of the front. This system was being replaced by a unified military along conventional lines, the Popular Army, but that did not yet fully extend to the Aragón front when Orwell arrived. Orwell fretted under the conditions of comparative inactivity, and yearned to transfer to the defense of Madrid, which would have meant switching to the Communist-controlled International Brigade. He argued with his fellow militiamen, defending the Communist line on the war against the POUM line.

Though he saw some action, Orwell increasingly felt that he was accomplishing very little and concluded that if he could not get to Madrid, he might leave Spain altogether. Orwell's supreme objective—to seek experiences he could turn into prose—meant that he could either go for higher-grade experiences in Madrid, or cash out the experiences he had accumulated already and start writing them up, back in England.

If Orwell had achieved his wish to enroll in the International Brigade and fight in defense of Madrid, he might have been killed in the fighting, more fierce than in Aragón, or he might have been bumped off by a Soviet commissar for talking back, or the two events might have been combined in the handy method applied to Uriah the Hittite. Orwell was not one to keep his mouth shut, so his death in Madrid would have been certain. He would have gone down in history with Christopher Caudwell, John Cornford, Julian Bell, and Ralph Fox, promising young Communist or fellow-traveling writers who died fighting for the glorious cause of Soviet Russian imperialism in Spain.

On April 25th, he took some leave that was due and applied for his discharge from the POUM militia. In Barcelona (where his wife Eileen had gotten a job at the POUM office) Orwell talked with Communists about joining the International Brigade, and taking some other POUM militiamen with him. This development was briefly put on hold because Orwell was undergoing a spell of illness and was waiting for boots to be made to fit his outsized feet.

As Orwell sat down to breakfast on the morning of May 3rd 1937, he was still a Popular Front socialist and Communist fellow traveler who had consciously rejected the revolutionary Left position. He was in for a shock. Later that day, street fighting—mainly with rifles and grenades—broke out between anarchist workers of the CNT and a Communist-led contingent of paramilitary police known as assault guards. In the next few days, several hundred people were killed and over a thousand wounded. The fighting commenced with an attack on the telephone exchange by the assault guards. The telephone exchange and other public buildings were manned by members of the CNT (the anarchosyndicalist trade union federation), who successfully resisted the police attack, for the moment. The workers at first held off the assault guards, but then, having run out of food, started trickling back to work. A few days later, a large force of assault guards arrived from Valencia and took complete control of the city.[6]

This event was crucial for Orwell's subsequent thinking. He was able to read an account of what he had witnessed which became blazoned throughout the world's media, and which Orwell knew to be, not merely distorted or garbled, but a fantastic fabrication. The story concocted by the Communists and successfully disseminated throughout the world, was that the POUM, acting under the orders of Franco and Hitler, had staged an armed rising against the Republic. In actuality the POUM played no part in initiating the fighting (there was no "rising," unless resisting a police attack is defined as a rising) and was taken by surprise. From this point dates Orwell's concern that objective historical truth might be lost forever, that no one would ever be able to establish what had really happened, and that, as O'Brien was to explain in *Nineteen Eighty-Four*, whoever controls the present controls the past and whoever controls the past controls the future. The value of objective truth might be disappearing from the world, along with the other values of classical liberalism.

Before Orwell ever came to Spain, Moscow had decided on the broad agenda of putting the revolutionary Left (the anarchists and the

6 VI, 101–124. In the original edition of *Homage to Catalonia*, Orwell mistakenly refers to the assault guards as "Civil Guards," a different organization of paramilitary police. Barcelona's public buildings had been seized and "collectivized" in July 1936, and the collectivization affirmed by government decree, so, quaint as it might sound, a good case can be made that the anarchosyndicalist workers of the CNT were the legally recognized owners of these buildings.

POUM) out of action under the pretext that they were fascist agents. Scholarly debate continues over whether the street fighting precipitated by the assault guards on May 3rd was a strictly premeditated part of this plan, or whether it involved unscheduled extempore elements (VI, 223; Thomas 2001, 636n2; Radosh et al. 2001, 172–78). The suppression of the POUM and then the anarchists was only part of a wider Communist plan: to disarm the civilian population, remove Premier Largo Caballero from office, replace him with the more compliant Juan Negrín, eliminate the CNT representation in the government, and silence all political voices except that of Communism and Communist-controlled Socialism.

Orwell abandoned his intention of getting to Madrid, where, it had now come home to him, he might very likely be ordered by the Soviet bosses to kill leftist workers (VI, 127). Instead of slipping out of Spain as quickly as possible to save his own and Eileen's lives, he returned to the front. There, at five o'clock in the morning, as he came on sentry duty, he was hit by a Nationalist sniper bullet, which went straight through his throat. In one of those little historical details which, like the length of Cleopatra's nose, made a big difference to subsequent events, the bullet happened to miss anything vital, passing within a hair's breadth of the trachea on one side and the carotid artery on the other. Orwell was sent to hospital, and soon recovered. He lost his voice, but it came back, though always to remain huskier and weaker than before. In the weeks that this was happening to Orwell, the POUM was declared illegal and anyone in Barcelona connected with it or with the recent fighting was imprisoned.

Having convalesced and received his discharge from the militia, Orwell returned to Barcelona, to find that he was a hunted fugitive, liable to be arrested at any moment. Catalonia had become, in fact, a Communist police state, a totalitarian regime, the population in a cowed state of terror. Eileen and other wives or girlfriends of leftist fighters had not been arrested, a police stratagem to encourage these combatants to make an appearance so that they could be picked up. After laying low for several days, Orwell and Eileen managed to make it over the border into France, posing as conventional English tourists. While Communist writers later scoffed at Orwell's apprehension that he was in some danger, we now know that he and Eileen did indeed have a narrow escape from being arrested and then murdered by the Communist-controlled police, following their instructions from Moscow (XI, 30–33).

On his return to England, Orwell wrote *Homage to Catalonia*, a flop at the time, though it is now far more widely read than anything else about the Spanish Civil War, except for Hemingway's novel, *For Whom the Bell Tolls*. Though Orwell had started out critical of the POUM line, he endeavored to defend the POUM and to expose the Communist behavior, but found major leftwing organs such as the *New Statesman* resolutely unwilling to publish anything reflecting badly on the Communist role in Spain.

Orwell's Conversion to the Revolutionary Left

When Orwell and others talk about "the revolution" in Spain, they are referring to three kinds of events: the seizure of land from the landowners by farm workers, and its conversion into collective holdings; the seizure of factories by the workers; and the destruction or desecration of churches, along with numerous physical attacks (often fatal) on priests and nuns. When Orwell arrived in Spain, these "revolutionary" actions, confined to a few parts of the country, had mainly occurred four or five months earlier, just after the commencement of the war.

The public Communist line was that these revolutionary actions should not be continued and where they had occurred should be reversed. Their argument was that socialist revolution was premature in Spain and that the revolutionary acts had hindered the Republican war effort. Priority should be given to winning the war, and for the sake of winning the war, it should be made clear that the Republic was defending conventional "bourgeois" democracy against fascism, not seeking to overturn capitalism. This was a recent switch for the Communists—before the generals' bid for power, they had strongly favored the revolutionary wave. The opposing POUM view was that the war and the revolution were inseparable, and that the way to win the war was to continue with the revolution.

Orwell reports that he started out in agreement with the Communist Party line on the war, but eventually came to see that the POUM had been right, or approximately right. The POUM position, he claimed, had been vindicated by events (XI, 168). There are two issues here—the narrower question of whether the POUM strategy would have been best for the Spanish Republic's military chances at the time and the broader question of Orwell's adoption of the general theory of the revolutionary Left, which he was to apply to all of politics, especially British politics, for the next two years and two months (and some parts of which he would continue to apply for years after that).

In *Homage to Catalonia*, Orwell outlines his arguments for the POUM position, focusing on the narrower question (VI, 211–13). He accepts that "the war was worth winning if the revolution was lost," in other words that it was worth striving for a Republican victory regardless of the revolution. This contradicts his repeated assertions that any two forms of capitalism are merely "Tweedledum and Tweedledee" so that neither side should be supported. It's also significant in that Orwell undertakes to show that the revolution is worth supporting, not merely because socialism is better than capitalism, but also because revolution is the best (or even necessary) method to win the war—an analysis he was to transpose to the British war against Germany in the years after August 1939.

First, he says that there were inadequate arms on the Aragón front, because the Communists refrained from supplying arms to the anarchists who would use them for revolutionary purposes. This argument rather misses the point because, first, the Communists withheld arms from political militias they couldn't control, irrespective of whether they might be used for revolutionary purposes, and second, if the Communist-supported policy of replacing all political militias with a unified military had been fully implemented (as it was being implemented), this would have ensured supply of arms evenly to all parts of the front (and would have had additional benefits for the efficiency of the Republican war effort). Orwell might have been thinking that the Comintern should have pursued a policy of encouraging revolution in Spain, as it no doubt would have done back in the 1920s, but that would be to ask for something out of the control of anyone in Spain.

Second, Orwell maintains that a non-revolutionary war in defense of democracy made it "impossible to make any large-scale appeal for working-class aid abroad." He says that workers in Britain could have raised more money for Spain and also supported the Republic by strikes and boycotts. Leaving aside the effectiveness of strikes and boycotts in behalf of one side in a foreign civil war, the vast majority of the British working class was non-revolutionary in outlook. The Labour Party was emphatically committed to achieving socialism through Parliament. The trade unions were consistently to the right of the Labour Party as a whole. If the Republic had been avowedly revolutionary, support from the British labour movement would therefore have been less than it was. The Communist depiction of the war as a defense of democracy was probably the most effective, judged by the standard of maximizing foreign support.

Third, Orwell states that a revolutionary policy would have roused the population in Franco's rear, so that he would have had to expend more resources on repressing the population under his control. However, political ideologies in Spain were regional in their strength, and the peasants in most regions were more likely to be victims than beneficiaries of land redistribution. It's understandable that Franco did not have much difficulty with his "rear," because Spaniards received daily evidence that life was better under the Nationalists than under the Republic—more food, regular payment for the troops, lower inflation, no attacks on churches, and fewer violent vendettas between political groups. There were some areas where guerilla fighters harassed the Nationalist forces (and would do so for years after the war had ended), but it's not clear that there would have been any more of this if the Republic had been more openly pro-revolutionary.

What Orwell thought was the strongest argument of all is an extension of the previous one. The Republic should have proclaimed Moroccan independence and tried to foment a rising in Spanish Morocco (a significant part of Franco's army was the Moroccan "Army of Africa"). However, the Republic could have proclaimed Moroccan independence without pursuing a revolutionary policy in Spain—decolonization and national self-determination are impeccably bourgeois. And Moroccan nationalism was not simmering among the Army of Africa. These Muslim professional soldiers answered to the Caliph, Mulay Hassan bin-al-Mahdi, who put them at the service of Franco (rather than the Republic) because the enemy was perceived as Communism. These troops had, in the overwhelming majority, remained loyal to Spain in the war against the Rif tribesmen in the 1920s, and were often employed as guards of the king, and (after Franco's victory) of Franco. They were the most lavishly honored and decorated of the Nationalist armed forces. Catholic Spain doted on its Muslim fighters.

Orwell probably did not know that the possibility of using Moroccan nationalism against the Nationalists was several times raised, both in public and behind the scenes.[7] Early in the war, the anarchists had pushed for a declaration of Moroccan independence, but had been outvoted by the rest of the Popular Front because of fears this would have discouraged possible support for the Republic from France and Britain, while the actual consequences in Spanish Morocco might be minor.

Orwell's awareness of the atrocious Communist behavior might be expected to make him more critical of the political strategy the Communists had been preaching, but people can conceivably pursue a basically sound strategy by brutal and dishonest methods. And further, Orwell admired and agreed with Franz Borkenau's analysis of the Spanish events (Borkenau 2000), yet the former Communist Borkenau drew different political conclusions, becoming skeptical about the prospects for any revolution.

In asserting that the POUM position had been vindicated, Orwell might merely have meant that the Communists had managed to get control over the Republic and still the war continued to go badly for the Republic. However this would have been open to the objection that the war was lost anyway, and in any case, at the time when Orwell began to say that the POUM had been vindicated, he was also predicting that the likely outcome of the war would be a Nationalist-Republican compromise settlement.

Much of what the Communists were saying—that a conventional army fights better than disunited militias, that foreign support and domestic middle-class support would diminish if the Republic were seen as revolutionary—was correct. It's not clear whether Orwell later came to accept this. In the years after 1939, there is a tendency in Orwell's remarks about Spain for his account to move closer to what had been the standard Popular Front line. Around 1942 he wrote that "The Trotskyist

7 See Thomas 2001, 561–62. Moroccan nationalism was weak at the time.

thesis that the war could have been won if the revolution had not been sabotaged was probably false" (XIII, 507). One possible explanation for this surprising statement is that Orwell, who always adapted his message to his audience and to the circumstances, was motivated immediately after the entry of the Soviet Union into the war, to make statements stressing his common ground with the Communists. But if we give this single, isolated utterance full weight, it registers a key step in Orwell's abandonment of the revolutionary Left position.

However, the Spanish Communists were not *simply* counter-revolutionary, as Orwell appeared to believe. Although they openly proclaimed that the war was a defense of bourgeois democracy, they really aimed to gradually convert Republican Spain, already a leftist dictatorship, into a "people's republic," a satellite dictatorship under Russian control (Radosh et al. 2001, 211–12). From the Communists' own subjective point of view, they were aiming at a kind of social revolution in Spain, to be achieved by bringing the country under the rule of Moscow, following the precedent in Mongolia. This was now the only kind of revolution the Communists understood. To a Communist, "socialist revolution" had come to mean conquest by the Soviet Union, however achieved, nothing more and nothing less. For a few months in 1938, Republican Spain was in effect ruled by the Soviet secret police, the NKVD, and thus by Joseph Stalin.

In Orwell's mind, his revolutionary leftism was fully compatible with democracy. This seems incongruous because we assume that a democrat will abide by the results of peaceful elections. In the 1930s, however, leftists imagined that the capitalists, the real controllers of states, would abolish democracy whenever it suited them. In their minds, such a view seemed to have been corroborated by their interpretation of the Spanish events of February–July 1936.

Tweedledum and Tweedledee

Orwell approvingly summarized the POUM position in these words:

> It is nonsense to talk of opposing Fascism by bourgeois "democracy." Bourgeois "democracy" is only another name

> for capitalism, and so is Fascism; to fight against Fascism on behalf of "democracy" is to fight against one form of capitalism on behalf of a second which is liable to turn into the first at any moment. The only real alternative to Fascism is workers' control. (VI, 203)

This position was then applied by Orwell, not just to Spain, but also to Britain for the next several years (except that Orwell would say "Socialism" rather than "workers' control").

On its face, there appear to be gaps in the reasoning. Who would buy the argument that it's pointless to fight cholera if you have malaria, because this is to fight against one form of ill-health on behalf of another form of ill-health? If we think of the kind of capitalism known as bourgeois democracy as preferable to the kind of capitalism known as fascism, why not take steps to have the former rather than the latter? But Orwell's wording "which is liable to turn into the first at any moment" gives us a hint of the assumptions which made this kind of argument persuasive to revolutionary leftists. Once we fill in these other assumptions of their belief system, the argument appears more natural.

According to revolutionary leftists, democracy and fascism are merely two form of capitalist government, "Tweedledum and Tweedledee" (XI, 44, 77). The capitalist class alone decides who the government shall be and what its policies shall be, whether they be democratic or fascist. (XI, 75). Capitalism in the 1930s is in its final throes and cannot possibly survive much longer. Fascist dictatorship is the inevitable recourse of the capitalist class faced with the terminal crisis of capitalism.[8] Because of this, democracy is not going to survive at all, unless capitalism is abolished, so trying to preserve democracy within capitalism is a hopeless waste of effort (XI, 168). Come what may, the revolutionary Left at this time does not see any future for "bourgeois democracy."

So far, none of this implies that the workers should not ally with democratically-minded capitalists to defend democracy. However, revolutionary leftists would go on to contend that any alliance between

8 Brockway 1938, 33.

workers and capitalists plays into the hands of the capitalists. Orwell is insistent upon this point (VI, 198; XI, 124). There's something inherently socialist about the working class: under the right circumstances they can become revolutionary and overthrow capitalism (XI, 43; XIII, 506), but they are easily sidetracked if they start to compromise with the capitalists.

If these propositions are accepted, then the Tweedledum and Tweedledee argument seems fairly plausible. This still leaves it a bit of a mystery why alliance or compromise with the capitalists is so fatal to the working class. Why does one side of the alliance always benefit? Why doesn't the working class sometimes use these alliances to its own benefit at the expense of the capitalists? After all, the workers are the majority of the population, and therefore in a democracy they can always control the government if they seriously want to.

Looking back from eighty years later, it has become harder to entertain these assumptions of the revolutionary Left. Since capitalism did not expire, its disease could not have been terminal, and fascism could not have been the only recourse of the capitalists in capitalism's death agony. So there must be a different explanation for the existence of fascism. The claim that the capitalists control democratic governments and that capitalists put fascism in power are both mistaken. Numerous interest groups, in shifting alliances, lobby and maneuver to achieve their ends in a democracy. Capitalists (people who receive a return on their savings) are not united in their goals or opinions. They are most likely to act together and be effective when seeking to modify legislation that directly affects their own businesses, though even here they sometimes lose skirmishes with other interest groups. Major business interests were not salient in promoting either Fascism or National Socialism. As Henry Ashby Turner demonstrated, quite contrary to leftist legend, "big business" funded, not National Socialism, but its opponents.[9] What Hitler actually did with power was not what business interests wanted. Who can suppose that the big German capitalists (if they had been consulted, which they weren't) would have voted to invade Poland on 1st September 1939?

9 Turner 1985.

Tweedledum and Tweedledee were similar characters (in a traditional rhyme and then in Carroll's *Through the Looking Glass*), often assumed to be identical twins, who engaged in sham fights. The implication is that democracy is no better than fascism. On this point Orwell and many revolutionary leftists were equivocal. Orwell often suggests that "capitalist democracy" is just as bad as fascism, but occasionally implies that the former is preferable. This inconsistency is even more glaring in the case of the Spanish Republic, because here Orwell says that the Republic is worth defending against the Nationalists ("fascists"), even though Republican Spain is itself turning into a kind of fascism and (in his judgment in 1937–38) cannot lead to democracy (XI, 45, 59). So here, Orwell concedes that it can be right to defend, not just democracy against fascism, but one kind of fascism against another!

The Instinctively Revolutionary Working Class

The fundamental assumptions of the revolutionary Left are not merely false; they have a dreamlike incoherence about them, especially when it comes to the role of the working class. The working class is perceived as simultaneously almighty and impotent—powerful enough to overthrow the capitalists and create a completely new social order unlike anything ever seen on planet Earth, and yet completely powerless to dissuade the capitalists from abolishing democracy. As we read the revolutionary Left, we find that the workers are easily distracted (by capitalist stooges or by incorrect variants of socialist theory) from executing the socialist revolution, while the capitalists never make any mistakes—they never believe, for example, that fascism is required when it isn't or that it isn't required when it is. The workers are like the sentient dogs in *Up*—all that's needed to stop them making the revolution is to shout "Squirrel!" (so therefore our most vital task must be to go after those pesky folks with the habit of shouting "Squirrel!"). Tacitly, then, the workers are perceived as a great, lumbering, well-meaning beast, which naturally pines for socialist revolution but is somehow always distracted by agents of the bourgeoisie, which in terms of observables means anyone with an opinion differing from that of the one correct faction of the revolutionary Left.

Orwell often stated with uncomfortable clarity what other people thought vaguely and tacitly:

> The struggle of the working class is like the growth of a plant. The plant is blind and stupid, but it knows enough to keep pushing upwards towards the light, and it will do this in the face of endless discouragements. (XIII, 506)

Setting aside the question of whether there really is an "it"—whether millions of wage-earners constitute a single organism with a single goal—the context here is Orwell's claim that the working class is inherently antifascist and pro-socialist, because fascism aims to reduce workers' wages. In fact Italian Fascism and German National Socialism aimed to increase workers' wages and, more urgently, to eliminate unemployment. We could consider how successful they were, or how successful socialism might be, compared with conventional capitalism, but it's not self-evident that blind and stupid growth will get us closer to the right answer. And, remember, this is the selfsame Orwell who also held that socialism might very well make life almost unbearable for centuries (XII, 459).

The Revolution Runs Out of Enthusiasm

When Orwell first arrived in Barcelona, "the revolution was still in full swing":

> Practically every building of any size had been seized by the workers and was draped with red flags or with the red and black flag of the Anarchists; every wall was scrawled with the hammer and sickle and with the initials of the revolutionary parties; almost every church had been gutted and its images burnt. Churches here and there were being systematically demolished by gangs of workmen. Every shop and café had an inscription saying that it had been collectivised; even the bootblacks had been collectivised and their

> boxes painted red and black. . . . All this was queer and moving. There was much in it that I did not understand, in some ways I did not even like it, but I recognised it immediately as a state of affairs worth fighting for. (VI, 2–3)

Orwell was caught up in the excitement of these events. He later witnessed the decline of this revolutionary enthusiasm and mentioned that at the peak of enthusiasm members of the bourgeoisie had been dressing like workers but had now reverted to displaying their bourgeois lifestyles (VI, 93). But of course, there were also many workers who were privately unsmitten by the revolution, keeping their heads down for fear of their lives.

Orwell claimed that there was great freedom of expression in the Republic (XI, 333). But this impression was superficial. Anyone openly arguing against the Left would be taking their life in their hands. Orwell himself points out that it would have been quite impossible to display a monarchist flag (VI, 232–33). When he writes about free debate, Orwell has in mind free debate among various brands of socialism, a small minority of the population. No one faction of the Left had yet succeeded in physically subjugating all the other factions, and until that was accomplished, there was indeed a kind of free debate among different denominations of socialism: some expressions of ideology punctuated the violent clashes. The moment that one of these factions had won—and it was to be the most unscrupulous, well-funded, and tightly organized, the Communists—all freedom of expression ceased. This is what happened in Catalonia in June 1937. It's inherent in the logic of the situation that if a group of parties (such as the Left) decides that it will not extend liberty of expression to others (the class enemies), then one member of this group will soon move to suppress the other parties in the group, and then to suppress differences of opinion within the membership of the sole surviving party—and then, of course, to invent differences of opinion which don't even exist, as a pretext to slaughter fellow members.

The revolutionary outbreak should have been terminated and reversed, not simply because it was advisable to put a good democratic face on the anti-Franco side, in order to maximize foreign support, but also because the agrarian and industrial components of "the revolution" were inefficient: they reduced output and thus impaired military effectiveness. But more than that, the revolution was inimical to human welfare and progress. Land is best farmed and factories are best operated under conditions of private property and free competition—best not only in terms of producing the most output for consumers with the least expenditure of resources, but best also in terms of the day-to-day emotional lives of the people working on those farms or in those factories. People are happier under capitalism than they are under collectivism, as well as "merely" materially better off.[10] And, aside from the fact that violent attacks on churches and priests are not the most effective way to win over the Catholic masses for the Republic, forcibly preventing people from going to church and being ministered to by priests of their chosen denomination is an attack upon their elementary rights.

Orwell's Defense of Leftist Atrocities

Lionel Trilling quotes with approval a graduate student who responded to Orwell's account in *Homage to Catalonia* with the observation, "He was a virtuous man" (Trilling 1952, viii). Trilling himself calls Orwell's stand on Spain "a genuine moral triumph" (vii).

Homage to Catalonia is a sincere attempt to get at the truth and is (despite some minor factual mistakes), a valuable source of information. But as we saw in Chapter 1 above, Orwell accepted the necessity for a government to employ misleading propaganda, including the dissemination of outright falsehoods, as a weapon of war. Although Orwell made the remark, "I hold the outmoded opinion that in the long run it does not pay to tell lies" (XI, 114), he did not, as a matter of principle, consistently reject the use of misrepresentation for political ends.

One of the three elements of the social revolution identified by Orwell was the destruction of churches and killing of priests. Orwell never voiced regret for these atrocities or condemned the killing of priests, monks, and nuns for no other reason than that they were priests, monks, and nuns. In the course of propounding his argument that the

10 Veenhoven 2000, 276.

Communist-influenced leftist press tried to deny the fact of the social revolution, Orwell states:

> Some of the foreign anti-Fascist papers even descended to the pitiful lie of pretending that churches were only attacked when they were used as Fascist fortresses. Actually churches were pillaged everywhere and as a matter of course, because it was perfectly well understood that the Spanish Church was part of the capitalist racket. In six months in Spain I only saw two undamaged churches, and until about July 1937 no churches were allowed to reopen and hold services, except for one or two Protestant churches in Madrid. (VI, 194; and see XI, 233–34)

Orwell here defends the Republicans against the calumny that they only attacked churches when these were used by the Nationalists. No, they attacked and pillaged churches on principle, and forcibly prevented them from holding services! If Orwell's telling the truth about the Communists was "a moral triumph," then his failure to criticize leftist violence against Catholics was a contemptible moral surrender. Orwell was doing exactly what many of his admirers believe he could never do: condoning vicious deeds because he was in the grip of a dogmatic orthodoxy.

It's unlikely that churches were attacked because they were seen as part of the capitalist racket, as very similar attacks go back in Spanish history to the early nineteenth century, when the secularizing reformers were not socialist. And anyway, the Church could hardly be part of the capitalist racket after the government had taken away all its privileges and almost all its property, and subjected it to numerous onerous restrictions.

The Conflict between Socialism and Syndicalism

In summarizing the POUM position, Orwell refers to "workers' control" but when advancing his own views he never writes of "workers' control" but only of "Socialism" (he always capitalized the word). A surprising fact about Orwell given some things we know about him is that he never advanced any even slightly unusual views about the way a socialist system would operate. Although he was surrounded in Spain by anarchism and syndicalism, he didn't write anything explaining why he rejected both of these, though reject them he certainly did. It's true that Orwell wrote, looking back on his arrival in Spain: "Had I had a complete understanding of the situation I should probably have joined the CNT militia" (XI, p. 136). However, this is easily explained: the CNT was by far the largest force on the Spanish left which was not under Communist control. All the displays of revolutionary fervor which appealed to Orwell's romantic conception of proletarian revolution would have involved CNT members. Even the Spanish working-class members of the POUM would also have been CNT members. When Orwell titled his book *Homage to Catalonia* what he meant was *Homage to the Revolutionary CNT Workers*, a continental turn of phrase which might not have helped sales in the English-speaking world but would have done wonders for sales among the Latins.

In the Spanish context Orwell encountered much talk of workers' control, but he never addressed the inherent tension between workers' control and socialism. When the workers seize the factories, the old factory owners are dispossessed and the workers themselves become the effective owners. However, for any movement in the direction of socialism, the new possessors, the workers, must in turn be dispossessed by the state. The factories can't be allowed to operate according to the wishes of the people who work in them; they must be subordinated to central direction by people who do not work in them—that is socialism. (The workers may be given the role of managers, but this doesn't make them the owners.) This ineluctable opposition between socialism and worker's control must have dawned on Orwell. A few brief comments in passing give a hint of something more involved going on in Orwell's mind, though unfortunately (from our point of view) never spelled out.

Orwell states that "The Communist's emphasis is always on centralism and efficiency, the Anarchists on liberty and equality" (VI, 204). In describing the process by which the Republican government thwarted the revolution he says that "the general movement was away from working class control, leading on to State capitalism or, possibly, towards the reintroduction of private capitalism" (VI, 219). Someone knowing only a few things about Orwell and reading remarks like these might easily suppose that he would reject the conception of socialism as entailing state monopoly ownership of industry, but this surmise is flatly contradicted by nearly everything that Orwell wrote referring to the organization of a socialist society. Orwell often stated what he meant by socialism, and had many opportunities to qualify it. In the 1930s he thought that socialism might somehow emerge from a revolutionary uprising; by 1945 he thought that socialism could come from a Labour government carrying out a lot of nationalization, but all the time he conceived of collectivism as essential to socialism, and collectivism as consisting in state ownership, not workers' control, of industry.

Spain in the Rearview Mirror

In his later references to the Spanish conflict, during World War II, Orwell asserted that the "fascists" had won in Spain because of the aid they received from outside the country. "The Fascists won because they were the stronger; they had modern arms and the others hadn't" (XIII, 507). Britain's policy had been suicidal, because "fascist" Spain would naturally support Nazi Germany. After 1939 Orwell said things which he thought would favor the Allied cause, regardless of their strict accuracy, and perhaps he believed that these simple and misleading formulas about Spain could be justified as war propaganda.

The Nationalist victory can't be adequately explained purely by German and Italian support. Italy put a lot of troops into Spain, but their combat performance verged on the embarrassing. Both sides in the civil war received foreign support, nearly all of which they had to pay for (though most writers, somewhat misleadingly, refer to it all as "aid"). From the standpoint of objective military analysis, this was a war with no brilliant generalship on either side, though somewhat more imagination with the Nationalists. The Republicans lost battles they might have had, purely in terms of men and ordnance, good chances of winning. For the first two years of the war, the Republic had more men, more tanks, and more planes than the Nationalists, the planes piloted at first by Russians, and later by Spaniards trained in Soviet Armenia.[11] Franco's victories in the North during 1936–1937 were all victories against superior numbers. The Republic controlled all the areas of heavy industry, so with a modicum of efficiency and resolute leadership, they could have organized their own production of weapons, but this didn't happen because of the squabbling of the leftist groups and the disastrous impact on the factories of revolutionary collectivization. The fundamental reason for ultimate Nationalist victory was the Nationalists' unity and single-minded sense of purpose, contrasted with the Republicans' division and disarray. Any budding General Bonaparte on the Republican side could only have remained mute and inglorious because of the bickering and mutual interference of contending factions in the Republican leadership.

It's a mistake to think that "fascist" nations are natural allies. For example, Britain went to war against Germany because of the guarantee to Poland, a nation which was at that time closer to the "fascist" stereotype than Nationalist Spain. And Mussolini's decision to go with Hitler in World War II was something that briefly hung in the balance in his mind. It's not clear that British support for the Republic would have favored British interests, for on the one hand, British support for a Republic which still lost (a distinct possibility) would have tended to put Spain in Hitler's camp, while if British support had been decisive, the Spanish Republic might yet have become a Soviet satellite, which would therefore have tilted to the German side from September 1939 to June 1941.

Orwell was in Spain for six months, and his experience was of a small, highly unrepresentative portion of the civil war. His knowledge of Spain and of the war itself was not extensive. His judgments on Spanish matters are often way off—for instance his predictions, quite late in the war, that it would be ended by a compromise between Nationalists and Republicans.

Yet eighty years later, Orwell's account of his experiences sells several hundred copies a week in the US alone and a public square in Barcelona has been named the Plaza George Orwell. Why is this? Partly because Orwell is a very good writer; he makes us live these events along

11 A summary of all the military supplies from abroad to the two sides in Spain is given in Thomas 2001, 934–944.

with him, in a way that no other writer on Spain was able to do. Partly because he had unusual insights into one particular aspect: the civil war within the Left and the Moscow-directed suppression of the Left. Partly because of the bigger issues he raises, such as the concoction of false history and the possibility that objective truth about historical events might actually vanish from the world. And mostly because so many people, having read *Animal Farm* and *Nineteen Eighty-Four*, want to read other things by this absorbing and entertaining writer.

Among the many issues Orwell did not pursue, and never began to understand, is the question of what led to the attempted military coup of July 1936 that precipitated the civil war. In a single brief mention of this period, Orwell wrote that the Popular Front government

> was not by any means under the control of extremists. It did not precipitate a crisis by violence towards its political opponents; on the contrary, it actually weakened itself by its moderation. (XI, 332)

These statements are not accurate. The Popular Front government made life increasingly unsafe for dissenters and constituted from the get-go an incipient "fascism of the Left."

The numerous leftist attacks upon democracy, rule of law, and civil liberties frightened the Right and Center into support or acquiescence for the attempted military coup.[12]

The governments which ruled Spain most of the time from 1931 until 1936 were coalitions nominally led by Republicans who were not themselves socialists. These Republicans were ardent reformists and enthusiastic anti-Catholics. They implemented a state-run education system and restricted the activities of the Church, effectively prohibiting priests from any teaching. They prided themselves on not adhering to merely "negative secularism," the liberal principle according to which the Church would be treated as a voluntary association without privileges or disabilities. Violent attacks on the Church by leftists were not

12 My main sources for the next few paragraphs are Payne 2006 and Payne 2012.

punished: law enforcement was applied to Catholics and the right, while the Socialists, responsible for most violence, walked free (though, as well as cracking down on the Right, the government would sometimes crack down on CNT members and others to the left of the Socialist Party). There were numerous burnings and sackings of church property, often involving the destruction of libraries and works of art, which went uninvestigated and unprosecuted.

A program was set up for expropriating land and giving it to the landless poor. In the south, there were big landowners and many landless laborers, but in other parts of Spain land was held by small or medium proprietors, who were targets rather than beneficiaries of land redistribution. So in these regions most rural people had no incentive to support the Republic. Fifty percent of Spain's population was rural.

The 1933 elections had been won by the Right, the CEDA party winning the most votes, though as all parties had received minorities of the vote, CEDA was kept out of actual government by the President, who had extraordinary powers under the constitution. The CEDA, supported by many monarchists and other opponents of the Republic, followed a policy of strict conformity with the law. With this victory of the Right, the most extreme measures against the Church were halted for a while; for example, Catholic schools were allowed to continue in existence.

Socialist violence escalated. In 1934 there was a Bolshevik-style insurrection, which sputtered out in most places, with some killings, but led to protracted violence in Asturias, the army being called in to suppress the insurgents.

In February 1936 the Popular Front won the election, though with a minority of the popular vote. The nominal leader of the Popular Front was the Republican Manuel Azaña, but he consistently pursued a policy of giving the Socialist minority everything they wanted, including effective immunity from any consequences of the increasingly frequent violent outrages by their supporters. The revolutionary Socialist tail wagged the Republican dog. The Socialists were led by Largo Caballero, known as 'the Spanish Lenin' and committed to a Bolshevik-style revolution. Having come to power, the Popular Front government retrospectively altered the election results by disqualifying some rightwing victories and giving these seats to the Left. The leftist parliamentary majority was thus made big enough for any measures to get automatic approval from the parliament. The effect was that the Socialists, who had received less than twenty percent of the popular vote in February, were getting their way in all important aspects of the running of the country.

A regular pattern was established: Socialist gangs would commit a violent outrage and the government would arrest rightists, that is, the victims, or associates of the victims, not the perpetrators. This pattern, in which the illegal actions of violent gangs of one political orientation are encouraged by the ruling group, also characterized the early phase of the rules of Fascism and National Socialism. The Republic was several times compared to Fascism (at least once by none other than Mussolini himself[13]). The government assumed arbitrary censorship powers. Any newspaper that criticized the government or disclosed embarrassing information might be shut down.

From the election until the outbreak of the civil war, there were daily murders and other political acts of violence, mostly by adherents of the Socialist Party. Leftist militants were appointed as special police deputies, effectively making the police into instruments of the violent leftist criminals. The distinction between police and criminal terrorists became blurred, as groups made up of police and non-police leftists carried out violent acts against rightists. The insurrectionists of 1934, including those who had committed murder, were unconditionally pardoned, let out of jail, and given their old jobs back, while members of the military who had followed the government's orders in suppressing the insurrection were prosecuted.

In all this time there were growing rumors of a military coup, but the military were mostly apolitical and quite divided in their political affinities. As politically-motivated violence escalated, preparations for a military takeover were discussed by a few officers. That a military coup would be attempted was almost taken for granted by nearly everyone, but the Left had no doubt the coup would be easily quashed, as General Sanjurjo's attempt had been in August 1932. The crucial difference was that now democracy had been abolished in Spain and the majority of the population were effectively powerless against the dictatorship of the Left.

13 Payne 2006, 24–25, 39.

Even this would probably have been passively accepted for quite some time, but for the daily acts of violence against non-leftists of all shades. Political killings and other attacks were overwhelmingly done by the Left, and those few by the right were mostly by the new and tiny Falange Española, which began to grow in direct response to the leftist violence. Unlike the leftist attacks, attacks by the Falange were of course prosecuted vigorously by the regime.

In July Falangists killed the socialist assault guard José Castillo. Upset by this, a group of leftist police and leftist civilians decided to kill the two most prominent parliamentary rightists but since one of these (Gil Robles) happened to be out of Madrid at the time, they settled on the other one, the leading monarchist politician, José Calvo Sotelo. Calvo Sotelo was not associated with the Falange or with any acts of violence or illegal behavior. Though not himself a believer in democracy, he was, like most of the Right, committed to strict adherence to the law. He was taken into custody by the now-typical mixed group of police and leftist militants, who put a couple of bullets in his head and left his body anonymously at the morgue.

This event is similar to the murder of Matteotti by Italian Fascists in 1924, which marks the transition to Fascist dictatorship. The chief difference between the two cases is that the Matteotti murder was a crisis for Fascism and a serious threat to Mussolini's continued premiership, with many resignations from the Fascist party—Mussolini's position was only rescued by the solid backing of the king—while the Republican government of Spain took the murder of Calvo Sotelo in its stride. The government had not ordered the killing, but again followed its standard procedure of failing to arrest or investigate the perpetrators, instead investigating associates of the victim. Though the actual identities of the killers were an open secret, they were not apprehended, and censorship was imposed to prevent public discussion of the crime. Following Calvo Sotelo's public funeral, police fired on mourners known to be unarmed (they had been searched), killing several. Police officers who voiced objections to this found themselves under arrest.

In the minds of the Spanish Right in mid-1936, disposed to go along with constitutional democracy as long as they themselves got a fair shake, the murder of Calvo Sotelo and the government's response were perceived as signs that their window for legal action had closed: the Bolshevik-minded Socialists, it appeared, were physically attacking the Right, including murder of anyone outspoken enough to criticize. The Spanish Right felt itself under increasing physical attack—and "the Right" now tended to encompass anyone who wanted a constitutional monarchy, anyone who favored elementary civil liberties for Catholics, and anyone who advocated consistent enforcement of the law against kidnapping, assault, and murder. The conspiring generals had hesitated and would have continued to hesitate but for the murder of Calvo Sotelo. Now they knew that more than half the population would acquiesce to a coup, and that if they didn't act soon, someone else would. Up to this point, Franco had repeatedly refused invitations to join preparations for a coup, but now he agreed.

It would be wrong to suppose that the murder of Calvo Sotelo was an unfortunate mishap. The opinion was widely held on the Left that a rightwing coup was highly likely, that it should be actively provoked, that it would be easily suppressed, and that this suppression would provide the opportunity for the Left to proclaim the dictatorship of the proletariat, outlawing all non-Left organizations (that is, the organizations which had invariably received the votes of more than half the electorate).

The point of these admittedly selective observations is not that the Left was solely responsible for the civil war. The Right, like the Left, contained a substantial segment who had no desire for democracy or equality before the law (though Payne's account makes clear that actual violence by the Right in the period up to July 1936 was a tiny fraction of violence by the Left). The point is that Orwell's account is exactly wrong: the Popular Front government was indeed under the control of extremists and did indeed precipitate a crisis by abolishing democracy and directing violence against its political opponents—though by enabling and protecting unofficial violence rather than by directly ordering official violence. When Orwell observed in 1937–38 that the Republic was turning into a kind of fascism (VI, 133), he did not realize that this had been the Republic's fixed course since February 1936.

Looking back on the Spanish Civil war from eighty years later, the most striking fact is the comprehensive unrealism and irrelevance of much leftwing thinking, including Orwell's. The Spanish Civil War occurred in large part because a minority, inspired by ideological passion, tried to violently impose a socialist revolution on a population that mostly didn't want it. The appalling outcome was also something that the population mostly didn't want—a brutal and oppressive dictatorship that lasted thirty-six years. The atrocities committed by the Franco regime between 1939 and 1949—exterminating all those who had any connection with the Republic—were horrendous, but, sadly, there's no reason to suppose that a victory for the Left would have turned out any better.

The victorious Nationalists were no more favorable to the free market than the Republic had been. For most of the civil war, the Nationalists pragmatically and flexibly ensured that everyone on their side had enough to eat. But near the end of the civil war and after it, to deal with problems of food supply, the Franco regime introduced price controls, very similar to those that had been introduced earlier by the Republic, and with the same results: shortages, hunger, and corruption. The Franco regime pursued a crippling policy of economic autarchy. Later, in a peculiar historical quirk, government policy began to be influenced by the religious order Opus Dei, one of whose oddities (as it seemed back then) was its espousal of free-market economic policy. The Spanish economy was liberalized. Spain soon enjoyed the highest rate of growth in Europe and was thus rapidly converted into an affluent, middle-class culture like other Western European countries. Such a culture, what we now call a latte culture, no doubt has its blemishes, but it does not seem to be conducive to political dictatorship.

On Franco's death in 1975, Juan Carlos de Borbón became king, and quickly took steps to move to a democratic constitutional monarchy. For a few years it seemed that all the old ghosts were still active, but it gradually became clear that Spain and the world had changed so much that none of the major ideologies of 1936 retained much potency. The Socialist Party won the election of 1982. It had evolved into a party whose membership accepted capitalism, democracy, the monarchy—and, yes, even freedom of worship for Catholics. This historical outcome would have seemed beyond incredible to the ingenious gentleman George Orwell.

8
The Class Warrior

. . . either we introduce Socialism, or we lose the war.
—George Orwell, August 1942 (XIII, 522)

In the early morning hours of 22nd August 1939, a man lies asleep in an English village. He is tall, good-looking, with big hands, big feet, and a thin mustache of the Douglas Fairbanks Jr. type. He is thirty-six years old but looks somewhat older. By his side in the bed lies a comely young woman, his wife. A close inspection of his eyelids with a flashlight would have shown a rapid flickering. This man is having a dream.

All we know about the actual storyline of that dream is that, in the dream, the long-expected and long-dreaded war with Germany had begun. It was to begin in reality only twelve days later. What we do know, however, is that this dream marks the dreamer's conversion—literally overnight—from one view of the impending war to a radically different view. In fact, the dreamer, George Orwell, was to devote a significant amount of his time and energy for the next six years to criticizing and denouncing precisely the view of the war he had maintained for the past twenty-six months, and during those twenty-six months he had aggressively criticized and denounced almost precisely the view of the war he would himself come to hold on August 22nd 1939.

In the period from June 1937 until August 22nd 1939, Orwell was strongly opposed to Britain's looming war with Germany. He repeatedly explained his views on this war with great precision and clarity.[1] Despite

1 See especially XI, 80–81, but also numerous other places, including XI, 74–76; 153–54, 182–84, 212–13, 242–46, 313–14, 340–41, 406.

this fact, *most published commentary on Orwell's views woefully misrepresents his attitude to war at this time*. Part of the problem is that Orwell changed his attitude to the coming war in May–June 1937 and again abruptly and radically changed it on 22nd August 1939. If this isn't understood, then the reader may try to harmonize Orwell's various remarks on the war from 1936 until, say, 1945. But many of these remarks are mutually and quite bitterly contradictory.

Writers on Orwell sometimes misrepresent him simply by omitting crucial aspects, but they also sometimes fill in the gaps with their own blithe fancies. I will confine myself to a couple of rich examples. Christopher Hitchens writes:

> So hostile was Orwell to conventional patriotism, and so horrified by the cynicism and stupidity of the Conservatives in the face of fascism, that he fell for some time into the belief that "Britain," as such or as so defined, wasn't worth fighting for. (Hitchens 2002, 127)

Here we see the phenomenon so common among admirers of Orwell of attributing to Orwell beliefs which have nothing to do with what he actually wrote. The principle seems to be "Orwell in his prose persona is such a congenial fellow that he must agree with me on just about everything, and if he doesn't agree with me on something, he must have been overcome by a powerful and essentially laudable emotion." So Orwell "fell," rather than reasoned his way, into his regrettable anti-war position. Because Orwell's anti-war standpoint up to August 1939 is an opinion that Hitchens disagrees with, it is implicitly attributed to Orwell's emotional reactions, and these reactions are presented sympathetically. We're invited to admire Orwell's motives and ignore his political position and the arguments he gave for it. But the motives are Hitchens's pure invention.

We would hardly guess from what Hitchens says here that Orwell's anti-war position was well thought-out and well-elaborated, that Orwell was opposed to British re-armament, and that Orwell explicitly identified the Left as the most culpable war-mongers ("The so-called left-wingers are now the jingoes."). Prior to August 22nd 1939, aside from the dwindling number of leftist pacifists, the main "peace" party was Sir Oswald Mosley's Blackshirts (the British Union of Fascists); Orwell wrote in January 1939, "I don't know whether Mosley will have the sense and guts to stick out against war with Germany, . . ." (XI, 341). As he wrote this, Orwell was planning to help form an illegal underground organization to sabotage the coming anti-fascist war. What "horrified" Orwell at this time was not any Conservative deficiency of anti-fascist zeal, but, as he described it, hearing "people tirading against Hitler" in anticipation of a war against Germany (XI, 321).

Here's a second example of misunderstanding, this time from historian Richard Overy. Overy maintains that Orwell's Spanish experience influenced him to abandon pacifism. Seeing the need to fight fascism in Spain, he abandoned his "absolute pacifism" and accepted the need to fight, thus preparing the way for his support for the British war against Germany.[2] This story sounds plausible but is quite false. It probably does roughly apply to many leftists at the time (such as, perhaps, Hubert Nicholson, Ellen Wilkinson, and Storm Jameson) but certainly not to Orwell. Orwell's "pacifist" position was continually reiterated from mid-1937 to mid-1939, that is, in the period of more than two years *after* he had returned from Spain. This was Orwell at his most "pacifist," though he was never at any time an "absolute pacifist," as Overy claims. Strange though it may seem at first blush, Orwell's Spanish experience had exactly the opposite effect to that alleged by Overy: the lessons Orwell took home from Barcelona made him a militant opponent of Britain's coming war with Germany.

Throughout this period, Orwell consistently held that it is right to kill capitalists, fascists, and priests in a domestic struggle such as a civil war or insurrection, but wrong to support one "imperialist" nation against another (for example Britain against Germany) in any war, even an anti-fascist war. This is a traditional leftist position—one might almost say *the* traditional leftist position, or at least the traditional position of the narrow Left. Orwell in this period saw no tension between fighting fascists in Spain and refusing to fight fascists by backing British war readiness against Germany. In his mind, there was no contradiction here

2 Overy 2009, 337.

(though years later, after he had abandoned this position, he would suggest that there had been a contradiction in it).[3]

Pacifism and the British Left

When Neville Chamberlain declared war on Germany on 3rd September 1939, he was the head of a National government, a mainly Conservative coalition which had ruled Britain for eight years. At this time the Labour Party was in opposition, and agreed with the Conservatives in support of the war. The Labour Party favored Churchill over Chamberlain to lead the country, even though Churchill was a long-time demon to the Left, in the belief that Churchill would more effectively prosecute the war. To employ an idiom which would not enter the English language until three years later, the Labour Party was more gung ho about the war than the government which had declared it.

Yet in September 1939 the Labour Party's readiness for war was a very recent turn. A few years earlier, the Party could fairly be characterized as predominantly pacifist, as long as we use the term "pacifism" in the loose way that it was most frequently employed at the time.

In World War I the narrow Left, meaning mainly the ILP, the Social Democratic Federation, and the British Socialist Party (the Communist Party did not yet exist and the Labour Party was still a federation with no direct membership), was anti-war, while the Labour Party in Parliament supported the war, though sometimes critically. Ramsay Macdonald, one of the two chief creators of the Labour Party, resigned from the Party leadership because of its support for the war (the other co-creator, Keir Hardie, who died in September 1915, criticized the war as a matter

3 In my review of Hitchens's book on Orwell (Steele 2003), I assumed, probably wrongly, that Orwell had been anti-war even before he went to Spain. We can't refute this assumption by direct evidence. Bearing in mind that Orwell was much less of a "political person" before 1936, and doesn't mention foreign policy per se in *Wigan Pier*, we don't have any comments by him on his favored foreign policy prior to 1937. However, since the Orwell of *Wigan Pier* is such an ordinary Popular Frontist, it now seems to me more likely that at that time he would have readily supported an "anti-fascist" war.

of mistaken national policy, though he also took the position that when the country was at war, the war had to be supported). After World War I the general assumption that it had been a good war was not at first widely challenged. But in the late 1920s and early 1930s, the view that the war had been unnecessary and wrong, formerly confined to a fairly small group of dissenting intellectuals, became much more widely held. As a result a broad range of Labour Party people who had supported the war came to agree in retrospect with the ILP. And the many Labourites who thought like this vowed: We must never permit ourselves to be fooled again; we must resolutely oppose any future wars among capitalist powers, no matter what the pretext.

The anti-war conviction really took hold after about 1928, with the publication of novels like Remarque's *All Quiet on the Western Front* (1929), Allington's *Death of a Hero* (1929), and Sassoon's *Memoirs of a Fox-Hunting Man* (1928), R. C. Sheriff's enormously successful play, *Journey's End* (1928), and Robert Graves's memoir, *Goodbye to All That* (1929). This swing in opinion sustained the continual high sales of Norman Angell's earlier *The Great Illusion* (1909), which was widely misinterpreted as implying support for a "pacifist" policy under all circumstances (what Angell actually argued was that modern wars could not pay, in the sense of being financially profitable for any of the warring parties). The term "pacifism" was employed loosely, to cover not only literal pacifists, who were opposed on principle to military force, but also many who were not literal pacifists, but were deeply concerned to avoid another major war. There was support for the League of Nations as an international deterrent to war, and there was support for general disarmament. There were substantial organizations, War Resisters' International and the Peace Pledge Union, in which individuals personally pledged themselves to refuse to participate in any future wars.

In the Labour Party, the high tide of anti-war sentiment was marked by the short-lived leadership (1932–35) of the charismatic socialist leader and outspoken pacifist George Lansbury (grandfather of the actress Angela Lansbury). With the growing military might of Nazi Germany, the National government embarked on a program of re-armament, which began in 1934 and was several times accelerated, as the perception of a German menace grew. This re-armament was opposed at every step by the Labour Party in Parliament. Although much of the opposition to re-armament was cast in terms of the way the re-armament was to be paid for, by government borrowing, anyone wholeheartedly behind re-armament would obviously have viewed this as a minor issue.

At this time there was a widespread view that wars were caused by preparation for war, as it seemed that the Great War had been. But there was also the view that wars ought to be prevented by collective security, by the League of Nations (founded in 1919) taking action, if necessary military action, against aggressors. It seemed natural to many people to oppose British re-armament and at the same to hope for the League to curb aggression. What they did not clearly see was that the League stopping aggression could only mean Britain taking military action against aggressors. The League had no troops of its own: its military power was only the military forces of the member states. The League of Nations was tested by two incidents of aggression: Japan's attack on China, and Italy's invasion of Abyssinia. In both cases, the League failed to do anything serious to oppose these aggressive actions, and the hopes that had been placed in the League as a guarantor of peace evaporated.

Many Labour Party members thought that a Labour foreign policy would be different in principle from a Conservative foreign policy, because it would resolve international disputes by law rather than by the assertion of national interest. This reasoning drove Labour Party leaders into a difficult position: they would favor re-armament by a Labour government to deter aggression, but they could not believe that a Conservative or National government would follow the same principles. As the heavily Conservative 1930s wore on, this took a more specific form in some leftwing circles: the fear—groundless—was that while the National Government was re-arming on the pretext of countering Germany, it might then go to war against Soviet Russia, perhaps in alliance with Germany. The upshot was that in the period 1934–1937, the Conservative-dominated National government, *always opposed by the Labour Party*, was rapidly building up armaments, to counter the German threat. As A. J. P. Taylor later made himself unpopular for pointing out, British re-armament was more rapid than German re-armament. The thinking of the "appeasers" was, predominantly, that if war could be postponed until 1941, Britain would by then be fully equipped to match Germany.

As it turned out, the Battle of Britain was fought by the RAF in August–October 1940, but had been won by the Chamberlain government in November 1938 (with the decision to accelerate re-armament, including increased production of the Spitfire).

As Germany recovered most of its lost territory and still seemed unsated, pacifist sentiment waned, and a few determined Labour rightwingers (led by Hugh Dalton, Ernest Bevin, and Walter Citrine) waged a determined struggle to persuade the Party to accept the need for war readiness. During the Spanish Civil war, the Labour Party objected to the National government's embargo on arms exports to the Spanish Republic, and trumpeted the slogan "Arms for Spain!" Dalton forcefully made the obvious point that voters found it incongruous for the Party to be demanding arms for Spain while obstructing arms for Britain. In 1937, the Labour Party, which had voted against the government's arms estimates for the past three years, this time voted to *abstain*. Although Labour was still not yet ready to vote *in favor* of re-armament against the Nazi danger, everyone recognized that this was a symbolic step in that direction.

The Class-War Anti-War Position

During this period when the Labour Party was shaking off its "pacifism" and getting ready for the likelihood of war, Orwell maintained a consistent, unswerving, and well-articulated position of opposition to the coming war. Within the ranks of those whom the press and other commentators called "pacifists," there were in fact various different motivations. One of these, embraced by Orwell and the revolutionary Left, I will call the "class-war anti-war" position. Its guiding principle was "The working class has no country." Its proponents believed that all wars between nation-states are "imperialist" conflicts between rival groups of capitalists. All modern war is caused by commercial rivalry, "nations" are nothing but groups of capitalists, and all that is at stake in war is the financial interests of these rival groups of capitalists.

Orwell at this time opposed the coming "anti-fascist war" on the grounds that it was an imperialist war between rival capitalist interests. He was not a literal pacifist: he had nothing against bloodshed, as long as it was directed against capitalists, fascists, and priests by the workers and their intellectual friends like himself (XI, 54). But he saw that his allies in opposing the war included the literal pacifists, and so he began to defend them. And he was not averse, on occasion, to describing his own position as "pacifism," though not usually in writings intended to be made public.[4]

This class-war anti-war position reflected what the POUM had been saying in Spain. But Orwell would certainly have come across this position long before he went to Spain. It was the view held by the most committed socialist intellectuals before World War I. It was quite close to the view maintained by the Communist Party in the years leading up to 1934. It was the view of the revolutionary anti-Stalinist Left, including the POUM and the ILP. Orwell joined the ILP in June 1938, though he was familiar with it earlier, in the period from late 1934 to early 1936 when he worked in a bookshop owned by two ILP members and had numerous discussions with ILP members and others about socialism. Orwell must also certainly have heard the class-war anti-war view preached by the Socialist Party of Great Britain (SPGB) in Hyde Park and elsewhere. The ILP leader James Maxton was to remain a sitting MP for the duration of World War II. Maxton and other ILP members maintained that they would not support the "imperialist" British war against Germany, but if the Germans invaded Britain, would favor a workers' uprising against the German occupiers.

Although Orwell argues for the class-war anti-war position with vigor and often with fresh turns of phrase, the fundamental position was not in the least distinctive to him. It was a standard position of the revolutionary anti-Stalinist Left. This is clearly illustrated in the "Manifesto: If War Comes, We Shall Resist," published at the time of the Munich conference in September 1938. This declaration appeared in the ILP journal, signed by 149 people of note, including Orwell, several other prominent writers, and five leftwing MPs. It blamed the Czechoslovak crisis on capitalist imperialism, especially British imperialism, stated that a war would lead to the imposition of "totalitarian regimes" in the

4 In a letter to his agent, Orwell says of *Coming Up for Air*, "its general tendency is pacifist" (XI, 352–53).

democratic countries, and concluded with a veiled indication that the way to combat the war was by a revolutionary uprising (XI, 212–13). In the leftist terminology of the time, the term "imperialist war" does not necessarily imply that the war is primarily about colonies. It simply means that the war should not be supported by the working class (translation: by leftist middle-class intellectuals identifying with the working class) because it is at root a war over the financial interests of different groups of capitalists.

Looking at the rise of leftwing pacifism in the early 1930s, it's sometimes hard to be sure who was a literal pacifist and who was a class-war anti-war proponent, and one could conceivably be both.[5] Fenner Brockway's writings and speeches, for example, often sound like class war, but there is an element of pure pacifism in his thinking, though he eventually abandoned it to support the war against Hitler's Germany.

In August 1937 Orwell reviewed a book by a retired general, advocating pacifism. (XI, 74–76). He naturally used it to explain his own position. There are, writes Orwell, two facts "which should be made the centre of all anti-war agitation":

> 1. That war against a foreign country only happens when the moneyed classes think they are going to profit from it.
>
> 2. That every war when it comes, or before it comes, is represented not as a war but as an act of self-defence against a homicidal maniac ("militarist" Germany in 1914, "Fascist" Germany this year or the year after). (XI, 75)

He also touches on the question of revolutionary violence:

> The test for any pacifist is, does he differentiate between foreign war and civil war? If he does not, he is simply saying in

5 Also, to be perceived as possibly a pure pacifist was safer. The authorities were very obliging with conscientious objectors who said they would never fight in any war, much less so with anyone who said he was not opposed to fighting in wars on principle but was opposed to *this* war.

> effect that violence may be used by the rich against the poor but not by the poor against the rich. (75)

Orwell's argument here is shaky, and even perhaps deliberately muddied, for he does not want his readers thinking about whether he is really a pacifist or not. But what's clear is that he regards it as important to differentiate between foreign war and civil war, in other words to support one side in a civil war or revolution (as in Spain) while opposing any war by one nation against another nation (as in Britain versus Germany).

Orwell's argument at this time is that the Communists, through the Popular Front movement, are trying to get Britain, allied with the Soviet Union, into a war with Germany. But he thinks it is futile to combat fascism by defending "capitalist democracy," because fascism is just a form of capitalism. To head off the obvious argument that capitalism with democracy is better than capitalism with dictatorship, Orwell maintains 1. that the British empire is even worse than fascism (that is, worse than Nazi Germany), because of its exploitation of colored peoples in the colonies, and 2. that the commencement of war will quickly lead to the imposition of fascism within Britain itself. This war will be presented as a war against fascism, just as the First World War was presented as a war against Prussian militarism. As soon as the war starts, says Orwell, effective fascism will be imposed in Britain, probably with Communist and broad left support. Like most of the Left, Orwell perceives fascism as an enemy, as an imminent threat, and as something inherent in capitalism on its death bed, but unlike many of the Left, Orwell judges that Sir Oswald Mosley and other overt fascists are too feeble ever to get into power in Britain. He sees fascism as likely to be imposed by the existing ruling class, or (as he believes had happened inside the Spanish Republic) by Popular Front progressives led by the Communists.

Here Orwell comes to the defense of Aldous Huxley's pacifism, as presented in Huxley's 1937 book, *Ends and Means*.

> So long as they [the workers] show themselves willing to fight "in defence of democracy," or "against Fascism," or for any other flyblown slogan, the same trick will be played upon them again and again: "You can't have a rise in wages *now*,

> because we have got to prepare for war. Guns before butter!" (XI, 153)

Orwell did not get into the details of Huxley's position, and pointedly did not defend any of Huxley's specifics. Orwell didn't think at all highly of the arguments in Huxley's book. But, as always, Orwell's way of framing his political position owed a lot to tactical expediency. As Orwell says, given the clamor for war from the mainstream Left and the Communists, "Anyone who helps to put peace on the map is doing useful work" (154).

Orwell identifies Popular Frontism with war preparation, and as part of his anti-war stance, points out that the Labour Party has nothing to gain electorally by falling in with a Popular Front. Labour without a Popular Front alliance would probably get more votes than Labour in a Popular front (XI, 242–46). On this point Orwell was undoubtedly correct. The Labour Party was huge in relation to the puny CPGB, and any connection with the CP would lose some appreciable number of Labour votes. However, the Labour Party from 1931 to 1939 had no chance of winning a general election anyway. Popular support for the National government was overwhelming.

Although Popular Frontists were hawks, many in the Labour Party who had no sympathy with a Popular Front were becoming supporters of war-readiness, in response to Germany's step-by-step expansion and continuing news of brutal repression within Germany.

Orwell observed that Chamberlain was re-arming, in readiness for a war with Germany (XI, 182–84, 359). He lamented the Labour Party's "tacit acquiescence in preparation for war" (XI, 242–46), an accurate characterization of the Labour Party's posture at this time. He hoped the Labour Party would return to its "anti-militarist and anti-imperialist line."

On 4th January 1939, Orwell wrote to his friend the anarchist Herbert Read: "I believe it is vitally necessary for those of us who intend to oppose the coming war to start organising for illegal anti-war activities." (XI, 313–14). Orwell argues here that anti-war people should oppose the war openly and legally, but "we might find it extremely useful to have an underground organisation *as well*." A later letter to Read continues the same argument, and states in passing: "I don't know whether Mosley will have the sense and guts to stick out against war with Germany, . . ." (XI, 341).

Essential to class-war anti-war theory is the assumption that the sole cause of all modern wars is financial gain. Governments, whether democratic or dictatorial, always do the bidding of the capitalists, and if they go to war, it is because the capitalists (or in some versions, a segment of the capitalists, such as big business or finance) order them to do so. Nations, which are essentially regional groupings of capitalists, compete for markets, raw materials, and trade routes, and this leads to war. Most commonly, people who think this way accept something like a Hobsonian view of imperialism. Underconsumption is built in to capitalism, the workers cannot buy what they have produced, therefore there is supposed to be a desperate urgency, inherent in capitalism, about finding new markets.

The Left believed that Hitler had been put in power by big business and continued to be a puppet of big business. The truth is that the Nazi Party got very little support from big business until Hitler was in office, by which time donating to the Nazi Party had become a matter of prudence. Until this final moment, political donations from German big business went overwhelmingly to opponents of the National Socialists. Once Hitler was in power, big business was unable to tell him what to do. German big business never had any influence over the Nazi movement and did nothing to bring this movement into being or put it into power.[6]

The socialists' assumption that democratic governments merely do what capitalists tell them is also mistaken. In a democratic capitalist system, there is certainly a ruling class in the sense that those with short-run influence on government policy are drawn from a very small segment of the population. But there is not a ruling class in the Marxist sense that a single social class, the capitalists, dictate the actions of the government. Geopolitical strategy is not determined by business interests. The influence of business owners on government is mainly a matter of lobbying to modify various proposed government measures which

6 Turner 1985.

might sharply affect particular industries. Growing sensitivity to a threat from Germany in the 1930s is easily explained by actual German expansion plus the traditional diplomatic doctrine of balance of power (which held that Britain should act to prevent any one nation achieving hegemony over the Continent).

A Dream Ends a Nightmare

Orwell switched very abruptly from an anti-war to a pro-war position. As he told the tale a few months later:

> For several years the coming war was a nightmare to me, and at times I even made speeches and wrote pamphlets against it. But the night before the Russo-German pact was announced I dreamed that the war had started. It was one of those dreams which . . . do sometimes reveal to you the real state of your feelings. It taught me two things, first, that I should be simply relieved when the long-dreaded war started, secondly, that I was patriotic at heart, would not sabotage or act against my own side, would support the war, would fight in it if possible. I came downstairs to find the newspaper announcing Ribbentrop's flight to Moscow.[7]

The real-time documentary record is consistent with Orwell's account of his conversion. While there is no reason to doubt that Orwell did have this dream and that it did mark his shift in position from anti-war to pro-war, there is every reason to think this cannot be the whole story. And indeed, a bit later in the same piece, Orwell writes: "If I had to defend my reasons for supporting the war, I believe I could do so. There is no real alternative to resisting Hitler and surrendering to

7 XII, 271. Ribbentrop's flight to Moscow to sign a non-aggression treaty with the Soviet Union was reported in the British morning newspapers on 22nd August, two days before the treaty was actually signed. Most sources give the date of signing as 23rd August; in fact it was the morning of the 24th (Moorhouse 2014, 29).

him . . ." This remark involves the debatable assumption that avoiding war with Hitler while he occupied the western half of Poland would be surrendering to him, but at least it is not the same as appealing to Orwell's own patriotic sentiments.

Orwell had a fully-worked-out position before this conversion, and a different fully-worked-out position afterwards—though, as it turned out, his pro-war position after the conversion evolved in details and emphasis, whereas his earlier anti-war position remained rigidly fixed for two years and two months (except for a gradually increasing emphasis on the anti-fascist left as the main war-mongering threat).

One of Orwell's calculated stratagems as a propagandist is to appear to lay bare his soul with a slightly shocking personal confession, as in this bizarre story of the dream. The report of the dream occurs in an article, "My Country Right or Left," which appears in *Folios of New Writing* for Autumn 1940. It would have been read by leftwing intellectuals, many of a "pacifist" orientation. The main goal of the piece is to convince his readers that one can and should be both patriotically pro-war and revolutionary. The article employs the usual Orwellian devices: the intimate personal confession, the emphatic assertion of sweeping generalizations with such confidence that the reader may not stop to think about them, the use of nasty ad hominems against those who disagree with him. It displays a longstanding Orwell worry: the consideration that leftwing intellectuals may be straying too far from the sentiments of "ordinary, decent people" to have much influence with them.

Up until 22nd August, Orwell has been stoutly maintaining: 1. that Britain is morally no better (and actually somewhat worse) than National Socialist Germany; 2. that Germany, as a collectivist economy, is more efficient than Britain in every way, including military capability; 3. that "capitalist democracy" has no future because it is so inefficient; 4. that the coming war is purely an imperialist squabble among rival groups of capitalists, in which nothing other than the financial interests of a tiny fraction of the population is at stake; 5. that while democracy has its gratifying aspects, democracy and fascism are merely two alternative ways in which the capitalists may choose to rule a country; 6. that Britain is liable to turn fascist at any moment, and will certainly do so in the event of war; and 7. that it is impossible to transform the British army into a more democratic structure without destroying its efficiency.

Following his conversion to a pro-war position, Orwell still maintains that "capitalist democracy" is doomed and that Nazi Germany is necessarily more efficient. But now he holds that the political order of the British Empire is somewhat morally superior to that of the Third Reich. He does not retract his view that wars occur because of financial rivalries among groups of capitalists, but he now accepts that in practice something more is also at stake. While before the conversion, Orwell observes, correctly, that the Chamberlain government is rapidly re-arming and in other ways getting ready for war, after the conversion he asserts, falsely, that the Chamberlain government had failed to re-arm, thus demonstrating the inability of a capitalist country to fight a war against a collectivist country (XV, 294).

Orwell's switch of position is facilitated by his new theme that to support Britain in the war is to call for a socialist revolution, since only a change to a socialist regime can enable Britain to win the war. And so, Orwell now believed, to be a patriot you must be a revolutionary:

> Only revolution can save England, that has been obvious for years, but now the revolution has started, and it may proceed quite quickly if only we can keep Hitler out. Within two years, maybe a year, if only we can hang on, we shall see changes that will surprise the idiots who have no foresight. I dare say the London gutters will have to run with blood. All right, let them, if it is necessary. But when the red militias are billeted in the Ritz I shall still feel that the England I was taught to love so long ago and for such different reasons is somehow persisting. (XII, 271–72)

This was written sufficiently early that Orwell supposed that a level of free speech which would allow it to be published would not long continue to be tolerated in wartime, and therefore this might be a last chance to get the new word out: become a patriotic revolutionary, support the war and turn it into a revolution. Many people were surprised by the degree of free speech that persisted for the duration of the war—much greater than in the First World War. Although the Fascist Blackshirts were all imprisoned and their literature suppressed, and although the Communist *Daily Worker* was suppressed, the Communist-led People's Convention, campaigning actively for acceptance of Hitler's peace offers, was able to operate publicly, and conscientious objectors to military service were generally able to remain at liberty, to argue publicly for their positions, and to publish journals and pamphlets.

Orwell switched from anti-war to pro-war at the precise moment when the Communists were switching from pro-war to anti-war. For the next twenty-two months the Communist Party would be the peace party, blaming the British government for failing to take up Hitler's repeated and generous offers of a negotiated peace. Comparatively little now separated Orwell from the non-Communist former Popular Frontists whom he has been excoriating for two years. It was now, to their regret, impossible for them to be Popular Frontists. Orwell had, in effect, rejoined the dominant faction of the Left with which he had broken in June 1937. Orwell and the leaders of the mainstream Left now had an obvious common program: support the war against "fascism" (that is, against Germany), oppose all demands for a negotiated peace, denounce the Communists for their betrayal of the anti-fascist cause, and press for a socialist transformation of Britain which would (in the opinion of all of them) enable the war to be fought more effectively. This common ground is symbolized in the 1941 volume, *The Betrayal of the Left*, consisting mainly of articles written in 1940 by Gollancz, with some by Orwell, Laski, and Strachey. After Germany invaded Russia in June 1941, this common ground still remained, though once Orwell had decided for himself, around the end of 1942, that the war was safely won, he felt less inhibition than the others about publicly criticizing Britain's Soviet Russian ally.

In August 1939, the bridge from Orwell's old anti-war position to his new pro-war position was class war. Whereas he had seen class war as a reason for opposing an imperialist war, his new idea was that Britain could not win the war against Germany without a socialist revolution, so the best way to pursue the class war was in fact to support the anti-fascist war—and vice versa. Orwell obviously relates this view to the POUM position during the Spanish Civil War, that the way to defeat Franco was to push forward with the social revolution. But this idea was in the air in Britain at the beginning of the war; it was held by other pro-war leftists at the time. It usually came from people who had been Popular Front supporters up to August 1939, like Harold Laski and John Strachey, but there were also former leftwing "pacifists," converted to a pro-war position, who had begun to see the coming war as an opportunity. While still in his class-war anti-war phase, Orwell wrote a piece about the British army, countering the view that it could possibly be democratized or proletarianized, without losing its efficiency as a fighting force (XI, 404–07); this piece was published in September 1939, when Orwell had already switched to embrace the position it implicitly attacked.

Orwell did not change his view that the British regular army could not be democratized, but he saw great potential in the Home Guard. The Home Guard armed and trained male civilians to defend against any possible German incursions: either invasion or commando raids. Orwell himself joined the Home Guard and saw it as potentially revolutionary (XII, 309–311, 348–49, 362–65). With a similar perception, the Marxist writer and military specialist Tom Wintringham founded the privately-run Home Guard training school at Osterley Park in 1940. The hugely popular socialist writer and broadcaster J. B. Priestley, without favoring violent revolution, also saw the Home Guard as a force that could popularize and democratize the war and thereby British political life. In 1940 Francis Williams published *War by Revolution*, advocating essentially the same view of war and revolution as Orwell.

The radical changes never happened during the war, and if they had happened, would have been purely "bourgeois." For example, it was difficult for a soldier with a regional accent—therefore either working-class or lower-middle-class—to become a commissioned officer. Officially there was provision for recommending lower ranks for officer training but in practice those who didn't fit socially tended to be weeded out. A university education gave chances, but universities were still dominated by the public schools.[8] Despite Churchill's interest in remedying

8 One of the exceptions was Enoch Powell, a brilliant classical scholar with a lower-middle-class background and a noticeable West Midlands accent. See Shepherd 1996, 40.

class discrimination in the military, it was never remedied during the war. To be a commissioned officer, you normally had to have been to public school,[9] except in the RAF (where all pilots were officers), and in the RAF you worked hard to lose your regional accent and talk like Biggles. This class discrimination in the selection of officers did not prevail to the same extent in Germany, for example, where individuals of comparatively lowly origin could much more easily become recognized as officer material and get into officer training programs.

Class discrimination in the British military must have led to officers being of lower average quality than would have been achievable with more open promotion, but maybe the solidly upper-crust quality of the officer corps enhanced their solidarity and thus their effectiveness. At any rate, the rectification of this problem, which did not happen during World War II, would have been entirely in accord with "bourgeois" principles and would have had nothing to do with socialism or revolution. Some socialists were calling for election of officers by vote of the lower ranks, as had been practiced in some Republican units in Spain, something seen as inherently revolutionary. Orwell was skeptical about this proposal, at least in Britain at the time, because of the likely reduction of military efficiency (XI, 404–07; XVI, 52).

Immediately following his pro-war conversion, Orwell had not abandoned his view that this war was an imperialist war between rival groups of capitalists, and nor had he abandoned his view that the ruling class, supported by most of the Left (but no longer by the Communist Party, now campaigning for acceptance of Hitler's peace offers) would try to impose fascism on Britain. But now he believed that a socialist uprising in Britain might be imminent. At the same time, he had come to acknowledge that internationalism had little potential appeal to the working class, most of whom were deeply patriotic.

From the outbreak of war until the end of 1942, a period of more than three years, Orwell consistently maintained that the war could not be won without a socialist revolution, and that a socialist revolution was likely (XII, 248–49, 311, 345–48, 379–381; XIII, 302–03). There was no socialist revolution during the war (though there was a peaceful and

9 British dialect for elite private school.

constitutional "socialist revolution" at the end of the war). Nor were there even any major disturbances, riots, mutinies, or strikes which could conceivably have become the early stages of an armed uprising. The non-occurrence of a socialist revolution was not a close thing: there was never the slightest prospect of any such event. The "idiots with no foresight" had been right.

No organization with more than a handful of members would have tried to facilitate an armed uprising, except possibly the ILP. The ILP would have welcomed an uprising if there had been any real prospect of one, but was not going to take the initiative in organizing an uprising in the face of overwhelming lack of popular support for any such course. During the war, general elections were suspended and there was an electoral truce between the Conservative, Liberal, and Labour parties. There were by-elections, due to the death or resignation of MPs, and anyone (except the interned Blackshirts) was free to contest these. A strong showing in these by-elections was made by a new party calling itself Common Wealth, led by a few prominent leftists who were opposed to the electoral truce. Aside from matters of electoral tactics and moralizing rhetoric, Common Wealth supporters were very similar to supporters of the Labour Party. They supported the war and the parliamentary system, and would not have favored any unconstitutional seizure of power. Common Wealth rapidly dwindled away to nothing in 1945.

Orwell's belief in an imminent British socialist revolution strongly colors all his thinking in the early years of the war. It's difficult to imagine how he could have switched so quickly and smoothly from anti-war to pro-war without this mistaken belief, as he continued to believe that the war was fundamentally an "imperialist" conflict between rival financial interests, that the capitalist economic system was facing its imminent demise, and that Nazi Germany was highly efficient because (and to the extent that) it has become collectivist.

Looking back in January 1941 Orwell claimed there had been a potentially revolutionary "swing of opinion" early in the war, but this had failed for lack of effective leadership. He offered very little evidence for the existence of this swing of opinion, other than such data as "conversations I listened to in pubs" (XII, 345).

If we did not have better evidence, we could speculate that Orwell might have modified his position by saying that Britain would have needed a socialist revolution to win the war alone, but did not need a socialist revolution once Russia and America had been pulled into the war. But this line of argument seems never to have crossed his mind. Instead, all through 1941 and 1942, he persisted with his claim that an imminent socialist revolution was likely and was the only way to win the war. In early 1943 there is the first clear expression of doubt when he refers to "the growing suspicion that we may all have underrated the strength of capitalism and that the right may, after all, be able to win the war off its own bat without resorting to any radical change" (XIV, 292).

Only around October 1944 did Orwell acknowledge in print that "up to at any rate the end of 1942 I was grossly wrong in my analysis of the situation." This candid admission of error is rendered somewhat less touching by what he says next. "It is because, so far as I can see, everyone else was wrong too that my own mistakes are worth commenting on" (XVI, 411). The next four pages (the remainder of this article) are largely a discussion of why "everyone" has been so wrong, along with the implication that Orwell is more perceptive than all those equally erroneous others because he can now diagnose why we have "all" been so mistaken.

Orwell maintains here that he was "often right as against the bulk of the leftwing intelligentsia" (414) because they had expected defeat for Britain whereas he had not. "The majority of leftwing intellectuals, *whatever they might say in print*, were blackly defeatist in 1940 and again in 1942" (XVI, 414, italics added). This is a common device with Orwell: when it suits him he will attack people for what he believes they are really thinking, rather than for what they actually say. Orwell's anecdotal evidence for this bleak defeatism is a couple of remarks by unnamed persons. Orwell himself, during 1940–42, had not displayed much confidence in a British victory. For most of the war Orwell was spectacularly mistaken to a degree that few others were, even though, as a BBC broadcaster, he had access to intelligence of a kind unavailable to most people. In May 1942 he believed that Churchill was about to be deposed (XIII, 304).

In December 1940, Orwell made his first mention of a new theme:

> The tremendous controversies that always rage in a democratic country at war, the endless discussion of strategy by more or less ignorant people, the free expression of near-seditious opinions, are sources of strength in the long run. They see to it that the conduct of the war shall not be entirely in the hands of the experts, who are generally right on the minor points and wrong on the major ones. (XII, 306)

Orwell puts the same argument four years later. Democracy allows "the common people" to influence decision-making, and this helps to avoid the gigantic mistakes committed by experts. Referring to the German decision to invade Russia and then declare war on the US, Orwell comments: "It takes an expert to make mistakes as big as that" (XVI, 61). However these blunders were not committed by experts at all, but by Hitler, who was an enthusiastic amateur military wonk but not accredited as an expert. Hitler made several serious blunders, and virtually every one of them would have been vetoed by the generals, if the generals had had a veto. Orwell has got hold of the important point, contrary to his earlier pronouncements, that democracies are likely to avoid some of the biggest blunders committed by dictatorships,[10] but Orwell has the reason for this almost exactly wrong. Democracy allows many points of view to be heard, including those of some of the experts, while totalitarian regimes suppress dissenting voices, including those of some of the experts.

Pacifism Favors the Enemy

On several occasions during the war, Orwell attacks pacifism, which has a substantial following among literary intellectuals (XIII 39–43, 396–99). His argument is that British pacifism objectively favors Nazi

10 This argument had been made by Russell in *Power* (1938), but Orwell showed in his review of that work that he did not fully appreciate Russell's point (XI, 311).

Germany. He further claims that pacifists themselves are psychologically attracted by fascism, and that they are often inclined to be selective, urging pacifism for Britain while not recommending it to Germans or Russians. From time to time (with phrases like "the pansy left") he hints that pacifists are homosexuals and therefore cowards.

Before June 1941, the real alternative to Orwell's policy of support for the war is a negotiated peace with Germany. Orwell dismisses this possibility in occasional brief remarks without any extensive argument. In his criticisms of pacifism, he speaks of the possibility of Germany conquering Britain, when he knows perfectly well that Germany has no interest in conquering Britain except to put an end to the war which Britain has declared and insists on pursuing.

In a negotiated peace, Germany would have withdrawn from France, Belgium, the Netherlands, and Norway. The Soviet Union would withdraw from the Baltic countries. Britain would recognize an enlarged German Reich incorporating Danzig and the Polish Corridor, while most of Western Poland would become a German protectorate along the same lines as Bohemia and Moravia. By way of symbolic tokens, Germany would probably have insisted on acquiring a couple of Britain's African colonies. Pursuit of a negotiated peace would not have been a pacifist policy for Britain; it could have been combined with a prudent level of armaments rather than disarmament. Tens of millions of lives would have been saved, and the fraction of Europe under totalitarian rule would not have been hugely greater than what actually transpired after 1945.

Class War to Cold War

During the Second World War Orwell gradually became aware, much to his surprise, that Western capitalism in alliance with Soviet Russia was defeating Germany, without any drastic change in the British political system. It also became clear to him that, while there was indeed a leftward movement of British public opinion, most people remained thoroughly democratic and constitutional in their general outlook.

Orwell had been susceptible to sudden conversion from one point of view to a radically different one, but here we see a gradual shift in emphasis. For Orwell, with fascism out of the way, Communism is replacing the capitalists as the main enemy. Orwell not only coined the phrase "Cold War" but also came down on the side of the West in that Cold War. Without renouncing democratic socialism, and even while urging the new Labour government to enact more sweeping extensions of state control, Orwell, as his death approached, saw Soviet Russia as the looming totalitarian enemy.

9
The Anti-Communist

> It's funny that when I met Mounier for only about 10 minutes in 1945 I thought to myself, that man's a fellow traveller. I can smell them.
> —George Orwell, May 1948 (XIX, 328)

Orwell wrote three books, each one of which could only make the Communist movement his enemy: *Homage to Catalonia*, *Animal Farm*, and *Nineteen Eighty-Four*. *Homage to Catalonia* was at first a commercial flop. Six years and a world war later, *Animal Farm* catapulted Orwell to fame and fortune.

Animal Farm is about a victorious socialist revolution gone wrong: the animals take over the farm, the former human owners are defeated, the pigs emerge as the new bosses. The story is intended as a satire on events in Russia (XVIII, 507; XIX, 234) and closely tracks the course of the Communist regime, even down to some very precise historical details. Yet there are major departures from a strict parallel. To make a better story, several historical characters are collapsed into one, or a historical character may be broken apart into aspects of separate characters, insofar as they illustrate key tendencies. For instance, there is no specifically Lenin figure: Snowball combines Trotsky with aspects of Lenin, while Major, who mainly represents Marx, also incorporates some of Lenin.

The actual Bolshevik coup of 1917 was a minority conspiracy opposed to the wishes of the majority of the population. As Orwell put it, "What actually happened in Russia, was the seizure of power by a small body of classless professional revolutionaries, who claimed to represent the common people but were not chosen by them nor genuinely answerable to them" (XIX, 269). In *Animal Farm* nearly all the animals favor the revolution, and it is because they favor it that it occurs. The more innocent account in *Animal Farm* can be justified as compelling narrative: it is dramatically more effective to give the ill-fated revolution an immaculate birth.

The biggest discrepancy between the facts and the way the story was interpreted by readers arose from the ending, and was due to a miscalculation on storyteller Orwell's part. The final scene of the story, where the pigs have become difficult to distinguish from the humans, understandably led many readers to conclude that the point of the book is that the new regime is becoming just the same as the old. This was not Orwell's view. As an attentive reading of *Animal Farm* makes clear, and as Orwell explicitly pointed out in many other writings, the new regime is inherently worse than the old, and the pigs and humans are never reconciled (XIX, 89). Orwell did not believe that Soviet Russia would evolve into anything like the West—quite the opposite, he believed there was the terrifying likelihood that the West would be transformed into something like Soviet Russia. The animals are considerably worse off under the pigs than they had been under Farmer Jones, just as Russian workers were considerably worse off under the Communists than they had been under capitalism.

This misunderstanding of the ending was probably a happy accident for the long-term sales of the book. It left the impression that a reasonable conclusion about the Soviet Union might be that it had become just as bad as the West. For those Western intellectuals highly disposed to become pro-Soviet but deflected from this stance by one Soviet atrocity after another, the conclusion that Russia had become just like the West because it had mislaid its socialist ideals was a comfortable resting place.

Orwell and the Communists

On several occasions after 1937, Orwell asserted that he had been opposed to Communism since the early 1930s or earlier. For example in 1946 he wrote: "I have never fundamentally altered my attitude towards the Soviet regime since I first began to pay attention to it some time in the nineteen-twenties."[1] Orwell's surviving references to the Soviet regime from before *Wigan Pier* are so few and so slight that we can't directly test this account, and his later recollections are not easy to harmonize completely.[2] However, assuming that such statements are literally true, they still tend to leave a misleading impression. Readers would suppose that there had been no great change in his attitude to Communism after 1930, and that is certainly false. In 1936, as we have seen in earlier chapters, he was a Popular Frontist and fellow traveler, and after June 1937 he was what the Communists would call an "ultra-leftist," contemptuous of the Popular Front movement and of the Left Book Club. When Orwell abandoned his revolutionary leftism (in stages, from August 1939 to late in 1942), he remained decidedly more critical of Communism than he had been in 1936. He ended his life, as we shall see, a supporter of the Western side in the Cold War.

Spain marked a change in Orwell's view of Communism. Before 1937, he evinced some distaste for "the cult of Russia" and therefore for its British tool the Communist Party of Great Britain (CPGB). We don't have to disbelieve his later statements that in this early period he had already accepted the diagnosis of Bertrand Russell and many others on the Left, that Soviet Russia was an oppressive dictatorship, worse than Western capitalism—though he does not say as much in any surviving document earlier than 1937. Contemporary readers of Orwell's later statements might generally not have been aware that before 1936 Orwell had not been a socialist and therefore might have opposed the Soviet regime along with socialism in general.

After his Spanish experience Orwell saw Soviet Russia as a slave-state closely akin to Nazi Germany and the Communists as fanatical, amoral liars and murderers. He asserted that "the existing Russian regime is a mainly evil thing" (XVII, 259) and "All people who are morally sound have known since about 1931 that the Russian regime stinks" (XII, 141). He dismissed the Moscow Trials as preposterous frame-ups—though for one who wrote so often about Communism, it took him rather a while to commit himself on this point in print (XI,

1 XVIII, 443; see also XIX, 87–88.
2 See for instance XIII, 436.

158–160). The amusing passage in which Orwell shows the ridiculous nature of the Stalinist allegations by imagining what their counterpart would be if something similar had occurred in Britain was no doubt suggested by a similar but less elaborated suggestion in Muggeridge's *The Thirties*.[3] Orwell thought that any seizure of power by a conspiratorial minority, on the model of the October coup, could only lead to a similar unhappy outcome.

One long-debated question about the USSR is whether it was fundamentally driven by the usual political forces, utilizing ideology as an instrument of more or less cynical rule by a self-interested group, or whether it was inherently the creation and the vehicle of a fanatical belief system. There were signs that Orwell was veering toward the former conception, suggested by remarks like: "The more vocal kind of Communist is in effect a Russian publicity agent posing as an international socialist" (XII, 101). But his later reading of Burnham (XIX, 97) and Plamenatz (XIX, 268–69) seems to have tilted him more to acceptance of the latter conception.[4]

For all his outspoken opposition to Communism, Orwell's anti-Communism was less consistent than that of many of his fellow-socialists. Orwell at times displayed a soft spot for Communism and the Soviet Union which we don't find in the writings of other anti-Communist socialists. Orwell described the USSR as "the real dynamo of the socialist movement in this country and everywhere else" (XVI, 122). We might have discounted this remark as a token gesture to wartime pro-Soviet platitudes, put in to help get his objections to totalitarianism published, except that he later defended this assertion in a letter to Dwight Macdonald, saying that "if the USSR were conquered by some foreign country the working class everywhere would lose heart, . . . I wouldn't want to see the USSR destroyed and I think it ought to be defended if necessary" (XVI, 381). Macdonald, like Koestler and numerous other leftists, would never have made any such favorable reference to the USSR and would have been delighted to see the USSR overthrown. Orwell's

3 Muggeridge 1971, 211.

4 Kotkin 2014 seems to be the final nail in the coffin of the first interpretation.

judgment here is remarkable because he also believed that the worst repercussion of Soviet Communism was the effect it had upon the thinking of socialists in the West. Orwell may have modified his position over the next few years, in view of his later statements on the need for the West to be ready for war with the USSR.

Orwell seemed at times to give the Communists much more than the benefit of the doubt (though this could have been a tactical rhetorical ploy, being ostentatiously over-generous in assessing the motives of the people he was attacking). Even in *Homage to Catalonia*, he said he didn't believe that the Communist suppression of the POUM was part of a pre-arranged plot (VI, 223). When Stalin officially dissolved the Comintern in 1943, an empty gesture as relations between Moscow and the Communist parties did not immediately change, Orwell reacted as though this were a serious move. He even stated that he thought the CPGB was no longer being funded by Moscow, but was instead receiving donations from wealthy sympathizers (XV, 107–08)—not considering that one of the most convenient ways for the Soviet Union to channel its subsidy was precisely through well-to-do supporters.

Communists in the British Left

In 1917 the Russian Bolsheviks defended their evidently un-Marxist action in seizing power in a largely unindustrialized country by claiming that countries in more industrialized Western Europe were about to undergo socialist revolutions. As late as the beginning of 1921, the Bolsheviks, now calling themselves Communists, still held to this belief; their statements at the time are filled with wildly erroneous assumptions about imminent socialist revolutions in western countries.

The Communist International (Comintern or Third International) was founded in Moscow in March 1919, an association of Communist Parties in every country, pledged to bring about socialist revolution by following the pattern of the Bolshevik capture of power. Every member party had to adhere to the Eighteen Points (later Twenty-One Points) of the Comintern program, and had to be subservient to the International, therefore in practical effect to the Soviet government. Really there was only One Point: Do what we tell you. Most national Communist Parties were founded in 1920–21, as it took a while for those who wanted to form each party to agree on their membership and organization. When serious differences of opinion emerged among the leadership of a national party, Moscow would make sure that the wrong faction would be expelled or cowed into submission. In the case of the Communist Party of the United States of America (CPUSA), the majority of members supported Jay Lovestone, who had had the misfortune to favor Bukharin against Stalin. Lovestone and his most faithful supporters were all driven out, while others were persuaded to denounce Lovestone and extol the new Foster-Browder leadership. This had to be done in such a way that most Lovestoneites did not leave the party, or there would have been almost no party left.[5] The British CP avoided any such convulsion: Pollitt and Dutt got control, with Moscow's blessing, comparatively smoothly in the 1920s and held it until 1960, when Pollitt died.[6] However it was managed, country by country, Moscow always insisted on getting what it was paying for.

These new Communist Parties all started life in an environment of long-established socialist parties. They had to justify their existence in the context of these existing parties and they had to decide how to behave in relation to those parties. They claimed to be the revolutionary party, as opposed to the established socialist parties which would sell out to the capitalists. The Communists would co-operate with these other parties, while seeking to expose them and supplant them. As Lenin happily put it, they would support the leaders of the democratic Left the way a rope supports a hanged man. Just as the Bolsheviks had outmaneuvered and eventually killed the Mensheviks and Socialist Revolutionaries, so the Western Communists would outmaneuver and eventually kill the Social Democrats and Labourites. The working class would be the infantry, manipulated by the vanguard party, which would destabilize the system so that power could be seized by the party.

5 Chambers 1987, 247–255. See Carr 1982, 5.

6 Pollitt was the recipient of an unusual example of latitude. He refused to take back his support for the British declaration of war against Germany in September 1939, and therefore had to resign as General Secretary of the CPGB, but was permitted to resume his position after 22nd June 1941.

The CPGB was founded in 1920 (and then re-launched on a different organizational basis the following year), it started life as a tiny segment of a massive labor and socialist movement and was always to remain so. Communism played a major role in the mental world of British intellectuals in the 1930s; it always played a negligible role in British political life.

Shortly after its formation, the CPGB applied for affiliation to the Labour Party and was rejected. CP members joined the Labour Party as individuals; the Labour Party responded by expelling them and expelling any branches in which they were active. The CP continued to apply for affiliation throughout its history and the Labour Party always said no. Antipathy to the CP predominated among the Labour Party rank and file, with anti-Communist resolutions winning by big majorities at party conferences. Labour Party members had well thought out, principled reasons for their anti-Communism, but there was also simple electoral arithmetic. The Labour Party has always been above all else a vote-acquiring enterprise, and any perceived combination of Labour Party and Communist Party would at any time (except, just conceivably, 1942–43, when, however, general elections were suspended) have gotten fewer votes than the Labour Party by itself.

Communist Zigs and Zags

A curious aspect of being a Communist or a Communist sympathizer was that "the Party line" would change, on matters minor and major, sometimes gradually and sometimes quite abruptly. This meant that a Communist might be required to preach today the opposite of what he had been required to preach yesterday. "Every Communist is in fact liable at any moment to have to alter his most fundamental convictions, or leave the party" (XII, 101). Someone who kept on saying today, after the line had changed, what he had been required to say yesterday, would get into trouble with the Party, and if he lived in the Soviet Union would be imprisoned, perhaps killed. If he lived outside the USSR, he might be ordered to travel to Moscow, and if he were obliging enough to comply, could be imprisoned, perhaps killed, upon arrival. (Sometimes the heresy-hunting would even be retrospective. Someone could be disciplined or killed simply because they had voiced the deviation at the time when it was still the party line.)

In the period when Orwell was aware of Communism, the Communist "line" went through the following broad phases (there were numerous more minor changes too). Note that in discussions of Communist policy, "left" means intransigent, revolutionary, not co-operating with other socialists, while "right" means patient, reform-oriented, and ready to form alliances with non-Communists.

> 1920–21. *Revolutionary, yet working within the Labour Party*.
>
> 1921. *Right turn. United Front*. Communists recognize that the revolutionary wave has subsided, and a "relative stabilization" of capitalism has occurred. Communists should stop trying to provoke immediate risings and should win over the masses.
>
> 1924. *Left turn.* United Front only from below.
>
> 1928–1931. *Sudden lurch to an extreme left standpoint*. This is the period of "Class against Class," in which non-Communist socialists were identified as the main enemy and branded as "social fascists." New Communist-controlled unions are formed in opposition to the existing unions.
>
> 1931. *Slight rightward movement: some softening of the revolutionary line*.
>
> 1933–34. *Continued gradual rightward movement*. United Front from below, followed by plain United Front.
>
> 1935–August 23rd 1939. *Right turn.* Communists promote a Popular Front, in which they would unite with various socialist and non-socialist parties in a great alliance against the rising threat of fascism.

> August 23rd 1939–June 22nd 1941. *Sharp left turn. Opposition to the war as imperialist.* The CPGB forms the People's Convention, a front organization demanding acceptance of Hitler's peace terms, and promotes strikes to hinder the war effort.
>
> June 22nd 1941–1945. *Right turn.* Complete support for the Churchill government. The CP discourages and breaks strikes to help the war effort.
>
> 1945–1947. *Continuation of rightist strategy.* Largely uncritical support of the Labour government, including discouragement of strikes.
>
> 1947– *Slight left turn.* More aggressive posture in line with ramped-up Soviet aggressiveness, though combined with acceptance of a purely constitutional road to power in Britain.

In Communist terminology, there's a big difference between a united front and a popular front. A united front means Communists co-operating with non-Communist leftists but not "bourgeois" parties; a popular front means Communist co-operation with non-socialists ("bourgeois" groupings, including those liberals and conservatives judged to be most "progressive") as well as with non-Communist socialists. A "united front from below" means that Communists will collaborate with individual members of non-Communist leftist organizations while denouncing and trying to undermine the leadership of those organizations, while a "united front from above" (or plain united front) means the Communists will collaborate directly with the leaderships of those organizations.

Communists maintained that these changes of line were decided by the International. But as everyone soon came to understand, the International was wholly owned and controlled by the Soviet government, and any changes were decreed by an individual sitting in Moscow. In the early years the Comintern had some autonomy, meaning that the person appointed as head of the Comintern (first Zinoviev and then Bukharin) had some independent role in determining Comintern policy. With the appointment of Dimitrov, Comintern policy was simply fixed by Joseph Stalin, who imposed the current line on all the Communist Parties in the world, including the CPGB. This was possible because Communists the world over were prepared to take their orders from Moscow and because Moscow provided crucial funding ("Moscow gold") for all the Communist Parties.

The current party line was always supposed to have been scientifically derived from an analysis of the world situation. A more aggressive or "left" strategy would usually be indicated by an analysis showing that world capitalism was in terminal crisis and therefore "objectively" ripe for revolution, a more convivial or "right" strategy would flow from an analysis showing that capitalism still had appreciable reserves of strength, and could therefore still be reformed to the benefit of the workers. So for example, the Comintern decided in 1928 that capitalism had entered a "third period" in which its resources for survival had been exhausted, and was in its terminal throes. This analysis seemed to be brilliantly confirmed by the 1929 financial crisis and the ensuing slump, from which it was believed capitalism could never recover (except temporarily by installing fascism and reducing the workers' wages to bare subsistence).

Since capitalism was tottering and fascism was merely an instrument of big business, fascism itself was nothing to fear, and was actually a welcome sign that the collapse of capitalism was imminent. Fascism was the prelude to socialist revolution and any movement towards controlled or regulated capitalism was inherently fascist. The really dangerous enemy was the non-Communist Left, which stood in the way of a direct confrontation between the working class (represented by the Communists) and terminally sick capitalism (represented by the fascists). While this analysis was in some ways novel within Marxism, elements of it were shared by others outside the Comintern. The revolutionary anti-Stalinist left, both the London Bureau and the Trotskyists, spoke of capitalism being in its death agony.

As an example of the way changes of line affected Communist behavior, the CPGB after 1928 attacked the ILP as "social fascists." In 1935 the CP began to cozy up to the ILP, and for more than a year there was much talk of the two parties permanently amalgamating, to form a new revolutionary party. But when the CP started to promote the Popular Front agenda, the ILP continued to reject co-operation with "bourgeois" (non-socialist) parties and was now therefore to the left of the CP. At the same time, the CP was pursuing its anti-Trotskyist witch-hunt, claiming that all ultra-leftists were Trotskyists and all Trotskyists allied with fascism. And so it came to pass that the ILP had the honor of being defamed as fascist, first at the beginning of the 1930s, because it was too rightwing, and then again, after 1936, because it was too leftwing. So we have two periods of ferocious denunciation separated by a brief interlude where the parties were so close they were publicly considering becoming one party, and all these changes in the relationship emanated from Moscow-decreed changes of line.

Recent scholarly work on the history of the CPGB has tended to focus more on the extent to which Communist Parties exercised autonomy and massaged Moscow directives into conformity with local conditions and local squabbles among Communists. This is entirely reasonable and salutary: all communications contain some room for interpretation, and Communists were not robots but passionate humans trying to make sense of their situation. But there were limits to local variation. Some writers go too far in suggesting that major changes of line were home-grown. This is highly improbable because (aside from direct testimony that the orders came from Moscow), with only a few minor qualifications, all the changes of line occurred in all the world's Communist Parties simultaneously.[7]

If we look at the zigs and zags of the party line, we see that in some cases, though not all, changes in the line are mechanically linked to Soviet foreign policy interests. So, Stalin makes a pact with Hitler, and the CPGB becomes the "peace" party, fomenting all the strikes it can to hinder the British war effort. Hitler invades Russia, and overnight the CPGB becomes the most enthusiastic war party, breaking strikes at every opportunity, and campaigning for a "second front" (really a third front), meaning a British and American invasion of France to relieve the

7 Studies of how seventeen different national Communist Parties experienced the "Class against Class" period are collected in Worley 2004.

pressure on Russia. The CP did not campaign for Russia to open a second front against Japan to relieve the pressure on the US in the Pacific. Other cases, such as the "Class against Class" line of 1929–1934, were still dictated by Moscow, but were not so clearly in Moscow's interests, though always reflecting Moscow's beliefs, which in this case were in error.

Aside from the merits of any particular line, the observed fact that the Communists would sometimes change their line overnight was a public embarrassment and was public evidence of their subservience to Moscow, as well as restricting their ability to shape their own strategy in the light of local political conditions. But the zigzags were less of an embarrassment than they might have been, because membership turnover was high, so that many members didn't know the Party had once had a different line.

To a latter-day outsider, these twists and turns may seem at first blush unaccountable. But they all occur within certain basic Communist assumptions which never changed in this period, and which were shared by all Bolshevik-influenced socialists, including Trotskyists, the POUM, and (in the 1930s) many leading members of the ILP. These were:

1. That socialism is a viable system and will be an improvement on capitalism;

2. That capitalism is in its final throes, with almost no resources left;

3. That the Russian Bolshevik seizure of power in 1917 was a successful socialist revolution and is the model for any future socialist revolution;

4. That the working class is somehow crucial to a socialist revolution (even though most members of this class observably have zero interest in socialism or revolution);

5. That there is some inherent connection between trade union activity (such as strikes) and a socialist revolution;

> 6. That (putting all the above together), there must be some scientifically correct way that a socialist party can behave that will lead to revolution.

Orwell, who definitely disavowed Bolshevik methods, rejected #3, accepted #1, #2, and #4, and had no clearly marked view about #5 and #6.

Most historical discussion of the British Communist movement has been conducted by Marxists or former Marxists who still accept some if not all of these propositions. This lends such writings a strange flavor, as they are always on the lookout for a stratagem which would have enabled the Communists to seize power, or at least exert some major influence on events.[8] It is as though scholars writing about nineteenth-century Christian sects were to be continually trying to discover what each sect could have done differently that would actually have precipitated the Second Coming of Christ. For a small conspiratorial group with no wide support and beliefs remote from the mainstream to have any major impact on a developed liberal-capitalist society is a rare event, so that if we demand to know why the CPGB didn't have greater success, the only mystery is what peculiar assumptions would incline us to ask such a question.

Most commentators can't make much sense of the Comintern's "Third Period" strategy of 1928–1933. But from a Bolshevik standpoint this strategy made perfect sense. In many ways it was a reversion to the Comintern's initial posture in 1920, and even more to the Bolsheviks' earlier views in 1917–1919. It was a more candid disclosure of what the Comintern intended at all times: the liquidation of the democratic Left. And if the world economic crisis of 1929–1935 was not capitalism's death agony, it could easily appear that way to those who lived through it and didn't know what was to come.

It's possible to imagine a party that was highly supportive of the Soviet system while able to make independent criticisms. This was the stance of most of the ILP in the early 1930s. Yet the Soviet state, which had bloodily suppressed all criticism from within its own population, was hardly likely to foot the bill for foreigners to make criticisms. Given

8 I am thinking of works like Eaden and Renton 2002.

that the CPGB was the party which put defense of the Soviet system above everything else, its long-term fortunes were bound to be heavily impacted by the perception of that system, and in the long run the perception was bound to be somewhat influenced by the wretched reality.

Exaggerating Communist Influence

Orwell helped to begin a legend which persists to this day: the legend that 1930s intellectuals were typically or predominantly Communists or Communist sympathizers. Recalling the youthful membership of his father, Kingsley Amis, in the Communist Party, Martin Amis makes the remarkable claim that "the overwhelming majority of intellectuals everywhere" accepted the Soviet government's version of the Moscow trials and other atrocities.[9] In Britain, at any rate, this amounts to a considerable exaggeration of Communist influence. Amis's claim can't be reconciled with the fact that the pre-eminent weekly organ of leftwing opinion, the *New Statesman*, consistently carried harsh criticisms of the Moscow Trials and the purges.

In one of his own reckless exaggerations, Orwell wrote in 1940 that "For about three years, in fact, the central stream of English literature was more or less directly under Communist control."[10] What could it even mean to control the central stream of English literature, unless it meant that most writers of importance were somehow controlled, which was obviously not the case? The statement might be true if the central stream of English literature meant the Left Book Club (and if "directly" were replaced by "indirectly"), but the Left Book Club was a small part of the output of the publishing industry, and far from the most prestigious or consequential. Allowing for Orwell's proclivity for preposterous generalization we should note that even here Orwell confines this extreme degree of Communist sway to three years, and later states that the Communists have lost nearly all their influence (XII, 353, 417). George

9 Amis 2003, 8.

10 XII, 101; see Wood 1959, 73. Neal Wood is one of the few to have attempted to correct the usual exaggeration of Communist influence, though many subsequent writers have failed to learn from him.

Woodcock refers to the "slashing inaccuracy" in Orwell's claims, and correctly points out that "most of the leading figures in the English literary world had never even in the Thirties been touched in any way by communism."[11]

What is true is that Communism was fashionable for a few years among intellectuals, and recruited a handful of the more prominent or promising writers, scientists, and others, something that would have been unthinkable before or since. I use the word "fashionable" in the sense that Wildean aestheticism in the 1870s, going topless in the 1960s, or dropping acid while listening to Captain Beefheart in the 1970s could all be described as fashionable—with no implication that very many people ever actually engaged in such activities.

A quite modest appraisal of Communist influence would be inferred from Orwell's comparison of the Communist literary influence in the 1930s with the Catholic influence in the 1920s and the Pacifist influence in the 1940s, "the successive literary cliques which have infested this country."

> The life of a clique is about five years and I have been writing long enough to see three of them come and two go—the Catholic gang, the Stalinist gang, and the present Pacifist . . . gang. (XIII, 399)

In other words the Communist fad in the mid-1930s was just one of a succession of briefly modish currents, affecting some but not most writers, and that episode was all over when Orwell wrote these words in 1942 (even though a different kind of pro-Sovietism, arising out of the wartime alliance, had by then come into vogue).

The Beliefs of 1930s Intellectuals

No quantitative study has been conducted of the affiliations of all 1930s intellectuals. However, we have various ways of making rough estimates. Wood cites questionnaires done at the time which go to show the

11 Woodcock 1984, 251–52.

limitations of Communist support among intellectuals, or indeed, of any serious political commitment (Wood 1959, 70–72). We know that membership of the CPGB rose to about 16,000 by the start of the war, and that the vast majority of CP members were "workers," not "intellectuals."[12] In other words the actual number of intellectuals who joined the Communist Party could only have been a minute fraction of all intellectuals, however that class might be precisely defined.

As a further rough gauge, we can run through some of the academic disciplines. In economics, there was Maurice Dobb, a well-known Cambridge economist who was a member of the Communist Party. There were hardly any other Communist economists, unless we count R. L. Meek, who wrote almost entirely about the history of economic thought and who did not become well-known until the 1950s. Among economists, Dobb was known simply as a spokesman for Communism. His writings were of little interest to economists except, very marginally, to those specializing in the history of industrialization. The 1930s was a heady, exciting time in economic theory, partly connected with the "Keynesian revolution." Yet more fundamentally, in price theory (what's now called micro-economics), neoclassical theory was unchallenged and was being refined and extended, in such works as Hicks's brilliant landmark *Value and Capital* (1939). These developments had nothing to do with Communism.

In philosophy there was Maurice Cornforth, a former student of Wittgenstein, who wrote books putting the Communist line on various

12 CPGB membership was less than 3,000 at the beginning of the 1930s. It grew rapidly to around 16,000, did not noticeably fall with the Nazi-Soviet Pact, and then increased dramatically when Russia became an ally, reaching an all-time peak of 56,000 following the Battle of Stalingrad. After the war, membership declined steadily—the sharp fall after 1956 was recouped in the early 1960s but the longer-term decline then resumed. Membership was below 2,000 when the party was wound up in 1991. At all times, membership turnover was high, sometimes over 30 percent per year and nearly always over 10 percent. Laybourn and Murphy 1999, 49; Morgan, Cohen, and Flinn 2007, 14–18; Wood 1959, 23. Until 1941 the CP was consciously a "cadre" party, and intellectuals might be refused membership, whereas subsequently the Party sought to maximize its membership.

developments in philosophy. These books, though in fact fairly well-argued and worth reading, were of little interest to professional philosophers at the time. No one but a committed Communist largely ignorant of philosophy would be likely to find anything appetizing in Stalin-era dialectical materialism.

The 1930s saw the arrival and departure of logical empiricism ("logical positivism"), followed in the 1940s by the beginnings of "linguistic philosophy" (including "ordinary language" philosophy). Not only were all these movements of ideas separate from Communism, not influenced by it and not influencing it, most of them were also actually forbidden to CP members. A comrade was not permitted to be a Keynesian, a neoclassical price theorist, a logical empiricist, or an ordinary-language philosopher. Nor was he permitted to say anything favorable about Freud, or Jung, or jazz, or stream-of-consciousness fiction, or serial music, or abstract painting. By the 1940s, it had become clear that he could not own up to a belief in genetics. All the new ideas which most energized mainstream intellectuals at the time were off-limits to CP members, except that they were allowed to denounce them as symptoms of capitalism's terminal malaise.

Only in the academic study of history did Communism have success in recruiting capable and productive thinkers, partly because a Marxist approach to historical studies has genuine strengths and partly because "social history" was deservedly coming into its own. The recruitment did not bear much fruit until after the war, when the eminent Communist historians recruited in the 1930s were all becoming disillusioned with Communism—Christopher Hill and E. P. Thompson left the Party, after years of friction, in the wake of the Hungarian revolt of 1956, and Eric Hobsbawm, who kept paying his dues, often spoke out as if he had left. The quirky A. J. P. Taylor (briefly a CPGB member in his youth) was pro-Soviet in terms of British foreign policy, but genuinely detested totalitarianism. His own historical method was distinctly un-Marxist. E. H. Carr and Geoffrey Barraclough were other leading historians who were pro-Soviet, though not CP members.

The CP did manage to get a number of leading scientists to adopt the peculiar Communist view of the social role of science. The journal *Nature* was a megaphone for this view for a few years before a reaction set in (Wood 1959, 123–34). But, just as the CP's Popular Front endeavors were hampered by its anti-Trotskyist crusade, so its attempt to co-opt scientists were eventually hampered by its rejection of Mendelian genetics, and therefore of Weismann's synthesis of Darwin and Mendel, the foundation of modern biology.

If we look at the Communist Party itself, we see the recurring names of R. Page Arnot, Emile Burns, Rajani Palme Dutt, James Klugmann, Pat Sloan, and a few others. These intellectuals had some modest talent as pamphleteers, but outside of the Communist Party itself they were basically nobodies. They were the CPGB's house intellectuals, with no influence except as workhorses of CP propaganda. Their books were nearly always published by Lawrence and Wishart, the CP's tame publishing house, and probably read by more people in Moscow than in London.

Christopher Hitchens refers to "the intellectuals of the 1930s" (p. 56), his context implying that most of them were pro-Communist. He mentions Orwell's "innumerable contemporaries, whose defections from Communism were later to furnish spectacular confessions and memoirs" (p. 59). There is a popular stereotype of the committed Communist who then breaks with the Party and confesses. But how many individuals conformed to this pattern? Were they innumerable? And how many of them were British?

There were a handful of intellectuals, like Dobb and Cornforth, who remained Communists throughout. There were promising young intellectuals like Christopher Caudwell who became Communists and died fighting for Communism in Spain. They would probably not have remained Communists for long had they survived a few more years. There were those who enjoyed weekend flings with Communism, like Auden and Spender, and who could never furnish spectacular confessions and memoirs because they had nothing spectacular to recall or confess. There were a few who left the Party or never joined it but remained devout fellow-travelers. There were some *sui generis* cases, like J. B. S. Haldane, whose wife left him and wrote an informative book that may be considered a slightly spectacular confession and memoir, and who himself faded away without publicly breaking with the Communists, or John Strachey, a non-CP member far more talented than any member, who preached the Communist line with great eloquence for a few years, then put it all behind him to resume his career as a Labour Party politician. Then there were the broad ranks of the Left, who had spasms of sympathy for Soviet Russia now and then, but who were not to be dislodged from their allegiance to the inherently anti-Communist Labour Party.

Some appreciation of the ideological climate at the time can be gleaned from the volume *The God that Failed* (1949). This popular collection brought together the stories of six notable writers who had become committed Communists and then been disillusioned and quit the Communist movement. The rarity of individuals who conformed to the pattern described by Hitchens is illustrated by the fact that the editor, Richard Crossman, couldn't find a single convincing British example of a former Communist intellectual turned anti-Communist, and not wishing to go to press without one home-grown British specimen, had to make do with Stephen Spender. Spender had been a member of the CP for a few weeks at most; he was disillusioned as soon as he joined.[13] Other writers often bracketed with Communism, like Auden, were never CP members or convinced Communists. They were fellow travelers for a year or two and then they moved on. Of course, there were some people who conformed with the pattern described by Hitchens—such as the other five contributors to *The God that Failed*, three continentals and two Americans. *The God that Failed*, a highly effective anti-Communist work, was entirely a product of the Left. All six contributors were democratic socialists, as was the editor.[14]

The virtual absence of any British examples did not arise because large numbers of intellectuals joined the CPGB and never left it. It arose because very few British intellectuals ever joined the Communist Party, and most of those who did left quickly before they could get up to any skullduggery worth memorializing. To say all this is not to belittle the propaganda achievement of the CPGB. It had an extraordinary impact

13 Although Spender's recruitment to the Party was announced in the *Daily Worker*, according to Sutherland (2005, 214), he was never technically a member.

14 Whittaker Chambers was invited (before his public revelations about Hiss) to contribute to *The God that Failed* but declined. If he had accepted, he would have been the only contributor who was not leftwing.

on politically minded intellectuals, *given that it was always such a tiny group of people with no popular support and with so many ideas out of sync with intellectual fashion.*

The CPGB worked hard to gain control of trade unions, with mixed results. The CP learned many times over that union influence does not lead to political influence. Often the very workers who would vote for a Communist union official or shop steward would not vote for a Communist parliamentary candidate, or even for permitting CP affiliation to the Labour Party.

It might be contended that the real influence of the Communist Party was not in its card-carrying membership or in its control of a few unions, but in the spread of pro-Communist ideas among non-CP members, particularly the manipulation of public opinion through front organizations and fellow-travelers. But this too can easily be over-rated.

Fellow travelers were certainly culpably uncritical of much in Communism, but usually not completely uncritical. *The New Statesman* was notoriously sappy about the Soviet Union but there were limits to its sympathy. Writers in the *New Statesman* did not try to deny that the USSR was an extremely repressive dictatorship; they excused the regrettable absence of democracy and civil liberties on account of the USSR's predicament of hostile "encirclement." They repeatedly and sharply criticized the Moscow Trials, the purges, and other acts of Soviet repression (Martin 1968, 229–236). The highly respected and prolific leftist journalist Henry Noel Brailsford was a keen critic of the Moscow Trials; the *New Statesman* gave him a platform and staunchly defended him against Communist attacks (Wood 1959, 48).

In the 1930s, and to a lesser extent in the 1950s after Sputnik, there existed a movement of opinion reflecting admiration of the advertised achievements of the Soviet Union. People who were caught up in this admiration did not automatically or necessarily adhere to Communism, just as people in the West who admired Japanese achievements in the 1970s did not believe we should take our orders from Tokyo. There were also many in the 1930s who saw the Communist movement as an ally in the struggle for peace or against fascism. A well-documented conclusion of David Caute's study of fellow travelers is that they were typically *not* ideological Marxists and did *not* want to see Communism come to power in their own countries (Caute 1988, 215–237). After all, fellow travelers all had this in common: they had not joined the Party. (In a few cases intellectuals might be refused membership but in the majority of instances, the Party would have welcomed fellow travelers who applied to 'join'; yet nearly all the fellow travelers were never motivated to take that step.) So, while the Communists were using others, the others were also using the Communists. Trade unionists and anti-fascists could gratefully lean on Communists doing a lot of hard work for their organizations, without themselves being seriously tempted by Communism.

In matters like the trials and purges, the CP probably had more success persuading non-intellectuals than convincing intellectuals. People only just "intellectual" enough to read the newspapers and to have heard about the trials and purges might be inclined to swallow the Communist account. The opinions of non-intellectuals in such matters tend to evaporate before they can leave any longer-lasting impression.

One very elementary point that unfortunately has to be made is that there was never any equivalence between "leftwing" or "far left" and "pro-Communist." It would only be a slight exaggeration to say that the far left were the original and always the most militant anti-Communists (in the usage of "Communism" where it refers, as it most frequently does, to Stalin's Comintern). To employ terms like "left-wing" or "far left" as synonyms for "favorable to Communism," as Peter Davison (XVI, 3) and John Rodden[15] sometimes do, is a confusing blunder.

Orwell's International Policy After 1944

> At some point or another a stand against Russian aggression will have to be made . . .
> —George Orwell, November 1945 (XVII, 339–340)

George Orwell coined the phrase "cold war"[16] quite casually in 1945 and he anticipated much of what was to follow, though he got some things

15 Rodden 2003, 178.

16 XVII, 321. He had earlier used the phrase to refer to the years immediately before World War II (XVI, 19).

wrong. It's sometimes asserted or implied that Orwell was opposed to Western interests in the Cold War. The truth is rather the reverse, but may be obscured by the fact that in most of his utterances on international relations, he advocated something he admitted to be highly unlikely at best: the creation of a United Socialist States of Europe, preferably incorporating Africa, independent of both Russia and America. This was an idea popular with the non-Communist narrow Left at the end of the war. It was supported by the ILP, which together with continental leftists launched the Movement for a United Socialist States of Europe.[17]

In the last few years of Orwell's life, many defining features of the postwar world were cloudy and only gradually becoming clarified. In 1945 many people expected a major slump; hardly anyone anticipated the long period of prosperity that got going in the 1950s. Many expected that Britain would hang on to its empire and (whether it did so or not) would remain a major world power. It took a while for some people to understand that the division of Europe by an "iron curtain" was absolute, and when they did begin to sense this, an imminent Third World War between Russia and the West seemed likely.

In these years it became apparent to everyone that when Stalin had demanded governments in Eastern Europe friendly to the Soviet Union, he meant that these countries would become Russian colonial possessions, with all dissent stamped out. These were the years of the killing of the Polish leadership, the blockade of West Berlin, the overthrow of democratic rule in Czechoslovakia, and the short-lived but brutal Soviet occupation of Austria. The implications of nuclear weapons were uncertain. Many people, including some on the Left, independently came up with the idea that the US should knock out Soviet Russia with nuclear weapons before Russia could acquire them.

In August 1945, Orwell asserts that Britain, under the new Labour government, has three alternatives:

17 Brockway 1977, 151–52. Orwell first broached the idea of a United States of Europe, though allied with Soviet Russia, in January 1943 (XIV, 296). Pro-Russian sentiment was at its height and apparently influenced Orwell here, though the passage is ambiguous because he is ostensibly reporting on what the British people at that time would prefer as the outcome of the war.

> One is to carry on as at present, acquiescing in "spheres of interest," and holding the Empire together as well as possible; another is to move definitely into the orbit of the USA; and the other is to liberate India, cut the links with the Dominions, and form a solid bloc of the western European states and their African possessions. (XVII, 248)

He goes on to say that the third option "seems to me a pipe dream," which is odd because, although it clearly was a pipe dream, a variant of this option soon becomes his preferred policy and the one he talked most about. Furthermore, the variant he talked about requires that the new federation also be socialist, something that even just by itself was extremely unlikely.[18]

In November he writes that the Labour government "is not obliged to adopt an appeaser attitude towards the USSR. At some point or another a stand against Russian aggression will have to be made." This reference to appeasement and the need to resist Russian aggression recurs in Orwell's subsequent discussions (XVIII, 287; XIX, 29, 250). Orwell argues that the Labour government's foreign policy will be similar to that of a Conservative government, except that Labour will be more pro-Zionist—which he dislikes—and will be better able to stand up to the USSR—which he likes (XVII, 339–341).

In March 1947 Orwell reviewed James Burnham's *The Struggle for the World* (XIX, 96–105). Burnham argued here that Communism was seriously bent on taking over the world, was infiltrating Western institutions, would succeed unless checked by American leadership, and that the US should quickly prepare for war against Soviet Russia before Russia was able to acquire nuclear weapons. Orwell largely agreed with Burnham's analysis but differed on one point. He agreed that the West needed to be ready to go to war to halt Communist expansion, but maintained that Communism was less powerful than Burnham believed and

18 To a socialist of Orwell's generation, post-war Western European welfare states would be examples of capitalism, definitely not socialism, because most industrial means of production are privately owned and total output is determined by the market. See Chapter 4 above.

that therefore the West did not need to take the immediate drastic measures recommended by Burnham, such as prohibition of all Communist activity and swift political unification of the USA with the British Empire. Again Orwell returns to his cherished idea of developing an alternative to Communism by making democratic socialism—"economic security without concentration camps"—work (103).

A couple of months later Orwell is arguing that there are three possibilities for the future: that America will use the atomic bomb pre-emptively against the USSR (which he sees as unlikely, though it is clearly not a proposal that horrifies him); that several countries will soon get the bomb so that a nuclear war ensues that would destroy civilization; and that the fear of the bomb will prevent its use—this last, he says, is "the worst possibility of all. It would mean the division of the world among two or three vast superstates, unable to conquer one another and unable to be overthrown by any internal rebellion"—the scenario he would develop in *Nineteen Eighty-Four*. After outlining these three possibilities, he says that the "only way of avoiding them" (thus, a fourth possibility) is for "democratic socialism" to be "made to work throughout some large area," the only practical possibility being Western Europe (XIX, 163–64). Orwell hoped that Britain wouldn't have to choose between America and Russia but he considered Britain would probably be forced to make this decision, and in that case the only possible choice would have to be America (XIX, 90, 103, 180–82).

We see Orwell grasping some of the realities of the postwar world while missing others. What actually happened didn't fit any of the scenarios he had allowed for. He correctly anticipated that Britain's days as a world power were over. There was indeed a nuclear standoff between two great "superstates," but the Western alliance didn't become politically unified or totalitarian. There was a European federation, of a sort, but it wasn't socialist, it was encouraged and supported by the United States, and Britain joined it, with lingering misgivings, only in 1973.

The biggest factor Orwell didn't foresee was that substantially private, free-market capitalism would spectacularly outperform state-controlled economies. Workers' living standards in the West quickly attained and surpassed levels Orwell hadn't considered remotely possible. In technology and output the Soviet system fell further and further behind the West. Experience of the Labour government's nationalizations immunized British voters against further extensions of state control, and far from a socialist movement emerging in America, Europe's nominally socialist parties all quickly and completely abandoned the goal of socialism as heretofore defined.

Although Orwell recognized federated European-African democratic socialism as a "pipe dream" he continued to promote it because, as he put it, a doctor should try to save the life of a patient he believes is very probably going to die (XIX, 163). At the same time as he recognized Communism as the major menace to freedom, he wanted the British economy to be brought more completely under state control, and hoped to see the emergence of a powerful socialist movement in America. In Orwell's mind, increased state control of the British economy and opposition to Soviet Communism—including alliance with the capitalist United States—went together. Since capitalism was objectively doomed, and the future could only lie with some kind of collectivism, he considered it vital to demonstrate in practice that democratic socialism, the only hopeful alternative to totalitarianism, could work.

I've Got a Little List

Around the end of the war, Orwell began to compile a list of prominent or influential individuals who might be covert Communists, crypto-Communists, or fellow travelers (earlier he had begun the same sort of exercise for those who might collaborate with the Nazis in the event of a German occupation of Britain). He did this for his own satisfaction and as background for things he might write. He mentioned the existence of the list to a few friends.

Under the postwar Labour government, the British Foreign Office set up a covert section known as the Information Research Department (IRD), with the job of counteracting Communist propaganda. One of Orwell's old flames, Celia Kirwan (twin sister of Arthur Koestler's wife), worked at the IRD, and in contact with her, Orwell mentioned the existence of his list. She showed interest, and Orwell turned over the list to her and through her to the IRD (XX, 88, 105, 318–321). From his sickbed, he apparently had numerous telephone conversations with her about the names on the list, and more generally about how to combat Communist activity. The list comprises 135 names, annotated with comments mainly on their possible Communist sympathies, but also their sexual habits, their characters, their ethnic backgrounds, and their political soundness generally (XX, 240–258). This list has presented some of Orwell's leftist admirers with a disquieting puzzle. Was Orwell a McCarthyist before McCarthy?

By 1945 Soviet agents had deeply penetrated several bastions of British and American government and society. The results were not merely transfers of information (such as the atomic secrets, enabling the Soviet Union to acquire the atomic bomb), but also interference with the actual behavior of government agencies—a trivial example being Smollett's dissuading Jonathan Cape from publishing *Animal Farm*, a more serious instance being the feeding of false information about the Yugoslavian resistance to Churchill, so that Britain backed Tito's partisans rather than Mihailovich's Chetniks.[19]

Before his passing of the list to Celia Kirwan, Orwell had publicly taken the stand that the government was fully entitled to discriminate against those whose ideological affiliation made them objective enemies. The British NCCL (National Council for Civil Liberties) is roughly equivalent to America's ACLU. For a few years after the war, the NCCL came under Communist control. Orwell and others were therefore active in an alternative group, the Freedom Defence Committee, which lobbied for civil liberties. At this time, the records of civil servants were being investigated for evidence of Communist or fascist connections. The Freedom Defence Committee issued a statement in August 1948, signed by twenty-four notables, including Orwell, calling for changes in procedures, so that an accused civil servant could be made aware of allegations against him and have legal representation to defend himself. The statement, however, firmly upheld the right of the government to refuse employment to those who might constitute a danger, the clear implication being that it was only right and proper for the government to dismiss

19 Martin 1990. See XVII, 255–56. One of the NKVD agents whose deceptions helped lead to Tito's capture of power was James Klugmann. Later, as an open CPGB member, when Tito broke with Stalin, Klugmann authored the remarkable tract, *From Trotsky to Tito* (1951).

any civil servants with Communist or fascist ties (XIX, 421–22). Privately, Orwell wrote that he found the government's investigation "vaguely disquieting" (XIX, 301).

Britain never experienced anything like the public American phenomenon known as "McCarthyism." There were no British politicians peculiarly identified with a crusade against Communist espionage and no public hearings on Communist penetration. It was never controversial that members of the CPGB or its front organizations would be security risks and should not be given access to secret information or hired for certain types of government jobs, because, obviously, they would do whatever Moscow ordered them to do. There was also the odd circumstance that Moscow had evidently ordered that agents caught in Britain would confess and get the matter tidied away as quietly as possible, whereas agents caught in the US would indefinitely stall, deny, and do everything possible to muddy the waters.

After the war there was a small group of Labour Members of Parliament who closely followed the Moscow line, essentially acting as political agents of the Russian government just as the Communist Party did, but without affiliating to the CP (which would have instantly prompted their expulsion from the Labour Party). Orwell several times attacked these people in print as "cryptos" (crypto-Communists) (XVIII, 286–87, 289–292; XIX, 179–184). He exaggerated their importance. The cryptos (notably Konni Zilliacus and D. N. Pritt) were a very tiny group and should not be confused with the left wing of the Labour Party, the *Tribune* group, represented in Parliament by Aneurin Bevan and Michael Foot. These Labour leftists were just as anti-Communist as anyone else, if not more so. Their general views on Communism, as on most political issues, were similar to Orwell's. At the end of his life, Orwell's political allegiance was Bevanite.

The late Christopher Hitchens was a strong admirer of Orwell as well as a long-time denouncer of McCarthyism, and when news came out that Orwell had passed on his list of suspects to the IRD, Hitchens sprang to Orwell's defense, presenting several arguments that what Orwell did was quite unlike what McCarthy did.

"A blacklist is a roster of names maintained by those with the power to affect hiring and firing," says Hitchens, evidently suggesting that this was not the intended effect of Orwell's list.[20] Yet Hitchens himself quotes Orwell as writing that "If it [the listing of "unreliables" by the IRD] had been done earlier it would have stopped people like Peter Smollett worming their way into important propaganda jobs where they were probably able to do us a lot of harm" (163). So Orwell's intention was that his list should be used as (or as part of) a blacklist by Hitchens's definition, to stop suspected Communists and fellow travelers from being hired for certain kinds of government jobs.

In another attempt at exculpating Orwell (while continuing to abominate McCarthyism), Hitchens says that "a 'snitch' or stool pigeon is rightly defined as someone who betrays friends or colleagues in the hope of plea-bargaining or otherwise of gaining advantage" (p. 166). But Hitchens's excoriations of McCarthyism included denunciations of people like Elia Kazan, who were not motivated by advantage but by conscience. And the fact that Orwell did not personally know most on the list doesn't help his case. Can it be right to report to the authorities one's uncorroborated suspicions of a stranger's Communist sympathies, intending that this will hurt his employment chances, and simultaneously wrong to report one's definite knowledge of an acquaintance's Communist Party membership?[21]

You can consistently defend the actions of George Orwell and Tail Gunner Joe, or you can consistently condemn both of them, but it's hard to see how you could consistently condemn McCarthy and defend Orwell, at least on the matter of lists. Whereas McCarthy's lists were lists of people credibly suspected (and, as we now know, for the most part actually guilty[22]) of illegal activity at the behest of Soviet controllers, Orwell's list mainly comprised people whose private beliefs Orwell had surmised from scraps of information, and whose beliefs had not

20 Hitchens 2002, 156.

21 Most of what is now called "McCarthyism" (the HUAC hearings and associated activities) did not involve McCarthy. McCarthy didn't personally know the individuals named in his lists, only that there was evidence they were security risks and yet had been shielded from prosecution or dismissal. See Evans 2007.

22 Evans 2007; Weinstein and Vassiliev 1999; Haynes, Klehr, and Vassiliev 2009.

necessarily resulted in illegal acts. The best defense of Orwell's actions here is that since some government agency to combat Communist penetration was necessary as a matter of elementary security, this agency might as well have the benefit of any relevant information, albeit of variable quality, that amateurs had managed to assemble.

10
The Inadvertent Antisocialist

> To accept an orthodoxy is always to inherit unresolved contradictions.
>
> —George Orwell, March 1948 (XIX, 291)

When it appeared in 1949, *Nineteen Eighty-Four* was a tremendous overnight success and over sixty years later it continues to find eager new readers every day across the world. From the beginning it reached readers who knew nothing about Orwell's other writings; many of those readers have understood this nightmarish tale as an attack upon Soviet Communism or upon the dangers of socialism in general.

Yet this view of *Nineteen Eighty-Four* as anti-Communist or antisocialist is disdainfully rejected by most people who write books and articles about Orwell. The overwhelmingly dominant view in these more exalted circles is that there's nothing antisocialist about *Nineteen Eighty-Four*, and that to suppose otherwise is pitiable ignorance. Not only that, but it is maintained that the use of *Nineteen Eighty-Four* by supporters of capitalism is an outrageous travesty, in which a great leftwing writer's work is distorted and defaced in aid of an evil political agenda.

The Anti-Antisocialist Interpretation of *Nineteen Eighty-Four*

I'll call the view, widespread among rank-and-file readers of fiction, that there is something antisocialist about *Nineteen Eighty-Four* the *antisocialist* interpretation. And I'll refer to the view, dominant among professional intellectuals who have a special interest in Orwell, that the antisocialist reading is at best an uneducated misunderstanding, more likely a sickening rightwing conspiracy, as the *anti-antisocialist* interpretation.

The main argument deployed in support of the anti-antisocialist interpretation is an appeal to Orwell's intentions. Advocates of this interpretation produce evidence that Orwell was a self-identified socialist, and they go on to show that Orwell himself objected to some statements of the antisocialist interpretation of *Nineteen Eighty-Four*. These advocates are usually confident that this disposes of the matter, but, as we shall see, there's a bit more to be said.

There are two fundamental objections to the anti-antisocialist reading as it is commonly presented. First, it ignores—or in some cases denies—a crucial fact about Orwell's intentions. That fact is that *Nineteen Eighty-Four* depicts a collectivist society in which capitalism and capitalists have been thoroughly eradicated. This anti-totalitarian novel is perfectly consistent with the view maintained by Orwell in his nonfiction writings: that totalitarianism is a disease of collectivism, not a disease of capitalism.

Second, the anti-antisocialist reading *confines* the discussion to Orwell's intentions, failing to consider the possibility that Orwell might have accomplished something he did not intend, or in other words that *Nineteen Eighty-Four* might be inadvertently antisocialist. For an author of fiction to stipulate the political significance of his work is not a privilege members of the literary intelligentsia are prepared to confer upon any writer other than Orwell. The reigning dogma among students of literary theory is (or was until quite recently) that the author's intentions ought to be discounted in interpreting a piece of writing such as a novel. Generations of American students of literature have been made to read Wimsatt and Beardsley's 1946 article, "The Intentional Fallacy," and (despite the sloppy reasoning of that work) have absorbed the doctrine that in interpreting any piece of writing, all attention to the author's intentions has to be discarded. The reason why this anti-intentionalism isn't reflected in much writing on Orwell is that most people who write about Orwell, even chiefly about his fiction, come from politics rather than literature. People who come to fiction from politics tend to make the opposite mistake to that of Wimsatt and Beardsley: they read a novel primarily as if it were an ideological manifesto or, perhaps, a confession.

The gist of the anti-antisocialist interpretation is that, since Orwell was a self-declared socialist, *Nineteen Eighty-Four* could not possibly carry an antisocialist message. According to Crick, *Nineteen Eighty-Four* was wrongly read as "a comprehensive anti-socialist polemic."[1] Woodcock, who knew Orwell, writes that although he possessed some Tory and some anarchist affinities, "Orwell's claim to have remained always a man of the Left must be respected."[2]

A similar position is taken by Anthony Burgess, himself a nonsocialist, or at least a Conservative Party supporter. Burgess remarks that

> even a few of the stupider British Tories rubbed their hands gleefully at what Orwell seemed to be doing for the Tory vote. None of these seemed to know, what was available for the knowing, that Orwell was a committed Socialist and was to remain so till his death."[3]

Yet even if Orwell did not intend for *Nineteen Eighty-Four* to increase the Conservative Party vote, it might still have had the result of doing so, therefore the stupidity of those Tories cannot be corroborated by the mere fact that Orwell was a socialist. These Tories were unwittingly echoing Fredric Warburg, far from stupid and far from a Tory, who, when he read the manuscript in December 1948, wrote that the book "is worth a cool million in votes to the conservative party [*sic*]" (XIX, 480).

All these writers share the premiss that a committed socialist cannot write an antisocialist work. Most of them, like Burgess, indicate that the whole matter is conclusively settled by Orwell's political allegiance to socialism, and that to read *Nineteen Eighty-Four* as antisocialist is simply ignorant. They generally intimate that Orwell's work has been illegitimately exploited by "the right." Some emphasize that it is wrong to depict Orwell as opposed to the Labour Party

1 Crick 1992, 565. And see Rodden 1989, 23–27.

2 Woodcock 1984, xii–xiii.

3 Burgess 1978, 24. In Britain, "Tory" is a popular term for the Conservative Party, just as in the U.S., "GOP" is a popular label for the Republicans.

(which came to power in Britain in 1945 and speedily nationalized a number of leading industries). Others go so far as to claim that it is incorrect to depict Orwell as anti-Communist or as pro-Western in the Cold War.

An underlying assumption of much of the leftist discussion of Orwell's reception is that it is wrong for an anti-Communist rightwinger to appeal to the anti-totalitarianism of *Nineteen Eighty-Four*, because its author was a leftist. The implication is that these rightists are doing something self-evidently wicked. Rodden applies the terms "septic treason" and "poisonous betrayal" to the use of *Nineteen Eighty-Four* by the Right.[4] Just what's bad about it? Are you debarred from quoting a writer sympathetically on one topic if you don't share all his views? And does this cut both ways? Orwell condemned "appeasement" of the USSR and considered the West should be ready to go to war against Communism.[5] Are those leftists whom Orwell would have judged to be appeasers of Soviet aggression also to be debarred from favorably citing Orwell's works? More broadly, did Marx commit septic treason when he quoted favorably from *Timon of Athens*?

Some leftist writers find it particularly incongruous that the John Birch Society once employed the digits "1984" for one of its phone numbers. If you start to read about Orwell, you soon lose count of the number of indignant references to this heinous incident. But what could possibly be wrong with it? Aside from its preference for democracy over dictatorship, the JBS also (like more than ninety percent of Americans and more than ninety-nine percent of the American working class) prefers capitalism to collectivism, and on this point therefore profoundly disagrees with Orwell. I see no reason why this should stop them alluding favorably to Orwell's horrific depiction of what could happen if the West succumbed to totalitarianism. Rodden says that *Nineteen Eighty-Four* was "shamelessly exploited by the John Birch Society and other rabid anticommunists."[6] Why should anti-Communists be ashamed of utilizing an anti-Communist work in support of their

4 Rodden 2011, 285.
5 See the previous chapter.
6 Rodden 2011, 286.

anti-Communist message, and why is Orwell's anti-Communism tacitly classified as non-rabid?[7]

Some statements of the anti-antisocialist position hold that the target of *Nineteen Eighty-Four* is not socialism or collectivism, but all forms of modern industrialized society.[8] Others even maintain that it is specifically aimed at capitalism. How do such writers account for the fact that the regime described in *Nineteen Eighty-Four* has stamped out capitalism and capitalists? Most of them never mention it. If you read what these writers say about *Nineteen Eighty-Four* without first having read the novel itself, you would never suspect it.

The Rightwing Response

The anti-antisocialist interpretation is often framed as though it is elementary, its denial merely ignorant. Yet not every knowledgeable critic agrees with it. There's a standard "rightist" response to the established leftist reading. For example Robert Conquest and Hilton Kramer each point out that Orwell was strongly anti-Communist and that he did not think that Western capitalism could become totalitarian (without first changing into something non-capitalist).[9]

Although, as a negation of the leftist interpretation, I think that this rightist interpretation is correct, its exposition has left some issues a little murky. After reading Conquest or Kramer, we're not entirely clear about the following questions: How could Orwell take the positions just mentioned, and still remain emphatically a socialist to the end of his days? How can we explain Orwell's objections to the use made of his work by overt supporters of capitalism? How can we harmonize the essentially collectivist nature of the Ingsoc regime (the political order depicted in *Nineteen Eighty-Four*) with the fact that *Nineteen Eighty-Four* is a kind of recreation of London in the 1940s? More broadly, how can we reconcile the fact that *Nineteen Eighty-Four* is aimed at collectivism, and not

7 For Orwell's comment on the use of the word "rabid" in connection with anti-Communism, see XIX, 182–83.

8 Crick 1992, 568.

9 Conquest 1989. Kramer 1999.

at capitalism, with the fact that it satirizes features of British capitalism? General answers to these questions have been given in earlier chapters of this book, but a little more can be said here.

The Anti-Orwell Leftists

I have mentioned the dominant leftists, who are fond of Orwell, and the rightists, who also admire Orwell. But there is a third group of writers who comment on Orwell: leftists who dislike Orwell. Leftists who dislike Orwell tend to agree in their interpretations with rightists who like Orwell. In other words, if you like Orwell and dislike socialism, you probably think that *Nineteen Eighty-Four* is anti-socialist, while if you dislike Orwell and like socialism, you probably also think that *Nineteen Eighty-Four* is anti-socialist. So there is some overlap between the views of Robert Conquest and Raymond Williams, between Hilton Kramer and Isaac Deutscher, much as this fact might make these four distinguished gentlemen feel queasy.

Political hostility to *Nineteen Eighty-Four* is almost always associated with sympathy for the form of state which prevailed in the Soviet Union. In the case of actual Communist Party members this is clear enough. It's also true of Trotskyists like Deutscher, committed to the view that the Soviet state, whatever its horrors, is essentially progressive, and always to be supported unconditionally in any conflict with capitalist states. But the most conspicuous leftist critic of *Nineteen Eighty-Four* is the non-Communist, though former Communist, Raymond Williams.

Williams calls the later Orwell an "ex-socialist," which is inaccurate, as Orwell continued to advocate the dispossession of the capitalist property owners, the nationalization of all major accumulations of wealth, and the approximate equalization of incomes. Williams recognizes its inaccuracy when he adds that Orwell's anti-Communist writing was all the more effective because he was not a defender of capitalism. This is quite true. Dislike for capitalism was fashionable among intellectuals, therefore many intellectuals were more likely to warm to an indictment of Communism if it came from someone who was avowedly anti-capitalist.

Why didn't Orwell's leftist detractors, notably Williams and Deutscher, react to *Nineteen Eighty-Four* by saying that this totalitarian nightmare wasn't essential to collectivism, that a way could be found to invent a collectivism that avoided totalitarianism, or in other words, that Orwell was simply right? Strangely, Williams and Deutscher sidestepped this issue and instead condemned *Nineteen Eighty-Four* because it conveyed hopelessness. Williams took the message of *Nineteen Eighty-Four* to be that everyone will always sell out,[10] and Deutscher similarly seemed bothered by the novel's depiction of "cruelty" as invincible.[11] Would Williams or Deutscher have condemned Kafka's *The Trial* because it "says" that all attempts to secure justice must fail and that the individual is forever powerless against the state? This is, after all, fiction, and fiction as satire. Deutscher commits the elementary error of equating the view implicit in *Nineteen Eighty-Four* as a literary device—that there is no hope of escaping totalitarianism—and Orwell's own political view, which encompassed the urgent need to develop a workable system of collectivism which would be democratic, not totalitarian.

Immediate Contemporary Reactions

We've seen that exponents of the anti-antisocialist reading often portray the antisocialist reading as pathetically ignorant. Yet when *Nineteen Eighty-Four* first appeared, some people who knew Orwell and were acquainted with his thinking immediately concluded that he had now finally broken with socialism. Orwell's publisher, Fredric Warburg, wrote that, in *Nineteen Eighty-Four*,

> The political system which prevails is Ingsoc = English Socialism. This I take to be a deliberate and sadistic attack on socialism and socialist parties generally. It seems to indicate a final breach between Orwell and Socialism, not the socialism of equality and human brotherhood which clearly Orwell no longer expects from socialist parties, but the socialism of marxism and the managerial revolution. (XIX, 480)

10 Williams 1981, 78–80.
11 Deutscher 1974, 131.

Quoting this passage, Wykes refers to Warburg as "sometimes obtuse,"[12] an undocumented allegation, implying that anyone who read the book this way would have to be obtuse. But Warburg was not the only one. Essentially the same conclusion about *Nineteen Eighty-Four* was reached by other early readers, for example the American socialist who knew Orwell's work very well, Philip Rahv.

Both these instances are cited by Crick. Crick is a standard pro-Orwell leftist, and duly sees the rightist interpretation of Orwell's work as monstrous, but unlike other writers, he holds Orwell partly responsible. "Orwell was at best incautious, at worst foolish."[13] Rodden and Newsinger each seem to agree.[14]

From writers like Crick, Rodden, and Newsinger, readers might infer that Orwell could and should have made his position clearer, by somehow writing *Nineteen Eighty-Four* as unmistakably pro-socialist and anticapitalist. This, they suppose, would have pre-empted the misunderstanding. As we will see, however, that would not have been practicable, for the world depicted in *Nineteen Eighty-Four* is rigorously conceived as a kind of society which might emerge only after capitalism has been abolished. On this point Orwell's position could not benefit from further clarification because it could scarcely have been any clearer to start with: the world of *Nineteen Eighty-Four*, taken as a whole, is an imaginable post-capitalist, collectivist society; it is decidedly not, in Orwell's judgment, an imaginable capitalist society.

Orwell's Response

Exponents of the anti-antisocialist interpretation frequently cite a passage from Orwell's letter to the American enquirer Francis A. Henson.[15]

12 Wykes 1987, 174.

13 Crick 1992, 569.

14 Rodden 1989, 25; Newsinger 1999, 121–24. This position is slightly different from that of Williams, who doesn't deny that Orwell *believed* that totalitarianism could emerge only from collectivism, but evidently doesn't believe it himself, and faults Orwell for propounding it (Williams 1981, 78).

15 Crick 1992, 569–70; Woodcock 1984, xi; Newsinger 1999, 122.

Those who quote it, however, often don't pay close attention to its precise wording:

> My recent novel is NOT intended as an attack on Socialism or on the British Labour Party (of which I am a supporter) but as a show-up of the perversions to which *a centralized economy* is liable and which have already been partly realized in Communism and Fascism. . .[16]

Orwell states that the Ingsoc regime illustrates the possible perversions of a centralized economy. He hopes for a centralized economy without those perversions, but he never allows, here or anywhere else, that such perversions could prevail to such an extreme degree except in a system where industry was controlled by the government and the free market had been eliminated.

By "Fascism," Orwell usually means primarily the National Socialism of the Third Reich. Orwell maintained, from 1940 on, that fascism, especially its National Socialist variety, was a revolutionary collectivist movement which had created a social order quite similar to Soviet Communism, and had it survived longer, would have taken the fascist countries even further in the direction of a completely centralized economic system on Soviet lines. On this key point, as on several others, Orwell completely agreed with James Burnham.

The Ingsoc Regime

In the imagined future world of *Nineteen Eighty-Four*, there is almost no private enterprise. The economy is fully nationalized: it is called "oligarchical collectivism," a term Orwell used in his nonfiction writings mainly to characterize Soviet Russia. The world is divided into three

16 XX, 135–36 (italics added). See Crick 1992, 569–570. Orwell subscribed to the common view of English style that it is best to use an Anglo-Saxon word where it can replace a Latinate word. He took this too far here, for the word "show-up," a replacement for "exposé," doesn't really work and has never caught on.

super-nations or power blocs, and the story is set in Airstrip One (Britain), which is part of Oceania, the North American entity—formerly the most capitalist of the three geographical territories. Yet in Oceania very little if any capitalist activity—private enterprise or production for profit—survives, even illegally. As far as we can tell, private commercial activity has been extirpated even more thoroughly than it ever was in the Soviet Union.

The one apparent exception, the little shop operated by Mr. Charrington, turns out to be no exception. Perhaps someone might argue that for such a shop to exist and pretend to be independently run, there must have been other such little shops which really were privately run. But that's as far as it can possibly go. Throughout the book, every hint of surviving freedom or individual dignity is associated with the past of free-market capitalism, and each disappointment, as another ray of hope for liberty is blocked off, is one more sign of how thoroughly capitalism has been eliminated.

The ruling party is called "Ingsoc" (English Socialism), and a major theme of its ideology is a hysterical hatred for top-hatted capitalists who, it's claimed, used to exploit and oppress the workers, in the days before capitalism was abolished. There are no capitalists, top-hatted or otherwise, around any longer. The Party constantly proclaims that conditions are steadily improving and are much better than in the days of capitalism, whereas the story's protagonist Winston Smith suspects and the reader knows that conditions are not improving and are much worse than they were under capitalism.

Orwell was consciously writing in the tradition of many utopias and dystopias which had been pouring out since the seventeenth century. For years he had made a special point of paying attention to dystopian works of fiction. A conscious opponent of capitalism, he could easily have followed such models as Wells's *The Sleeper Awakes* (1899; revised 1910) or London's *The Iron Heel* (1907) and presented his dystopia as capitalist. Yet he chose instead to ruthlessly purge his horrific future of all but vestigial traces of capitalism, and such traces are presented as mementoes of a sadly lost past. The Ingsoc economy comes close to pure, distilled essence of collectivism.

The Challenge to Socialists

The rise of Communism in Russia, Fascism in Italy, and National Socialism in Germany compelled socialists to make momentous choices. Socialists had to decide whether they approved of Soviet Russia, and whether they considered it an example of what they called socialism.

Following his conversion to socialism in mid-1936, Orwell made sharply critical comments about some features of Soviet Communism, but did not directly address the question of whether Soviet Russia could be called socialist. After his experiences in Spain, Orwell became strongly anti-Communist and emphatically asserted that the Soviet Union was not socialist, though he frankly acknowledged that this presented socialists with a problem, as they had traditionally supposed that the abolition of private property and its replacement by planned state-owned industrial administration were the defining features of socialism.

Immediately after Hitler's accession to power, Orwell had underrated the significance of this event. Though not yet himself committed to the Left, he apparently did not dissent from the general view of most leftists at the time that Hitler was a mere pawn of capitalist interests, and would be removed as soon as he inconvenienced those interests. Orwell soon changed his mind, however, and later argued that National Socialism was a revolutionary collectivist movement. Communism and fascism were similar in their thrust, and would tend to become more similar:

> National Socialism *is* a form of Socialism, *is* emphatically revolutionary, *does* crush the property owner as surely as it crushes the worker. The two régimes, having started from opposite ends, are rapidly evolving towards the same system—a form of oligarchical collectivism. . . . It is therefore nonsense to talk about Germany "going Bolshevik" if Hitler falls. Germany is going Bolshevik *because* of Hitler and not in spite of him. (XII, 159)

"Oligarchical collectivism" is the term Orwell was to apply to the society described in *Nineteen Eighty-Four*. A few months after writing the above, Orwell argued that the recent defeats of Britain by Germany, provided a conclusive demonstration that "private capitalism . . . does not work." These military outcomes have proved once and for all that "a planned economy is stronger than a planless one" (XII, 409–410). Orwell goes on to define fascism, "at any rate the German version," as "a form of capitalism that borrows from Socialism just such features as will make it efficient for war purposes." He then repeats the analysis he has given earlier, that the German economy is nominally privately owned but in fact completely controlled by the state, and adds: "The mere *efficiency* of such a system, the elimination of waste and obstruction, is obvious" (410).

At one point, then, Orwell calls the Nazi regime "a form of Socialism" and a little later "a form of capitalism." Despite such terminological fluctuations, the actual meaning of his analysis is clear and has not changed: Nazi Germany has the elements of a planned, centralized economy, which is one of the essential qualities of socialism. It lacks other essential qualities of socialism, such as democracy and equality of incomes, just the same qualities lacked by Soviet Russia. Orwell explains what he means by calling the Nazi economy a form of capitalism: for the most part, the same individuals "own" property and continue to get incomes comparable to what they received prior to the Nazi revolution. However, he says, the factory "owner" has in essential function become a state employee.

The fundamental similarity of the Third Reich and the Soviet Union, summed up in the phrase "Red fascism and brown Bolshevism," was a common view after 1933, and naturally received even more attention after the Nazi-Soviet pact. Orwell's agreement with this analysis had no doubt been confirmed by reading Franz Borkenau's hurriedly-written yet pivotal book, *The Totalitarian Enemy* (1940). However, as early as *The Road to Wigan Pier*, Orwell already sees "the objective of Fascism" as a slave state which is "economically collectivist—that is, with the profit principle eliminated" (V, 200), though he doesn't at that point identify it as the same system as Communism.

On another occasion Orwell remarked that "one country after another is adopting a centralised economy that one can call Socialism or state capitalism according as one prefers" (503). Orwell is here taking the stance (for a wider audience than he normally reached) that terminology doesn't matter. On the few occasions where Orwell calls Soviet Russia "state capitalism," he is not abandoning his "oligarchical collectivism" analysis. The analysis doesn't change: we just have to remember that, in these contexts, what he most often calls "capitalism" would have to be called "private capitalism" to distinguish it from state capitalism.

We can sum up the position Orwell had arrived at by 1940 by saying that while Communism and Nazism are different in origins, different in ideology, and different in the kind of people they initially appeal to, they become increasingly similar in practical administration. They both impose a planned economy (which Orwell along with almost the entire Left believes to be axiomatically more efficient than a competitive one), they both eliminate democracy, and they both fail to bring about even approximate equality of incomes. Orwell never subsequently departed from this assessment; his later remarks are all consistent with it.

Two Definitions of Socialism

Socialists wanted a new kind of social order because they believed it would have desirable qualities and would therefore be an improvement upon capitalism. They were faced with the reality of new societies which did not look like the traditional leftist model of capitalism but also did not possess the anticipated desirable qualities of socialism. In the eyes of many socialists, of whom Orwell was one, these new societies were manifestly worse than capitalism as they had known it.

If socialism meant replacing competitive capitalism with central direction of the economy, then the Communist and National Socialist societies would have to be called socialist. Alternatively, socialists could simply deny that Communism and National Socialism were socialist, by defining the word "socialism" so that it necessarily included the hoped-for desirable qualities.

Socialists like Orwell would often vacillate between two tacit definitions of the word "socialism." According to the first definition, "socialism" is a society in which industry is collectively owned. According to the second definition, 'socialism' means that industry is collectively owned *and* that life is wonderful. On this second definition, then, if we look at any society and find that life is not wonderful, we must infer that this society is not socialist even if industry is collectively owned.

Some people said "Soviet Russia has abject poverty, mass killings, and a total absence of democracy, therefore it cannot be socialist." Others said "Soviet Russia has abject poverty, mass killings, and a total absence of democracy. This is where socialism has led." These two statements agree completely on the facts. They differ only on the terminological convention of how the word "socialism" is to be defined. The first group adheres to definition 2 and reasons that since life in Soviet Russia is not wonderful, it cannot be socialist. The second group adheres to definition 1 and reasons that since Soviet Russia is, by this definition, socialist, socialism has led, at least in this instance, to a less than wonderful life.

Most of the time, Orwell followed definition 2, and therefore maintained that Soviet Russia was not socialist, but he occasionally slipped into definition 1, which implies that Soviet Russia is socialist, as in his view is Nazi Germany.

In Russia the Communists had nationalized almost the whole of industry except for very tiny firms. The vast majority of industry was not privately owned but state-owned. This was certainly understood by the Left and by Orwell himself to be the most essential point of socialism, as Orwell often acknowledged. What Orwell means by denying that Russia is socialist is that none of the anticipated desirable qualities of socialism have appeared in Russia (especially democracy and equality of incomes). Instead, Orwell observes, Soviet Russia is, for the ordinary worker, even worse than Western capitalism.

The various statements by Orwell seem to contradict each other, until we realize that he is slipping from one definition of socialism to another. In his remark about the Third Reich, Orwell wants to stress that it is decidedly different from countries like France, Britain, and the U.S.: it is not "just capitalism," as many leftists were then assuming. He goes so far as to call the Third Reich "a form of Socialism" (Orwell always capitalizes "Socialism"), meaning that it has a collectivized economy. Orwell often liked to provocatively overstate his point for shock value, and this explains his lapse into definition 1 on this occasion. Mostly, he sticks to definition 2, which is what I have done in this book except where otherwise noted: "collectivism" is employed to signify any social order which has collective ownership of industry. "Socialism" is a subset of "collectivism"; if something is true of collectivism generally, it is ipso facto true of socialism, whatever socialism may be.

Orwell's usage of the terms "socialism" and "collectivism" fluctuated somewhat. For instance, in a 1945 book review he disputes that communism and fascism are "collectivist" because they have inequality and class privilege (XVII, 22). Here I consistently stick to the usage Orwell followed most of the time: "socialism" is a subset of "collectivism"; collectivism has abolished private, competitive profit-making; socialism is collectivism with additional attributes (democracy and equality) of which Orwell approves. If he had stuck to his predominant usage, Orwell would not have written "National Socialism *is* a form of Socialism," but "National Socialism *is* a form of collectivism."

By the time he came to write *Nineteen Eighty-Four*, Orwell had held for at least eight years that the Soviet Union was neither socialist (in the sense that socialists like him had favored) nor moving toward socialism, and that fascism had been moving in the same direction as the Soviet Union. Orwell called the kind of society towards which both the Soviet Union and Nazi Germany were moving "oligarchical collectivism" and his own preferred social order "democratic Socialism." Naturally, we ought to bear in mind that the Soviet Union and the fascist regimes actually existed, whereas Orwell's democratic socialism never has existed.

This view would prompt the conjecture that, purely as a factual matter, independent of any value judgments we might make, society is not moving in the direction of socialism (collectivism with income equality and with liberty of thought and expression) but toward oligarchical collectivism, a society more oppressive than capitalism had been, with worse conditions for the workers and greater inequality, and with a totalitarian form of state. Could it be that a collectivist organization of industry inherently favors political totalitarianism? This point did indeed occur to Orwell and became a major preoccupation.

He took the position, sometimes voiced with confidence, sometimes with a perceptible lack of confidence, that collectivism could possibly be democratic if it were to be established in countries with a strong liberal tradition. In a broadcast talk in which he was arguing that literature as we have come to know it (creative works like novels) must cease to exist under totalitarianism, Orwell comments:

> . . . I believe the hope of literature's survival lies in those countries in which liberalism has struck its deepest roots . . . I believe—it may be no more than a pious hope—that though a collectivised economy is bound to come, those countries will know how to evolve a form of Socialism which is not totalitarian, in which freedom of thought can survive the disappearance of economic individualism. (XII, 505)

Capitalism Is Doomed

Having read this far in this chapter, a twenty-first-century reader new to Orwell might be baffled. Most of the puzzlement can be dispelled by identifying a simple fact about Orwell's outlook. Along with most other socialists and even many nonsocialists of the time, he holds that capitalism is, as a matter of objective fact, doomed to disappear in the near future. Irrespective of the merits of capitalism or socialism, and quite independent of any arguments about totalitarianism, he thinks that nothing can save capitalism from imminent disappearance. This is something Orwell reiterates in tones of confident certainty from 1936 until his death (XII, 503; XVI, 386; XVIII, 57, 272; XIX, 166).[17] Capitalism is doomed, not because people don't like it, but because of inexorable economic and political forces which no one can deflect. Orwell sometimes adjusts his identification of the precise nature of these forces, but always within the assumptions that we cannot escape the mechanization of life, and the mechanization of life decrees the replacement of capitalism by collectivism.

17 It's true that in such statements Orwell sometimes (not always) refers to "laissez-faire capitalism." However, we can infer from the totality of his remarks that Orwell's worldview did not allow any possibility of the indefinite survival even of regulated capitalism. He employs the term "laissez-faire capitalism" rather loosely to refer to the social system actually prevailing in western countries. In other words, Orwell's position excludes any possibility of saving capitalism by modifying it.

If capitalism is about to pass away and cannot be rescued, it follows that the comparative merits of capitalism and socialism have become an issue of little urgency, whereas the comparative merits of "oligarchical collectivism" and "democratic Socialism," supposing the latter to be feasible, becomes an issue of the utmost importance. Oddly, the premiss that capitalism is inevitably going to disappear can be used in an argument for abolishing it as soon as possible, since the success of a true democratic socialist revolution might, Orwell supposes, help to tip the balance for democratic socialism and against oligarchical collectivism. If we hurry up and establish collectivism, we'll get to have a say in what sort of collectivism it will be, whereas if we do nothing we're still bound to get collectivism soon, and maybe a type of collectivism we don't much care for (XII, 460–62).

Orwell never abandoned one of the key beliefs of the 1930s Left, that capitalism spontaneously and ineluctably evolves in the direction of collectivism.[18] Traditionally, this belief involved the Marxian proposition that large-scale organization beats out small-scale organization in competitive markets because large-scale organization is always more efficient. Free competition therefore automatically leads to increasing concentration of organization and ownership, and so to the abolition of free competition. Though he may not have been completely convinced by this hypothetical mechanism, Orwell thought he could see other, additional mechanisms by which capitalism was doomed. He would not give up trying to make collectivism tolerable largely because he had never seriously questioned his orthodox leftist conviction that collectivism of some sort is implicit in the evolution of modern industry.

Orwell sometimes looked forward to the possibility of totalitarian states like the USSR becoming more democratic (XVIII, 71). In the light of history since Orwell, we might be inclined to interpret this as meaning that totalitarian states would retreat from collectivism and re-introduce

18 Contrary to Lebedoff (2008, 119–120). Orwell acknowledged that the most productive and powerful country in the world was capitalist, but he did not doubt that the United States would become collectivist. In July 1947 he wrote: "In North America the masses are contented with capitalism, and one cannot tell what turn they will take when capitalism begins to collapse" (XIX, 164).

elements of the free market or private property. But if we carefully read all of what Orwell says on such matters, we see that he does not mean this at all. For Orwell, the triumph of collectivism is inevitable and final; there is to be no return of capitalism or free markets, not even a partial return. He is simply referring to unspecified provisions for individual liberty within a fully collectivist system, thus enabling oligarchical collectivism to be "liberalized" in the sense of becoming democratic collectivism.

For Orwell, the danger of worldwide totalitarianism arises only because capitalism cannot survive. Orwell never suggests that capitalism ("private capitalism") might become totalitarian, except only in the process of ceasing to be capitalism ('private capitalism'). "The real question . . . is whether capitalism, now obviously doomed, is to give way to oligarchy or to true democracy" (XVIII, 272). Totalitarianism, for Orwell, is not a conceivable political form of private, competitive capitalism (which most of the time he calls simply "capitalism"), but it is the political form of the oligarchical replacement of capitalism. The only possible alternative he can see to oligarchical collectivism (beyond universal destruction or a relapse into primitive conditions) is a democratic form of collectivism, for which he prefers to reserve the label "socialism."

Bad, Bad Capitalism

It would be wrong to conclude from the above that Orwell would have instantly become a supporter of capitalism if he had become convinced that the evolution of capitalism towards collectivism was not inevitable. Although A. M. Eckstein wrote a perceptive article bringing out Orwell's comparatively favorable view of laissez-faire capitalism,[19] we can't get around the fact that Orwell was a doctrinaire 1930s leftist intellectual. Orwell believed that unregulated capitalism causes unemployment and slumps and that government intervention could greatly reduce human suffering. Piecemeal state interventions in capitalism would not be socialism, but they would always tend to move the economy in the direction of socialism by replacing *laissez faire* with more and more central direction.

19 Eckstein 1987.

If capitalism is an inefficient, morally odious system, producing much unnecessary misery, which can be ameliorated by government intervention, this has two consequences for Orwell. First, he supports such measures on the obvious compassionate grounds. Second, aside from his own preferences, he reckons that such measures will inevitably be introduced, and the accumulation of such measures will take society away from capitalism towards collectivism. So even if the orthodox Left is wrong about central planning being the culmination of free competition, there is another spontaneous process which will, Orwell believes, culminate in replacing capitalism by central planning: the political process of successively doing things which relieve the misery caused by capitalism. In his brief, sympathetic review of Hayek's *Road to Serfdom*, Orwell appeals to this argument against Hayek's contention that monopoly is not the outcome of competition (XVI, 149), though he also gives a nod to the traditional leftist theory of competition destroying itself by indefinite increase in the size of firms.

Since Orwell is convinced that capitalism cannot be saved, and is bound to be supplanted by collectivism before long, he wants that collectivism to be "democratic" and therefore in his terminology "socialist." In using the term "democratic," Orwell is not referring chiefly to rule by majority vote, but to the continuation, or even expansion, of the liberty of thought and expression which has been attained under liberal capitalism.

Is *Nineteen Eighty-Four* about Capitalism?

A burden of much leftist writing on Orwell is that *Nineteen Eighty-Four* is not specifically about a collectivist system. It is not about Soviet socialism, nor about Labour Party socialism. It's about modern society in general, and therefore it's as much about capitalism as it is about socialism or collectivism. Once this position has been established to the writer's satisfaction, it's a short slide to the view that *Nineteen Eighty-Four* is specifically directed at capitalism. I don't contend that this kind of reading is to be ruled out of court. But, just as much as the antisocialist reading, it clashes with a key component of Orwell's intentions.

An extreme variant of this reading is the view that *Nineteen*

Eighty-Four is not about an imaginary future at all. It is, rather, about aspects of the society in which Orwell lived. It is a satire on features of British life in the 1940s. Therefore, it's just a mistake to suppose that the book is about a different kind of society. We are then free to apply its lessons to any society where they seem applicable, and if we are good leftists, even this view ends up with *Nineteen Eighty-Four* as an attack upon capitalism.

It's quite correct that *Nineteen Eighty-Four* is on one level a depiction of life in 1940s Britain. But this should be taken in something of the same sense as that the Eloi in *The Time Machine* "are" Wildean aesthetes. It does not entitle us to throw out the "imagined future" aspect of the narrative. A rich work of literary art like *Nineteen Eighty-Four* is "about" more than one thing. Many aspects of *Nineteen Eighty-Four* are utterly different from anything experienced in England at any time: the complete absence of a profit incentive, the one-party state, the reduction of Britain to a small component in one of only three world powers. These aspects are identical with likely future outcomes Orwell had seriously discussed in his non-fiction writings. As backstory to the novel, Orwell had clearly worked out the fictional history of Britain from the 1940s until the 1980s. And when trying to combat unwelcome interpretations of *Nineteen Eighty-Four*, Orwell did not retort that it was just about 1948. He said that it depicted a future that might, in essence, come about but was not bound to come about.

It is, however, quite true that Orwell saw the society of *Nineteen Eighty-Four* as a culmination of trends which existed in all modern societies including western capitalist ones. Orwell believed that capitalism would inevitably be replaced by collectivism in all industrialized societies (XII, 123), and this opened up the possibility of totalitarianism, which would be more likely if totalitarian ideas came to prevail in the capitalist societies prior to their transition to collectivism.

For example, Orwell criticized the popular "bad books" of his day for their formulaic approach, and wrote derisively of the "How to Invent Gripping Plots" mail-order industry for aspiring writers (XVI, 464). In *Nineteen Eighty-Four* (written before people like Orwell were even remotely aware of the possibilities of computers), literature for the masses, called "prolefeed," is composed by machines. In one of the book's many comical touches, Julia, who cares nothing for any kind of writing, works on one of the machines which 'writes' prolefeed, and at one point injures her arm operating the machine. Orwell thought that the mechanical approach to composing stories would come into its own under totalitarianism, but he did not suppose that any such cultural development could actually bring totalitarianism into being—that requires the replacement of competition by central economic planning. The triumph of totalitarianism, in Orwell's conception, has become likely because the abolition of capitalism has become certain.

According to Crick:

> *Nineteen Eighty-Four* is a long premeditated, rational warning against totalitarian tendencies in societies like our own rather than a sick and sudden prophecy about a Soviet or neo-Nazi takeover . . ." (Crick 1992, 568)

Crick here presents the alternatives in a false light. A "totalitarian tendency" in a society like Britain of the 1940s is, in Orwell's conception, a tendency to become like the Soviet Union and Nazi Germany. No one has claimed that Orwell's "prophecy" was "sudden." Orwell's preoccupation with the likelihood that Britain would experience a totalitarian (Soviet-style or Nazi-style) transformation was at least ten years old when *Nineteen Eighty-Four* was published; it is hauntingly present in *Coming Up for Air* (1939). The backstory to *Nineteen Eighty-Four* is something akin to a Communist or neo-Nazi takeover, though specifically one perpetrated by an anti-Semitic movement whose roots are in the British Left.

Newsinger suggests that Orwell thought of Ingsoc as a "rightwing" movement like Nazism.[20] For Orwell, this would have been a minor issue, since he held that leftist oligarchical collectivism (Communism) and rightist oligarchical collectivism (National Socialism) produce similar and convergent forms of society. However, it's clear that Ingsoc is leftist in origin: it arises from an ideological takeover of the British Left, which involves antisemitism; the antisemitism survives in the hatred of Emmanuel

20 Newsinger 1999, 121.

Goldstein, but has apparently been discarded in practice by the time of the action of the novel. In Orwell's backstory, a key role is played by a collectivist demagogue named Baker (the name presumably suggested by General Georges Boulanger, the political adventurer who could have become dictator of France in the 1880s if only he had tried a little harder). If Ingsoc had been conceived as specifically quasi-Nazi, why wouldn't Orwell publicly announce this simple fact when he was trying to counter the anti-Labour Party interpretation of *Nineteen Eighty-Four*? But if he had done so, this might not have carried conviction, because the Ingsoc rhetoric in the book is obviously closer to Communism than to Nazism.

In Burnham's *Managerial Revolution*, Soviet Socialism, National Socialism, and the New Deal, are all different expressions of managerialism: the form of collectivism which is actually replacing capitalism. They all take society in the direction of the complete elimination of capitalism, though Soviet Socialism has so far gone further in that direction than National Socialism or the New Deal. The trappings of the Ingsoc regime are more like the Communist than the Nazi example, simply because the former had moved further than the latter along the predetermined path which led to pure oligarchical collectivism, the topic of *Nineteen Eighty-Four*.

As the example of the Third Reich shows, many of the most appalling features of totalitarianism can exist alongside substantial nominal private ownership of capital, and Orwell would not, of course, have denied this. But in Germany the nominally private industry was controlled and directed by the government. Orwell thought of the surviving elements of the market inside the Third Reich as vestiges of capitalism which would have been gradually wiped out if the regime had survived.

Thus, Crick's statements are seriously misleading. Orwell did indeed think of *Nineteen Eighty-Four* as a culmination of existing tendencies in both collectivism and capitalism, but he thought of capitalism as tending to become ever more collectivist, ever less capitalist, until all but a few tiny vestiges of capitalism were stamped out, as in the world of *Nineteen Eighty-Four*. He thought that existing capitalism contained collectivist tendencies, and it was from these collectivist tendencies, as they grew and became all-pervasive, eliminating capitalism in the process, that the danger of a society like *Nineteen Eighty-Four* arose. He never for one moment allowed the possibility that private, competitive capitalism could continue to exist and itself become totalitarian.

In addition to the letter to Henson quoted above, another, longer statement was issued about *Nineteen Eighty-Four* on 15th June 1949. This is headed "Orwell's Statement on *Nineteen Eighty Four*," but it actually seems to be a statement composed by Warburg after a discussion with Orwell (this is suggested by, among other things, a reference to Orwell in the third person). While there is no doubt that this statement is a broadly accurate interpretation of Orwell's intentions, it's likely that Warburg was responsible for some of the exact wording and for some decisions as to what to include and what to emphasize. The statement asserts that *Nineteen Eighty-Four* portrays what "*could* happen." The danger of its happening lies in the structure imposed "on Socialist and on Liberal capitalist communities" by the need to prepare for war with the USSR,[21] and also in "the acceptance of a totalitarian outlook by intellectuals of all colours." The statement envisions that in Britain, new "tougher" leaders will take over, "drawn probably from the ranks of the Left." The present Labour Party leaders (Attlee, Cripps, Bevan, "and in general the older men") are "safe," but the younger generation "is suspect and the seeds of totalitarian thought are probably widespread among them" (XX, 134–35). And so, even in this statement, so often cited to rebut the notion that Orwell saw danger in the Labour Party, there is an explicit indication that the younger men in the Labour Party could be the ones to take Britain in a totalitarian direction.

David C. Smith maintains that both Zamyatin's *We* and *Nineteen Eighty-Four* "provide an extremely graphic idea of what capitalism, carried to its end, will become."[22] This statement could be rescued by recalling Orwell's belief that industrial capitalism, carried to its end, must lead to its own abolition. However, the immediate context of Smith's

21 If this statement had actually been written by Orwell, then it would be significant that he focuses on nuclear rivalry with the USSR as a cause of the West's going totalitarian, and does not mention any internal economic or political cause, as he always does in other places. But this is just the sort of nuance that might have been missed by Warburg in writing up his conversation with Orwell.

22 David C. Smith 1986, 79.

remark shows that he is not thinking along those lines. He says that "for some" *We* "provided a Marxist analysis of capitalism which is useful. In fact the book was also read as an attack on the early years of Soviet society" (78–79). There is nothing that looks remotely like Marxist analysis (or remotely like capitalism) in *We*. It is not an attack on the early years of Soviet society but on the fundamental premisses of Communism as Zamyatin understood them.

A particularly crude assertion of the view that *Nineteen Eighty-Four* is about capitalism occurs in David Smith's[23] *Orwell for Beginners*. According to Smith, "Orwell did, in fact, have a taste of the anti-Communist interpretation to be conferred on *Nineteen Eighty-Four*, and he strenuously protested."[24] Orwell did indeed strenuously protest against the anti-socialist or anti-Labour Party interpretation, but never against the anti-Communist interpretation, which he explicitly endorsed, even in the oft-quoted letter to Henson.

Orwell for Beginners ends by quoting a "statement" attributed to Orwell. The statement is actually a running together of two passages. The first passage is by Orwell, from the letter to Henson, the second is from the statement composed by Warburg. The latter passage refers to the speculative possibility that "100 percent Americanism" might be the name of a future Western totalitarian ideology. Smith's concocted "statement" is accompanied by a cartoon by Mike Mosher headed "BIG BUSINESS, 100% Americanism" and a picture of Henry Ford saying "History, my friends, is Bunk!"

As Warburg's statement was made following a conversation with the hospitalized and feeble Orwell, it is possible (though not certain), that Orwell accepted "100 percent Americanism" as one possible name, along with "Ingsoc" and others, for a future western totalitarian ideology. The notion that an ideology glorifying big business could be totalitarian is, however, not connected even dubiously with anything stated by Orwell or by Warburg, and is Smith's (or Mosher's) pure invention.

If the possibility had been suggested to him, Orwell would probably

23 As far as I can tell, this author is not the aforementioned David C. Smith and has no connection with him.

24 Smith 1984, 189.

not have ruled out that a totalitarian ideology might in practice be associated with glorification of big business. We know from Orwell's statements about the National Socialist economy that he accepted that capitalism could be abolished while nominally private business leaders might survive. But the Nazi ideology did not single out big business for unique glory in the manner of Mosher's cartoon. A collectivist economy accompanied by this kind of explicit ideological identification with big business has never existed and would be a bizarre fluke. Smith and Mosher's presentation conveys the distinct impression that it would be quite natural, and that *Nineteen Eighty-Four* is specifically directed against big business, a complete travesty of the novel and of Orwell's views generally. It is with all deliberate purpose that there is no big business in the world of *Nineteen Eighty-Four*.

What if There's No Such Thing as Democratic Socialism?

What if freedom is somehow tied to the absence of a collectivist economy, and therefore (in an industrial system) tied to capitalism? What if there can be no such thing as a democratic form of collectivism, democratic socialism? This question troubled Orwell.

Nowadays, some people are liable to respond by citing the twentieth-century examples of Britain, France, or Sweden, especially after 1945. However, if Orwell or most of the 1930s Left could have looked at these developments, they would have had no hesitation in saying that these are clear examples of capitalism, whether or not governed by people who style themselves "socialist." A state-welfare system, progressive taxation, and some piecemeal regulation do modify the operation of capitalism. We might even say that they take society somewhat in the direction of collectivism. But societies with these features remain obviously and palpably capitalism, because most of industry is privately owned, with dividends going to stockholders, there are flourishing financial markets (capital and money markets), and there is no serious attempt to predetermine the magnitudes of major economic aggregates by central direction.

Is *Nineteen Eighty-Four* an anti-collectivist book? If, as Orwell held, capitalism is doomed and democratic socialism is a possibility, then *Nineteen Eighty-Four* is not an anti-collectivist book. But if capitalism is not doomed and democratic socialism is an impossibility, then *Nineteen Eighty-Four* becomes an anti-collectivist book, regardless of its author's intentions. (If capitalism is doomed and democratic socialism is impossible, then it's not an anti-collectivist book in any pragmatic sense, because it presents us with a future we can do nothing about.)

Orwell was committed to "democratic Socialism." However, he also sometimes entertained the possibility that this might never come about, and that capitalism would then be replaced by a form of society much like Soviet Russia, decidedly worse than capitalism. Since Orwell publicly maintained to the end of his days that capitalism was doomed and that democratic socialism was possible (or hopefully might be possible), he was bound to defend the book as not anti-collectivist. Indeed following the terminology he most commonly employed, it would be natural to see *Nineteen Eighty-Four* as anything but antisocialist. In this terminology, *Nineteen Eighty-Four* depicts a horrific collectivist society which is, precisely, *not* socialist, which is to say, not democratic collectivist but oligarchical collectivist.

Intentionalism is not, in my view, a fallacy. If I find a note from a family member on my refrigerator door, then in trying to make sense of it I am trying to reconstruct the writer's intentions, and it's exactly the same with "Le bateau ivre" or *Nineteen Eighty-Four*. However, it has always been understood that a work may in some special cases have a character and direction quite distinct from or even contrary to the author's intentions. This, however, has to be shown by specific arguments.

A chemist writes a book effectively demonstrating the perils of cyanide poisoning. This chemist happens also to be an enthusiastic member of a sect which preaches that a non-poisonous type of cyanide will one day be found, and will prove to be no poison at all but a wondrous panacea. According to the liturgical conventions of this sect, the as yet undiscovered non-toxic cyanide is alone truly worthy of the name "cyanide," and it would therefore be better to call by a different name the cyanide we have actually observed. Now if in fact non-poisonous cyanide does not exist, then the chemist's book makes a contribution to showing the dangerous character of all cyanide, cyanide in general, even though that was not his intention, and almost the opposite of his intention.

Orwell is a democratic socialist who doesn't want to call 'socialist' those collectivist systems which turn out to be undemocratic, inegalitarian, and oppressive. *Nineteen Eighty-Four* is a horrendous depiction of a kind of collectivist society instantiated by Soviet Russia and Nazi Germany. To someone with Orwell's theoretical outlook, observing events in the 1930s and 1940s, it seems entirely plausible that this form of society is in the ascendant and may soon take over the entire world.

It should go without saying that *Nineteen Eighty-Four* is a work of literary art, in which various aspects of the imagined social order are selected because they "work" aesthetically within the narrative. It is above all a satire with moments of grim humor. No doubt some people have cut their throats after finishing *Nineteen Eighty-Four*, but they have had a few chuckles first. We should avoid the fallacy of thinking of *Nineteen Eighty-Four* as an expression of Orwell's "mood of despair." Orwell outlined the work in 1943 and wrote it in 1948. During those five years, as it happens, he became slightly *less* inclined to think that a totalitarian future was imminent. This is no more mysterious than the commonplace fact that a happy composer may cheerfully write a melancholy piece of music. When Orwell sat down on the Isle of Jura to write *Nineteen Eighty-Four*, he was performing the exercise of working out a conception he had been carrying around in his mind for some years, a conception with an artistic logic of its own.

If, as a matter of objective fact, a society with a collectivist economy is by its nature totalitarian, if democratic socialism is impossible, or even just highly unlikely, then *Nineteen Eighty-Four* changes from being an indictment of a specific kind of collectivism to being an indictment of collectivism per se. In evaluating the proposition that collectivism is by its nature totalitarian, Orwell's mere opinions have no relevance.

If collectivism can be other than oligarchical, or if we reserve the term 'socialism' for non-oligarchical collectivism, then we may say that *Nineteen Eighty-Four* is not anti-socialist, but if collectivism cannot be other than oligarchical, and if we may apply the term "socialism" to any actual collectivism, then *Nineteen Eighty-Four* is anti-socialist.

The above would hold even if Orwell had not himself considered the possibility that collectivism might be necessarily totalitarian. One of the admirable things about Orwell is that he often pursues a line of thought somewhat further, in a direction unwelcome to his preconceptions, than we might expect someone in his situation to do. Orwell did indeed raise the possibility that collectivism was inherently totalitarian, and he was unable to dismiss it. It became a nagging worry. But this is immaterial to the main point, which would apply even if Orwell had never contemplated that possibility.

Similarly, we can speculate that Orwell might have abandoned his commitment to socialism if he had lived longer. Speculations over such matters are not unreasonable but they are somewhat trivial—not because "we can never really know what he would have thought," but because it doesn't much matter what he would have thought. Ideas have an objective content independent of the wishes of their creators. If Darwin had, as Christian preachers routinely and falsely used to claim, renounced evolution on his deathbed, this would have exactly no bearing on the truth of Darwin's theory.

Orwell wrote a story which is, as he intended, an attack upon oligarchical collectivism. If there is no other kind of collectivism—and that is a purely factual issue, independent of Orwell's beliefs—then the book turns out to be an attack upon collectivism *per se*, irrespective of Orwell's intentions and even contrary to them.

Raymond Williams considers *Nineteen Eighty-Four* objectively anti-socialist, and Orwell less than honorable for having written it. Williams never faces up to the possibility that democratic socialism may be impossible. This is not merely a pedantic conceptual point: if there were such a thing as democratic socialism, and if anyone had any idea how to bring it about, it would have been a live issue in European politics after 1949, and *Nineteen Eighty-Four* would have fallen into place as an attack on one pathological form of collectivism, just as Orwell conceived it. What occurred instead was that democratic socialists remained democrats and in practice abandoned socialism. In other words, it is not Orwell's fault that a democratic form of collectivism cannot exist. It is that reality in the world, not some defect in Orwell, that makes *Nineteen Eighty-Four* objectively anti-socialist.

Socialists like Williams and Deutscher condemn *Nineteen Eighty Four* because it is an attack upon socialism itself, or because it spreads discouragement or even despair by its depiction of what collectivism must turn into. But it is impossible to make this charge without tacitly appealing to the premise that socialism is inherently totalitarian—that there is no alternative type of socialism than that which was embodied in the Soviet state and is parodied in *Nineteen Eighty-Four*. If there existed any such alternative, it would be natural to say that *Ninety Eighty-Four* was an attack on just one type of collectivism, or that it was an indication we ought to promote the other type of collectivism. This was precisely Orwell's position. The socialist who concludes that *Nineteen Eighty-Four* is objectively antisocialist is a socialist who tacitly recognizes that he has no persuasive answer to the proposition that collectivism can only be totalitarian. The severest socialist critics of Orwell, like Williams, Deutscher, and E. P. Thompson, were generally people who generated an immense quantity of verbiage about socialism, which they believed ought to be democratic, without ever grappling with the arguments indicating that socialism can never be democratic.

Now of course, someone might still argue, even at this late date, that democratic socialism *is*, after all, feasible, despite the absence of any actual example, and despite the formidable arguments against its feasibility by writers like Michels, Mises, Hayek, or Schumpeter. That's certainly worth discussing, but it's not crucial to the issue I have been looking at in this chapter. As long as some people do hold the view that democratic socialism is not a realistic option, and if such people view *Nineteen Eighty-Four* as objectively antisocialist, they are not thereby committing any kind of error about *Nineteen Eighty-Four* or about Orwell. This book by a socialist is open to just such an antisocialist reading.

11
Must Freedom Die?

> Almost certainly we are moving into an age of totalitarian dictatorships.
> —George Orwell, March 1940 (XII, 110)

From 1917 through 1939 one European country after another moved from democracy to dictatorship—Russia, Italy, Lithuania, Poland, Albania, Yugoslavia, Germany, Austria, Latvia, Bulgaria, Estonia, and Spain. While some of these regimes looked much like traditional dictatorships, others had qualities which were quite novel. What was different was unrestrained promotion of an empowered ideology through a one-party state.

Under the new dictatorships, the rule of law disappeared. Those in control of the state gloried in the fact that they were now empowered to do what they liked to anyone. No area of human life was off-limits to government intrusion. In Soviet Russia, in Fascist Italy, and in National Socialist Germany, there was the same lip-smacking glee at the fact that all traditional, constitutional, or moral constraints on the behavior of the ruling gang had been swept away.

This impression of rapidly disappearing democracy was exaggerated, as these toppled democracies had been installed quite recently on shaky foundations. None of the countries with really strong liberal traditions had abandoned democracy.[1] Yet the abolition of so many liberal democracies in such a short time impressed many people with the suspicion that liberty, democracy, and even capitalism were together disappearing from the world, perhaps forever.

1 Chamberlin 1937, 240–41.

Socialism as Ultimate Democracy

Socialism, as the idea prevailed between, say, 1880 and 1920, was identified with the fullest possible democracy. Socialists wanted to extend and enhance the democracy that already existed; hence "socialism" and "social democracy" became virtually synonymous terms. If socialists denigrated the democracy that existed under capitalism, it was only by maintaining that this democracy was imperfectly developed, because the system was unfairly weighted in favor of the owning class and against the workers. Once the classes of capitalist and worker had been abolished, then democracy would flourish as never before.

Now this identification of socialism with democracy was actually fairly new. Most socialists in the 1850s and after didn't know that their intellectual ancestors in the 1820s had been frankly authoritarian and reactionary—reactionary in the sense that they hated the turbulence of rapid social change, and wanted to terminate the unsettling revolution of liberalism by reinstating a higher form of aristocracy, in which the new lords of the world would be industrialists, bankers, and scientists. The 1820s ideology of Saint-Simonianism was boldly totalitarian.[2] The new socialism of the 1840s was democratic and equalitarian, and by the 1880s, when socialism was rapidly expanding its political following across Europe, the older Saint-Simonian socialism was largely forgotten: millions of socialists now saw socialism not merely as democratic, but as pure democracy, democracy in full flower.

Collectivism without Democracy

In the early twentieth century the easy identification of socialism with maximum democracy continued undiminished in the minds of many socialists. As Orwell pointed out (XVIII, 60), most socialists had just assumed that if we converted industry to public ownership, democracy would be maintained and expanded. Yet, around 1900, more and more

2 Hayek 1952; Manuel 1965; Iggers 1958; Iggers 1972. On the injection of liberal and democratic ideas into previously undemocratic socialism, see Bakunin 1976.

people had begun to question this assumption. If we have a publicly-owned industrial economy, in which deliberate planning of the whole of industry has replaced the spontaneous process of the profit-driven market, just why should we assume that such a system is automatically or naturally democratic and equalitarian? Could it be an instrument for the rule of a small minority of the population? Could it even be a new form of slavery, in which the liberal achievements of freedom of speech, freedom of movement, freedom of association, and freedom of belief would all be swept away?

The first writer to make a serious attempt to understand how democracy worked in practice was Moisey Ostrogorsky (1902). He showed how the electoral system is a structure with its own imperatives, not merely a conduit for the wishes of the voters. Although today Ostrogorsky's findings—the influence of party caucuses and the potential for demagoguery—seem mild, at the time they were disturbing to some. In H. G. Wells's *When the Sleeper Awakes*, there is an oppressive future political system; the Sleeper's antagonist and villainous would-be dictator masquerading as a democrat is named Ostrog. The Sleeper represents the basically sensible but lethargic educated middle class which potentially could control the world, but which Wells fears will never "wake up."

Jack London's *The Iron Heel* (1908) depicts the oppressive rule of a class of "Oligarchs." London considered himself a Marxist and therefore saw the Oligarchs as the final stand of capitalism. He assumed that they would be overthrown eventually—though he has them in power for three centuries. A speculation like this naturally prompts the question: what assurance can we have that such a powerful ruling class couldn't stay in power indefinitely?

In 1911 Robert Michels published the work to be known in English as *Political Parties*.[3] Where Ostrogorsky had set off tremors, Michels produced an earthquake. Michels had been a Social Democrat, then a syndicalist, and then had given up altogether on the possibility of "real" democracy. He explained that in any large, complex organization, no matter what attempts might be made to keep the officials as servants of the membership, in practice the leadership separates from the

3 Michels 1962.

rank-and-file and develops its own distinctive interests. Democracy requires organization; organization requires leaders; the larger and more complex the organization, the greater the gulf between leaders and led. He illustrated this process by a study of the German Socialist Party and explained some of the mechanisms by which it occurred.

The term "participatory democracy" had not yet been coined, however the concept without the name was popular among socialists. In later parlance, what Michels purported to show—and few readers of his book have been able to resist the conclusion—was that *participatory democracy is forever impossible*. This doesn't imply that ordinary, representative democracy is impossible—some checks can be placed upon the leaders. But many socialists, especially syndicalists, and including Michels himself, had vested their hopes in something stronger, some way in which the people's will could directly control the administration of a movement—or an entire society's industrial structure. Michels finally disposed of that notion in 1911, a momentous intellectual achievement. Michels moved on to become a theoretician of Fascism, but his book had been widely read before that became known, so the Law of Oligarchy had already become famous before its discoverer could be dismissed on account of his adherence to Fascist social theory.

From a very different quarter came Hilaire Belloc's *The Servile State* in 1912. Belloc and his followers, including G. K. Chesterton, detested capitalism, which they saw as a product of the Reformation. In their account the Catholic medieval system had abolished slavery and instituted a system of widespread property ownership. Capitalism, a consequence of Protestantism, had rendered the masses propertyless, and thus prepared the way for socialism. However, socialists could not achieve what they wanted; instead, their struggle to abolish capitalism would lead to the return of slavery. *The Servile State* was widely read—Belloc was an extremely popular writer at the time. The Belloc-Chesterton "distributists" had amicable discussions with socialists. The phrase "servile state" became a cliché in socialist circles by the time of World War I; socialists were concerned to distinguish the servile state from socialism, and to guard against the possibility that they might be unwittingly working for the former rather than the latter.[4]

4 Bullock 2011, 156.

The emergence of Bolshevik rule in Russia also made Western socialists uncomfortably aware of the fact that collectivism need not be democratic. Many socialists might cut the USSR some slack because the regime was "isolated and encircled," and might assume that "socialism" when it arrived in the West would naturally be less oppressive. But still, the point was brought home that collectivism does not inherently or intrinsically favor democracy, equality, or personal liberty. A malign future collectivism was projected in such works as Zamyatin's *We* (1924) and Huxley's *Brave New World* (1932). Whereas Wells's and London's dystopias had been capitalist; the later dystopias of Zamyatin and Huxley were collectivist.

One result of these currents of thinking was that G. D. H. Cole was not saying anything terribly controversial among British socialists when he wrote in *The Simple Case for Socialism*:

> . . . collectivism is as compatible with the Slave State as with Socialism; and if we seek Socialism without assiduously preaching to mankind a new way of living together we are in grievous danger of making only the Slave State where bureaucrats will rule and the quality of life decay. (Cole 1935, 13)

Cole holds that collectivism of some sort is coming, whether we like it or not. We may get bad collectivism ("the Slave State") or we may get good collectivism ("Socialism"), and which we do end up getting is something we can help to determine by our own efforts. This position is echoed by Orwell just two years later in *The Road to Wigan Pier*:

> Industrialism, once it rises above a fairly low level, *must* lead to some form of collectivism. Not necessarily to Socialism, of course; conceivably it might lead to the Slave-State, of which Fascism is a kind of prophecy. (V, 175)

Whereas Cole allows the possibility that we might work for socialism and inadvertently help to bring about the slave state, Orwell does not mention this scenario and merely connects the slave state with fascism. As early as 1936 Orwell sees fascism as possibly leading to a stable non-capitalist future—a totalitarian world "with the profit principle eliminated—but with all political, military, and educational power in the hands of a small caste of rulers and their bravos" (V, 200). Both Cole and Orwell accept that collectivism may be a slave state rather than socialism; neither of them broaches the possibility that there may be something inherent in collectivism which actually favors the slave state over democracy—though perhaps that is tacitly conceded in Cole's assertion that we may end up with the slave state unless we assiduously preach a new way of living together. Soon after *Wigan Pier* and his Spanish experience, Orwell begins to mention the disturbing possibility that collectivism can *only* be the slave state—totalitarianism.

Orwell had an additional reason for being pessimistic about the future of democracy. He held to a theory which, as it happened, he did not mention in his general discussions of totalitarianism: the theory that prospects for democracy are determined by the prevailing type of weaponry. Some weapons are easy to use by the many against the few, and where these are superior, they favor political clout for the common people, whereas other weapons are easy to use by the few against the many, and if these have the upper hand, democracy's chances are slim. Orwell strongly favored plenty of firearms in the hands of the mass of ordinary people, but it seemed to him that the tendency of modern weaponry, the machine gun, the tank, the plane, the missile, and the atomic bomb, boded ill for democracy (XII, 306, 365, 439–440; XVII, 319–320).

What to Make of the USSR?

The Bolsheviks' theory explaining why they had seized power in 1917 was that socialist revolutions in the West were imminent, and together the revolutionary socialist governments would convert their economies from capitalism to socialism. But then it gradually became clear that Bolshevik Russia was on its own. Marxist theory indicated that in this situation socialists should work for a democratic republic and allow capitalism to develop. But that would have meant acknowledging that the Bolshevik coup had been, at best, a horrible blunder. So instead the

Bolsheviks outlawed all their political opponents and made a dash for socialism in the period 1918–1921.[5] The result was industrial collapse, starvation, and growing working-class resistance to Bolshevik rule.

In March 1921, the Communists (as the Bolsheviks now called themselves), retreated from their attempt to institute socialism and permitted some scope for the market—the New Economic Policy. So far, things were going exactly as classical Marxism (maintained by people like Kautsky and Martov) had predicted. Evidently, the new regime could not be socialism or an approach to socialism, because it lacked both democracy and income equality. The premature attempt to establish socialism in a single, comparatively backward country had failed, "commodity relations" could not be forcibly abolished under conditions of extreme scarcity (just as Marx and Engels had always insisted), and now the trappings of bourgeois society would be gradually restored.

The leading Communists were determined not to let this happen. After Stalin's dictatorship had become a settled matter in the mid-1920s, the government renewed its drive, abandoned in 1921, to transform the economy into a socialist order. In the countryside the peasants were forcibly recruited into collectives—essentially, they were made chattel slaves of the state, something that could only be accomplished by slaughtering many millions of them.

In industry, new attempts were made to administer the state enterprises according to non-market principles. This too led to disasters, but instead of the restoration of private capitalism, something else emerged. The regime now instituted as a fixed matter of principle certain features hitherto assumed to be outmoded peculiarities of capitalism, or at best temporary expedients: wide differences in wages, the prevalence of piece-work, one-man management of each enterprise, and the requirement that each enterprise aim for an accounting profit. Alongside these unsocialist aspects, every enterprise was to remain state-owned and

5 The background to this innovation was the recent development in Marxist thought which perceived the installation of socialism as an outcome of national planning for war, reflected, for example, in the title of Otto Neurath's 1919 book, *Through the War Economy to the Natural Economy*. (A "natural" economy means a moneyless economy.)

subject to the system of planning by "material balances": every enterprise was to receive a copy of the central plan, specifying its physical inputs and outputs, and was expected to comply with this plan, with bonuses and other rewards going to those enterprise directors who "overfulfilled" the plan, and disciplinary measures, not excluding execution as a saboteur, going to those who underfulfilled.

As Michael Polanyi astutely pointed out, the "planners" at the center had no idea, and could have no idea, how the economy should develop.[6] The planners asked the enterprise managers what they intended to do, and then fed back to them a selection of their own projections in the form of plan directives. Soviet five-year plans were compiled a year or two after the official date of the plan's commencement, and were continually adapted during the remaining period, so that the plan finally proclaimed as fulfilled at the end of the period was different from the original plan. This freakish system, which had to be rescued from collapse daily by the immense black market, remained in place until 1991.

At first, the Communist description of what they were doing was "building socialism." In 1936 it was announced that socialism had been built, and that the Soviet Union was now "building communism," the moneyless society without wages which Marx had seen as the successor to capitalism, but which Lenin had defined as the stage after socialism.

One big question for Western socialists such as Orwell in the 1930s was how to classify the USSR. Was it socialism (which implied that if you blinked hard and looked again, it would turn out to be really quite nice)? Was it a new form of capitalism? Was it a new, non-socialist, non-capitalist type of society ruled by a bureaucracy, akin to age-old oriental despotisms?

According to Trotsky (who had conducted the Bolshevik seizure of power in November 1917) it was none of these things. Instead, it was a society in transition from capitalism to socialism which had got stuck in the transitional stage, neither relapsing into capitalism nor moving forward to socialism. Sooner or later, it would have to do one or the other. He called it a degenerated (or deformed) workers' state, an odd classification for a Marxist, since it said nothing about the social relations of

6 Polanyi 1940, 50–55.

production but only something about the political superstructure—and what it said seemed to be demonstrably wrong, for the workers had no control over the Soviet state; in fact members of the working class, or representatives of the "organized" working class, had far less political influence or scope for self-development in Soviet Russia than in France or Britain.

So what was Trotsky getting at? For him the decisive point was that Soviet industry was state-owned—private ownership had not been restored. What followed was that the Soviet system, however brutally it crushed the workers, was an advance on capitalism and should be supported in any conflict with capitalism—because and only because Soviet industry was state-owned. This makes a sort of sense given the twin assumptions that some mysterious force in "history" is tending to propel us towards socialism and that socialism will necessarily be better than capitalism. Socialism requires state ownership—even if you think that the expected "withering away of the state" is going to happen quickly, the first step has to be to bring about state ownership of industry. And so the establishment of state ownership is one necessary step towards a better world. But if we drop these assumptions, and assume instead that nothing (except intellectual fashion) is propelling us toward socialism—socialism is merely one suggestion by a bunch of intellectuals as to how we might try to organize things—then the argument doesn't look so persuasive.

Was the Soviet Union then "state capitalism"? According to Marx, wage labor and "capital" presuppose each other.[7] The general prevalence of wage labor is a sure sign of the predominance of bourgeois relations of production—of "capitalism." In this sense, the new Soviet order was capitalist: the workers had essentially the same relation to their employer as they did in openly capitalist societies. Only they were worse off, because they faced a single monolithic employer instead of a multitude of separate employers. Also (though this was harder for most people to understand at the time) they were worse off because state monopoly is necessarily less efficient than competition, output will be lower, and therefore total wages can only be lower.

7 Marx and Engels 1977, 214.

However, the conclusion that the Soviet system was a form of capitalism was not very persuasive to most socialists. In the period from roughly 1890 to 1910, German socialists (who provided Russian socialists with most of their ideas) had moved on from Marx's prediction that in the first phase of "communism," the day after the revolution, workers would be paid in non-circulating labor-vouchers. They concluded two things: first, that being paid in labor-vouchers was pretty much similar to being paid in money, and no more appetizing, and second, that the practical convenience of being paid in money rather than labor-vouchers was decisive. Karl Kautsky, the "pope of Marxism," knowing that he was overturning the traditional Marxist view, declared in 1902 that money would persist for a long time after the revolution, "until something better is discovered."[8] Marx's "revolutionary watchword," "Abolition of the wages system!"[9] became a dead letter. From this revised Marxist point of view, fully accepted by Lenin in such works as *The State and Revolution*, socialism retains money, and therefore it retains wages. The USSR could not readily be analyzed as being any more "capitalist" than any feasible socialist system which retained the payment of money wages. And ultimately, only a system which severed all connection between people's incomes and what they contributed to output could escape this broad conception of "capitalism."

The wider context here is that socialists were fitfully coming to understand that aspects of modern society they had once supposed optional and tied to capitalism are actually indispensable and equally essential under any alternative to capitalism, if it hopes to retain modern industrial technology.

What to Make of Fascism?

Until 1914 Benito Mussolini was the leading personality in Italian Marxism. He was imprisoned several times for his involvement in strikes and anti-war protests. He became editor of the Socialist Party journal *Avanti!* and his reputation as an activist, intellectual, and journalist grew from

8 Kautsky 1902, 129.
9 Marx and Engels 1985, Volume 20, 149.

1910 to 1914. He was a glamorous figure of the militant left, the Che Guevara of his day.[10]

Mussolini's rise to prominence as a Marxist *duce* coincided with the growth of syndicalism as the revolutionary alternative to social democracy. Socialists who wanted to be as left as they could be became syndicalists. Syndicalists favored revolution by direct action and a general strike, defying those socialists who favored electoral methods. Unlike others who embraced syndicalism, Mussolini remained within the Socialist Party, yet he closely followed the arguments of those syndicalists who had left it. Within syndicalism, new currents of thought developed. "Revolutionary revisionists," while determined to overthrow the liberal bourgeois order, acknowledged that capitalism had not turned out as Marx had predicted. They placed a new emphasis on "myths" (inspiring abstract ideas) rather than material interests and on action by active minorities rather than the majority of workers. They saw that workers had little interest in class struggle and harbored patriotic sentiments. A new form of syndicalism emerged—national syndicalism—based on the most productive elements of all classes and geared to the accelerated industrialization of backward economies like Italy.

In 1913 Mussolini began to publish and edit his own Marxist discussion journal, *Utopia*, a forum for controversial discussions among leftist intellectuals. Mussolini's articles here were signed "The man who is seeking." Two of those who collaborated with Mussolini on *Utopia* (Amadeo Bordiga and Angelo Tasca) would go on to help found the Communist Party of Italy and one (Karl Liebknecht) to help found the Communist Party of Germany while others, with Mussolini, would found the Fascist movement. Fascist doctrine grew directly out of the determination of highly intelligent Marxist militants to cast off all dogmatic blinkers and face the world as it really is.

A major issue in Italian politics in 1914 was whether Italy should join Britain and France against the Central Powers or remain neutral. The leading socialists were opposed to joining the war, but in November Mussolini abruptly changed his position and started a new independent socialist newspaper calling for entry into the war. He himself joined up

10 This parallel was first drawn by Adam L. Buick.

and was wounded, emerging after the war as a popular pro-war socialist. His socialist newspaper became the paper of the new Fascist movement, officially launched in 1919. Five of the seven individuals who organized the launch were of socialist or syndicalist background, though the bulk of the first rank-and-file recruits came from the Nationalist movement of Enrico Corradini.

The Left at first had no precise theory of what Fascism was, but leftists thought they knew that, since Fascism was opposed to the Socialist and Communist parties, it must have been devised by one or another group of capitalists. This conclusion owed nothing to any examination of facts, but was created to satisfy the narrative requirements of the drama of capitalism in its terminal crisis.[11] Other dictatorships which came along in the years after 1924 were also called "fascist" by the Left and a theory emerged to explain this entire phenomenon. Because of the fact that capitalism was in its death agony, dictated by objective and ineluctable economic laws, the capitalists had hired the fascists to prolong the life of the system by reducing workers' wages. This was the Comintern analysis, faithfully reproduced in such works as Strachey's *The Coming Struggle for Power*, but it was roughly accepted by almost all the Left; at least, there was no clear leftist alternative to the Comintern's theory.

Though the Nazis were encouraged by the prior example of Fascism, German National Socialism was not Fascist. While Fascist doctrine was produced by advanced intellectuals, many of whom became involved in the Fascist movement, generally speaking the leadership of the NSDAP was no more theoretically-minded than the leaderships of other political movements. In this respect the NSDAP was more like the common run of political parties—it accepted ideas developed by earlier intellectuals who were not themselves members of the movement.

From the earliest days of the socialist movement in Germany, many people noticed that it had points of affinity with the antidemocratic conservatism of the aristocracy. Both were hostile to liberalism and to the "English" system of free trade. More specifically, after World War I there were those who wanted to combine the new Bolshevik system with

11 Gregor 2000 19–35; Sarti 1971; Turner 1985.

nationalism. The current of political thought that became "national socialism" was originally called "national bolshevism," combining Soviet collectivist methods with nationalism. The basic doctrines were laid down by Marxists such as Ludwig Woltmann and Werner Sombart. Woltmann tried to give a more precise elaboration of Marx's historical materialism, and in doing so took account of racial differences, finding superior hereditary qualities in the Nordics. Woltmann directly influenced Hans F. K. Günther, the most eminent of the race theorists favored by the Third Reich.

Some writers helped prepare the ground for National Socialism even though they were eventually not favored by the regime. Arthur Moeller van den Bruck's book of 1923, *The Third Reich*, preached a form of national bolshevism and popularized the term "Third Reich," though this book was eventually burned by the Nazis, mainly because of Moeller's advocacy of an alliance between Germany and Russia and perhaps partly because of his personal contempt for Hitler. Moeller committed suicide in 1925.[12] Oswald Spengler was an international best-selling writer, whose *Downfall of the West* (1918) disseminated a worldview broadly favorable to a national socialist regime. Admired by many Nazis including Goebbels, Spengler in 1933 was critical of the new regime and disrespectful of its Fuehrer. He died of natural causes in 1936.

Bolshevism, Fascism, and National Socialism were all intellectual products of the crisis of Marxism in the 1890s. They were reactions against traditional socialism, which was considered to have failed, but reactions which retained many assumptions of traditional socialism. Bolshevism stridently insisted on certain aspects of Marxism, in a "fundamentalist" style, while casually abandoning essential elements of Marxism—democracy and working-class self-emancipation. Fascists and National Socialists had a more accurate grasp of what they were really doing—they were Bolsheviks with their eyes open.

12 The suggestion by Stan Lauryssens in his popular book on Moeller Van Den Bruck (Lauryssens 2010) that Moeller committed suicide because he foresaw, in the Nazi movement, where his ideas were leading, is not accepted by other historians.

The Myth of Irrational Fascism

The Left in the 1930s held that "fascism" (both Fascism and National Socialism) was something got up by the capitalists to save capitalism from the imminent destruction inherent in its economic laws. We now know that this explanation must have been wrong, since eighty years have passed and private, competitive capitalism is flourishing as never before, while Fascism, National Socialism, and Communism have all been consigned to history's trash cans.

How did fascism, supposedly a creature of business interests, gain the necessary mass support? The Left's answer was that the capitalists paid the fascist leaders to whip up this support. But how could this support be whipped up, especially as fascist movements were strongest in countries with large socialist movements, and the fascists converted many socialists into their own supporters? The Left's answer to this puzzle was that fascism appealed to the irrational.

It's true that the non-rational has a special place in Fascist theory, but the contention that Fascism is "irrational" is a misunderstanding. The writers whose ideas fed into Fascist doctrine, like Tarde, Le Bon, Bergson, Sorel, Pareto, and Mosca, believed they were drawing attention to irrationality, or at least a-rationality, in human thinking and behavior, but they did not consider what they themselves were doing to be anything other than entirely rational.[13] Fascism sees itself in relation to the irrational in much the same way that psychoanalysis does. Both Fascism and psychoanalysis see themselves as rationally taking account of the irrational springs of human action. This doesn't mean that the Fascist analysis of the irrational consists of propaganda tricks. It means, for example, that Fascist theory came up with a cultural explanation for the fact that workers were bound to be patriotic and not internationally-minded. Working-class national sentiment was not a result of trickery, which could be overcome by learning through struggle, but was the determinate outcome of specific cultural forces. In the context of Italian underdevelopment, talk of international solidarity was a distraction. Italy was a proletarian nation in a world ruled by bourgeois nations. Since the

13 Gregor 2000, 224n45.

goal of Fascism was to accelerate the modernization of backward Italy, nationalism was seen as more fruitful than appeals to class solidarity. On this point, at least, Fascist theory has been corroborated: international proletarian solidarity never amounted to much. Similarly, Fascist theoreticians, building on the ideas of Pareto, Mosca, and Michels, constructed a theory showing that "hierarchy" is unavoidable in complex societies.

Whereas Fascism explicitly rejected epistemological anti-rationalism, this doctrine was influential in National Socialism. Epistemological anti-rationalism was a major current in German intellectual history, arising from Johann Gottfried Herder, from romanticism, and later from the tendency to reject as un-German the mores of the calculating and money-grubbing English.[14]

The Myth of Unintellectual Fascism

The belief that fascism was peculiarly irrational often went along with the belief that it had no intellectually respectable theory of its own and that its leaders were cynical opportunistic adventurers ignorant of any theory.

Such works as Drucker's *The End of Economic Man* and Silone's *The School for Dictators* presented fascism as bereft of serious ideas. Even Borkenau repeated this interpretation in *The Totalitarian Enemy*. John Strachey wrote in 1935 that "fascism has no theory and needs no theory."[15] This was a staggering misjudgment. Fascist theory was immensely more subtle and elaborate than the theory of Comintern Marxism espoused by Strachey.[16]

Orwell knew almost nothing about the ideas animating Fascism. He remarked that this might be something worth pursuing, but never did get around to it. As with any elaborate ideology that attains practical political

14 Butler 1942.

15 Strachey 1935, 271.

16 On the ideas which came together in the intellectual movement that would become Fascism, see Sternhell, Sznajder, and Asheri 1994; on the development of these ideas within Fascism, see Gregor 2005.

success, there's a gulf between the underlying theory and what may be gleaned from political speeches, adapted as they must be to ephemeral circumstances, but even in the latter context, Orwell misunderstood Fascism, seeing it as nostalgically anti-industrial, when Fascism was observably infatuated with high-tech and rapid growth. He underrated the common ground between socialism and fascism—and did not realize that in some respects he was treading in the footprints of Fascist thinkers, as when he argued that patriotism was essential to any viable society and therefore tried to reconcile his revolutionism with patriotism. Orwell believed that fascist regimes were impelled by their situation to move towards collectivism, underrating the collectivist element that was in their thinking from the beginning.

Orwell on Totalitarianism

When Orwell began to employ the word "totalitarian" in the mid-1930s, this term was already a dozen years old. It was coined in 1923 as a label for Fascist Italy, but was soon extended to other antidemocratic rightwing movements, and from 1929 was extended by some writers to all one-party regimes including Soviet Russia.[17] In *Wigan Pier*, the term is used only in relation to fascism, but after Spain, Orwell gave it the more inclusive sense.

Nineteen Eighty-Four has become the classic depiction of totalitarianism. Because of the well-known phenomenon in cultural history, where a few authors' works survive while their contemporary peers are mostly forgotten, people now tend to exaggerate the originality of *Nineteen Eighty-Four*. As a picture of totalitarianism, it is a brilliant literary presentation of what were already commonplaces in certain circles.

The glorification of a leader who can do no wrong, the rule of a single party, children spying on their parents, the repeated rewriting of history—all these things had been familiar for years from the writings of Silone, Borkenau, Koestler, and others. *Nineteen Eighty-Four* skillfully takes some of these well-known features of totalitarianism to an absurd extreme, in the interests of satire. The constant surveillance of the

17 Gleason 1995, 14–50.

intellectually active members of the population becomes the installation of two-way TV sets in every party member's home. In *We*, Zamyatin had made the same point by having the walls of all the living quarters made of glass.

The idea in *Nineteen Eighty-Four* that the political leaders want power for its own sake, and not for anything they can do with it, is also presaged in Silone.[18] This is a Swiftian satirical twist, it does not have to be taken literally as a statement about real-world politics. The real-world counterpart is simply that totalitarians defend what they are doing without feeling the need to show any good results. Orwell coined the term "catastrophic gradualism" for those who combined advocacy of brutal methods with low expectations of perceptible results (XVII, 342–44), so *Nineteen Eighty-Four* takes the natural next step: the sadistic exercise of power is its own reward; it does not have to be justified by results. Similarly, it is no criticism of Orwell the satirist to point out that the motivations of the rulers in *Animal Farm* and *Nineteen Eighty-Four* are completely contradictory: naked self-interest in the first case, fanatical dedication and absence of almost any self-interest in the latter. These are *stories*, works of art, not sociological treatises, and they may each isolate a single influence, while in reality both will be combined.

Most of the British Left assumed that the undemocratic and inegalitarian aspects of Soviet Russia were due to peculiar circumstances and that western, especially British, collectivism would automatically be democratic. But Orwell, after Spain, entertained the possibility that the same economic and sociological forces which made collectivism inevitable might also make it inevitable that collectivism would be oligarchic—that economic totalitarianism would require political totalitarianism. Yet since a non-collectivist future was, in his view, out of the question, all we could do was to try to make collectivism as democratic as possible.

At times, Orwell implies that the worldwide triumph of totalitarianism is inevitable, or highly likely, and at other times, that there is hope for a non-totalitarian form of collectivism, worthy of the name "socialism" (XII, 505). In the essay "Inside the Whale," Orwell stated that "Almost certainly

18 Silone 1963, 70.

we are moving into an age of totalitarian dictatorships." In response to a comment from Victor Gollancz, Orwell wrote to him:

> You are perhaps right in thinking that I am over-pessimistic. It is quite possible that freedom of thought etc. may survive in an economically totalitarian society. We can't tell until a collectivised economy has been tried out in a Western country. (XII, 5)

Orwell criticized James Burnham for maintaining that totalitarianism is inevitable—though here, as on several points, Orwell was unfair to Burnham. Burnham, like Orwell, judged the worldwide victory of totalitarianism to be probable (XVI, 61–63). In fact Burnham was more hopeful than Orwell about the survival of liberty, partly because he was not so convinced of the inevitable demise of capitalism.

For Orwell, it's an urgent requirement to establish socialism, defined as democratic collectivism, not because socialism will be better than capitalism—that's immaterial because, whatever we may say or do, capitalism's days are numbered—but because socialism will be better than the only alternative he can see, totalitarianism.

From early 1940, Orwell asserted that Communism and National Socialism were converging on the same system of oligarchical collectivism, though occasionally he described Nazism as a form of capitalism (XII, 409), the more standard left assumption. These differing formulations can be rescued from contradiction by the theory that (in Orwell's view) fascism begins as an attempt to save capitalism but then automatically becomes, despite itself, a road to replacing capitalism with collectivism.

Totalitarian Influences in Culture

One way to conduct the fight against totalitarianism is to write explicitly political works, like *Animal Farm* and *Nineteen Eighty-Four*. But Orwell conceived this fight as much broader. He was concerned that many intellectuals seemed to *want* totalitarianism, and even more alarmed that this partiality might be spreading to the non-intellectual masses.

In "Raffles and Miss Blandish" (1944), Orwell compared E. W. Hornung's nineteenth-century stories about the gentlemanly jewel thief, A. J. Raffles, with the recent gangster novel *No Orchids for Miss Blandish*, by James Hadley Chase, a successful British imitator of such hard-boiled American storytellers as James M. Cain. Orwell expresses his distaste for the book's sadistic brutality and lack of any noble character or honorable motives, agrees with others that it is "pure fascism," and adds that it is "a daydream appropriate to a totalitarian age" (XVI, 355). He asserts that "serious" novels had long abandoned the conventions of heroes and villains, while the extension of this amoralism to popular fiction is something new. *Miss Blandish* is dominated by worship of brutal power: the lowbrow reader's admiration for these sadistic gangsters parallels the *New Statesman* reader's admiration for Stalin.[19]

Orwell's argument that such cultural developments are favorable to totalitarianism is not convincing. Contrasting Raffles and Hadley Chase is an example of what's now called "cherry-picking"—even Orwell sounds a dubious note about the fairness of the comparison. For example, the Victorian era had its "penny bloods"—it might have been more appropriate to compare *Miss Blandish* with *Sweeney Todd* (though there were much "worse" things, now largely forgotten, than *Sweeney Todd*) and the 1940s still had Miss Marple and Lord Peter Wimsey. Even if there were a proportionate growth of amoral or sadistic fiction, this could just be a broadening of the range of the acceptable, alongside such trends as the emergence of more latitude for explicit sex or disrespect for religion. Most of the characters in *Miss Blandish* are brutal and uncompassionate but they mostly harbor at least some uneasiness about their foul deeds and there are a few fundamentally benevolent characters, notably Fenner. The innocent Miss Blandish meets a horrible fate—life's tough—but all the really nasty characters come to really nasty ends, and Fenner ends up in the money.

Orwell's theory is that people like to read accounts of brutality because they worship power; a more straightforward alternative is that

19 The shock of some Europeans at "amoral" American thrillers of the 1920s and later is rather similar to the shock of some Americans at the "amoral" Italian westerns of the 1960s.

people like to read narratives of individuals struggling hard and overcoming opposition: descriptions of physical violence, whether in *Beowulf*, the *Iliad*, or *Miss Blandish*, appeal to the reader's appetite for the spectacle of a struggle. Fights are always fascinating, as any observer of a school playground can testify. Orwell is concerned that readers are enthralled by gangsters like Capone; he forgets that lowbrow Victorian readers were enthralled in much the same way by the exploits of highwaymen. In his discussion of the "poisonous rubbish" of violent American science-fiction comics, Orwell does not explicitly link these with totalitarianism, but he does identify their appeal with "fantasies of power" (XVII, 221). Yet these comics do have what Orwell bemoans the lack of in the gangster novels—a clear distinction between good and bad characters. And surely it might be relevant that actual totalitarian literature, such as the socialist realist novels favored by the Stalin regime, were, precisely, traditional stories in which the good guys can easily be discriminated from the bad.

There's also an element of snobbery in Orwell's response to this genre of fiction. Immediately before discussing Miss Blandish, he says "Now for a header into the cesspool." He did not say anything like this when he wrote about *Voyage au bout de la nuit* or *Tropic of Cancer*. The widening of the possibilities of fiction to encompass works in which there are few or no unambiguously good guys was a highbrow as well as a lowbrow trend, but Orwell reacts more viscerally against the lowbrow trend, because he is fond of supposing that the unintellectual working class are more healthy-minded than middle class intellectuals.

Orwell wrote a number of articles in which he connects bad prose—jargon-ridden, pretentious, and foggy writing—with totalitarianism. Orwell's examples of bad writing are generally witty and convincing, his broader conclusions, both literary and political, are less so. The most popular of these works, "Politics and the English Language" (XVII, 421–430), is the one that says least about politics and dwells least on Orwell's broader conclusions, which are generally erroneous. As W. F. Bolton has demonstrated in detail,[20] Orwell's views on the supposed deterioration of English were widely held at the time and embody considerable

20 Bolton 1984.

ignorance about the history and structure of the language. Orwell's theory of how written language works (that you typically have a wordless thought and then search for a word which accurately conveys that thought) is manifestly untenable.

While Orwell is correct to say that ugly, obscure wording can be both produced by and then can further produce unclear thinking, Orwell's theory that bad prose is somehow specifically conducive to totalitarianism is probably wrong. We have seen many similar examples of such prose in areas like social science, popular theology, and psychotherapy, often without any political implication. Orwell occasionally mentions examples, such as "the horrible dialect of the American psychologist" (XII, 280). Bad prose flourishes in areas where writers wish to give a bogus impression of technical expertise, or where writers allude to some system of ideas which has gained prestige and is therefore worth associating with their argument, or where writing is being done (as in most scholarly journal articles today) for motives other than that it shall be read and understood.

The Death of Literature

Orwell maintained that literature must cease to exist under totalitarianism (XVII, 372–80). As we read his repeated assertions of this claim it's hard to resist the feeling that, at least at times, he intended it quite literally: there would no longer be such things as novels, short stories, or even essays. At one point he actually says, "God knows . . . whether such things as publishing novels will still be happening two years hence" (XII, 146–47).

Orwell asserts that

> the imaginative writer . . . cannot misrepresent the scenery of his own mind: he cannot say with any conviction that he likes what he dislikes, or believes what he disbelieves. If he is forced to do so, the only result is that his creative faculties dry up. (XVII, 375)

This may be true of some imaginative writers, perhaps even true of the best of them, but it's hardly true of all of them. The history of literature is full of examples of writers modifying their work for extra-artistic motives. One could even argue that clinging to an ideologically sensitive point of view is itself the product of an extra-artistic motive. An artist, such as a writer, is above all a technician; he may want to discredit the king, but once it's suggested to him that it would be safer to praise the king, the writer will start to think of ways in which this could be done most effectively, and this challenge will probably appeal to him as a technical problem, however much he loathes the king.

Orwell does state that worthwhile literature is not being produced in Soviet Russia or Nazi Germany, but this is a judgment about quality, not sheer existence. As far as fiction goes (including drama and film), people always have an appetite to read or hear stories and individuals can be found to compose these stories, working within the limits of what's permitted. Some writers will spontaneously write in agreement with the official line while others will depart from their own preferences to fit what's permitted even though they might prefer not to.

Orwell assumed that the official doctrine in a totalitarian society would be spelled out in great detail and would be subject to change at any moment. In other words, he thought that totalitarian societies would be like Stalin's Russia, moving towards the Ingsoc regime. This is doubtful: a totalitarian society could permit some latitude and merely impose the official line on a comparatively small number of essential points of doctrine, much like the medieval Church. Something like this happened in the USSR under Khrushchev and again later. It might be countered that the "reform Communism" of Khrushchev and his successors was only a stage in the breakdown of the system, but if true that arises from the system's economic failure—precisely the point where Orwell believed collectivism must be more efficient than capitalism. In terms of the interaction of ideology, popular art, and political power, there seems to be no intrinsic unfeasibility in a totalitarian system which is much less fidgety and heavy-handed than Stalin's USSR. As we know from the phenomenon of "cults," fanatical insistence on minute points of doctrine is a general pathological feature of organized belief systems, not a specific product of any political order. We can even imagine a totalitarian system which has a special name for the dreadful heresy that every little point of doctrine has to be correct, and tortures people to death for advocating this. A hypothetical Nazi system might have called this "Talmudic compulsive thinking," a Communist system, "petty-bourgeois pedantry."

The arts flourished under Communism—not in the sense that the art produced was good (that's a separate question), but in the sense that the customers' demands for art—for stories, music, and visual images—were catered to. Novels were written and read, symphonies were composed and performed to appreciative audiences, paintings were made and hung in galleries. Soviet fiction was expected to comply with the tenets of Socialist Realism—in general shape Soviet novels were much like Ayn Rand's, with traditional literary forms, heroic characters wrestling with villainous characters, the dialogue verging on sublimated slogans, and a happy ending. In general the Soviet line on the arts, like the Nazi line, accorded with popular taste: the masses always spontaneously agree with totalitarian regimes in being averse to baffling artistic experiments. Much that was then permitted in the West was forbidden in Russia and Germany, but for most of preceding Western history, much that was permitted by the early twentieth century had also been effectively forbidden. The Third Reich lasted for only twelve years, half of them wartime, so not much can be concluded (though, outside literature, we observe that significant works like Orff's setting of the *Carmina Burana* and the drawings of M. C. Escher could be produced, disseminated, and appreciated under National Socialist rule), but the Soviet Union survived for over seventy years, and literature, whatever we might think of its quality, showed no sign of disappearing. Novels like *Cement* and *How the Steel Was Tempered* were revised numerous times, which would be unusual for Western novels. My guess is that those changes reflected the changing political line and that they usually reduced literary quality, but looked at dispassionately, this still shows literature as being of enduring importance to the political system.

In *Nineteen Eighty Four* there is prolefeed, reading material for the masses composed by machines. Presumably Orwell excludes this from "literature" because no thought goes into it. Yet its existence acknowledges the eternal appetite for stories, and therefore the permanent need for fiction. From what we know of even the crudest fiction, it doesn't look as though composition by machine could ever seriously compete with composition by human minds.

The End of Truth

> We know that Ones and Ones make Twos—
> Till Demos votes them Three or Nought.
> —Rudyard Kipling, "The Bonfires" (1933)

While Kipling thought that democratic politics was a menace to truth, Orwell considered that totalitarianism would mean "the end of truth" (the phrase itself is Hayek's). The notion of the end of truth has two distinct meanings, both of which preoccupied Orwell. First, there's the possibility that the state will have a single interpretation of events (and possibly of all factual matters, even encompassing astrophysics) and will try to destroy all the evidence which might support any deviant opinions. Thus, if Communism had triumphed rapidly everywhere after 1939, the only view freely circulated of the events of May 1937 in Barcelona would have been that this was an attempted coup by the POUM in the pay of Franco and Hitler. All documents testifying to a different story would have been destroyed, and any outspoken eyewitnesses or critics would have been removed from circulation. The ideal aim is that everyone will believe just one version—though experience of the Soviet Union and even of Western governments (which have at times been known to assert untruths) suggests that some disobliging folks will respond by believing the opposite of whatever the government tells them.

This idea of the end of truth doesn't involve any novel interpretation of the concept of truth. For example, the truth about a past event is what actually happened, independent of what anyone thinks about it. This notion of truth is indispensable in the conduct of everyday life and everyone understands it. The idea that some single account of some topic might become accepted as the standard account, even though it contains falsehoods—that untruths can become accepted as truths—is also something that everyone can easily understand. Not only that, but the untruthful account of the May Events *requires* continued acceptance of that traditional and everyday notion of truth. Any regime, totalitarian or otherwise, must always rely on the fact that everyone applies that notion of truth. A habitual liar does not want his listeners to adopt some strange new theory of truth—quite the contrary. If the Communists were to have announced: "The POUM, in the pay of Franco and Hitler, attempted a coup in May 1937, but when we say this we don't mean that this actually happened. Instead we mean . . . something different, which we can explain by a lengthy disquisition whose verbiage, we hope, will confuse you," then the whole exercise in presenting untruth as truth would have been pointless. If you claim that something is true, and then add that by "true" you don't mean absolutely and objectively true, independent of what anyone says, you are simply taking back your claim. It's tantamount to saying: "*x* is true—Oh, I didn't mean that." This is of no use to a totalitarian regime. Orwell wrote in 1945 that "Totalitarianism demands . . . the continuous alteration of the past, and in the long run probably demands a disbelief in the very existence of objective truth" (XVII, 374). But if disbelief in the existence of objective truth became general, then there could be no possible point in altering the past.[21]

The other meaning of the end of truth is that people would cease to believe that there is any such coherent notion as objective truth—truth would mean just what the Party said, and nothing else. This is the theory—"collective solipsism"—propounded by O'Brien in *Nineteen Eighty-Four*. This second meaning of the end of truth, that the very notion of absolute objective truth can be made to disappear, is the topic of the debate between O'Brien and Winston Smith.

We can imagine two likely alternatives to O'Brien's position in *Nineteen Eighty-Four*. First, O'Brien might have said to Winston, "What the Party says is often false, but we have the power to make people accept it, and even make it so that most of them believe it." Nothing important would be different in the actual situation described in the novel or in the operation of the Ingsoc regime. O'Brien would be less of a muddlehead.

21 This somewhat parallels the observation made by Mises about Sorel's conception of the "myth." Sorel held that Marxist ideas like the class struggle are not literally true, but are vital "myths" of the socialist movement. Mises pointed out that for these myths to be effective *in Sorel's sense*, the adherents had to accept them as literal truths, not myths (Mises 1969, 126).

The debate between O'Brien and Winston would be less entertaining, or at least different, for O'Brien would not try to convince Winston of the truth of all the Party's claims. Instead the debate would move to the desirability of imposing a single comprehensive doctrine, which a few people (the Inner Party, or perhaps not even all of those) would know contained untruths.

The other alternative would be for O'Brien to insist that the Party is right in everything it says, and to argue this point by point, for example: some of Winston's memories are false; he never did see such and such a photograph but just hallucinated seeing it, and so forth. At times O'Brien does seem to be arguing like that (IX, 258), but entirely in the context that there is no standard of truth independent of the Party. Instead of that, we can imagine O'Brien admitting that there is such an independent standard, and insisting that the Party just happens to be always right by that standard. (A slightly more sophisticated version would be that on some detailed points of current policy the Party could be wrong, but in those instances it's the duty of Party comrades to endorse the Party's version anyway, for after all, we are at war.) This possibility has the advantage, for O'Brien, that he would be able to torture Winston to see if this could get him to change his beliefs—something O'Brien gets a kick out of, and which would be pointless in the first alternative. This is a familiar dramatic situation: it's the basic plot of *Gas Light* and other stories where the victim's sanity is called into question by someone with power over them (and who may in many versions, as in *Gas Light*, themselves be insane). Another example is Nuñez, in "The Country of the Blind," who faces an operation to remove his eyesight, the source of his insane delusion that he can "see."

Which of the three scenarios, O'Brien's collective solipsism or one of the two alternatives—prevailed in actual totalitarian systems? The two alternatives have the advantage over collective solipsism that they are not self-evidently absurd. What did Stalin and Beria really think about the idea that Trotsky, Bukharin, and the rest were collaborating with Hitler to perpetrate acts of sabotage and terror across the USSR? Obviously neither Stalin nor Beria accepted the theory of collective solipsism or even gave it a thought. My guess is that Beria maintained the first alternative—he knew that the confessions were false, but felt obliged to give Stalin what he wanted—and that Stalin maintained the second alternative: he believed in the Trotskyist conspiracy. Alternatively, he might have believed it was mostly true, and probably false in some patches, which were still worth imposing as official policy, because, as the crime boss in *Casino* asks, "Why take a chance?" (It's entirely conceivable, of course, but I just don't think it's the case, that Stalin simply knew the allegations were all false and adopted them purely as an instrument to eliminate his rivals.)

Why does Orwell have O'Brien favor the doctrine of collective solipsism? It makes for a more gripping story. Exactly why it does so is more tricky to pin down, as literary effects often are. The feeling of the victim in *Gas Light* that she's in a closed world where she is powerless to challenge certain false assumptions which are being used to menace her is taken to the ultimate: there is no possibility of challenging false assumptions because the possibility of Winston being in possession of the truth is defined away. And the fact that the person inflicting pain on you is totally dotty can add to the terror of such an experience. Even the most preposterous theories, asserted glibly, can take someone unfamiliar with them off-guard. O'Brien gets Winston to agree that the past exists in the form of present documents and memories (IX, 260). A better account would be to say that the past does *not* exist except in the sense that it is the fact that some things actually happened (and others didn't), that documents and memories are not the past (obviously there are no documents or memories for the vast majority of past events) but are present clues to what happened in the past, and that people can always be mistaken about what happened in the past.

Collective solipsism requires that you be able to change your beliefs and memories in an instant to comply with a change in what the Party says. This is only possible by mastery of the technique of doublethink. In real life, "doublethink" simply means "not paying attention to what you're doing." As Peter Van Inwagen has pointed out, O'Brien simultaneously appeals to his theory of "collective solipsism" *and* to the ordinary notion of objective truth, and he could not have done otherwise.[22]

22 Van Inwagen 2008. In Van Inwagen 1993, a popular introduction to metaphysics, the author recommends *Nineteen Eighty-Four* as "the greatest of all attacks on anti-Realism" (69). Richard Rorty, a philosopher who advo-

Proponents of totalitarianism in Orwell's lifetime did not generally preach collective solipsism.[23] *The Social Construction of Reality* lay a quarter century in the future—and even then would not be accepted by such overt totalitarians as Communists—but a beginning had been made with Karl Mannheim and the "sociology of knowledge."[24] The use of this notion in *Nineteen Eighty-Four* is Swiftian satire, a literary approach which takes real-world tendencies and exaggerates them to bring out their absurdity.

The Birth of Brainwashing

Winston's conversion to loving Big Brother introduced to the world in 1949 the new notion of "brainwashing." The people who originated the English term claimed it was a translation from the Chinese, but these people didn't know any Chinese, and actually the idea (though not the precise word) comes straight out of *Nineteen Eighty-Four*.[25]

If you torture someone long enough, you can get them to say any-

cated rejection of realism, analyzed the O'Brien-Winston Smith debate to show that one could be an anti-realist and still regard O'Brien as being in the wrong (Rorty 1989). Rorty was criticized by James Conant (Conant 2000) and replied to him (Rorty 2000). Van Inwagen then commented on this exchange in Van Inwagen 2008.

23 In his 1955 comments on *Nineteen Eighty-Four*, the Communist doctrinal authority R. Palme Dutt duly pointed out that Winston Smith's view that "reality is something external, objective, existing in its own right" is precisely the Communist view (quoted in Walsh 1975, 287–88). But collective solipsism was not completely without contemporary antecedents. In an amusing passage in his William James Lectures of 1940, Bertrand Russell criticized the views on truth of the logical empiricists Neurath, Hempel, and Carnap, and caustically observed that, for Neurath, the implication is that "empirical truth can be determined by the police" (Russell 1995, 140–48). While Neurath was by conviction a totalitarian leftist, his philosophical views were very unlike the dialectical materialism of Communist orthodoxy.

24 It's not clear that Mannheim or even Berger and Luckmann were really equivalent to collective solipsism, though my impression is that some of their admirers have taken them that way.

25 Gleason 1995, 246–47.

thing, and if you preach to someone a hitherto unfamiliar point of view, there's always the possibility they may undergo a conversion and accept it as true. But "brainwashing" implies that there's a specific technique (other than persuasive argument) for getting someone to believe something they're initially not inclined to—a foolproof conversion method. From here it's a short step to *The Manchurian Candidate* and *Homeland*—though if anything like that were possible, you might expect it to happen at least once in real life. For patriots, the brainwashing theory serves as a polite narrative to excuse the embarrassing fact that our boys will generally give in to torture.

A post-socialist to the end, Orwell gave a new twist to the post-socialist theory that it's possible to control people's minds. As with all fabulous "magic potion" theories—hypnosis, the madness of crowds, the instincts of the herd, the regimentation of the population by propaganda, the subliminal persuasion of advertising—Orwell's invention of brainwashing, something just barely imaginable under certain impossibly strange conditions, once accepted, becomes expanded into a routine part of everyday life. So now we're brainwashed when we read Shakespeare, when we watch TV, and when we solve crossword puzzles. Orwell, however, didn't go as far as the later theorists of "brainwashing," since to convert Winston required electrical shocks to his brain. Julia proved to be even tougher—her case needed actual brain surgery (IX, 304).

The Stability of the Ingsoc Regime

"If there is hope," muses Winston Smith, "it lies in the proles" (IX, 72). It's still debated whether this was Orwell's view, or whether it was one more example, in Orwell's judgment, of Winston's pathetic delusions. Whatever Orwell thought, there can be no hope of any initiative from the proles as they are described in *Nineteen Eighty-Four*. Indeed, the whole notion that the proletariat is one day going to do something dramatic is a pathetic delusion of leftist intellectuals, of which Winston is a kind of pale copy. The actual instability of a real-world Ingsoc regime would arise from its economic unsustainability and from the interests of members of the ruling group, the Inner Party.

Orwell conceives of the Ingsoc regime as being able to provide high real incomes for the population, but choosing not to do so, deliberately restricting and wasting technology to maintain general poverty (IX, 196). Yet the Ingsoc regime produces ICBMs and highly sophisticated surveillance equipment, and it's dubious whether this could be feasible in a fully collectivized world. At any rate, to operate these systems would require a lot of trained engineers and other specialists, and these would have the means to manoeuver somewhat within the system, especially as a flourishing black market would ineluctably arise.

Orwell sees the military competition between the three superpower blocs as being largely pretense. However, pretense could become reality if any one of the blocs were to become actually more efficient than the other two, and this could occur if one of them were more loosely regulated, thereby unleashing greater efficiency due to spontaneous market co-operation. The policymakers in the three blocs would soon discover, as third-world governments did in the 1970s, that doses of liberalization, marketization, and privatization could yield benefits, even to the ruling gang, and even in the short run. The rulers would face a continuous incentive to deregulate, and sometimes it would pay one faction in its struggle with another faction to press for more deregulation.

Orwell supposes that the rulers (either the Inner Party or some group within the Inner Party) are motivated by pure fanaticism without any trace of self-interest. But even fanatics have some self-interested motivation. The book does show Inner Party members as being better off materially than anyone else—any other circumstance would lack credibility. We can be sure that the members of the ruling group would maneuver in various political factions, and that sometimes groups would ally with other groups. They would do this even if we assume that they harbored no desires for more personal consumers' goods, but simply desired to protect themselves and to acquire power. In the evolution of the Soviet Union we see the gradual pressure of the people at the top to protect their interests, for example by guaranteeing themselves against sudden execution at the whim of the General Secretary. Changes within the privileged elite are always a more likely source of substantial political change than anything emanating from the proles.

None of this means that Orwell's conception of the Ingsoc regime was faulty from an artistic point of view, as fiction. To apply my remarks that way would be like criticizing Gulliver's adventures in Lilliput by pointing out that there can't be full-grown humans five inches tall. But we can lift certain ideas from their literary context and analyze them as they reflect upon political theory. My excuse for doing this here is that the inescapable political dynamics of a state system are less obvious than the constraints on human body mass.

The Strange Death of Democratic Collectivism

The socialist movement of the period 1880–1920 perceived collectivism and democracy as each implying the other. Yet in practice socialists, whether they knew it or not, faced a choice: give up collectivism or give up democracy. Few people saw this; the choice played itself out in a confused and messy way over several decades, with many partial glimpses of the dilemma and many partial adjustments. Over a long period, the inherent logic of this choice could not be evaded. And so it came to pass, that those who remained committed to collectivism gave up democracy (though they usually did so by applying democratic labels to undemocratic procedures), while those who remained committed to democracy gave up collectivism (though they often did so by applying collectivist labels to capitalist practices).

By the 1950s, in Europe, we see nominally socialist parties which have abandoned any practical attempt to abolish capitalism, and alongside them, we see the Communist parties and other groups in the Bolshevik tradition, which continue to push for collectivism while proclaiming their adherence to "democracy" in the form of a one-party police state, which is to say, the abolition of democracy.

Within both of these broad groupings, there were people with affinities for the other. There were people in the Labour and social democratic parties who wanted to resume the pursuit of collectivism, but they were continually discouraged and always eventually lost out, this outcome being aided by the fact that further extension of state control had become unpopular with voters. By the 1970s, there arose "Euro-Communism," members of the Western Communist parties becoming infected, despite all Moscow's best efforts, with an interest in democracy.

There are two fundamental reasons why the democratic socialists of

Orwell's day faced, without knowing it, a choice between democracy and collectivism. One is that collectivism reduces output and therefore reduces workers' incomes. Workers want higher wages, and therefore objectively have a powerful interest in retaining (or retrieving and extending) private ownership of the means of production. Workers always want what only private, competitive capitalism can give them.

The other reason was stated with unprecedented clarity by F. A. Hayek in *The Road to Serfdom*. Serious attempts to institute collectivism must abolish democracy. Yet this is no cause for despair, since a collectivist future is not inevitable after all. Orwell briefly reviewed *The Road to Serfdom* along with a now forgotten work by the fellow traveler Konni Zilliacus (XVI, 149–150). Orwell affects to treat the two books as roughly on a par, while tacitly sending the message that the Hayek work is more interesting. Yet there is no indication anywhere that Orwell came to entertain Hayek's view that free-market capitalism might have a long-term future.

It Didn't Happen

Orwell's conviction that capitalism was in its terminal throes was entirely typical of 1930s political intellectuals, Marxist and non-Marxist alike, but this belief was to evaporate rapidly after Orwell's death. Socialists had generally held that there was an automatic tendency in capitalism for increasing industrial concentration. Marx maintained that big firms always outcompete small firms, so that the size of firms gets bigger and bigger without limit. As Orwell phrased this theory, "the trouble with competitions is that somebody wins them" (XVI, 149).[26] And yet, in its most obvious interpretation, this claim is observably false. We see many firms co-existing and competing over generations or centuries, and no one ever "wins," in the sense of permanently eliminating all the others. Marx had memorably said, "One capitalist always kills many."[27] Yet we do not see a diminishing number of firms, so the assassinated capitalists must be replaced somehow.

26 As early as 1928 he had written, "In all competition there must be a winner and a loser" (X. 122).

27 Marx 1974, 714.

Eduard Bernstein had drawn attention to some of the relevant facts in the 1890s. There is no tendency within competitive capitalism for the total number of firms to dwindle. Competition does not destroy itself, but regenerates itself indefinitely; only government intervention can create enduring monopoly. Marx's expectation that capitalism itself would centralize the economy in a few vast organizational units has turned out to be mistaken. Some firms become big, but new firms enter all the time, and the biggest firms are never secure in their position. In 1937 Ronald Coase published "The Nature of the Firm," opening up a fruitful theoretical approach to analyzing the size of firms, and incidentally, explaining the fact that this has no observable long-term tendency to increase.[28]

By the 1930s, many socialists, even if they had not quite given up the theory that capital tends to become concentrated into one immense organization as a result of market competition, had at least accepted that this was occurring far too slowly to be of any help to the practical institution of socialism for many generations to come. In Germany, many socialists thought that the monopolizing activities of the bourgeois state, especially in wartime planning, constituted an alternate mechanism for centralizing capital, a current of thinking which influenced the Bolsheviks.

In 1936 Orwell stated that machine production in itself (not competition) tended to bring about collectivism, though he offered no explanation for this contention. While occasionally echoing the standard argument that competition leads to ever-increasing size of firms, he mostly appealed to a different theory of his own: the majority of workers and voters value security above both personal freedom and income. They therefore don't care that state intervention curtails their liberty and may reduce total income. This implies that the mass of ordinary employees will always tend to support more government intervention rather than less, and if this is pursued indefinitely it will lead to the indefinitely growing role of the state and therefore ultimately to the demise of private capitalism (XVI, 149; XVIII, 58, 71).

We can understand why this argument seemed so persuasive to Orwell, especially given the situation in Britain in 1945, along with the

28 Coase 1937; Alchian and Demsetz 1972; Williamson 1975.

general conviction that a new slump was imminent. But there are serious objections to it. At the most abstract level, how much income and freedom a worker will sacrifice for a gain in security depends on the terms of the trade-off, and that worker's existing "holdings" of income, liberty, and security. We observe that workers often take risks to increase their income and their freedom (leaving a modestly paid secure job for a more highly paid but riskier job), and so there cannot be any law that security will always trump income and freedom. Income and freedom also permit workers to buy increments of security, in the form of savings for retirement and for emergencies. And experience has shown that, even with generous state welfare systems, personal savings, help from family members, and voluntary charity continue to be important. As capitalism develops, workers' savings form a large and growing segment of the ownership of total capital; a steadily increasing proportion of workers enjoy the security that derives from possessing substantial private means. The long-term direction under capitalism is for every household to own sufficient assets for its members to live comfortably without the necessity to work.

A remarkable absence in Orwell's writing is any attention to half-measures—reforms of capitalism which modify the system without abolishing it. For example, he never once mentions Keynesian demand management, one of the hottest of public policy topics after 1936. And even though he lived through the debate over the Beveridge proposals for an all-encompassing welfare state, and saw these proposals enacted into law, along with a free National Health Service, there is no sign that he ever considered the possibility that such supplements to capitalism might give the workers enough "security" to forestall further movement in a collectivist direction.

What we have seen since Orwell's day is that a large proportion of the working population comes to dislike public support for people on welfare. The state welfare system creates social problems as severe as the insecurity it was designed to cure. And so, though there may be a drift towards more and more generous state welfare, there are periodic bouts of politically motivated tightening up of the system ("welfare reform"), supported by a major segment of working-class voters. An equilibrium is approached where state welfare persists at some level, but the survival of private, competitive capitalism is not endangered.

After Orwell's death events occurred which he had not foreseen. Not only was there rapid growth of real wages in Britain and many other countries, but, across the world, private, competitive capitalism unmistakably out-performed collectivism in every instance. Wherever we looked, West and East Germany, South and North Korea, Taiwan and Mainland China, capitalism made workers dramatically better off while collectivism held workers down in wretched misery.

We can learn many things from our dissection of the now-deceased worldview of George Orwell and the 1930s Left. One of them is that politically-minded intellectuals in any generation are adamantly convinced of propositions which no one takes seriously a few decades later. There's no safety in consensus. The future is full of surprises.

Select Bibliography

Abrams, Mark. 1945. *The Condition of the British People, 1911–1945*. London: Gollancz.

Adamson, Walter L. 1983. Benedetto Croce and the Death of Ideology. *Journal of Modern History* 55:2 (June).

Alchian, Armen A., and Harold Demsetz. 1972. Production, Information Costs, and Economic Organization. *American Economic Review* 62:5.

Aldington, Richard. 1929. *Death of a Hero*. London: Chatto and Windus.

Amalrik, Andrei. 1970. *Will the Soviet Union Survive Until 1984?* New York: Harper and Row.

Amis, Martin. 2003 [2002]. *Koba the Dread: Laughter and the Twenty Million*. New York: Vintage.

Angell, Norman. 1912 [1909]. *The Great Illusion: A Study of the Relation of Military Power to National Advantage*. London: Heinemann.

———. 1938. *Peace with the Dictators?* New York: Harper.

———. 1939. *For What Do We Fight?* New York: Harper.

———. 1951. *After All: The Autobiography of Norman Angell*. London: Hamilton.

Atkins, John. 1954. *George Orwell*. London: John Calder.

Attlee, Clement R. 1937. *The Labour Party in Perspective*. London: Gollancz.

Ayling, Jean. 1930. *Retreat from Parenthood*. London: Kegan Paul.

Baker, John Randal. 1945. *Science and the Planned State*. London: Allen and Unwin.

Bakunin, Jack. 1976. *Pierre Leroux and the Birth of Democratic Socialism 1797–1848*. New York: Revisionist Press.

Barltrop, Robert. 1975. *The Monument: The Story of the Socialist Party of Great Britain*. London: Pluto Press.

Basily, Nicolas de. 1938. *Russia under Soviet Rule: Twenty Years of Bolshevik Experiment*. London: Allen and Unwin.

Baumer, Franklin L. 1977. *Modern European Thought: Continuity and Change in Ideas, 1600–1950*. New York: Macmillan.

Bebel, August. 1904. [1879]. *Woman under Socialism: Translated from the Original German of the 33rd Edition by Daniel De Leon*. New York: New York Labor News Company.

Becker, Gary S., and H. Gregg Lewis. 1974. Interaction between Quantity and Quality of Children. In Schultz 1974.

Beevers, John. 1935. *World without Faith*. London: Hamilton.

Bellamy, Edward. 1889. *Looking Backward, 2000–1887*. New York: Houghton, Mifflin.

———. 1898. *Equality*. New York: Appleton.

Belloc, Hilaire. 1912. *The Servile State*. London: Foulis.

Benedict, Bertram. 1921. *The Larger Socialism*. New York: Macmillan.

Berger, Peter L., and Thomas Luckman. 1966. *The Social Construction of Reality*. New York: Random House.

Bernays, Edward L. 1928. *Propaganda*. New York: Liveright.

Bernstein, Eduard. 1911 [1899]. *Evolutionary Socialism: A Criticism and Affirmation*. New York: Huebsch.

Bevan, Aneurin. 1952. *In Place of Fear*. London: Heinemann.

Bilan, R. P. 2010. *The Literary Criticism of F. R. Leavis*. New York: Cambridge University Press.

Blaazer, David. 1992. *The Popular Front and the Progressive Tradition: Socialists, Liberals, and the Quest for Unity, 1884–1939*. Cambridge: Cambridge University Press.

Blatchford, Robert. 1897 [1894]. *Merrie England*. Chicago: The Social Democracy of America.

Böhm-Bawerk, Eugen von. 1959 [1884–1921]. *Capital and Interest.* South Holland: Libertarian Press.

———. 1962. *Shorter Classics of Eugen von Böhm-Bawerk, Volume I.* South Holland: Libertarian Press.

Bolloten, Burnett. 1961. *The Grand Camouflage: The Communist Conspiracy in the Spanish Civil War*. New York: Praeger.

———. 1991. *The Spanish Civil War: Revolution and Counterrevolution*. Chapel Hill: University of North Carolina Press.

Bolton, W. F. 1984. *The Language of 1984: Orwell's English and Ours*. Knoxville: University of Tennessee Press.

Borkenau, Franz. 1933. Zur Soziologie des Faschismus. *Archiv führ Sozialwissenschaft und Sozialpolitik.*

———. 1936. *Pareto*. New York: Wiley.

———. 1937. *The Spanish Cockpit: An Eye-Witness Account of the Political and Social Conflicts of the Spanish Civil War*. London: Faber and Faber.

———. 1938. *The Communist International*. London: Faber and Faber.

———. 1939. *The New German Empire*. New York: Viking.

———. 1940. *The Totalitarian Enemy*. London: Faber and Faber.

———. 1953. *European Communism*. New York: Harper.

———. 1962 [1939]. *World Communism: A History of the Communist International*. Ann Arbor: University of Michigan Press.

Bounds, Philip. 2009. *Orwell and Marxism: The Political and Cultural Thinking of George Orwell*. London: Tauris.

Bowker, Gordon. 2003. *Inside George Orwell*. New York: Palgrave Macmillan.

Brailsford, Henry Noel. 1918 [1914]. *The War of Steel and Gold: A Study of the Armed Peace*. London: Bell.

———. 1943. *Subject India*. New York: John Day.

Bramah, Ernest. 1995 [1907]. *The Secret of the League*. Originally titled *What Might Have Been: The Story of a Social War*. Atlanta: Specular Press.

Brander, Lawrence. 1954. *George Orwell*. London: Longmans.

Brandom, Robert B., ed. 2000. *Rorty and His Critics*. Malden: Blackwell.

Brockway, Fenner. 1937. *The Truth about Barcelona*. London: Independent Labour Party.

———. 1938. *Workers' Front*. London: Secker and Warburg.

———. 1942. *Inside the Left*. London: Allen and Unwin.

———. 1977. *Towards Tomorrow: The Autobiography of Fenner Brockway*. London: Hart-Davis, MacGibbon.

Brown, Alec. 1936. *The Fate of the Middle Classes*. London: Gollancz.

Buber-Neumann, Margarete. 2008 [1948]. *Under Two Dictators: Prisoner of Stalin and Hitler*. London: Random House.

Buchanan, D. H. 1934. *The Development of Capitalistic Enterprise in India, 1900–1939*. London: Macmillan.

Buddicom, Jacintha. 1974. *Eric and Us*. London: Frewin.

Buitenhuis, Peter, and Ira B. Nadel, eds. 1988. *George Orwell: A Re-assessment*. New York: St. Martin's Press.

Bullock, Ian. 2011. *Romancing the Revolution: The Myth of Soviet Democracy and the British Left*. Edmonton: AU Press.

Burdekin, Katharine ["Murray Constantine"]. 1985 [1937]. *Swastika Night*. New York: Feminist Press.

Burgess, Anthony. 1978. *1985*. Boston: Little, Brown.

Burnham, James. 1941. *The Managerial Revolution: What Is Happening in the World*. New York: John Day.

———. 1945. Lenin's Heir. *Partisan Review* 12 (Spring).

———. 1943. *The Machiavellians: Defenders of Freedom*. New York: John Day.

———. 1947. *The Struggle for the World*. New York: John Day.

———. 1950. *The Coming Defeat of Communism*. New York: John Day.

Butler, Rohan D. 1941. *The Roots of National Socialism, 1783–1933*. London: Faber and Faber.

Cain, Peter J. 2002. *Hobson and Imperialism: Radicalism, New Liberalism, and Finance, 1887–1938*. Oxford: Oxford University Press.

Cain, Peter J., and A. G. Hopkins. 2002. *British Imperialism 1688–2000*. Harlow: Longman.

Canovan, Margaret. 1978. *G. K. Chesterton: Radical Populist*. New York: Harcourt, Brace.

Čapek, Karel. 1923 [1920]. *R.U.R. (Rossum's Universal Robots)*. Garden City: Doubleday.

———. 1937 [1936]. *War with the Newts*. London: Allen and Unwin.

Carey, John. 1992. *The Intellectuals and the Masses: Pride and Prejudice among the Literary Intelligentsia, 1880–1939*. New York: St. Martin's.

Carr, E. H. 1951. *The New Society*. London: Macmillan.

———. 1982. *Twilight of the Comintern, 1930–1935*. New York: Pantheon.

Caudwell, Christopher. 1937. *Illusion and Reality*. London: Macmillan.

———. 1938. *Studies in a Dying Culture*. New York: Dodd Mead.

Caute, David. 1973 [1964]. *The Fellow-Travellers: A Postscript to the Enlightenment*. New York: Macmillan.

Cervantes Saavedra, Miguel de. 1991 [1605]. *Don Quixote*. New York: Knopf.

Chamberlin, J. Edward, and Sander L. Gilman, eds. 1985. *Degeneration: The Dark Side of Progress*. New York: Columbia University Press.

Chamberlin, William Henry. 1935. Russia and Germany: Parallels and Contrasts. *Atlantic Monthly* (September).

———. 1937. *Collectivism: A False Utopia*. New York: Macmillan.

Chambers, Whittaker. 1987 [1952]. *Witness*. Washington: Regnery.

Chakhotin, Sergei. 1971 [1940]. *The Rape of the Masses: The Psychology of Totalitarian Political Propaganda*. New York: Haskell House.

Charles, Enid. 1934. *The Twilight of Parenthood: A Biological Study of the Decline of Population Growth*. London: Watts.

———. 1936. *The Menace of Underpopulation: A Biological Study of the Decline of Population Growth*. London: Watts.

Chase, James Hadley. 1939. *No Orchids for Miss Blandish*. London: Jarrold.

Chesterton, G. K. 1904. *The Napoleon of Notting Hill*. London: Bodley Head.

———. 1908. *The Man Who Was Thursday: A Nightmare*. London: Arrowsmith.

Ciliga, Ante. 1979 [1940]. *The Russian Enigma*. London: Ink Links.

Clarke, Ben. 2007. *Orwell in Context: Communities, Myths, Values*. Basingstoke: Palgrave Macmillan.

Coase, Ronald H. 1937. The Nature of the Firm. *Economica* n.s. 4 (November).

Cohen, Gidon. 2007. *The Failure of a Dream: The Independent Labour Party from Disaffiliation to World War II*. London: Tauris.

Cole, G. D. H. 1934. *What Marx Really Meant*. London: Gollancz.

———. 1935. *The Simple Case for Socialism*. London: Gollancz.

———. 1937. *The People's Front*. London: Gollancz.

———. 1948 [1934]. *The Meaning of Marxism*. Ann Arbor: University of Michigan Press.

Cole, G. D. H., Francis Williams, Harold Laski, George Orwell, and Mary Sutherland. 1942. *Victory or Vested Interest?* London: Routledge.

Conant, James. 2000. Freedom, Cruelty, and Truth: Rorty versus Orwell. In Brandom 2000.

Connolly, Cyril. 1944. *The Unquiet Grave: A Word Cycle*. Pseudonymous, as "Palinurus." London: Hamilton.

———. 1938. *The Enemies of Promise*. London: Routledge.

———. 1985 [1945]. *The Condemned Playground: Essays 1927–1944*. London: Hogarth.

Conquest, Robert. 1989. *Tyrants and Typewriters: Communiqués from the Struggle for Truth*. Lexington: Heath.

Coppard, Audrey, and Bernard Crick, eds. 1984. *Orwell Remembered*. New York: Facts on File.

Corrin, Jay P. 1981. *G. K. Chesterton and Hilaire Belloc: The Battle against Modernity*. Athens: Ohio University Press.

———. 2003. *Catholic Intellectuals and the Challenge of Democracy*. Notre Dame: University of Notre Dame Press.

Corthorn, Paul. 2006. *In the Shadow of the Dictators: The British Left in the 1930s*. London: Tauris.

Crick, Bernard. 1989. *Essays on Politics and Literature*. Edinburgh: Edinburgh University Press.

———. 1992 [1980]. *George Orwell: A Life*. Harmondsworth: Penguin.

Croce, Benedetto. 1911. La Morte del Socialismo. *La Voce* (February). Reprinted in Croce 1955 and quoted in Adamson 1983.

———. 1955. *Cultura e Vita Morale*. Bari: Laterza.

Crosland, Anthony. 1956. *The Future of Socialism*. London: Cape.

Crossman, Richard, ed. 1949. *The God that Failed*. New York: Harper.

Cushman, Thomas, and John Rodden, eds. 2004. *George Orwell: Into the Twenty-First Century*. Boulder: Paradigm.

Dante Alighieri. 2014 [1320]. *The Divine Comedy: Inferno, Purgatorio, Paradiso*. New York: Penguin.

Darnton, Robert. 1968. *Mesmerism and the End of the Enlightenment in France*. Cambridge: Harvard University Press.

Davis, Lance E., and Robert A. Huttenback. 1986. *Mammon and the Pursuit of Empire: The Political Economy of British Imperialism, 1860–1912*. Cambridge: Cambridge University Press.

Davison, Peter. 1996. *George Orwell: A Literary Life*. London: Palgrave Macmillan.

Deutscher, Isaac. 1955. *Heretics and Renegades and Other Essays*. London: Hamilton.

———. 1974. The Mysticism of Cruelty. In Williams 1974. Reprinted from Deutscher 1955.

Diener, Ed, and Carol Diener. 1996. Most People Are Happy. *Psychological Science* 7:3 (May).

Diener, Ed, John F. Helliwell, and Daniel Kahneman. 2010. *International Differences in Well-Being*. New York: Oxford University Press.

Diener, Ed, and Shigehiro Oishi. 2000. Money and Happiness: Income and Subjective Well-Being across Nations. In Diener and Suh 2000.

Diener, Ed, and Eunkook M. Suh, eds. 2000. *Culture and Subjective Well-Being*. Cambridge: MIT Press;

Dowse, R. E. 1966. *Left in the Centre: The Independent Labour Party, 1893–1940*. London: Longmans.

Drucker, Peter F. 1939. *The End of Economic Man: The Origins of Totalitarianism.* Originally *The End of Economic Man: A Study of the New Totalitarianism*. New York: Harper and Row.

———. 1942. *The Future of Industrial Man: A Conservative Approach*. New York: John Day.

Du Maurier, George. 2009 [1894]. *Trilby*. New York: Oxford University Press.

Durbin, Evan. 1940. *The Politics of Democratic Socialism*. London: Routledge.

———. 1949. *Problems of Economic Planning*. London: Routledge.

Dutt, Rajani Palme. 1934. *Fascism and Social Revolution*. London: Martin Lawrence.

Dutt, Romesh C. 1902. *The Economic History of India under Early British Rule: From the Rise of the British Power in 1757 to the Accession of Queen Victoria in 1837*. London: Kegan Paul.

———. 1904. *The Economic History of India in the Victorian Age: From the Accession of Queen Victoria in 1837 to the Commencement of the Twentieth Century*. London: Kegan Paul.

Eaden, James, and David Renton. 2002. *The Communist Party of Great Britain Since 1920*. Basingstoke: Palgrave.

Eastman, Max. 1937. *The End of Socialism in Russia*. London: Secker and Warburg.

———. 1940. *Stalin's Russia and the Crisis of Socialism*. New York: Norton.

Eckstein, A. M. 1987. *Nineteen Eighty-Four* and George Orwell's Other View of Capitalism. In Wemyss and Ugrinsky 1987.

———. 1992. George Orwell's Second Thoughts on Capitalism. In Rose 1992.

Elson, R. V., Milosh Sekulich, Maurice Vitou, and Harold Gray. 1945. The Truth about Mihailovich. Series of five articles. *World Review* (January–November).

Evans, M. Stanton. 2007. *Blacklisted by History: The Untold Story of Senator Joe McCarthy and His Fight against America's Enemies*. New York: Random House.

Ezard, John. 2003. Blair's Babe: Did Love Turn Orwell into a Government Stooge? *The Guardian* (21st June).

Fielden, Lionel. 1943. *Beggar My Neighbour*. London: Secker and Warburg.

Fischer, Ruth. 1948. *Stalin and German Communism*. Cambridge: Harvard University Press.

Fischer, Louis. 1941. *Men and Politics: An Autobiography*. New York: Duell, Sloan, and Pearce.

———. 1943. *Empire*. New York: Duell, Sloan, and Pearce.

Forster, E. M. 1909. The Machine Stops. *The Oxford and Cambridge Review* (November).

———. 1951. George Orwell. In *Two Cheers for Democracy*. New York: Harvest.

———. 1951. Two Cheers for Democracy. New York: Harcourt, Brace.

France, Anatole. 1910 [1905]. *The White Stone*. London: Bodley Head.

———. 1922 [1899]. *The Amethyst Ring*. London: John Lane.

———. 1947 [1908]. *Penguin Island*. New York: Heritage.

———. 1979. [1912]. *The Gods Will Have Blood*. London: Penguin.

Frolov, Y. P. 1938. *Pavlov and His School*. London: Kegan Paul.

Fyvel, T. R. 1971. The Years at *Tribune*. In Gross 1971.

———. 1982. *George Orwell: A Personal Memoir*. London: Macmillan.

Gardner, Averil. 1995 [1987]. *George Orwell*. Boston: Twayne.

Garratt, G. T. 1932. *The Mugwumps and the Labour Party*. London: Hogarth.

———. 1940. *What Has Happened to Europe?* New York: Bobbs Merrill.

George, Henry. 1881 [1879]. *Progress and Poverty: An Inquiry into the Cause of Industrial Depressions and of Increase of Want with Increase of Wealth—The Remedy*. New York: Appleton.

Gide, André. 1936. *Retour de l'U.R.S.S.* Paris: Gallimard.

Gillie, Christopher. 1975. *Movements in English Literature, 1900–1940*. Cambridge: Cambridge University Press. Cited in Slater.

Gillis, John R., and Louise Tilly, and David Levine, eds. 1992. *The European Experience of Declining Fertility, 1850–1970: The Quiet Revolution*. Oxford: Blackwell.

Gilmour, David. 2002. *The Long Recessional: The Imperial Life of Rudyard Kipling*. London: Murray.

Ginneken, Jaap van. 1992. *Crowds, Psychology, and Politics, 1871–1899*. New York: Cambridge University Press.

Gissing, George. 1961 [1903]. *The Private Papers of Henry Ryecroft*. New York: Signet.

———. 1968 [1891]. *New Grub Street*. Harmondsworth: Penguin.

———. 1970. *Essays and Fiction*. Baltimore: Johns Hopkins University Press.

———. 1972 [1886]. *Demos: A Story of English Socialism*. Brighton: Harvester.

———. 1992 [1889]. *The Nether World*. Oxford: Oxford University Press.

———. 2000 [1893]. *The Odd Women*. Oxford: Oxford University Press.

Gleason, Abbott. 1995. *Totalitarianism: The Inner History of the Cold War*. New York: Oxford University Press.

Gollancz, Victor, John Strachey, and George Orwell. 1941. *The Betrayal of the Left*. London: Gollancz.

Goode, John. 1978. *George Gissing: Ideology and Fiction*. London: Vision.

Graubard, Stephen Richards. 1956. *British Labour and the Russian Revolution: 1917–1924*. Cambridge: Harvard University Press.

Graves, Robert. 1960 [1929]. *Goodbye to All That*. London: Penguin.

Graves, Robert, and Alan Hodge. 1963 [1940]. *The Long Week-End: A Social History of Great Britain 1918–1939*. New York: Norton.

Greene, Graham. 1939. *The Lawless Roads*. London: Longmans.

———. 1940. *The Power and the Glory*. London: Heinemann.

———.1943. *The Ministry of Fear*. London: Heinemann.

———. 1948. *The Heart of the Matter*. London: Heinemann.

Greenwood, Walter. 1933. *Love on the Dole: A Tale of Two Cities*. London: Cape.

Gregor, A. James. 1968. *Contemporary Radical Ideologies: Totalitarian Thought in the Twentieth Century*. New York: Random House.

———. 1974. *The Fascist Persuasion in Radical Politics*. Princeton: Princeton University Press.

———. 1979. *Young Mussolini and the Intellectual Origins of Fascism*. Berkeley: University of California Press.

———. 2000. *The Faces of Janus: Marxism and Fascism in the Twentieth Century*. New Haven: Yale University Press.

———. 2005. *Mussolini's Intellectuals: Fascist Social and Political Thought*. Princeton: Princeton University Press.

———. 2009. *Marxism, Fascism, and Totalitarianism: Chapters in the Intellectual History of Radicalism*. Stanford: Stanford University Press.

Gregory, Owen. 1918. *Meccania: The Super-State*. London: Methuen.

Gross, Miriam, ed. 1971. *The World of George Orwell*. London: Weidenfeld and Nicolson.

Haldane, Charlotte. 1949. *Truth Will Out*. London: Weidenfeld and Nicolson.

Halévy, Élie. 1966 [1936]. *The Era of Tyrannies: Essays on Socialism and War*. New York: New York University Press.

Hamburger, L. 1943. *How Nazi Germany Has Controlled Business*. Washington, DC: Brookings Institution.

Harrison, J. R. 1967. *The Reactionaries: Yeats, Lewis, Pound, Eliot, Lawrence—A Study of the Anti-Democratic Intelligentsia*. New York: Schocken.

Hayek, F. A., ed. 1935. *Collectivist Economic Planning*. London: Routledge.

———. 1944. *The Road to Serfdom*. London: Routledge.

———. 1949. The Intellectuals and Socialism. *University of Chicago Law Review* (Spring). Reprinted in Hayek 1967.

———. 1967. *Studies in Philosophy, Politics, and Economics*. Chicago: University of Chicago Press.

———. 1952. *The Counter-Revolution of Science: Studies on the Abuse of Reason*. Glencoe: The Free Press.

Hayes, Carlton J. H. 1941. *A Generation of Materialism*. New York. Harper.

Haynes, John Earl, Harvey Klehr, and Alexander Vassiliev. 2009. *Spies: The Rise and Fall of the KGB in America*. New Haven: Yale University Press.

Hearnshaw, F. J. C. 1929 [1928]. *A Survey of Socialism*. London: Macmillan.

Heiden, Conrad. 1944. *Der Führer*. London: Gollancz.

Hemingway, Ernest. 1940. *For Whom the Bell Tolls*. New York: Scribner's.

Heppenstall, Rayner. 1960. *Four Absentees*. London: Barrie and Rockcliff.

Heston, A. 1983. National Income. In Kumar 1983.

Hewison, Robert. 1977. *Under Siege: Literary Life in London, 1939–45*. London: Weidenfeld and Nicolson.

Hicks, John R. 1946 [1939]. *Value and Capital: An Inquiry into Some Fundamental Principles of Economic Theory*. Oxford: Clarendon.

Hillegas, Mark R. 1967. *The Future as Nightmare: H. G. Wells and the Anti-Utopians*. New York: Oxford University Press.

Hilton, Jack. 1935. *Caliban Shrieks*. London: Cobden-Sanderson.

Hitchens, Christopher. 1983. An Exchange on Orwell. *Harper's* (February 1983).

———. 2002. *Why Orwell Matters*. UK title, *Orwell's Victory*. New York: Basic Books.

Hobson, J. A. 1965 [1902]. *Imperialism: A Study*. Ann Arbor: University of Michigan Press.

Hollis, Christopher. 1956. *A Study of George Orwell: The Man and His Works*. London: Hollis and Carter.

Hoover, Calvin Bryce. 1932. *Bolshevism, Fascism, and Capitalism*. New Haven: Yale University Press.

———. 1933. *Germany Enters the Third Reich*. New York: Macmillan. Not HW

———. 1937. *Dictators and Democracies*. New York: Macmillan. Not HW

Horowitz, I. L. 1961. *Radicalism and the Revolt against Reason: The Social Theories of Georges Sorel*. London: Routledge.

Howe, Irving, ed. 1982. *1984 Revisited: Totalitarianism in Our Century*. New York: Harper and Row.

Hughes, H. Stuart. 1975 [1952]. *Oswald Spengler: A Critical Estimate*. Westport: Greenwood.

———. 2002 [1958]. *Consciousness and Society: The Reorientation of European Social Thought, 1890–1930*. Piscataway: Transaction.

Humphrey, R. 1951. *Georges Sorel, Prophet without Honor: A Study in Anti-intellectualism*. Cambridge: Harvard University Press.

Hurley, Kelly. 1996. *The Gothic Body: Sexuality, Materialism, and Degeneration at the Fin de Siècle*. Cambridge: Cambridge University Press.

Huxley, Aldous. 1932. *Brave New World*. London: Chatto and Windus.

———. 1936. *Eyeless in Gaza*. London: Chatto and Windus.

———. 1937. *Ends and Means*. London: Chatto and Windus.

———. 1945. *The Perennial Philosophy*. New York: Harper.

———. 1994. *Aldous Huxley between the Wars: Essays and Letters Edited by David Bradshaw*. Chicago: Dee.

———. 2000. *Complete Essays. Volume I: 1920–1925*. Chicago: Dee.

———. 2000. *Complete Essays: Volume II: 1926–1929*. Chicago: Dee.

———. 2001. *Complete Essays. Volume III: 1930–1935*. Chicago: Dee.

———. 2001. *Complete Essays. Volume IV: 1936–1938*. Chicago: Dee.

———. 2002. *Complete Essays. Volume V: 1939–1956*. Chicago: Dee.

———. 2002. *Complete Essays. Volume VI: 1956–1963*. Chicago: Dee.

Hyndman, H. M., and William Morris. 1884. *A Summary of the Principles of Socialism*. London: Reeves.

Hynes, Samuel. 1968. *The Edwardian Turn of Mind*. Princeton: Princeton University Press.

Iggers, George G. 1958. *The Cult of Authority: The Political Philosophy of the Saint-Simonians, a Chapter in the History of Totalitarianism*. The Hague: Nijhoff.

———, ed. 1972. *The Doctrine of Saint-Simon: An Exposition, First Year, 1828–1829*. New York: Schocken.

Ingle, Stephen. 1993. *George Orwell: A Political Life*. Manchester: Manchester University Press.

———. 2006. *The Social and Political Thought of George Orwell: A Reassessment*. London: Routledge.

Isherwood, Christopher. 1939. *Goodbye to Berlin*. London: Hogarth.

Jackson, Ashley. 2006. *The British Empire and the Second World War*. London: Continuum.

Jay, Douglas. 1937. *The Socialist Case*. London: Faber and Faber.

Jefferson, Carter. 1965. *Anatole France: The Politics of Skepticism*. New Brunswick: Rutgers University Press.

Jones, Bill. 1977. *The Russia Complex: The British Labour Party and the Soviet Union*. Manchester: Manchester University Press.

Jones, William David. 1999. *The Lost Debate: German Socialist Intellectuals and Totalitarianism*. Urbana: University of Illinois Press.

Kahneman, Daniel, Ed Diener, and Norbert Schwartz, eds. 1999. *Well-Being: The Foundations of Hedonic Psychology*. New York: Russell Sage Foundation.

Kalechofsky, Roberta. 1973. *George Orwell*. New York: Ungar.

Kateb, George. 1963. *Utopia and Its Enemies*. New York: Free Press.

———. 1966. The Road to 1984. *Political Science Quarterly* 81 (December).

Kautsky, Karl Johann. 1902. *The Social Revolution*. Chicago: Kerr.

Keenan. John L. 1943. *A Steel Man in India*. New York: Duell, Sloan, and Pearce.

Ker, Ian. 2003. *The Catholic Revival in English Literature, 1845–1961*. Notre Dame: University of Notre Dame Press.

Kingsmill, Hugh. 1944. *The Poisoned Crown*. London: Eyre and Spottiswoode.

Klemperer, Victor. 2000 [1947]. *The Language of the Third Reich: LTI–Lingua Tertii Imperii*. London: Athlone.

Klugmann, James. 1951. *From Trotsky to Tito*. London: Lawrence and Wishart.

Koestler, Arthur. 1940. *Darkness at Noon*. London: Macmillan.

———. 1943. *Arrival and Departure*. London: Cape.

———. 1945. *The Yogi and the Commissar and Other Essays*. New York: Macmillan.

———. 1952. *Arrow in the Blue: An Autobiography*. New York: Macmillan.

———. 1954. *The Invisible Writing: Being the Second Volume of* Arrow in the Blue. New York: Macmillan.

Korg, Jacob. 1963. *George Gissing: A Critical Biography*. Seattle: University of Washington Press.

Kotkin, Stephen. 2014. *Stalin, Volume I: Paradoxes of Power, 1878–1928*. New York: Penguin.

Krafft-Ebing, Richard Freiherr von. 1965 [1886]. *Psychopathia Sexualis*. New York: Bell.

Kramer, Hilton. 1991. An Orwell for the Nineties. *The New Criterion* (November). Reprinted in Kramer 1999.

———. 1999. *The Twilight of the Intellectuals: Culture and Politics in the Era of the Cold War*. Chicago: Dee.

Kubal, David. 1972. *Outside the Whale: George Orwell's Art and Politics*. Notre Dame: University of Notre Dame Press.

Kumar, Dharma, ed. 1983. *The Cambridge Economic History of India. Volume 2: c. 1757–c. 1970*. Cambridge: Cambridge University Press.

Lal, Deepak. 2004. *In Praise of Empires: Globalization and Order*. New York: Palgrave Macmillan.

———. 2005. *The Hindu Equilibrium: India c. 1500 B.C.–2000 A.D.* Oxford: Oxford University Press.

Laqueur, Walter, and George L. Mosse, eds. 1966. *The Left Wing Intellectuals between the Wars, 1919–1939*. New York: Harper and Row.

Larkin, Emma. 2011 [2004]. *Finding George Orwell in Burma*. London: Granta.

Laski, Harold J. 1925. *Socialism and Freedom*. London: Fabian Society.

———. 1943. *Reflections on the Revolution of Our Time*. London: Allen and Unwin.

———. 1944. *Faith, Reason, and Civilisation: An Essay in Historical Analysis*. London: Gollancz.

Lauryssens, Stan. 2010 [1999]. *The Man Who Invented the Third Reich: The Life and Times of Arthur Moeller van den Bruck*. Stroud: The History Press.

Lawrence, D. H. 1990 [1922]. *England, My England and Other Stories*. Cambridge: Cambridge University Press.

Laybourn, Keith, and Dylan Murphy. 1999. *Under the Red Flag: A History of Communism in Britain*. Thrupp: Sutton.

Le Bon, Gustave. 2002 [1895]. *The Crowd: A Study of the Popular Mind*. Mineola: Dover.

Lea, F. A. 1960. *The Life of John Middleton Murry*. New York: Oxford University Press.

Leavis, F. R. 1930. *Mass Civilisation and Minority Culture*. Cambridge: Minority Press.

———. 1932 "Under Which King, Bezonian?" *Scrutiny* 1. Reprinted in Leavis 1986.

———. 1952. *The Common Pursuit*. London: Chatto and Windus.

———. 1986. *Valuation in Criticism and Other Essays*. Cambridge: Cambridge University Press.

Leavis, Q. D. 1932. *Fiction and the Reading Public*. London: Chatto and Windus.

Lebedoff, David. 2008. *The Same Man: George Orwell and Evelyn Waugh in Love and War*. New York: Random House.

Lenin, Vladimir. 1964 [1916]. Imperialism: The Highest Stage of Capitalism. In *Collected Works*, Volume 22. Moscow: Progress.

Lewis, Peter. 1981. *George Orwell: The Road to 1984*. New York: Harcourt, Brace.

Lewis, W. Arthur. 1970. *Tropical Development, 1880–1913*. Evanston: Northwestern University Press.

Lewis, Wyndham. 1952. *The Writer and the Absolute*. London: Methuen.

Lidman, R., and R. I. Domrese. 1970. India. In Lewis 1970.

Lifka, Thomas E. 1988. *The Concept 'Totalitarianism' and American Foreign Policy, 1933–1949*. New York: Garland.

London, Jack. 1903. *The People of the Abyss*. London: Macmillan.

———. 1948 [1908]. *The Iron Heel*. New York: Grayson.

Lucas, Scott. 2003. *Orwell*. London: Haus.

———. 2004. *The Betrayal of Dissent: Beyond Orwell, Hitchens, and the New American Century*. London: Pluto Press.

Lumley, F. E. 1933. *The Propaganda Menace*. New York: Appleton.

Lyons, Eugene. 1991 [1937]. *Assignment in Utopia*. New Brunswick: Transaction.

Macdonald, Dwight. 1946. The British Genius. *Partisan Review* 9:2 (March–April).

———. 1974. *Discriminations: Essays and Afterthoughts, 1938–1974*. New York: Grossman.

Macmillan, Harold. 1938. *The Middle Way: A Study of the Problems of Economic and Social Progress in a Free and Democratic Society*. London: Macmillan.

Maddux, Thomas R. 1977. Red Fascism, Brown Bolshevism: The American Image of Totalitarianism in the 1930s. *The Historian* 40.

Malia, Martin. 1994. *The Soviet Tragedy: A History of Socialism in Russia, 1917–1991*. New York: The Free Press.

Mallock, W. H. 1907. *A Critical Examination of Socialism*. London: Murray.

Manuel, Frank E. 1962. *The Prophets of Paris*. Cambridge: Harvard University Press.

Mann, Erika. 1940. *The Lights Go Down*. London: Secker and Warburg.

Mannheim, Karl. 1936 [1929]. *Ideology and Utopia*. London: Routledge.

Martin, David. 1990. *The Web of Disinformation: Churchill's Yugoslav Blunder*. San Diego: Harcourt.

Martin, Kingsley. 1968. *Editor: A Second Volume of Autobiography 1931–45*. London: Hutchinson.

Marx, Karl. 1974. *Capital: A Critical Analysis of Capitalist Production*. Three volumes. London: Lawrence and Wishart.

Marx, Karl, and Frederick Engels. 1977. *Marx Engels Collected Works*. Volume 9. Moscow: Progress.

———. 1985. *Marx Engels Collected Works*. Volume 20. Moscow: Progress.

Maugham, Robin. 1943. *The 1946 Ms*. London: War Facts Press.

Maugham, W. Somerset. 1922. *On a Chinese Screen*. London: Heinemann.

McCarthy, Mary. 1969. The Writing on the Wall. *New York Review of Books* (January 30th). Reprinted in McCarthy 1970.

———. 1970. *The Writing on the Wall and Other Literary Essays*. San Diego: Harcourt Brace Jovanovich.McClelland, J. S. 1989. *The Crowd and the Mob: From Plato to Canetti*. London: Unwin Hyman.

McPhail, Clark. 1991. *The Myth of the Madding Crowd*. New York: de Gruyter.

Meerloo, [J.] A. M. 1944. *Total War and the Human Mind: A Psychologist's Experience in Occupied Holland*. London: Allen and Unwin.

Meyer, Michael. 1989. *Not Prince Hamlet: Literary and Theatrical Memoirs*. London: Secker and Warburg.

Meyers, Jeffrey, ed. 1975 [1965]. *George Orwell: The Critical Heritage*. London; Routledge.

———. 2000. *George Orwell: Wintry Conscience of a Generation*. New York: Norton.

Michels, Robert. 1962 [1911]. *Political Parties: A Sociological Study of the Oligarchical Tendencies of Modern Democracy*. New York: Free Press.

Mirsky, Dmitri. 1935. *The Intelligentsia of Great Britain*. New York: Covici Friede.

Mises, Ludwig (Edler von). 1935 [1920]. Economic Calculation in the Socialist Commonwealth. In Hayek 1935.

———. 1951 [1922]. *Socialism*. New Haven: Yale University Press.

———. 1969 [1944]. *Omnipotent Government: The Rise of the Total State and Total War*. New Rochelle: Arlington House.

Moeller Van Den Bruck, Arthur. 1934 [1923]. *Germany's Third Empire*. London: Allen and Unwin.

Moore, R. J. 1983. *Escape from Empire: The Attlee Government and the Indian Problem*. Oxford: Oxford University Press.

Moorhouse, Roger. 2014. *The Devils' Alliance: Hitler's Pact with Stalin, 1939–1941*. New York: Basic Books.

Morgan, Kevin, Gidon Cohen, and Andrew Flinn. 2005. *Communists and British Society, 1920–1991: People of a Special Mould*. London: Rivers Oram.

Morris, William. 2003 [1890]. *News from Nowhere: Or, an Epoch of Rest, Being Some Chapters from a Utopian Romance*. Oxford: Oxford University Press.

Morrison, Arthur. 1896. *A Child of the Jago*. London: Methuen.

Mosse, George L. 1964. *The Crisis of German Ideology: Intellectual Origins of the Third Reich*. New York: Grosset and Dunlap.

Muggeridge, Malcolm. 1934. *Winter in Moscow*. London: Eyre and Spottiswoode.

———. 1940. *The Thirties, 1930–1940, in Great Britain*. London: Hamilton.

———. 1981. *Like It Was: The Diaries of Malcolm Muggeridge*. New York: Morrow.

Murry, John Middleton. 1944. *Adam and Eve*. London: Dakers.

———. 1948. *The Free Society*. London: Dakers.

Neurath, Otto. 1919. *Durch die Kriegswirtschaft zur Naturalwirtschaft*. Munich: Callwey.

Newman, Michael. 1989. *John Strachey*. Manchester: Manchester University Press.

Newsinger, John. 1999. *Orwell's Politics*. New York: St. Martin's Press.

Nordau, Max. 1993 [1892]. *Degeneration*. Lincoln: University of Nebraska Press.

Norris, Christopher, ed. 1984. *Inside the Myth: Orwell, Views from the Left*. London: Lawrence and Wishart.

Noyes, Alfred. 1940. *The Last Man*. London: Murray.

———. 1944. *The Edge of the Abyss*. London: Murray.

Nye, R. A. 1975. *The Origins of Crowd Psychology: Gustave Le Bon and the Crisis of Mass Democracy in the Third Republic*. London: Sage.

O'Brien, Connor Cruise. 1965. *Writers and Politics*. New York: Random House.

Orwell, George [Eric A. Blair]. 1952 [1938]. *Homage to Catalonia*. Introduction by Lionel Trilling. New York: Harcourt Brace Jovanovich.

———. 1956. *The Orwell Reader: Fiction, Essays, and Reportage*. Introduction by Richard Rovere. San Diego: Harcourt.

———. 1968. *The Collected Essays, Journalism, and Letters of George Orwell. Volume I: An Age Like This, 1920–1940. Volume II: My Country Right or Left, 1940–1943. Volume III: As I Please, 1943–1946. Volume IV: In Front of Your Nose, 1946–1950*. London: Secker and Warburg.

———. 1986 [1933]. *Down and Out in Paris and London*. The Complete Works of George Orwell, Volume I. London: Secker and Warburg.

———. 1986 [1934]. *Burmese Days*. The Complete Works of George Orwell, Volume II. London: Secker and Warburg.

———. 1986 [1935]. *A Clergyman's Daughter*. The Complete Works of George Orwell. Volume III. London: Secker and Warburg.

———. 1986 [1936]. *Keep the Aspidistra Flying*. The Complete Works of George Orwell. Volume IV. London: Secker and Warburg.

———. 1986 [1937]. *The Road to Wigan Pier*. The Complete Works of George Orwell, Volume V. London: Secker and Warburg.

———. 1986 [1938]. *Homage to Catalonia*. The Complete Works of George Orwell, Volume VI. London: Secker and Warburg.

———. 1986 [1939]. *Coming up for Air*. The Complete Works of George Orwell. Volume VII. London: Secker and Warburg.

———. 1987 [1945]. *Animal Farm: A Fairy Story*. The Complete Works of George Orwell. Volume VIII. London: Secker and Warburg.

———. 1987 [1949]. *Nineteen Eighty-Four*. The Complete Works of George Orwell. Volume IX. London: Secker and Warburg

———. 2000–2001 [1903–1936]. *A Kind of Compulsion, 1903–1936*. The Complete Works of George Orwell, Volume X. London: Secker and Warburg.

———. 2000 [1937–1939]. *Facing Unpleasant Facts, 1937–1939*. The Complete Works, Volume XI. London: Secker and Warburg.

———. 2000 [1940–1941]. *A Patriot After All, 1940–1941*. The Complete Works of George Orwell, Volume XII. London: Secker and Warburg.

———. 2001 [1941–1942]. *All Propaganda Is Lies, 1941–1942*. The Complete Works of George Orwell, Volume XIII. London: Secker and Warburg.

———. 2001 [1942–1943]. *Keeping Our Little Corner Clean, 1942–1943*. The Complete Works of George Orwell, Volume XIV. London: Secker and Warburg.

———. 2001 [1943]. *Two Wasted Years, 1943*. The Complete Works of George Orwell, Volume XV. London: Secker and Warburg.

———. 2001 [1943–1944]. *I Have Tried to Tell the Truth, 1943–1944*. The Complete Works of George Orwell, Volume XVI. London: Secker and Warburg.

———. 2001 [1945]. *I Belong to the Left, 1945*. The Complete Works of George Orwell, Volume XVII. London: Secker and Warburg.

———. 2001 [1946]. *Smothered Under Journalism, 1946*. The Complete Works of George Orwell, Volume XVIII. London: Secker and Warburg.

———. 2001 [1947–1948]. *It Is What I Think, 1947–1948*. The Complete Works of George Orwell, Volume XIX. London: Secker and Warburg.

———. 2001 [1949–1950]. *Our Job Is to Make Life Worth Living, 1949–1950*. The Complete Works of George Orwell, Volume XX. London: Secker and Warburg.

———. 2006. *The Lost Orwell: Being a Supplement to the Complete Works of George Orwell*. London: Timewell.

Ostrogorsky, Moisey. 1902. *Democracy and the Organisation of Political Parties*. Two volumes. London: Macmillan.

Overy, Richard. 2009. *The Twilight Years: The Paradox of Britain between the Wars*. UK title: *The Morbid Age*. New York: Viking.

Parrinder, Patrick. 1995. *Shadows of the Future: H. G. Wells, Science Fiction, and Prophecy*. Syracuse: Syracuse University Press.

Patai, Daphne. 1984. *The Orwell Mystique: A Study in Male Ideology*. Amherst: University of Massachusetts Press.

Pavlov, I. P. 1941. *Lectures on Conditioned Reflexes, Vol. 2: Conditioned Reflexes and Psychiatry*. London: Lawrence and Wishart.

Payne, Stanley G. 2004. *The Spanish Civil War, the Soviet Union, and Communism*. New Haven: Yale University Press.

———. 2006. *The Collapse of the Spanish Republic, 1933–1936: Origins of the Civil War*. New Haven: Yale University Press.

———. 2012. *The Spanish Civil War*. Cambridge: Cambridge University Press.

Pick, Daniel. 1989. *Faces of Degeneration: A European Disorder, c. 1848–c. 1918*. Cambridge: Cambridge University Press.

Pimlott, Ben. 1977. *Labour and the Left in the 1930s*. Cambridge: Cambridge University Press.

Podhoretz, Norman. 1983. If Orwell Were Alive Today. *Harper's* (January). Reprinted in Podhoretz 1986.

———. 1986. *The Bloody Crossroads: Where Literature and Politics Meet*. New York: Simon and Schuster.

Polanyi, Michael. 1940. *The Contempt of Freedom: The Russian Experiment and After*. London: Watts.

Popper, Karl Raimund. 1945. *The Open Society and Its Enemies*. Two volumes. London: Routledge.

Porter, Andrew, ed. 1999. *The Oxford History of the British Empire. Volume III: The Nineteenth Century*. Oxford: Oxford University Press.

Potts, Paul. 1960. *Dante Called You Beatrice*. London: Eyre and Spottiswoode.

Powell, Anthony. 1976. *Infants of the Spring: Volume 1, To Keep the Ball Rolling*. London: Heinemann.

Preston, Paul. 1983. *The Coming of the Spanish Civil War*. London: Methuen.

Priestley, J. B. 1934. *English Journey*. London: Heinemann.

———. 1967. *All England Listened: The Wartime Broadcasts of J. B. Priestley*. New York: Chilmark.

Radosh, Ronald, Mary R. Habeck, and Grigory Sevostianov, eds. 2001. *Spain Betrayed: The Soviet Union in the Spanish Civil War*. New Haven: Yale University Press.

Ranald, Ralph A. 1967. George Orwell and the Mad World: The Anti-Universe of 1984. *South Atlantic Quarterly* 66.

Rand, Ayn. 1938. *Anthem*. London: Cassell.

Rappard, William. 1938. *The Crisis of Democracy*. Chicago: University of Chicago Press.

Reade, William Winwood. 1875. *The Outcast*. London: Chatto and Windus.

———. 1924 [1872]. *The Martyrdom of Man*. London: Watts.

Rees, Richard. 1961. *George Orwell: Fugitive from the Camp of Victory*. London: Secker and Warburg.

Reilly, Patrick. 1986. *George Orwell: The Age's Adversary*. London: Macmillan.

———. 1989. *Nineteen Eighty-Four: Past, Present, and Future*. Boston: Twayne.

Remarque, Erich Maria. 1929. *All Quiet on the Western Front*. New York: Little, Brown.

Richter, Eugen. 1907 [1891]. *Sozialdemokratische Zukunftsbilder: Frei nach Bebel*. Berlin: Verlagsanstalt Deutsche Presse.

Roberts, David D. 2006. *The Totalitarian Experiment in Twentieth-Century Europe: Understanding the Poverty of Great Politics*. New York: Routledge.

Rodden, John. 1989. *The Politics of Literary Reputation: The Making and Claiming of 'St. George' Orwell*. New York: Oxford University Press.

———. 2003. *Scenes from an Afterlife: The Legacy of George Orwell*. Wilmington: ISI.

———. 2006. *Every Intellectual's Big Brother: George Orwell's Literary Siblings*. Austin: University of Texas Press.

———, ed. 2007. *The Cambridge Companion to George Orwell*. Cambridge: Cambridge University Press.

———. 2011. *The Unexamined Orwell*. Austin: University of Texas Press.

Rorty, Richard. 1989. *Contingency, Irony, and Solidarity*. Cambridge: Cambridge University Press.

———. 2000. Reply to James Conant. In Brandom 2000.

Rose, Jonathan. 1986. *The Edwardian Temperament, 1895–1919*. Athens: Ohio University Press.

———, ed. 1992. *The Revised Orwell*. East Lansing: Michigan State University Press.

Rousset, David. 1947. *The Other Kingdom*. New York: Reynal and Hitchcock.

Russell, Bertrand. 1896. *German Social Democracy*. London: Longmans.

———. 1916. *Principles of Social Reconstruction*. London: Allen and Unwin.

———. 1918. *Roads to Freedom: Socialism, Anarchism, and Syndicalism*. London: Allen and Unwin.

———. 1920. *The Practice and Theory of Bolshevism*. London: Allen and Unwin.

———. 1934. *Freedom and Organization, 1814–1914*. London: Allen and Unwin.

———. 1936. *Which Way to Peace?* London: Cape.

———. 1938. *Power: A New Social Analysis*. London: Allen and Unwin.

———. 1956. *Portraits from Memory and Other Essays*. London: Allen and Unwin.

———. 1975 [1967, 1968, 1969]. *The Autobiography of Bertrand Russell*. One-volume edition. London: Allen and Unwin.

———. 1995 [1940]. *An Inquiry into Meaning and Truth*. London: Routledge.

———. 2002. *Yours Faithfully, Bertrand Russell: A Lifelong Fight for Peace, Justice, and Truth in Letters to the Editor*. Chicago: Open Court.

Salvemini, Gaetano. 1936. *Under the Axe of Fascism*. New York: Viking.

Samuels, Stuart. 1966. The Left Book Club. In Laqueur and Mosse 1966.

Sandison, Alan. 1986 [1974]. *George Orwell after 1984*. Dover: Longwood.

Sargant, William. 1959 [1957]. *Battle for the Mind: A Physiology of Conversion and Brainwashing*. London: Pan.

Sarti, Roland. 1971. *Fascism and the Industrial Leadership in Italy, 1919–1940: A Study in the Expansion of Private Power under Fascism*. Berkeley: University of California Press.

Sassoon, Siegfried. 1928. *Memoirs of a Fox-Hunting Man*. London: Faber and Gwyer.

Schultz, Theodore W., ed. 1974. *Economics of the Family: Marriage, Children, and Human Capital*. Chicago: University of Chicago Press.

Schumpeter, Joseph Alois. 1942. *Capitalism, Socialism, and Democracy*. New York: Harper.

———. 1955 [1919, 1927]. *Imperialism and Social Classes*. Cleveland: Meridian.

Séché, Alphonse. 1929. *La Morale de la Machine*. Paris: Malfère.

Seidman, Michael. 2002. *Republic of Egos: A Social History of the Spanish Civil War*. Madison: University of Wisconsin Press.

———. 2011. *The Victorious Counterrevolution: The Nationalist Effort in the Spanish Civil War*. Madison: University of Wisconsin Press.

Shay, Robert Paul, Jr. 1977. *British Rearmament in the Thirties: Politics and Profits*. Princeton: Princeton University Press.

Shelden, Michael. 1991. *Orwell: The Authorized Biography*. New York: Harper Collins.

Shelley, Mary. 2004 [1826]. *The Last Man*. Ware: Wordsworth.

Shepherd, Robert. 1996. *Enoch Powell: A Biography*. London: Hutchinson.

Sherriff, R. C. 1929 [1928]. *Journey's End*. New York: Brentano's.

Silone, Ignazio [Secondo Tranquili]. 1937 [1936]. *Bread and Wine*. New York: Harper.

———. 1960 [1934]. *Fontamara*. New York: Atheneum.

———. 1963 [1938]. *The School for Dictators*. New York: Atheneum.

Slater, Ian. 1985. *Orwell: The Road to Airstrip One*. New York: Norton.

Small, Christopher. 1976 [1975]. *The Road to Miniluv: George Orwell, the State, and God*. London: Gollancz.

Smith, David. 1984. *Orwell for Beginners*. London: Writers and Readers Publishing Co-operative.

Smith, David C. 1986. *H. G. Wells: Desperately Mortal*. New Haven: Yale University Press.

Soloway, Richard A. 1982. *Birth Control and the Population Question in England, 1877–1930*. Chapel Hill: University of North Carolina Press.

———. 1990. *Demography and Degeneration: Eugenics and the Declining Birthrate in Twentieth-Century Britain*. Chapel Hill: University of North Carolina Press.

Sorel, Georges. 1915 [1908]. *Reflections on Violence*. London: Allen and Unwin.

Souvarine, Boris. 1937. *Cauchemar en U.R.S.S.* Paris: Revue de Paris.

Spender, Stephen. 1937. *Forward from Liberalism*. London: Gollancz.

———. 1978. *The Thirties and After*. London: Fontana.

Spengler, Oswald. 1932 [1918–1923]. *The Decline of the West: Complete in One Volume*. New York: Knopf.

Spurling, Hilary. 2003. *The Girl from the Fiction Department: A Portrait of Sonia Orwell*. New York: Counterpoint.

Stanley, J. L. 1981. *The Sociology of Virtue: The Political and Social Theories of Georges Sorel*. Berkeley: University of California Press.

Stansky, Peter, ed. 1983. *On Nineteen Eighty-Four*. San Francisco: Freeman.

Stansky, Peter, and William Abrahams. 1972. *The Unknown Orwell*. New York: Knopf.

———.1980 [1979]. *Orwell: The Transformation*. New York: Knopf.

Stapledon, Olaf. 1942. *Darkness and the Light*. London: Methuen.

Steele, David Ramsay. 1992. *From Marx to Mises: Post-Capitalist Society and the Challenge of Economic Calculation*. La Salle: Open Court.

———. 2001. The Mystery of Fascism. *Liberty* (November).

———. 2003. My Orwell Right or Wrong. Review of *Why Orwell Matters* by Christopher Hitchens. *Liberty* (May).

Steinhoff, William. 1975. *George Orwell and the Origins of "1984."* UK title: *The Road to "1984"*. Ann Arbor: University of Michigan Press.

Stern, Fritz. 1961. *The Politics of Cultural Despair: A Study in the Rise of Germanic Ideology*. Berkeley: University of California Press.

Sternhell, Zeev. 1986 [1983]. *Neither Right nor Left: Fascist Ideology in France*. Berkeley: University of California Press.

Sternhell, Zeev, Mario Sznajder, and Maia Asheri. 1994 [1989]. *The Birth of Fascist Ideology: From Cultural Rebellion to Political Revolution*. Princeton: Princeton University Press.

Strachey, John. 1933. *The Menace of Fascism*. London: Gollancz.

———. 1935 [1932]. *The Coming Struggle for Power*. New York: Modern Library.

———. 1935. *The Nature of Capitalist Crisis*. London: Gollancz.

———. 1936. *The Theory and Practice of Socialism*. New York: Random House.

———. 1938. *Why You Should Be a Socialist*. London: Gollancz.

———. 1938. *What Are We to Do?* London: Gollancz.

———. 1940. *A Programme for Progress*. London: Gollancz.

———. 1941. *A Faith to Fight For*. London: Gollancz.

———. 1963. *Lenin's Theory on Imperialism Reconsidered*. London: Today Publications.

Sudaplatov, Pavel, and Anatoli Sudaplatov, with Jerrold L. Schechter and Leona P. Schechter. *Special Tasks: The Memoirs of an Unwanted Witness—a Soviet Spymaster*. Boston: Little, Brown.

Sutherland, John. 2005 [2004]. *Stephen Spender: A Literary Life*. Oxford: Oxford University Press.

Sweezy, Paul M. 1942. *The Theory of Capitalist Development: Principles of Marxian Political Economy*. New York: Oxford University Press.

———. ed. 1949. *Karl Marx and the Close of His System by Eugen von Böhm-Bawerk and Böhm-Bawerk's Criticism of Marx by Rudolf Hilferding*. New York: Kelley.

Swift, Jonathan. 1970 [1726]. *Gulliver's Travels*. New York: Norton.

Symons, Julian. 1975 [1973]. *The Thirties: A Dream Revolved*. London: Faber and Faber.

Taylor, D. J. 2003 [2002]. *Orwell: The Life*. New York: Holt.

Tawney, R. H. 2013 [1921]. *The Acquisitive Society*. London: Martino.

———. 2015 [1926]. *Religion and the Rise of Capitalism*. London: Verso.

Teitelbaum, Michael S. 1984. *The British Fertility Decline: Demographic Transition in the Crucible of the Industrial Revolution.* Princeton: Princeton University Press.

Teitelbaum, Michael S., and Jay M. Winter, eds. 1985. *The Fear of Population Decline.* Orlando: Academic Press.

———. eds. 1988. *Population and Resources in Western Intellectual Traditions.* Cambridge: Cambridge University Press.

Terrill, Ross. 1973. *R. H. Tawney and His Times: Socialism as Fellowship.* London: Deutsch.

Thomas, Hugh. 1973. *John Strachey.* New York: Harper and Row.

———. 2001 [1961]. *The Spanish Civil War.* New York: Modern Library.

Thompson, E. P. 1978. *The Poverty of Theory and Other Essays.* New York: Monthly Review Press.

Thorpe, Andrew. 1992. *Britain in the 1930s: The Deceptive Decade.* Oxford: Blackwell.

Tindall, William York. 1947. *Forces in Modern British Literature 1885–1946.* New York: Knopf.

Tomlinson, B. R. 1993. *The Economy of Modern India, 1860–1970.* (*The New Cambridge History of India* III:3.) Cambridge: Cambridge University Press.

Tressell, Robert. 2008 [1914]. *The Ragged Trousered Philanthropists.* Oxford: Oxford University Press.

Trilling, Lionel. 1952. Introduction to Orwell 1952. Reprinted with minor changes as "George Orwell and the Politics of Truth" in Trilling 1978.

———. 1978 [1955]. *The Opposing Self: Nine Essays in Criticism.* New York: Harcourt Brace Jovanovich.

Trotsky, Leon. 1972 [1937]. *The Revolution Betrayed: What Is the Soviet Union and Where Is It Going?* New York: Pathfinder.

———. 1973 [1930–1940]. *The Spanish Revolution, 1931–39.* New York: Pathfinder.

Trotter, Wilfred. 1923 [1916]. *Instincts of the Herd in Peace and War*. London: Fisher Unwin.

Tugan-Baranowsky, Michael I. 1966 [1908]. *Modern Socialism in Its Historical Development*. New York: Russell and Russell.

Turner, Henry Ashby, Jr., ed. 1975. *Reappraisals of Fascism*. New York: New Viewpoints.

———. 1985. *German Big Business and the Rise of Hitler*. New York: Oxford University Press.

Upward, Edward. 1962. *In the Thirties*. London: Heinemann.

———. 1969. *The Rotten Elements: A Novel of Fact*. London: Heinemann.

Utley, Freda. 1948 [1940]. *Lost Illusion*. London: Allen and Unwin.

Van Inwagen, Peter. 1993. *Metaphysics*. Boulder: Westview.

———. 2008. Was George Orwell a Metaphysical Realist? *Philosophia Scientiae*.

Vassiliev, Alexander, and Allen Weinstein. 1999. *The Haunted Wood: Soviet Espionage in America—The Stalin Era*. New York: Random House.

Veenhoven, Ruut. 2000. Freedom and Happiness: A Comparative Study in Forty-Four Nations in the Early 1990s. In Diener and Suh 2000.

Voigt, F. A. 1938. *Unto Caesar*. London: Constable.

Wadhams, Stephen. 1984. *Remembering Orwell*. Harmondsworth: Penguin.

Wagar, W. Warren. 1961. *H. G. Wells and the World State*. New Haven: Yale University Press.

Wain, John. 1963. *Essays on Literature and Ideas*. London: Macmillan.

———. 1973. *A House for the Truth: Critical Essays*. New York: Viking.

Walsby, Harold. 1947. *The Domain of Ideologies: A Study of the Origin, Development, and Structure of Ideologies*. Glasgow: McLellan.

Walsh, James. 1975 [1956]. [Untitled]. In Meyers 1975. Originally in *Marxist Quarterly*, January 1956.

Walton, David. 1982. George Orwell and Antisemitism. *Patterns of Prejudice*, 16: 1.

Ward, Mrs Humphrey. 1987 [1888]. *Robert Elsmere*. Oxford: Oxford University Press.

Warburg, Fredric. 1959. *An Occupation for Gentlemen*. London: Hutchinson.

———. 1973. *All Authors Are Equal*. New York: St. Martins.

Warren, Bill. 1980. *Imperialism: Pioneer of Capitalism*. London: NLB.

Webb, Sidney. 1907. *The Decline in the Birth-Rate*. London: Fabian Society.

Webb, Sidney, and Beatrice Webb. 1923. *The Decay of Capitalist Civilisation*. London: Allen and Unwin.

———. 1935. *Soviet Communism: A New Civilisation?* London: Longmans.

Weber, Eugene. 1986. *France Fin de Siècle*. Cambridge: Harvard University Press.

Weinstein, Allen, and Alexander Vassiliev. 1999. *The Haunted Wood: Soviet Espionage in America—the Stalin Era*. New York: Random House.

Wells, H. G. 1895. *The Time Machine: An Invention*. London: Heinemann.

———. 1901. *Anticipations of the Reaction of Mechanical and Scientific Progress upon Human Life and Thought*. London: Chapman and Hall.

———. 1903. *Mankind in the Making*. London: Chapman and Hall.

———. 1905. *A Modern Utopia*. London: Chapman and Hall.

———. 1908. *New Worlds for Old*. London: Macmillan.

———. 1909. *Tono-Bungay*. London: Macmillan.

———. 1910 [1899]. *The Sleeper Awakes*. Formerly *When the Sleeper Wakes*. London: Collins.

———. 1920 [1919]. *The Outline of History*. London: Newnes.

———. 1921. *Russia in the Shadows*. New York: Doran.

———. 1924. *The Dream*. London: Cape.

———. 1927. *Meanwhile: The Picture of a Lady*. London: Benn.

———. 1928. *The Open Conspiracy: Blue Prints for a World Revolution*. London: Gollancz.

———. 1932 [1931]. *The Work, Wealth, and Happiness of Mankind*. London: Heinemann.

———. 1934. *Experiment in Autobiography: Discoveries and Conclusions of a Very Ordinary Brain (Since 1866)*. New York: Macmillan.

———. 1940. *The New World Order*. London: Secker and Warburg.

Wemyss, Courtney T., and Alexej Ugrinsky, eds. 1987. *George Orwell*. Westport: Greenwood.

West, Anthony. 1957. *Principles and Persuasions: The Literary Essays of Anthony West*. New York: Harcourt, Brace.

West, Geoffrey. 1930. *H. G. Wells*. New York: Norton.

West, W. J. 1992. *The Larger Evils: Nineteen Eighty-Four—The Truth Behind the Satire*. Edinburgh: Canongate.

Williams, Francis. 1940. *War by Revolution*. London: Routledge.

———. 1948. *The Triple Challenge: The Future of Socialist Britain*. London: Heinemann.

Williams, Ian. 2007. Orwell and the British Left. In Rodden 2007.

Williams, Raymond. 1958. *Culture and Society, 1780–1950*. London: Chatto and Windus.

———. ed. 1974. *George Orwell: A Collection of Critical Essays*. Englewood Cliffs: Prentice Hall.

———. 1971. *George Orwell*. New York: Columbia University Press.

———. 1981 [1979]. *Politics and Letters: Interviews with New Left Review*. London: Verso.

Williamson, Oliver E. 1975. *Markets and Hierarchies: Analysis and Antitrust Implications*. New York: The Free Press.

Wimsatt, W. K., and Monroe C. Beardsley. 1946. The Intentional Fallacy. *Sewanee Review* 54.

Winslow, E. M. 1948. *The Pattern of Imperialism: A Study in the Theories of Power*. New York: Columbia University Press.

Wintringham, Tom. 1940. *New Ways of War*. London: Penguin.

———. 1940. Armies of Freemen. London: Routledge.

Wood, Neal. 1959. *Communism and British Intellectuals*. New York: Columbia University Press.

Woodcock, George. 1948. *The Writer and Politics*. London: Porcupine Press.

———. 1984 [1966]. *The Crystal Spirit: A Study of George Orwell*. New York: Schocken.

Wykes, David. 1987. *A Preface to Orwell*. London: Longmans.

Worley, Matthew. 2004. *In Search of Revolution: International Communist Parties in the Third Period*. London: Tauris.

Young, John Wesley. 1991. *Totalitarian Language: Orwell's Newspeak and Its Nazi and Communist Antecedents*. Charlottesville: University Press of Virginia.

Zamyatin, Yevgeny. 1993 [1924]. *We*. New York: Penguin.

Zwerdling, Alex. 1974. *Orwell and the Left*. New Haven: Yale University Press.

Index